Writings on Architecture and the City

George Baird

Introduction by Francesco Garofalo

This book is for my London friends:

David Chipperfield, Peter Cook, Ted Cullinan, Jamie Fobert and Dominique Gagnon, Kenneth Frampton, Adrian Forty, Tony Fretton, Bruno and Mavis Giordan, Bruno Jr and Gill Giordan, Charles Jencks and Louisa Lane Fox, Pamela Jencks, Edward and Margo Jones, Mark Lewis and Janice Kerbel, Robert Maxwell and Celia Scott-Maxwell, Robin Middleton, John and Sue Miller, Graham Morrison, Laura Mulvey, Joseph and Anne Rykwert, Mary Stirling, Madelon Vriesendorp, Michael Wilford, and Brendan Woods.

And in fond memory of London friends deceased:

Leonie Cohn, Alan Colquhoun, Sam Stevens, Jim Stirling and Peter Wollen.

Contents

6   Introduction by Francesco Garofalo

Architecture and Semiotics

20   *La Dimension Amoureuse* in Architecture, 1969

38   The Dining Position: A Question of *Langue* and *Parole*, 1976

54   A Critical Reflection on the Theory and Practice of Architectural Symbolism in the Work of Venturi, Rauch, and Scott Brown, and Their Colleagues, 1976

70   Semiotics and Architecture, 1998

Architectural Theory Between Structuralism and Phenomenology

78   Alvar Aalto, 1970

94   Rome and Modern Architecture: A Personal Reminiscence, 2000

98   On the Phenomenology of Spatial Sequences: Frank Gehry's Disney Hall and Hans Scharoun's Berlin Philharmonic, 2012

Urban Morphology and Building Typology

106   Theory: Vacant Lots in Toronto, 1978

124   Studies on Urban Morphology in North America, 1988

132   Mutant Urbanity: Revisiting Las Vegas, 2004

146   Thoughts on "Agency", "Utopia" and "Property" in Contemporary Architectural and Urban Theory, 2013

Critical Biography

Part 1: Rem Koolhaas, OMA, and some other Dutch architects

162   *Les Extrêmes Qui se Touchent*, 1977

166   OMA, Neo-Modern and Modernity, 2001

178   Review of *Mart Stam's Trousers* by Crimson, with Michael Speaks
       and Gerard Hadders, 2001

184   An Open Letter to Rem Koolhaas, 2007

Part 2: Ignasi de Solà-Morales

190   Review of *Differences: Topographies of Contemporary
       Architecture*, 1997

Part 3: Colin Rowe

196   Oppositions in the Thought of Colin Rowe, 1997

208   The Work, Teaching and Contemporary Influence of Colin Rowe:
       A 1999 Status Report, 1999

Part 4: Joseph Rykwert:

222   "A Promise as Well as a Memory":
       Notes Towards an Intellectual Biography of Joseph Rykwert, 2002

Public Space

238   On Publicness and Monumentality in the Work of Machado
       and Silvetti, 1994

246   Review of "Free University Berlin: AA Publication/Exhibition
       in the Members' Room 21 May–18 June, 1999", 1999

254   The New Urbanism and Public Space, 2007

On the "Critical" in Contemporary Architectural Theory

262   Criticality and Its Discontents, 2004

270   Why Can't Architecture Just Be Happy? 2009

274   Index

287   Image Credits

291   Acknowledgements

Introduction

Francesco Garofalo

An introduction to a volume of collected essays can hardly be a spoiler. Despite that, it is not uncommon to meet people who prefer to read such introductions after they have read the book. To help the reader make a decision in this case, it could be said that the structure adopted here resembles that of a classical building. It starts with a podium, an intellectual/biographical account that follows George Baird from his journey to London in 1964 to his present continuing involvement in teaching and writing. It is not nearly as sophisticated as the critical exercises he devoted to his colleagues Joseph Rykwert and Colin Rowe, but it contextualises this collection in the many aspects of his career.

Above the podium there is a mezzanine, a brief discussion of the similarities and differences between this book and others published by characters that have intersected with George Baird's ideas and biography. Trying to learn a lesson from his insightful criticism, a venue—or in this case a format—should not be taken for granted and left unquestioned.

The *piano nobile* consists of a series of sometimes diverging and sometimes diagonal paths with respect to the thematic sections of the book, an exploration of correspondences and conceptual structures beyond the ones proposed by its author. For example, one of them is the possibility of addressing architecture as a product *per se*, besides being the manifestation of theoretical positions; another is the never-ending friction between architecture and the city.

The reader will discover in this collection, even without the need of this introduction, a rare author who is optimistic at the same time that he is radical and critical about the chances of architecture in the contemporary world.

Architect, educator, theoretician?
George Baird retired in 2009 from his tenure as Dean at the University of Toronto, crowning a remarkable career that began in London in 1964 and included teaching at Harvard University's Graduate School of Design from 1993 to 2004.

A conference held in Toronto in 2012 (George Baird: A Question of Influence), was the first opportunity to reflect on the complexity of his career and now this collection of 24 essays spanning over 40 years provides an opportunity to explore the triangle formed by theory, history and practice, which shows how theory, 'surfaced' with Baird's generation, and has irrevocably influenced practice without leaving history unaffected.

Having met Joseph Rykwert and Alan Colquhoun through Robert Maxwell, who was his doctoral advisor at the Bartlett School of Architecture, he was able to obtain his first teaching positions at the Royal College of Art and the Architectural Association. All three of these mentors will eventually move to the United States, as Colin Rowe had already done and Kenneth Frampton will also do, to play a very influential role in American academia.

Together with Charles Jencks, Baird publishes *Meaning in Architecture* in 1969. The status of the book is unusual for a collection of essays, notwithstanding the emerging reputation of several contributors such as Françoise Choay, Reyner Banham and Aldo van Eyck. It is the first time that British architecture culture confronts fundamental questions: the relationship with mass media and semiology, the sharp criticism of Functionalism and the inadequate attempts to overcome its limitations, and finally the discovery of the typological paradigm. His essay *"La Dimension Amoureuse"* in architecture acquired the status of a small classic and was the point of departure for some contributions at the 2012 Toronto conference.

At the end of the 1960s, however, George Baird decides to return to Canada to establish a professional practice. The office from which he is now partly retired has involved as partners successive generations of his students. This circumstance reveals a continuity of production that is less dependent on signature than it is on a transmission of knowledge.

Compared with the biographies of others who began as practitioners to eventually put down roots in academia (notably Colquhoun and Frampton), the architecture of George Baird's office in Canada and the United States, even if it did not reach the heights of commercial success, played a significant role, and formed a bridge with his main interest in the urban dimension of projects.

In the 1970s, in addition to teaching in Toronto and maintaining a connection with the Institute for Architecture and Urban Studies (IAUS) founded by Peter Eisenman in New York, he produced a series of studies on the city. They present an original mix of perceptual and structural aspects suggesting the possibility to combine the specificity of North America with European theoretical urban inventions. Examples of this work were presented in the exhibition at the University of Toronto in 2012 (Meanings in Architecture: the early works of George Baird 1957–1993), but could be reproduced in this book only to a limited extent.

Learning not only from Las Vegas, but also from Barcelona and Paris, tools of urban analysis were put to the test in Toronto. Inviting to the University of Toronto designers and theoreticians from Europe, made it possible to reduce the linguistic gap and disseminate new ideas.

"Onbuildingdowntown" was published in 1974, "Vacant Lottery" (included in this collection) in 1978. The relevant aspect of these studies is that they left a mark on Toronto urban planning, penetrating in a limited way the city administration, but more deeply the professional establishment through the collaboration of younger generations of architects in the research projects.

In the 1980s, however, this prudent reformist approach does not unfold to its full potential. There is no leap towards a programme linking urban goals to public architecture commissions, except for rare competitions in which Baird is a strategy maker such as the one for Mississauga City Hall, won by Edward Jones and Michael Kirkland. It is for this reason that, after taking over the direction of the architecture school for some years, he focuses again on research.

Even if they are both published in 1995, two books are preceded by a decade long investigation. The one on public space edited with Mark Lewis, Queues, Rendezvous, Riots, explores the social and urban dimension of questions central to his other book

published by MIT Press, The Space of Appearance. Ambitious and not as popular as expected, it is difficult to fit into a genre: a powerful reflection on the twentieth century, but not a history of architecture. It is a selective examination of the crisis of Modernity extensively predicated on critical and philosophical thought dominated by the figure of Hannah Arendt, as revealed by the title.

A new detachment from the politics of Toronto is manifest in the decision to accept a professorship at Harvard in 1993. Despite the continuity and commitment of the practice, an engagement in the urban transformation of North American cities is no longer possible for architects. Research moves more and more exclusively to academia, a trajectory already followed by the protagonists of IAUS in the previous decade. Many of the articles in this book come from the 1990s that saw him as a contributor to old and new journals like Perspecta, Assemblage and Harvard Design Magazine.

Having returned to the University of Toronto as Dean in 2004, the voice of George Baird has been heard since in more European locations, like London, Graz and Rotterdam, at the Berlage Institute. The publication of another book in 2012, Public Space: Cultural/Political Theory; Street Photography, proves the vitality of questions that are also examined in this collection.

Format and form of writing

A collection of essays is not a banal matter, the answer to a mere need to sum up. In the case of George Baird, it arrives after an initial book that was an instrument of debate (Meaning in Architecture), an ambitious monograph laboured on for a long time (The Space of Appearance), and other significant endeavours.

There is a group of authors of collections that may seem arbitrarily assembled (Banham, Colquhoun, Eisenman, Rowe, Solà-Morales), all of whom have had a connection to George Baird. Colin Rowe and Ignasi de Solà-Morales, for example, are discussed in different depth, but with equal involvement in this book.

At one end of the spectrum could be placed Reyner Banham who was a militant critic and wrote several books, but is the only one in the group fully trained as an historian. Colin Rowe's As I Was Saying, presents a much more fragmentary structure because the collection is a systematisation assisted by a compliant editor, reflecting blocks of work and blocks of biography. This may have to do with Rowe's playing a role in the debate on architecture and the city that was more directly operative than the critical one of Banham.

At the opposite end of the spectrum is Peter Eisenman, whose relationship between theoretical reflection and practice cannot be separated, even though his largest collection to date, *Inside out: Selected writing 1963–1988*, deliberately does so. Eisenman's style is for the most part dispassionate, neutral and abstract, as though to compensate for it being the counterpart to the translation of strict procedural manoeuvres from the page to the drawing board (or the computer).

There are two particular authors with whom George Baird presents a strong affinity: Alan Colquhoun and Ignasi de Solà-Morales. They share his commitment to design, and have had a long experience in practice. They have a common passion for historical and philosophical depth, a search for the paradigm that goes beyond the individual architectural work. Their writings are no less influential than those of others, but they take explicitly and almost exclusively the form of a collection of essays (*Differences: Topographies of Contemporary Architecture*—de Solà-Morales, *Essays in Architectural Criticism. Modern Architecture and Historical Change*, and *Modernity and the Classical Tradition*—Colquhoun). In each case the volumes were not the summation of a career coming to an end, but the framing of a cultural phase in architecture.

Is this form of writing inherent to architecture theory as we came to know it? At the conference on George Baird in 2012, Michael Hays introduced one of the sessions by saying that what we call theory emerged in the 1960s in two places: London and Venice (which could be *pars pro toto* for Italy, as in Venice converged Aldo Rossi from Milan, Manfredo Tafuri and Carlo Aymonino from Rome).

Without underestimating the ambitious oeuvre of the long monograph, it is the article, the essay that constituted the specific medium of discussion. This collection presents yet one more difference with most of the ones already mentioned: it has a thematic structure that reflects George Baird's intellectual mobility.

The argument for the essay as the influential genre could be supported by its association with the author as an architect involved in academia, rather than a scholar. If one then sees writing as a project, invited or commissioned, does it make it less relevant? It is like its equivalent in design: an inextricable mix of ongoing research and circumstance. None other than Ignasi de Solà-Morales, quoted by Baird, warns in the

beginning of his book that he "'found it impossible' in selecting the texts and in writing an introduction, 'to construct a systematic discourse'".

Having made a number of comparisons with other authors of theory and criticism in architecture it is time to identify an aspect of the writing style that is so peculiarly "Bairdian". He uses the first person very frequently in the habit of beginning the text by 'positioning' the issue, telling the circumstances of it becoming relevant, and its connections and associations. This is done in a richly anecdotal style, which sounds always spontaneous and there is nothing condescending or instrumental about it: "I almost managed to visit Frank Gehry's Disney Hall on the day that it opened. As it happened, I had a business appointment in downtown Los Angeles that day, and Gehry's administrative staff made a special arrangement for me to slip in and explore the building before the official opening later in the day…."

It makes you think of conversation (an art in which George Baird excels), which the text appears to be continuing. The format of conversation is linked to a dialogical structure. The initial part of his text is more often than not a way to bring the reader in a circle. The next part, if it is appropriate, is the development of the dialogical nature of the argument. George Baird has a unique way of presenting all sides, positions and relevant opinions. It could be said that anybody does or should do that when writing an essay, yet it is hard not to notice a certain rhetorical use of this laying the issue on the table, such that it could be difficult for the polemical target to recriminate for having been misunderstood (if it happens anyway, Baird will incorporate it in the text!).

This little stylistic detour leads to a more fundamental question about his position in intellectual-architectural matters. The following parts of this introduction will seek to demonstrate that George Baird is both radical and anti-dogmatic, by analysing a number of his writings.

Addressing architecture

Browsing the table of contents, five titles, well distributed over time, mark the recurrent interest for architecture "in the flesh". They are sometimes a comparison and other times a review. Each text has a different occasion and agenda, presenting a circular movement from the phenomenological appreciation of Alvar Aalto, to that of the concert halls in Berlin and Los Angeles.

There are references to contemporary debate emerging at each instance: in Aalto, questioning of orthodox Modernism; in Venturi, Scott Brown and Rauch, the symbolic dimension; in Machado and Silvetti, typology; in Woods the exemplary; and finally the phenomenology of the audience in the buildings by Scharoun and Gehry. In each case there are built works that can be called "emblematic".

The relatively short text on Aalto is not biographical, contextual or stringently theoretical. In its premise, it declares that Aalto had until then scarcely probed, and contains no reference to the then recent discovery of semiology in *Meaning in Architecture*. Instead it begins immediately with the exploration of the element that plays a metonymic role in Aalto's architecture: the balustrade. The description of its features takes up one third of the space and establishes for the first time what George Baird will define as a phenomenological approach: "a mode of criticism that is resolutely personal, first hand and experiential; in short phenomenological".

This term has had wide circulation in the English speaking architecture world, but remains uncomfortable from a European—or maybe just Italian—perspective. The slight ambiguity of the meaning implied—literal, metaphorical and strictly philosophical—has always made it suspect, not unlike other architectural-philosophical contaminations of Postmodernism and deconstruction.

The 'corporeal' role of the balustrade opens a possibility of experiential intensification in a building, which is the opposite of the potential quality harboured by the 'typical' and even the 'ordinary' as it will be discovered in other writings.

The other two keys to unlock Aalto are the urban and the political. Since *"La Dimension Amoureuse"* had already introduced the symbolic element, with these three concerns (physical, urban, political) we are equipped already with the questions that are central to all the texts in this book.

Another precocious sign of his critical architecture framework is in the discussion of the urban attitude of Aalto's buildings conducted in 'compositional' terms adopting the metaphor of the ruin, or as Tafuri would rather say, the fragment. Equally significant is the coincidence of the political dimension with the phenomenon of public space.

Six years later, a lecture at Cornell University provides the opportunity to scrutinise the work of Venturi and Scott Brown. This time there is a lot of personal positioning to do, and this is one of the texts where we discover an early instance of the dialectic style already mentioned.

Meaning in Architecture falls chronologically in between *Complexity and Contradiction*, and *Learning from Las Vegas*. By then, there had already been the well-known polemic between Denise Scott Brown and Kenneth Frampton over the legitimacy of a realist or populist approach to the city. But the question of how the influence of the symbolic dimension imported by semiotics can be "confused and confusing" for Venturi interests George Baird more in strictly architectural terms than on account of any political or ethical overtones.

Confronting the growing historicist curiosity, he tries to elaborate a definition, a "theory of decorum" that will not become popular but is very interesting as an early symptom and concern for a direction that in the work of the Philadelphia office will become much more explicit and will cause a significant loss of depth in the following decades.

The reference to a number of projects by Venturi and Scott Brown to that date, makes it possible to identify a list of elements that sit on either side of a threshold of the symbolic, and measure their potential to be incorporated in the composition, rather than 'applied' to it. Baird questions the schematic dilemma between the decorated shed and the duck. For example in the Guild House, the sculpture in the form of a TV aerial, soon removed from the roof, is contrasted with the treatment of the chain-link fence delineating the space around the building, evoking a classical reference by using a mundane object; a way to resolve the contradiction between being "heroic and original or ugly and ordinary".

It could be argued today that George Baird's explicit preference for *Complexity and Contradiction* over *Learning from Las Vegas* would be met by popular consensus. At the time, he found that in the latter book, the structural dimension of the Nolli appropriation was quickly lost. In choosing his preferred book he was aware that the city is altogether a field in which it is impossible to adopt a univocal position, whereas *Complexity and Contradiction* was more productively about architecture and its inner workings.

The essay on the work of Machado and Silvetti is written from a very different point of view. It is sympathetic enough that it could be wondered if George Baird is taking the opportunity to state positions that could be his own. The points of this manifesto represent a potential common ground: the claim of the unity of the architectural and urban dimensions of design, the preoccupation for context that could articulate the third dimension beyond the flattened definition of Colin Rowe's figure-ground, the commitment to materiality (despite the fact that the projects discussed are all on paper) and finally, realism and typicality.

This is a recurrent interest for the elements of standard construction, especially belonging to the public realm, that in the work of Machado and Silvetti acquires a "delirious quality". Except for Colin Rowe, the polemical targets are not identified. In 1994, however, it may be accurate to say that he retrospectively counted them among those who opted for "the literal politicisations of the practice", or for the "more popular modalities of so-called "Postmodernism" in architecture, especially in its consumerist North American version" and finally those who "chose to look to the art gallery rather than the street".

If these had been some of the risks for architecture in the time since writing *Meaning in Architecture*, during which Machado and Silvetti developed their distinctive position, more currently the nihilist claim of "otherness" has seemed to challenge the possibility of creating any space in which an architectural practice could be relevant in the public realm.

Nothing could be more distant from the work of the Boston firm than Candilis-Josic-Woods' Free University in Berlin. In the review of a monograph on the building the context is accurately set up. This time the question is the controversial nature of a building as a model, or its being 'exemplary'.

While he recognises this as a necessity against the mainstream, he is not indulgent with the problematic features of the mat building itself, removed from the city and disliked by the students. These limitations are projected against the revolutionary ideas of Team 10, but without driving the knife too deep in its contradictions. He has rarely confronted the ideas and works of the group that sought to subvert Modernism: none of the protagonists appears in the critical biographies, except for passing references to Aldo van Eyck.

The analysis of the Free University reveals a mix of criticism and sympathy that does not lower the guard, but certainly refuses to consider the impact of Team 10 as ultimately destructive. George Baird belongs to a generation involved more with the aftermath of Team 10 than its inception but, characteristically, with the urban realists and even with the historicist camp, there is a conspicuous hesitation to condemn it wholesale.

The last architectural scrutiny makes an explicit claim of closing a circle: "from the beginning of my career I have tried to make my architectural criticism phenomenological". It is the story of visits to two celebrated buildings: Disney Hall in Los Angeles and the Philharmonic in Berlin.

It is the experience that propels not only the comparative judgment, but the inspiration to write the text. This is why the author does not position the buildings as he normally does, in the context of the architectural debate, but rather in the circumstance of the visit. The conclusion is clear and explicit in favour of the older masterpiece.

To a certain extent, Baird does not want to fully elaborate on the reasons that prevented Gehry from providing the user with an equally satisfying experience as Scharoun. The criticism of architecture production in the Gehry manner—or the Gehry age—is left suspended, almost implicit after having analysed routes and spaces with great precision. The difference with the young author of the introduction to Aalto, whose continuity is claimed, as we saw in other instances, is in the cautious yet non-diplomatic or reticent way in which the message discovered in the building is delivered, and indicates the need for a distinct approach to the architectural, urban and social-political spheres.

Critical biographer

The career of George Baird as a "critical biographer" begins later than it appears in the chronology. The seminal article on OMA in 1977, for the purpose of this introduction, should be seen as an instrument for retrospective reading in the context of the interview with *Perspecta* of 2001. In fact these investigations take place in a decade of full maturity in his career.

In-depth analysis of such eminent figures is not free from the risk of being too laudatory, or too polemical or conditioned by personal association. This does not prevent the texts from displaying a spectrum of tonalities from complicity to severe criticism.

The review of Ignasi de Solà-Morales' book is slightly different. It is less of an excavation than a selective reading, but nonetheless very productive. George Baird could not help being fascinated by an author with whom he bears certain similarities. To simplify, their writings suggest that new philosophical material leads to new interpretations of architecture. This is proved by the appearance of a Heideggerian Mies displacing the traditional Schinkelian one. Another example is the debt to existentialism, discovered as an undercurrent of different radical revisionist critiques of Modernism in the post-war period.

The productive use of Solà-Morales becomes manifest in these words: "Finally—and perhaps for me most brilliantly—Solà-Morales' point of departure leads him to make an affirmative (but of course subtle) case for two architectural ideas that he sees as currently being in disrepute: 'decoration' and 'monumentality'." In qualifying these two words, Baird comes across a famous quote by Benjamin that he himself has adopted since the 1970s, if not earlier, on the distracted versus the attentive reading of architecture.

The appreciation of Solà-Morales is mirrored in his own efforts. It is a short review constructed like others—and more than others—by letting the subject speak. It is a sort of introduction to the more elaborate critical enquires.

Solà-Morales explains what architecture was—"an exquisite material labour capable of producing beautiful results", and what it is—"a global discourse addressing the great questions filling individual consciences with uncertainty". These words set the challenge faced by George Baird for much of this book, to overcome a separation of theory and practice, but at the same time to acknowledge the constant need to rely on 'external' intellectual sources without being deterministic or derivative.

There is continuity between the questions raised by de Solà-Morales and the two-part assessment of Colin Rowe's influence. The first, published in *Assemblage*, ("Oppositions in the Thought of Colin Rowe"), is the *pars construens*, and the second, in *Zodiac* three years later, is the *pars destruens* at the expense of *Collage City*. The two texts complement each other in several ways. The first hinges on a question asked with a self-reflexive tone by Colin Rowe in his famous introduction to *Five Architects*: "Can an architecture which professes an objective of continuous experiment ever become congruous with the ideal of an architecture which is to be popular, intelligible and profound?" The second ends with another question that again Rowe seems to ask himself: "do the words exist?"—referring to his inability to give full expression to his great admiration for James Stirling's Leicester Engineering Building.

Starting with the first question, its implications are examined both within the structure of Rowe's thought and in themselves. But only the readers of Baird, not the readers of Rowe, will have the privilege of knowing a tentative answer, because it is provided in the careful montage of the quotations.

To succeed in this difficult exercise, George Baird has to demonstrate that there is a more ambitious project than the one associated with the formalist Rowe. Its "conceptual techniques" are carefully unravelled: the trans-Atlantic opposition, the attention to "high and low", the seed of the appreciation of the ordinary—not entirely different from Robert Venturi's ambiguities around "elitist" versus "commonplace". The last challenge is the confutation of the widely accepted organically anti-Modernist Rowe. The provisional conclusion is that in the theory-conscious architecture world, the question remains with us, and continues to resonate against any alternately regressive or avant-gardist shortcut.

Having avoided *Collage City* in the first essay, Baird makes it the object of criticism in the second one. At the time, 15 years ago, Baird began by observing that it is a problematic book in terms of its structure and its ability to deliver what it promises. Further time having now passed, and not disagreeing with his opinion, there are signs that historical research is beginning to invest all the 1960s and 1970s classics (Venturi, Rossi, Tafuri, and several others) with a secular acceptance of their evident defects as books. If *Collage City* can be put in question for its ideological perspective as well as for its formal structure, so are other books in PhD programmes around the world, perhaps implying that a coherently organised argument is fundamentally incompatible with the intellectual frame of a contemporary architect. George Baird's *Space of Appearance* is probably too recent to be invested, and will be safe for some time, but it represents a conspicuous exception to the dis-homogeneous structure of the others.

The attack on *Collage City* is conducted on three fronts. The first is the asymmetry with the European discourse of typology and morphology, a dialectic in which Rowe entertains only the second term, and which, therefore is exposed to the charge of formalism. The second criticism concerns his philosophical reliance on Popper: "For my part, I am more troubled by the insufficiencies of Rowe's argument, than I am by his problematic political references", and the third is addressed to the uncertain results of Rowe's theorisation in the field of practice.

He discards one by one the architects who could have been said to be influenced by Rowe. As the result of this proceeding by exclusion, it turns out that Stirling remains the only possibility, as already mentioned, and it is when Rowe attempts to explain the beauty of the

Engineering Building that he asks whether "the words exist?". But even Stirling is eventually not congruent with Rowe's urban polemic, and this leads Baird to ask if in the future it will be the architecture critic rather than the advocate of urban contextualism that will be rediscovered in Colin Rowe. It is hard to say: if it is true that some renewed interest has invested the figure of the British critic; appreciation is emerging for his pedagogic project, and his canonisation by his many students continues.

The series of texts that revolves around OMA, Rem Koolhaas and Dutch architecture, reveals how much more difficult it is to conduct a conclusive investigation on a 'prey' that continually eludes the hunt. Does it have to do with the target's mobility? Or is it inherent to the fact that half of the production in question is actual architecture? A situation not confronted by the masterly inquiries on Rowe and Rykwert that 'anchor' this section.

One way or another, the effort is spread over a larger number of texts, each peculiarly belonging to a different genre, as if trying to overcome the difficulty in dissecting OMA by frequently changing tools. The first assessment of 1977, "Les Extrêmes qui se Touchent", becomes a sort of archival document in the interview with Perspecta's editors, "OMA, Neo-Modern, and Modernity". The review of Mart Stam's Trousers adds some contextual keys, and finally the epistolary formula is adopted ("An Open Letter to Rem Koolhaas") conferring a personal tone of resignation to the endless chase.

Since the last article came out, in 2007, the least that could be said is that the rhythm of Rem Koolhaas' "manifesto" production has even increased. One could mention the interrupted Harvard Project on the City, the use of new words like "education" (he founded Strelka, a private school in Moscow), "preservation" (presented at Unesco and other venues), and finally "research" (the exhibition Elements of Architecture, in the Venice Biennale of 2014 for which he was the director, after having been behind the scenes of the 2010 edition).

This acceleration had the consequence of creating a yet unacknowledged split between Koolhaas the thinker, OMA the office and AMO the agency. From this point of view, "An Open letter to Rem Koolhaas" might be a last attempt to examine the connections between the different spheres, an attempt that George Baird himself seems to find inconclusive, maybe anticipating the further shift he had suspected, but was not evident at the time.

Tracing back our steps for a moment, it is interesting to contrast the assertiveness of "Les Extrêmes Qui se Touchent" with the cautious and methodical reconstruction of the Perspecta interview. In the latter, the arguments from 1977 are thrown like stones in a pond creating broader and broader chronological circles. For example, each declination of Modernist revisionism is discussed in a fashion that reveals the impatience of the young editors to reach conclusions, and the prudence of George Baird in examining, for example, the inertia of form (the comparison of KPF buildings in New York and Montreal), or his warnings to historicise the positions of "The Grays" and Venturi which were more interesting (and to a certain extent remain more interesting) than mainstream opinion subsequently established.

If dealing with Rem Koolhaas was difficult, working on the intellectual biography of Joseph Rykwert is not easy either. The trajectory is the resultant of two vectors: the close association of Baird to Rykwert—not quite as that of student to teacher—with on one side a vast common ground of interests in the 1960s and an intense exchange afterwards—and on the other the evolution of a critical position by Baird in a direction different to that of Rykwert.

His reconstruction opens with what could be seen as a minor episode: three instances in which Rykwert entered a vigorous polemic which ended with the decision by those who commissioned his texts not to publish them. It is interesting that at least in two cases—the attack on the artists Yves Klein and Piero Manzoni, and especially on the Triennale exhibition curated by Aldo Rossi in 1973—it is likely that George Baird would not subscribe to Rykwert's position. Nonetheless, his rigorous method uncovers one by one issues that are at the centre of the Rykwert theoretical web, issues that he deals with more 'scientifically' in the second part of the essay.

In the case of Rykwert's polemic with Aldo Rossi, George Baird hints at the fact that the Italian's structural reading of the city has established a long-lasting hegemony in architectural circles in Europe. This goes with the assumption that it is possible to conveniently separate Rossi's theory from his architectural vocabulary (his—and especially his followers), both of which are problematic for Rykwert, but not for Baird who examines what the two opponents have in common: the rejection of naive Functionalism.

However, for Rykwert, in addition to the lack of an anthropological dimension (despite Rossi's strong claim of Lévi-Strauss), it is the "aggressive rhetorical demeanour" that cannot be acceptable. In retrospect, it is possible to argue that the aggressive ideological-political demeanour could have been a problem too. The polemic remains today not completely understandable, in that it is about an exhibition that meant to establish a "*Tendenza*", a party line, but was in fact more inclusive than exclusive, especially if compared with later label-making exhibitions like the 1981 Biennale by Paolo Portoghesi, The Presence of the Past, or the 1988 Deconstructivist Architecture curated by Philip Johnson and Mark Wigley.

In reaching a conclusion about the influence of Rykwert's ideas on architecture, Baird recognises that "the central analytic focus of his research is (speaking almost archaeologically) several levels below the operative layer within which most cultural and, even more particularly, design praxes have been promulgated". This does not prevent those who can access the layers from discovering links between a historical critical message and the present. For a final example of this, Baird uses Rykwert's re-examination of Perrault definitions of "positive" and "arbitrary" beauty in *The First Moderns*. In analogy to Baird's own use of the reference in his "*La Dimension Amoureuse*", they represent the blueprint for contradictions still operating "in a series of episodes of style, theory and polemic in architecture that typify the century and a half to follow".

The underlying structure of urban life
In trying to grasp the essence of George Baird's position on urban phenomena (and on their metonymic complement—public space), one has to bring together again texts from various parts of the book. For the sake of symmetry it is possible to identify two groups of three articles that show both differences and continuities.

The first is composed by the older morphological and typological studies on Toronto and North America, that can be read together with the "personal reminiscence" of Rome. The second starts with the study of Las Vegas and ends with the argument for "agency", via the discussion of the New Urbanist's quest for public space.

The three earlier texts look at North America and Europe through knowledge acquired on the field in Toronto, an observation conducted wearing European theoretical spectacles borrowed especially from Rossi and Ungers. This already makes him a pretty rare and interesting voice, as it emerges from the review that he compiles for the French dossier in "Studies on Urban Morphology in North America".

The second group of texts ("Las Vegas", "New Urbanist", "Agency") recognises implicitly the limits of both the analytical and the political instruments that were trusted in the earlier phase. By observing new unexpected manifestations of urbanity in Las Vegas; in making concession for the usefulness of limited changes in the urban spaces *a propos* New Urbanism; and finally by reframing the question at a global scale in his opposing agency to utopia, Baird is possibly hinting at a new *episteme*. There are nonetheless several specific continuities in these two periods, from the importance of land ownership patterns in urban evolution, to the criticism of the Modernist Heroic Period's lack of realism *vis a vis* the urban structure.

Is George Baird's 'catalogue' of cities limited? They certainly are paradigmatic. Toronto is studied for its specificity, but also as a specimen of the North American city. Rome and Las Vegas are reflected upon for their influence as models across time and space, and in a way confirming the original intuition of Venturi and Scott Brown that they are somewhat complementary.

40 years ago George Baird and a group of students embarked on applying "evolving methodologies" to Toronto. The need to understand the history of the city was closely linked with that of establishing a normative approach to its transformation. This experience, limited to the downtown, is theorised more profoundly in the report on urban studies in North America prepared for a research initiative of the French Ministry. Here we find a pertinent criticism of the relatively young urban design practices introduced in Boston, Philadelphia and New York, but also a friendly criticism of the attempt to make urban design stronger undertaken by Colin Rowe, in a way that will reappear in Baird's later critique.

Figure-ground disconnected from a structural dimension, such as that implied by "patterns of land ownership", becomes more formal (like "cardboard and cheese"), but less effective. Beyond this example, Robert Stern's survey of the suburbs and Mario Gandelsonas' analytical drawings, are admittedly lacking the ambition to define an operative position.

This is the first time that he points to the fact that all progressive urban models, as far back as Tony Garnier, were 'distracted' about the fact that "the lot is the basis of urban morphology", not for an aesthetic preference, but for a fallacious ideological and political project predicated on a "collectivist form of land tenure".

In retrospect, his cautionary observation that the Second World War created in many European cities the possibility of experimenting with a *tabula rasa*, should be supplemented by the consideration of the techniques used for the formidable expansion of the cities in the years after reconstruction. Planners adopted models of varying density in Europe, with private development opting in general for denser settlement patterns, and public development unfortunately for more sparse ones. So zoning came from Europe with norms that tended to preclude the development of contemporary urban fabric.

Starting from the years in which he was testing urban analysis in North America, it has to be said that in Europe new forms of large-scale development were encouraged (public, private and mixed), in which it would be possible to recreate conditions of normative design regulations beyond the street pattern. In France, this is the story of the *projet urbain*, which often produced contrived 'islands', not quite as dense as the traditional city, and with very controversial results.

A measure of how the urban transformations globally justify the generalising tone of Baird's "agency" manifesto, is provided by the three specific aspects of the North American city that he felt necessary to identify to move beyond the European categories: the urban land grid, the tall building and the suburb.

If it is true that the urban grid continues, negotiating geography, to dominate American cities, the other two have colonised Europe to an extent that was not foreseeable, and for which no useful recipes like the ones proposed by George Baird have been possible to reimport from North America.

The lesson of Rome that he learns is not completely different from the one that is possible to learn in Las Vegas: at a very different pace, the city evolution is incremental and overlapping. At the same time, the history of the city as a model (according to Baird, from the age of reason, to that of instrumentality, to that of modernity) goes in an opposite direction, that of simplification. At least this seems to be the schema until Brasilia, but also until the last essay on "agency" opens the view on a range of situations wider than those created by Western urbanisation.

So Rome is not Baroque, and its Modernism is not Heroic, but it is intriguing how Baird reads Libera and Moretti in the same way that Le Corbusier read Michelangelo—outside orthodoxy. Italian architecture of the twentieth century remains important precisely because it is modern—without the movement. In this

historical perspective, it could be useful to dust off morphology and typology as universal tools. Following the interesting comparisons made in the text on Rome, it would be possible to explain the rupture between the Parisian 'hotel' and Haussmanian tenement, in contrast with the continuity of Roman Renaissance palazzo and nineteenth-century apartment building.

How different is the research conducted with students first in Toronto, and 30 years later in Las Vegas? This is another opportunity to appreciate not only the evolution of the research, but the context in which it takes place. The first descent into the city was highly selective, normative, projected in the past to orient the future. The second is open and multi-layered, no less curious and systematic, but certainly less hopeful to determine consequence. It could be said that we all have to accept the shift from the paradigm of 'learning from' derived from the original Las Vegas fieldtrip of Venturi and Scott Brown, to that of 'understanding' Dubai of the Harvard Project on the City fieldtrips led by Rem Koolhaas.

Whereas a part of architecture culture (the one that George Baird polemically labels "neo-avant-garde"), contents itself with contemplating the crisis of the city, or at most is engaged in documenting or aestheticising it, he is willing to recognise the operable limits of design. The last two essays are in this respect once again complementary without being contradictory. In cities where small variations can be negotiated and put to the test (like the Canadian examples provided in "The New Urbanism and Public Space"), a street rather than a square and its layout can make a difference.

In the global metropolis, where masses of population arrive and settle, human agency can be more politically effective than indulgence in Utopia.

In this particular polemic, the way of constructing the argument that is a reason to admire George Baird's writing, leaves room for a more passionate opposition. In the first part of the text, the two influences of Jameson and Arendt are perfectly staged, as usual, with their ramifications from the philosophical to the political dimension, all the way down to the marginal arena of architectural theory. However, when it is time to provide examples, the camp of Utopia remains inevitably empty, and the opposite camp is rich with references from all continents.

On the other hand, it is legitimate to ask: where is Utopia in architectural thinking past the age of instrumentality in the nineteenth century? It is even uncertain whether the use of the word Utopia is nothing more than a retrofitting exercise on the radical positions of Modernism, unless it refers to more recent revivals of the Utopia in the version of Archigram, Yona Friedman, etc.

Architectural Diagnostics

This last section of the introduction intends to discuss texts that are very far from each other chronologically and thematically. Here and there I have remarked on the special ability of George Baird to convey the full spectrum of positions on the way to a discussion of the main topic, whether it is architectural, urban, or presents itself under the veil of a biographical exploration. This strategy produces even more remarkable results when the architectural debate is the topic. This is the reason to compare "Semiotics and Architecture" and the article "Criticality and Its Discontents", further developed by the short text in response to the question of why architecture can't just be happy.

It will be a premise of mine to close the circle by returning to the oldest essay, "*La Dimension Amoureuse*" and to its currently productive role as a small 'classic'. Despite the very different occasion and purpose, "Semiotics" and "Criticality" share the large breadth of a reconstruction, spanning two long overlapping arches and bringing us an open question about the future.

In "Semiotics and Architecture" he identifies the moments and places in which the post-war crisis of Modernism led to the search for alternatives based on the trust in a 'scientific' paradigm which would purge the exhausted Functionalism of any remaining arbitrary trace of the pre-war identification of ideologies and styles with the charismatic 'masters'. ULM's Hochschule für Gestaltung was certainly one of these crossroads, in that it hosted Maldonado, Rykwert and Norberg-Schulz. But Baird also thoroughly documents the two influential strands of anthropology and semiology emerging in Italy, and especially in France.

The reconstruction is far from narrowly specialised. On account of the rapid decline of the possibility of a fully theorised semiology in architecture, he examines the fertilisation operated across the architectural discourse in the 1970s and 1980s. He concedes that his co-editor Charles Jencks was able successfully to popularise the unwanted consequences of the rediscovery of the symbolic, implicitly evoking a Faustian pact to which he remained a spectator in Toronto where he had returned at the end of the 1960s. So

it was not with too much a regret that he noted "By the mid-1990s, the impact of the combination of neo-avant-gardist and phenomenological attacks on Postmodernism—and by implication on semiotics and Structuralism as well—was effective enough to largely destroy the intellectual legitimacy that architecture and urban design had inherited from that body of theory."

Interestingly, in this article there is no mention of the term "Deconstructivism", despite the fact that a show by the same title opened at MoMA in 1988. Could it be said that Deconstructivism unified the two positions that he calls "neo-avant-gardist" and "phenomenological?" He does not blame them for killing the semiotics baby in the cradle, given that it had been raised to become a young Postmodernist man. However, their unification delayed by a decade the realisation that he anticipated: "It has become apparent that the architecture of critique is now a largely exhausted trope and cannot any longer sustain substantial new design creativity."

In the meantime, George Baird could find some consolation in the arrival of a new pragmatism, which was not alien to a sophisticated intellectual dimension. Certain works of architecture on both sides of the Ocean seemed to materialise the theory of decorum that he began advocating already at the end of the 1960s, now as a form of "new sobriety". This in turn should not be confused with minimalism, a vague term nowhere to be found in his writings.

The interest in Solà-Morales, already discussed, reflects that for architects put under his lens by the influential Spanish critic: Eduardo Souto de Moura, Herzog & de Meuron, and in addition to these, Tony Fretton, Atelier Bow-Wow.

It may be bending George Baird's words instrumentally to say that these developments begin to close the "split (in) the intelligentsia of the profession off from its mainstream practitioners more severely than any time since the early part of twentieth century" that he denounced at the end of his encyclopedia entry in 1998.

With the article on "Criticality and Its Discontents" in 2004 George Baird punctured the balloon of another controversy. He did it so well that the opposing factions of advocates of critical and post-critical architecture have not been able to reorganise.

The point of departure is the reference to a seminal text by Michael Hays from 20 years before: "Critical Architecture: Between Culture and Form". Given its notoriety, he does not quote from it in writing for the *Harvard Design Magazine*, a publication from the school where both he and Hays taught. In rereading Hays' "Critical Architecture", I found two passages towards the conclusion that are very relevant for Baird's argument, but also for the decade between then and now: "Authorship can resist the authority of culture, stand against the generality of habit and the particularity of nostalgic memory, and still have a very precise intention", and "if critical architectural design is resistant and oppositional, then architectural criticism—as activity and knowledge—should be open and contentious as well".

The political dimension of "Criticality and Its Discontents" is more important than the authorial one in the argument mounted by Baird, because it is the principal point polemically used by the younger advocates of a projective/efficacious architecture (M Speaks, R Somol, S Whiting, S Allen). The other aspect, the need for critical architecture to legitimise authorship remains behind the scene. Seen from today it appears equally important. The cult of authorship is the corner stone of the "efficacy" of the star system especially in its "critical" version.

George Baird's argument fuels a possible interpretation (which he would, of course, be free to reject) that could be synthesised as follows.

In the late 1960s and 1970s two relevant questions emerged in architecture: one having to do with referential content and symbolism, the other with the urban in a structural mode of thinking. These questions are at the centre of the historicist wave in architecture known as Postmodernism. The wave was powerful, but was wrecked on the rocks of a nostalgic and shallow formal vocabulary (George Baird was one of the first to blow the whistle, as can be read in his essay on Venturi of 1976). The criticality that arrived after historicism was questioned on grounds that were more political than formal (from Kenneth Frampton to Mary McLeod). With the Deconstructivist exhibition, the unquestioned heart of the historicist paradigm is displaced by an apparently "critical" one. Baird warns: "it became apparent that the putative tropes of the then-ascendant 'Deconstructivism' were much less 'critical' than many had expected them to be".

To be sure Michael Hays is not responsible: the MoMA exhibition was curated four years later by Johnson and Wigley. However it could be said, forcing slightly George Baird's accurate reconstruction in his article, that critical architecture was the powerful amplifier of the professional efficacy of a specific group of architects, once a label and a medium were provided by MoMA.

The fact that some of the most interesting protagonists, such as Frank Gehry and Rem Koolhaas, have always manifested a discomfort for the label and its unintended consequences, is in the end less important. Anyone who had a conversation with Robert Venturi on the subject of Postmodernism could have heard the same complaints 20 years before.

The post-critical authors argue for inspiration to be found in "popular culture and the creativity of the marketplace", yet most architects of note seem reluctant to make this visible and explicit—are they stuck in a "critical" position? Even Rem Koolhaas seen in conversation with Tony Fadell (the CEO of Nest, inventor of the self-teaching thermostat) at the opening of the Venice Biennale in 2014, came across as "critical" compared to the "post-critical" entrepreneur, notwithstanding the latter's social and environmental good intentions. Maybe George Baird would agree that the interesting architecture seen in the last decade has been more elusively realist (Caruso & St John), than aggressively projective (Bjarke Ingels Group).

Not appearing to take sides, George Baird recruits Manfredo Tafuri (who was negative on utopias and considered avant-garde completely deflated), against Peter Eisenman, the target of the post-critical assault. This partiality is legitimate in light of the negative meaning that for George Baird has always tainted the term neo-avant-garde (past the original ones at the beginning of the twentieth century). In the future it would be interesting to read one of his formidable essays to put this polemical target sharply in focus.

It is worth noting that the conclusion of the "Criticality and Its Discontents" text in 2004 is quite skeptical since "A number of questions remain to be asked… before a truly robust and durable new professional stance will be able to be achieved." It is maybe the emerging of new architectures by a number of practitioners to which he has devoted critical attention that inspire a less doubtful answer in a more recent text, recognising "that even if architecture 'can't just be happy', it does have the capacity to find numerous, engaging ways to insert itself into the consciousness of its users, so as to evoke equally engaging responses, among which one might well be 'happiness'."

Closing the circle brings us back to the "La Dimension Amoureuse", written by George Baird at the age of 28. In concluding the re-examination of "Semiotics and Architecture", he was hoping that "perhaps the combination of the inadequacies of the once-ascendant avant-gardist project, combined with the aura of historical rediscovery, will yet reinvigorate the historic project of semiotics and architecture".

The fate of "*La Dimension Amoureuse*" is perhaps not the sign of that, but rather of its specific productivity. After all, Michael Hays paired it up with Manfredo Tafuri's critique of ideology, to open his collection of essays in architectural theory: *Architecture Theory Since 1968*, of 1998. At the 2012 Conference on Baird in Toronto, Louis Martin put the essay at the centre of another reconstruction of revisionist efforts that will eventually echo in "Criticality and Its Discontents". Pier Vittorio Aureli, on the same occasion, actualised the dialectic of Eero Saarinen and Cedric Price from which the essay started, to "argue that a return to the importance of the "*La Dimension Amoureuse*" of architecture invoked by Baird in 1969 today must be connected with the reality of political economy in which the social sphere is not a domain free from economic instrumentality (if it ever was), but rather its most fertile terrain of reproduction". Aureli continued: "In such context, language, rhetoric and any semiotic construct is not just a means of interpersonal communication, but one of the most powerful means of production...."

Having crossed many of the texts contained in this book along diagonal lines, one is confronted in conclusion with the question whether George Baird's intellectual and professional biography belongs to a past for which we should feel only nostalgia.

The world in which his research has taken place has changed, and he has evolved with it. The venues and instruments of architectural theory have been transformed; in urban politics there are new zones and non-conventional forms of action; next to traditional schools, institutions have been established that support architectural research, and not only historical research; the status of the printed text vacillates, but new opportunities have presented themselves under the rubric "curatorial".

New forms of intellectual labour will surely produce new biographies. To deal with this complex reality, among the intellectual protagonists that emerged in the 1960s, there is no one who can provide us with greater assistance than George Baird.

Architecture
and Semiotics

In the fall of 1964, I arrived with my wife in London England, where I was to commence a doctoral dissertation at the Bartlett School of Architecture in University College London, under the supervision of Robert Maxwell. Maxwell, who remains a friend to this day—and is now 92 years old—proved to be an extraordinarily generous and well-connected mentor. A rather naive young architect upon my arrival in London, I had no idea that I was about to become part of the most intellectually stimulating architectural milieu extant in the world at that time. Over time, through Maxwell, I became acquainted with, among others, Alan Colquhoun, Peter Cook, Kenneth Frampton, John Miller, Monica Pidgeon, Joseph Rykwert, Sam Stevens and James Stirling.

Colquhoun assisted me in obtaining a teaching position at the Architectural Association School, and I became an occasional contributor to the Association Journal, then called *Arena*. In 1966, its editor, Francis Duffy invited me to edit a guest issue on the theme of "Meaning in Architecture", which, by that time, had become the focus of my work on my prospective dissertation. At the Bartlett, along with Maxwell, I had already become a dissenter to the increasingly well established tendency there that was coming to be known as "systematic design methodology". In my intellectual efforts to counter that problematic tendency, I found myself turning to theories of symbolism and to anthropology. And in that quest, I came upon the work, first of the literary critic Roland Barthes, then, of the anthropologist Claude Lévi-Strauss, and finally, of the linguist, Ferdinand de Saussure.

La Dimension Amoureuse in Architecture, 1969

… la rhétorique, qui n'est rien d'autre que la technique de l'information exacte, est lié non seulement à toute littérature, mais encore à toute communication, dès lors qu'elle veut faire entendre à l'autre que nous le reconnaissons; la rhétorique est la dimension amoureuse de l'écriture.[1]

It was out of that intellectual brew that I developed the argument of *"La Dimension Amoureuse"*, which was my own contribution to the June 1967 issue of *Arena* that also included the first publication of the seminal text of Joseph Rykwert, "The Dining Position: A Question of Method", and the equally seminal one of Alan Colquhoun: "Typology and Design Method". By the time I was preparing the special issue, I had also met and become friends with an American who was also a fellow doctoral scholar at the Bartlett, Charles Jencks. An enthusiastic collaborator in the undertaking, Charles contributed a review of the recently published and very relevant book of Robert Venturi: *Complexity and Contradiction in Architecture*.

The special issue caused a sufficient stir in architectural circles in London, that Charles and I were invited to turn it into a book. Since I was already in the process of leaving London to return to Toronto, it was agreed that Charles would shoulder the bulk of the editorial work of producing the book version of "Meaning in Architecture", which appeared in 1969.

It is not unprecedented to suggest that architecture occupies its place in human experience through some kind of communication. By the mid-eighteenth century, Germain Boffrand had already speculated that "the profiles of mouldings and the other parts which compose a building are to architecture what words are to speech".[2]

Nowadays we know all too well that Eero Saarinen's TWA terminal at Kennedy Airport symbolises "flight"; we have heard him say that the "beauty" of his CBS building "will be, I believe, that it will be the simplest skyscraper statement in New York".[3] In fact, even discussions of "symbolism" and "statement" provoke vigorous protest today. The young English architect, Cedric Price, for instance, recently criticised architects' preoccupation with the "role of architecture as a provider of visually recognisable symbols of identity, place and activity". Call it a fix or the "image of a city", said Price, "such overt self-consciousness is embarrassing only to a few—in general, it is both incomprehensible and irrelevant".[4] Familiar as it may be, then, the issue is a contentious one.

Now Saarinen's and Price's importance for this paper does not only lie in their having made their positions as clear as that. As Saarinen was, so Price is a designer of facility and sophistication. As one might expect, then, both of them have produced designs which aptly reflect their respective views. This means that it is possible to see even more clearly in their work than in their remarks, just how fundamentally they have both misconceived the question which presently concerns me; the question of just how it is that architecture occupies its place in human experience. The designs I mean to discuss are Saarinen's CBS building,[5] and Price's Potteries Thinkbelt project for a technical university in the English Midlands.[6]

There is no doubt that CBS, the prominent seat of a prestigious American corporation, is a definitive example of what Robert Venturi calls "establishment Modern architecture"; it is well-known that the Thinkbelt, conceived in terms of minimum cost and maximum efficiency, has been proposed as the antithesis of a building like CBS.[7] Yet the designs' similarities are really more extensive and more important than their differences. That CBS and the Thinkbelt are thought of as antithetical seems to me only to show the shallowness of the controversy they represent; the depth of their designers' misconception of architecture's place in human experience.

This misconception is neatly summed up in the respective approaches of the two designs to the detailed organisation of human occupation of space. In the Thinkbelt project, the designer stops well short of offering the occupant, say, an ash-tray (on the grounds that there is no guarantee that the designer and the occupant have the same cultural values), while at CBS, the designers only *allow* him one approved by Florence Knoll (since there is no guarantee that the designer and the occupant have the same cultural values). But this is just an ironic illustration of my point. To grasp the full scale of the misconception involved requires examination of these designs' historical context. After all, the concept of "total design" underlying CBS, following Gropius' "total theatre" and "total architecture", is nothing more nor less than a Wagnerian *Gesamtkunstwerk*.[8] And Price's idea of architecture as "life-conditioning" rests on essentially the same view of human experience as Jeremy Bentham's *Panopticon*. Both designs' conceptual premises then, lie deep in the intellectual history of the nineteenth century. What we ought eventually to understand, is how CBS and the Thinkbelt, as manifestations of *Gesamtkunstwerk* and "life-conditioning", show the bizarre consequences which even today follow from that century's loss of faith in rhetoric.

The first of those consequences is that modern designers, especially those like Saarinen and Price, become caught up in partly conscious, partly unconscious attempts to assume privileged positions with respect to the groups of people who will occupy the environments they design. The architectural *Gesamtkünstler* assumes a stance towards those groups analogous to that of Wagner *vis a vis* his audiences. He takes quite for granted his capacity to enhance the lives of the occupants of his buildings; he believes that enhancement ultimately depends upon the occupants' conscious experience of their environment being dramatically heightened; he is thus committed to a "total" predetermination of their experience of the environment, from every conceivable point of view. In short, were he successful, he would occupy a privileged position in the sense that he would stand utterly *over and above his fellows'* experience of the environment he had designed.

The "life-conditioner", on the other hand, is not paternalistic, but scientistic. He assumes a stance towards his fellows analogous to that of a nineteenth-century natural scientist towards and experiment he is conducting. He is anxious to take nothing for granted, to sustain an absolute neutrality with respect to the experience the occupants have of the environments he has designed. He believes his neutrality precludes his taking any account of their experience of it and he thus resorts to a designed anonymity, the purpose of which is a 'total' non-determination of the occupants' experience of that environment. Were the life-conditioner successful, he would occupy a privileged position in the sense that he would stand utterly *outside* his fellows' experience of the environment he had designed. To sum up, the *Gesamtkünstler* treats his fellows as children; the life-conditioner treats them as objects. Now I introduced this matter of the attempt to assume a privileged position, as one of the bizarre consequences of the nineteenth century's loss of faith in rhetoric. What I should really in the first instance say is that the *Gesamtkünstler* and the life-conditioner forget—or else take completely for granted—just how inescapably the design act is always a gesture in a social context. Their oversight can be seen to have been a part of a loss of faith in rhetoric only in the light of the current revival of interest in the ancient subject, which surrounds the work of men such as Roland Barthes, Ernst Gombrich, Claude Lévi-Strauss, and Marshall McLuhan.[9] This revival is due, of course, to the fact that all of these men have attempted to analyse and understand various kinds of gesture-in-a-social-context, by means of either the traditional categories of rhetoric, or the concepts of modern communication theory.

In criticising Saarinen's and Price's misconceptions, in discussing how it is that architecture occupies its place in human experience, I shall rely most heavily upon the ideas of Lévi-Strauss. The reason is that he has staked the most audacious, yet most intellectually tenable claim of the four, proposing anthropology as the intellectual discipline of most comprehensive

Entry to Eero Saarinen's CBS building.

human relevance, and doing so in an expansive fashion which appears to accommodate many of the others' most impressive ideas. Lévi-Strauss has explained his claim for anthropology, by calling it the "bona-fide" occupant of the domain of *semiology*. This, the comprehensive theory of communications, the linguist Ferdinand de Saussure introduced half a century ago as the study of life of signs at the heart of social life.[10] Taking its cue from Lévi-Strauss' "structural" anthropology, modern semiology looks on *all* social phenomena as communication systems; not just the obvious ones such as literature and films, but also kinship systems, culinary customs, clothing habits, and, of course, architecture.

The part of semiological theory which bears most directly on the problem of modern designers' attempts to assume privileged positions, is the part Saussure described by means of the *langue/parole* distinction. For semiology, any social phenomenon is made up of both and *langue* and *parole*. In the first of three senses, the *langue* is the collective aspect of the phenomenon, and the *parole* the individual aspect. Thus, semiology incorporates the fundamental sociological insight that human experience, in so far as it is social, is simultaneously collective and individual.

In the second of the three senses, semiology sees the *langue* as the unconscious aspect of a social phenomenon, and the *parole* as the conscious aspect. In this way, it incorporates one of the most obvious insights of post-nineteenth-century psychology, and posits that any conscious gesture in a social context always involves an unconscious component. With respect to these two senses of the *langue/parole* distinction in language, Barthes has said:

The *langue* is both a social institution and a system of values. As a social institution, it is never an act; it utterly eludes premeditation; it is the social part of language; the individual can, by himself, neither create it, nor modify it; it is essentially a collective contract, which, if one wishes to communicate, one must accept in its entirety. What is more, this social product is autonomous, like a game which has rules one must know before one can play it…. As opposed to the *langue*, institution and system, the *parole* is essentially an individual act of selection and actualisation….[11]

Montage drawing showing a general view of the Madeley Transfer Area: a part of Cedric Price's Thinkbelt project.

In the most modern sense of the distinction, the *langue* of a social phenomenon is considered to be its "code", and the *parole* its "message". In some respects, this new sense of the distinction is the most interesting, because it introduces into semiology a number of precise mathematical techniques of analysis, commonly grouped under the term "information theory". In terms parallel to collective/individual and unconscious/conscious senses of the distinction, we may say that the particular "message" which any gesture in a social context constitutes, necessarily involves the use of the "code" which that context entails.

Of course, information theory goes even further than that nowadays, viewing communication systems as dynamic. While the relation holding between the *langue* and the *parole* is necessarily constant, the system as a whole is in a continuous process of development. More specifically, "information" occurs as a function of "surprise" within a matrix of "expectancy". In order to register, a message must be somewhat surprising, yet not utterly unexpected. If it is too predictable, the message won't register at all. It is in this sense that "background noise" tends to slip below the threshold of awareness, and that we speak of clichés as not having enough "information value". Conversely, if the message is too unpredictable, the result is the same. As Paul McCartney has said, "… if music… is just going to jump about five miles ahead, then everyone's going to be left standing with this gap of five miles that they've got to

all cross before they can even see what scene these people are on…".[12][13]

We can now, I think, begin to see how the *Gesamtkünstler* and the life-conditioner become involved in their own attempts to assume privileged positions. If, for example, we examine their stances in the light of the collective/individual sense of the *langue/parole* distinction, the following becomes apparent. In undertaking "total design", the *Gesamtkünstler* presumes *ipso facto*, either individually, or as part of a small elite, to take over comprehensive responsibility for the *langue* of architecture, and to do so, moreover, in a fashion which leaves the *langue*'s collective validity unimpaired. In other words, "total design" amounts to an attempt to shift the impact of the individual design act from the level of *parole* to that of *langue*. On the other hand, in making his individual design gesture, the life-conditioner pretends to act altogether independently of the *langue* of architecture. But of course, since he like the *Gesamtkünstler*, is only an individual acting in a social context, his presence really amounts to a single-handed attempt at a radical modification of the *langue*. And that is just another way of saying that he too attempts to shift the impact of the individual design away from the level of the *parole* to that of *langue*.

Then, too, the unconscious/conscious sense of the *langue/parole* distinction throws further light on their attempts at privileged positions. As I have said above, the *Gesamtkünstler* makes his attempt for the purpose of dramatically heightening the occupants' conscious experience of the environment he has designed. The life-conditioner, on the other hand, makes his for exactly the opposite purpose. But what they both do, in this respect, is to take for granted their own capacity for consciously manipulating their fellows' threshold of awareness of the environment in question.

An examination of such designers' attitudes in terms of code and message only confirms the picture now emerging. Neither sees fit to modulate his design gesture in terms of either its "surprise" or its "expectancy". Indeed, were it not the case of architecture under consideration, I would say that the emphatic manner in which the CBS environment has been imposed upon its occupants would no doubt result in its being sensed only as "background noise", while Price's look-no-hands gesture would leave the Thinkbelt's occupants with their own gap of five miles to cross before they could make any sense of the environment in which they found themselves. But alas, it *is* the case of architecture under consideration, and analogies from music don't apply perfectly straightforwardly. Unlike music, architecture is inescapably operative in human experience. When music becomes background noise, its unconscious impact is incidental; when architecture becomes background noise, its unconscious impact is still far from incidental.

The illumination provided by the *langue/parole* distinction is also capable of graphic representation. Extracting from it two of its particular senses, unconscious/conscious, and code/message, one can portray the field of meaning of any social phenomenon, as shown in the adjacent diagram. The line across the top of the diagram represents increasing expectancy, and that across the bottom, increasing surprise. In terms of the capacity for registering messages which I described above, the extent of the overlap between the line indicating the threshold of minimum awareness, and that indicating maximum awareness, defines the field of meaning. The length of the bottom line then, from the one threshold to the other, represents the scope of articulation of the social phenomenon in question. In the language of information theory, the *langue* of architecture is the gamut of conceivable perceptible articulations, which the *parole* comprises the possibility of selective combination across that gamut. But that is only the abstract formation of the relation. Since, as Barthes says, the *langue* is a

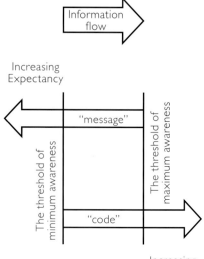

"social institution and a system of values", one can say much more. Take as examples those very concepts "house", "overcoat", "commuter service", and "shop", whose "existing definitions" Price deprecated in his introduction to the Thinkbelt.[14] We can consider the *langue* as the gamut of articulation defined in such complex environmental concepts as those. The *parole*, then, comprises the selective possibility of variation implicit in the gamut. To suggest that the *langue* comprises such a gamut is not to imply that there is anything inherently significant or stable about those particular, or any particular concepts. For the *langue* lies in the gamut of articulation, and not in any primary functional category those concepts might be thought to represent. To suggest that there were such categories would be to fall into the historicism and/or the functional Platonism which, one presumes, have provoked Price's objections.

On the other hand, to suggest that the *langue* comprises such a gamut is very much to claim that the place as "social institution", which such albeit non-primary concepts hold, can be ignored only at the risk of diminishing the scope of articulation of the whole of the environment. In short, as *langue*, such concepts establish the fixes which allow the corresponding variability of *parole*. The greater the scope of *langue*, the greater the possible variation of *parole*.

In fact, Price's attack on the "ephemerality" of those definitions is most noteworthy in the way it recalls the linguistic crusade which was launched in immediately post-revolutionary Russia, and which has been described by Roman Jakobson.[15] In that case, a number of theorists argued that phrases such as "the sun is setting" ought to be expunged from Communist speech, on the grounds that they were obsolete remnants of a non-scientific mentality. Obviously, a success in either of these cases would have as its chief result simply an impoverishment of the existing cultural situation.

Up to this point, I have concerned myself with modern designers' attempts to assume privileged positions. But that is only the first of the consequences of the nineteenth century's loss of faith in rhetoric. For the premises underlying the *Gesamtkunstwerk* and life-conditioning also involve such designers in a belief that their designs embody what we might call an *absolute perceptual transparency*: a belief that they can take for granted their fellows' capacity to see each design "as it itself really is".[16] And, of course, the corollaries of that belief, typical of both the *Gesamtkunstwerk* and life-conditioning, are an aversion to ambiguity, and an incapacity for ever sustaining irony.

Consider again Saarinen's conviction concerning the CBS building. "Its beauty will be", he said, "that it will be the simplest skyscraper statement in New York". Later on, he continued, "when you look at this building, you will know exactly what is going on. It is a very direct and simple structure."[17] What Saarinen has done, it seems to me, is to take the "objectivist" aesthetic of orthodox Modernism in its most literally expressionist sense, and then to assume that his design was capable, through its transparent "simplicity", of rendering directly accessible to his fellows an ultimate, universal, even meta-physical reality.

Price, for his part, looks on all such concerns with considerable contempt. He prefers, like his Utilitarian predecessors, to affect a matter-of-fact pragmatism with respect to all aspects of human experience. Nevertheless, his pragmatism rests on an assumption of architecture's perceptual transparency which is just as absolute as Saarinen's. For he takes for granted the capacity of a configuration of built form as elaborate as the Thinkbelt, to unfold *itself* in his fellows' experience as nothing more nor less than a "servicing mechanism", that is to say, as unambiguously and unobtrusively as, say, a coffee-vending machine.

If however, we take seriously the proposition put above, that there is nothing *inherently* significant, or stable, about any particular environmental concepts, then we must at the same time recognise the impossibility of taking it for granted that architecture can be perceptually transparent, or that people can *a priori* perceive any environment "as it in itself really is". Indeed, it has been one of the preoccupations of modern philosophers to indicate that we do not even possess any criteria for deciding *in advance* how to measure our fellows' estimates of reality "as it in itself really is". To use Merleau-Ponty's words, "the phenomenological world is not pure being (as Saarinen and Price assume), but rather the sense which is revealed when the paths of my various experiences intersect, and also where my own and other people's intersect and engage each other like gears".[18]

Semiology takes account of these matters in defining the *langue* of a social phenomenon as a set of signs, each of which comprises a signifier and a signified. That is to say, each signifier is something which stands for something else. It is because social phenomena are coded as such sets of signs, that the reality of human experience is socially representable. In the most general perspective, one can say that the ultimate signifier is the social phenomenon's set of signs itself, and the ultimate signified is the 'reality' which that set of signs discloses, and which is accessible to us only through those signs. In other words, for semiology, there is no "getting to the bottom of" any social phenomenon.

Furthermore, semiology looks on the relations holding between signifiers and signifieds, as having been established arbitrarily, or non-isomorphically. For instance, it is not necessary for the purposes of communication, that the signifier "tree" must be the most "tree-like" signifier to describe the phenomenon "tree". So long as once a tree is called a "tree", everyone involved agrees to call it that (or at least to call it that sufficiently frequently that occasional ironic, or humorous exceptions will still make sense). Alternatively, it is this same non-isomorphism that accounts for the simultaneous precision and flexibility of a signifier such as "the season of the year following winter", "a natural source of fresh water", or "a mechanical device for providing flexible support for weight". In short, semiological theory holds that the relations of signifiers and signifieds depend on both a conceptual arbitrariness and an operative non-arbitrariness. And that means, of course, that it is exactly the extent to which signs are capable of misinterpretation, that they are also capable of reinterpretation. To return to the case of architecture, it is just this fact that enables Aldo Van Eyck to say that "it is not merely what a space sets out to define in human terms that gives it place-value, but

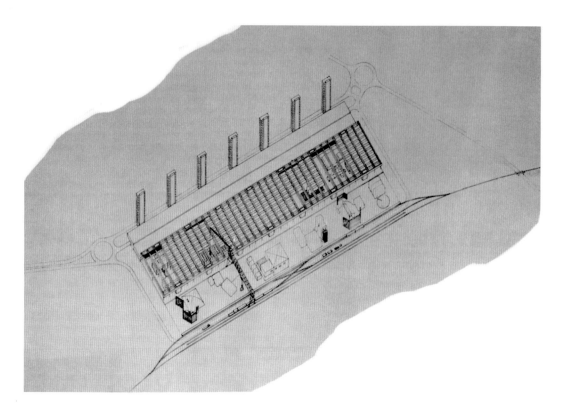

Axonometric view of the Madeley Transfer Area.

what it is able to gather and transmit".[19] We can now see why the beliefs underlying the *Gesamtkunstwerk* and life-conditioning both entail such an aversion to ambiguity, such an incapacity for ever sustaining irony. In so far as either conception still allows any appreciation of the fact that the environment consists of a set of signs, it involves designers in an attempt to cut through all that, to "get to the bottom of the situation" in exactly the fashion I have just described as impossible.

Take the case of Saarinen. In assuming that the "ultimate reality" which he intended his design to reveal depended so completely upon its "directness" and "simplicity", he would obviously feel that he could not afford to leave any part of the detail of that design "unsimplified", that is to say unclear or less than utterly straightforward. On the other hand, in taking for granted the capacity of the Thinkbelt to unfold *itself* in human experience "as it in itself really is", Price would obviously see no reason to concern himself with such "ephemeral" matters. The life-conditioner, like the *Gesamtkünstler*, always sees ambiguity as compromise, and irony as hypocrisy.

The irony of ironies is that there is no ambiguity less controlled, no irony less sustained, than that which follows from these naivetes. But to show that requires two further tenets of semiological theory. I have already quoted Merleau-Ponty to the effect that what we perceive is "the sense which is revealed where the paths of my various experiences intersect, and also where my own and other people's intersect and engage each other like gears". In other words, not only are we able to perceive only in terms of a past and present context, but we inevitably do perceive in such a context, if we perceive at all. Semiology takes account of this by positing that the signs which make up the *langue* of a social phenomenon carry meaning through the fact of their total mutual interrelatedness. It is in this sense that Colin Cherry said: "Signals do not convey information as railway trucks carry coal."[20] That is, any individual sign in a code has a particular meaning by virtue of its distinctiveness from every other sign in that code. To understand a sign means in this sense to be aware of the set of alternative possible signs from the code that could conceivably take that sign's place. This dimension of meaning Saussure characterised as "the relationship of substitution" between the signs in the code.

However, the distinctiveness of all the signs in the code—one from another—needn't be absolute. For a sign, or to be more precise, a signifier, can stand for, or substitute for, a range of signifieds, the precise reference to be established through the actual context of the sign in question. (Recall again the example of "spring" discussed above.) To understand a sign in this sense means to be aware of the extent to which the signs surrounding a particular sign qualify its particular significance. This dimension of meaning Saussure characterised as "the relationship of contiguity" between the signs assembled in any particular message.

Saussure illustrated this distinction by an actual architectural analogy himself, saying:

> Each linguistic unit is like a column of an antique temple: this column is in a real relation of contiguity with other parts of the building, the architrave for example; but if this column is Doric, it reminds us of the other architectural orders, Ionic or Corinthian, and this is a relation of substitution.[21]

Jakobson has subsequently argued that Saussure's distinction between contiguity and substitution is capable of further elucidation.[22] While, in Saussure's sense of the distinction, any message would necessarily be defined in terms of both contiguity and substitution, Jakobson thought that at the level of "style", one could point to a possibility of emphasis on one or other of the two poles. He claimed that certain works of art were characterised primarily through relations of substitution (metaphor, in his terminology) while others were characterised more through relations of contiguity (metonymy, in that terminology). Thus, he saw romanticist and symbolist poetry, and Chaplin's films, as emphasising the pole of metaphor, and realist literature and Griffith's films as emphasising metonymy. In architecture, one can point to a work like Mies' Farnsworths House as emphasising the pole of metaphor, not only because of the reductive substitution from the norm "house" which that design involves, but also because each element which remains is thereby super-charged with metaphorical significance. On the other hand, works like Carlo Scarpa's renovation of the Medieval palace of Verona, or an interior by Alexander Girard, emphasise the role of metonymy, since they do not substitute reductively from their norms, nor powerfully metaphorise their individual elements, but rather build up their significance out of the assembly of relatively diverse parts.

When, however, in this perspective, we get to designs like CBS and the Thinkbelt, we encounter what can only be described as a radical polarisation between metaphor and metonymy. The Thinkbelt makes a radical substitution, both reductive (through the complete elimination of anticipated academic elements), and non-reductive (through a major shift from academic to industrial iconography), from the norm "university". CBS on the other hand, undertakes a radical intensification of the assembly of all its diverse elements (from the details of the window wall right down to the relations of the already-mentioned ash trays and potted plants).

It is this radical polarisation which results first in the uncontrolled ambiguity and unsustained irony and eventually in the impoverishment of the existing cultural situation, which I referred to above. The first result occurs because polarisation has the effect of eroding the occupants' capacity for detecting *in the particular design itself* any very helpful evidence of its relation to the historic and present context in which it has taken place. Thus, the occupants are obliged all by themselves to bring to their experience of the environment that awareness of alternative possible environments on which that particular environment's whole distinctiveness rests. Far from being perceptually transparent then, CBS and the Thinkbelt are in fact highly opaque; they tend to confront their occupants in the first instance as uncontrollably ambiguous, except in so far as those occupants' previous experience lends any stability to the situation. Subsequently, of course, when that previous experience is no longer so effectively operative, the second result of polarisation occurs. The precarious ambiguity and irony of the first stage collapse altogether, and the occupants are no longer even able to *conceive of* those alternative possible environments. And that, effectively, amounts to an impoverishment of the existing cultural situation.

Of course, in discussing the results of this polarisation, I have moved on a stage in my general argument, from a consideration of the consequences of the nineteenth century's loss of faith in rhetoric, to a consideration in turn, of those consequences' own effects. Let me briefly go back over my argument so far, so that I may try to indicate, in the light of semiological theory, just what *those* effects might be.

Interior view of a secretarial area in the CBS building.

My first conclusion in these terms was that both the *Gesamtkünstler* and the life-conditioner attempt to shift the impact of the individual design gesture from the level of *parole* to that of *langue*. Just what that involves is neatly illustrated in the now-so-fashionable quotations from *Through the Looking-Glass*.

"When I use a word", Humpty Dumpty said in a rather scornful tone, "I mean just what I choose it to mean, neither more nor less." "The question is", said Alice, "whether you can make words mean so many different things". "The question is", said Humpty Dumpty, "who is to be master".[23]

Now, short of establishing a dictatorship which is either ruled or managed by designers, neither the *Gesamtkünstler* nor the life-conditioner is likely to have much success on this front. Nor would it seem that their failure in this respect would have any serious consequences. But there is the assumption that they are in a position to consciously manipulate their fellows' threshold of conscious awareness. In this case, it seems to me, the situation is more complicated. After all, it *is* possible to manipulate others' thresholds of awareness, at least to some extent. And not only that. An attempt at such manipulation which fails has consequences almost as serious as one which succeeds.

Take the case of CBS. To the extent that its designers fail to heighten the occupants' conscious awareness of their environment, the occupants will end up in the position described above, their capacity to conceive of, let alone to respond to alternative possible environments having been correspondingly reduced. On the other hand, to the extent that the designers succeed, they beg the question as to what

those occupants will be so dramatically conscious of. After all, the chief part of their extraordinary effort at intensification has been devoted to making the building a ruthlessly simplified symbolic 'object' as a whole, and a highly formalised continuum in its minutest details. No effort of equivalent power has been devoted to a reconsideration of peoples' experience of the environment at the crucially important level intermediate between those extremes, the level of work a day experience of an 'office-building' in central Manhattan. At the same time, as I indicated above, the designers' extraordinary effort (at the levels where it has been made) erodes the occupants' capacity for detecting in the building itself any evidence of its relation to its context. In other words, it erodes that evidence at every level but the workaday one. This combination of circumstances will guarantee that any heightened awareness of the environment of CBS will reveal not an "ultimate reality" at all, but rather just a monumentalisation of the already familiar phenomenon of mass bureaucracy.

In the case of the Thinkbelt, the situation is slightly different. If Price were to fail to leave the Thinkbelt's occupants unconscious of their environment, those occupants would become consciously aware of their environment. The question then arises, what would they perceive? Well, they would perceive a configuration of built form which, in the terms of both the historic and the present kinds of context we have discussed, would demonstrate a quite particular and identifiable set of characteristics. Among those characteristics, as I see it, would be the following: first, a fundamental organisational scheme in terms of a mechanical flow pattern; second, a pattern of human occupation of built form, which is itself articulated mechanicalistically; third, the restriction upon the potential psychological intensity of any particular space to a maximum level of a "zone"; fourth, a construction technique which formalises the actual temporariness of the built form involved. In short, although Price claims to have succeeded in devising an environment which stands for no particular "values" at all, what he has in fact done is simply to exchange one set of values for another. What the occupants of the Thinkbelt would consciously perceive would, in my view, be the most concrete symbolisation there has yet been of bureaucracy's academic equivalent, the "education-factory".

On the other hand, what of the consequences if Price were to succeed, to some extent, in leaving those

Interior view of a corridor in the CBS building: refinement of detail, in the name of an objectivist aesthetic, approaches an approximate present-day limit, and any perception of such a space, which is not absolute and ultimate, in metaphysical terms, is probably either blunted or ridiculous.

occupants unconscious of their environment? The environment would correspond to "background noise", in the sense I discussed above. But of course, as I said at that point, when architecture becomes "background noise", its unconscious impact is still far from incidental. To cite one of the most apt recent McLuhanisms, "The most successful television commercial is the one you are least aware of." So if Price were successful the Thinkbelt's occupants would be *processed* without realising that was what was happening to them. Faced with an "educational service" that made no claims on their values, the students would be unable to make any claim on that education's values. They would, in short, have become part of the "servicing mechanism".

It seems unnecessary, in conclusion, to do more than repeat; the *Gesamtkünstler* treats his fellows as children; the life-conditioner (and we can see now with what unwitting aptness Price chose that term) treats them as objects.

The question that now arises is why, in the mid-twentieth century, there should arise two such strikingly distinctive architectural schemes, which both betray a conception of architecture's place in human experience, and which do so in terms I have described as the bizarre consequences of the nineteenth century's loss of faith in rhetoric. To answer that question, or at least to try to answer a part of it, will require an even larger historical context than I have used so far. But here as before, the precepts of semiological theory offer illumination.

The issues at stake really began to be unmanageable two centuries before the concepts of *Gesamtkunstwerk* and life-conditioning gained their definitive, nine-teenth century formulations. It was at that particular time in European history when, to use Pascal's terms, the relation of "nature" and "custom" in human experience was first seen as such an urgent philosophical question. In 1683, Claude Perrault's *Treatise on the Five Orders* was published, a work which outlined the particularly architectural implications of that question, with astonishing clarity and foresight.

Perrault was convinced that the twin tenets of traditional architectural theory, the authority of classical precedent, and the assumption that "beauty" was a kind of Platonic absolute, were too seriously discredited to guide contemporary practice any longer. Regarding the traditionally acknowledged authority of ancient precedent, he said:

> We cannot find, either in the remains of the Buildings of the Ancients, or among the great Number of Architects that have treated of the Proportions of the Orders, that any two Buildings, or any two Authors, agree, and have followed the same rules.[24]

So much then, for classical precedent. As for the assumption of "beauty" as a Platonic absolute, Perrault was so unconvinced of that as to speculate:

> Whether that which renders the proportions of a building agreeable be not the same thing as that which makes a modish Habit please on account of its Proportions, which nevertheless have nothing positively beautiful, and that ought to be loved for itself; since when Custom, and other reasons not positive, which induc'd this Love, come to change, we affect them no longer, tho' they remain the same.[25]

Perrault's controversial suggestion, based on that argument, was:

> To judge rightly in this case suppose two sorts of Beauties in Architecture, namely those which are founded on solid convincing Reasons (positive beauties, in that terminology, corresponding to nature in Pascal) and those that depend only on Prepossession and Prejudice (arbitrary beauties for Perrault, corresponding to custom in Pascal).[26]

CBS building: the urban office building as symbolic object.

It is this argument in terms of a relationship between "positive" and "arbitrary" beauty, which can instructively be set alongside Saussure's distinction of *langue* and *parole*, where the *langue* is the "invariant" and the *parole* the "variant" aspect of a communication system. I have said that in information theory, "information" is a function of "surprise" within a matrix of "expectancy". Or, to return to Perrault's terminology:

> Architecture has no Proportions true in themselves; it remains to be seen whether we can establish those that are probable and likely ('*vraysemblable*', in the original French text) founded upon convincing Reason, without departing too far from the Proportions usually received.[27]

As well known as Perrault's argument is the extraordinary theoretical dispute that followed it. For over a century after its publication, Perrault's treatise dominated French architectural writing. Each successive writer from Blondel to Boullée established his own position primarily with respect to the concepts of "positive" and "arbitrary" beauty as originally discussed by Perrault. However, no influential contributor to that dispute attempted to sustain his concern for "those [proportions] that are probable and likely". Rather, each laid a particular emphasis on either "positive" or "arbitrary" beauty.

Although, as I have said, Perrault's argument and the ensuing dispute are well-known, the consequences of the split emphasis laid by his important successors are not, as far as I can see, well-known at all. If they were, I do not think we should be faced with such designs as CBS and the Thinkbelt. Generally speaking, we seem to be as yet too much a product of that split to recognise the extent of its influence upon our thinking. All the same, I would suggest that all subsequent architectural theory lies in the shadow of its distinction.

Consider the school of thought which, upon following Perrault, chose to assert the primacy of "positive" beauty.[28] Their commitment involved them in a moral obligation to "get to the bottom of" architecture, an effort whose modern guises I have already discussed. In the three centuries since Perrault, there have of course been numerous proposals put forward, purporting to reveal what solid "bottom" was, among them Laugier's ethnological primitivism, Choisy's technological determinism, Guadet's elemental geometry, and Hannes

Meyer's dialectical materialism. However, as Perrault knew quite well, it is not possible to lay such an exclusive emphasis upon the "positive" aspects of architecture, to the exclusion of the "arbitrary". Indeed, for those who wished to see, the persistent quest for a solid bottom for architecture was shown to be pointless before the eighteenth century was half over. The philosophical experience of a David Hume demonstrated that such sceptical rationalism as the advocates of a solid bottom to reality were required to exercise towards the whole of *apparent* reality would end up leaving indubitable virtually no aspect of human experience whatsoever.[29]

Alternatively, consider the school of thought which chose to assert the primacy of "arbitrary" beauty. Their commitment involved them in resolutely sticking close to the diverse surface of architecture as they saw it in all its forms. Once again, three centuries have produced various approaches to the "arbitrary", ranging through early versions of cultural relativism, such as Fischer von Erlach's, Loudon's and Schinkel's calculated eclecticism, Gilbert Scott's uncalculated eclecticism, and Philip Johnson's "Camp". But of course, here again, by the mid-eighteenth century, the theoretical premises of the position were already (albeit inadvertently) demolished in Hume's claim that "beauty is no quality in things themselves: it exists merely in the mind which contemplates them, and each mind sees a different beauty".[30]

With that celebrated remark, Hume both out-flanked and superseded the advocates of arbitrary beauty. For were he correct—and all he did was to take the argument for "arbitrary" beauty to its radically subjective conclusion— then there was no such thing about which one could generalise at all. From the time of Hume, until that of Marcel Duchamp and John Cage, the unqualified commitment to the "arbitrary" has always ended in utter silence.

Now semiology does not only offer us a simulacrum of the relation of "positive" and "arbitrary" beauty, in terms of *langue* and *parole*. It also suggests a means of correlating the approaches of the various theorists that succeeded Perrault. I have discussed the semiological poles of metaphor (the relationship of substitution) and metonymy (the relationship of contiguity). In the light of those concepts, I think we can see that the three-centuries-old drive to "get to the bottom of" architecture, has been characterised by a continual, radically reductive pattern of substitution for the given architecture at any particular time; while the corresponding effort to stick close to the given architecture's diverse surface has been equally characterised by a pattern of radically inclusive correlation of the forms of that given architecture.

Consider again the first tradition. As each successive proposal of a truly solid "bottom" for architecture was made, the very force of exclusion of some factor previously taken for granted was what imbued the new proposal with a certain plausibility, not to say moral authority. Thus, Laugier proposed to substitute for the accepted architecture of his day a new one which excluded arches, niches, and applied pilasters. And the force of that exclusion lent his argument sufficient plausibility to dominate the development of architecture (especially in France) for several years. In his turn, Choisy proposed to substitute for the history of architecture which was accepted in his day a new one which excluded legitimate formal intention, and that exclusion lent his argument its conviction. And, of course, Hannes Meyer proposed to substitute for architecture in his day simply "building", deriving his moral authority from the exclusion of "architecture" altogether. Thus, the quest for the solid "bottom" has proceeded. In every case, only the passage of time revealed that the particular reductive substitution involved was insufficient to guarantee the indubitability of the new proposal.

As for the second tradition, the defenders of "arbitrary" beauty have taken the opposite tack. Instead of effecting reductive substitutions for the given architecture at a particular time, they have always attempted to correlate all that architecture's forms to the greatest extent possible. Both Loudon and Schinkel, for example, devised theoretical systems in which the various stylistic motifs used in their period were carefully correlated, so that each would have a particular programme significance (Gothic style for churches, Greek style for public buildings, etc).[31] For that matter, Saarinen's well-known effort to find the "style for the job" is only another version of the Loudon-Schinkel approach. But this school of thought has never established any real authority, since, in the face of its adversaries' reductive scepticism, it has continually failed to demonstrate any conclusive "authenticity" for its elaborate sets of stylistic distinctions.

Now, what I suggest, in the face of designs such as the CBS building and the Thinkbelt, is that we regard both of those traditions as bankrupt. The attempt to "get to the bottom of" architecture has now clearly shown that there is no such "bottom". In this respect, it is only appropriate that Price, who has in the Thinkbelt taken radical reduction to one of its extremes, should

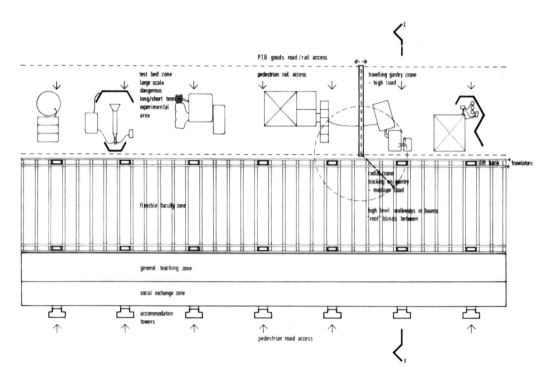

The following are labels within the diagram:

P.T.B. goods road / rail access

test bed zone
large scale
dangerous
long/short term
experimental
area

pedestrian rail access

travelling gantry crane
- high load

flexible faculty zone

radial crane
tracking on gantry
- medium load

lift bank   travelators

high level walkways in beams
roof blinds between

general teaching zone

social exchange zone

accommodation
towers

pedestrian road access

Plan of the Madeley Transfer Area.

himself have been publicly chastised by Reyner Banham, for his unwarranted presumption in taking it for granted that he could even describe himself as "in the enclosure business".[32] In its latest stages, "getting to the bottom of" architecture has turned into a game of nihilist one-upmanship. At the same time, the parallel struggle to stick close to architecture's diverse surface would seem to have shown itself as finally self-defeating. When the commitment to the "arbitrary" has been serious, it has always fallen into the trap of making "comprehensibility" an end in itself. In seeking "the style for the job", and in undertaking a *Gesamtkunstwerk* such as CBS, Saarinen has in just this way promoted a kind of petrification of architecture's communicativeness. On the other hand, frivolous commitment to the "arbitrary" has always tended to dissolve that communicativeness. To see this, one has only to think of any modern hotel interior, with its Bali Hai Room, its Charles Dickens Pub, its Old West Saloon, etc, etc. As William Burroughs puts it: "Nothing is true; everything is permitted."[33]

The bankruptcy of both those traditions, and the illumination cast upon them by semiological theory, suggest to me that there would be good reason to look again at Perrault's long-forgotten query as to "whether we can establish those [proportions in architecture]

that are probable and likely, without departing too far from the proportions usually received". If Perrault's tone seems cautious, it is no more so that Paul McCartney's. The point is simply the abstract one made by Norbert Wiener: "The essence of an effective rule for a game… is that it be statable in advance, and that it apply to more than one case…. In the simplest case, it is a property which is invariant to a set of transformations to which the system is subject."[34]

The possibilities for architecture which open up in the perspective of semiological theory are numerous and even exhilarating. Consider again the diagram which I used to illustrate the "field of meaning" of a social phenomenon. As I said at that point, one dimension of that field can be considered to represent the "scope of articulation" of architecture. Then too, in terms of the overall "social context" of which I spoke, that "scope of articulation" is co-extensive with our society's total social awareness of architecture, both historically and geographically.

Take the case of our relation to architecture which is distant in time, yet clearly within our own cultural tradition. A semiological perspective reveals how it is that so long as we take the trouble to observe the buildings of the past, they will assume a greater

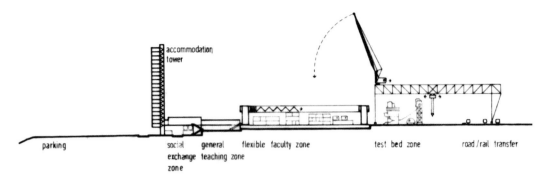

SECTION X-X

Labels on the diagram: accommodation tower · parking · social exchange zone · general teaching zone · flexible faculty zone · test bed zone · road/rail transfer

Section through the Madeley Transfer Area in Cedric Price's Thinkbelt project showing the particular organisational principle assumed. Lateral layering of areas occupied by specific functional activities, including a "zone" for "social exchange".

and greater distinctiveness, simply by virtue of the "perceptual distance" as it were, which separates us from, yet connects us to them. In other words, semiology provides a kind of theoretical apparatus to back up T S Eliot's famous remark: "What happens when a new work of art is created is something that happens simultaneously to all the works that preceded it."[35] We may even conclude that there is a sense in which Wiener's "effective rule" applies to history. Like the human unconscious, it is inexhaustible, since present action perpetually transforms it. At the same time, an acknowledgement that the distinctiveness of our architectural heritage is so largely a function of "perceptual distance", has an important reverse implication. For example, once we recognise that the "visual coherence" which we admire in Medieval towns is so much due to our own historical perceptual position, then we can see that attempts to reproduce that coherence are really attempts to seize hold of our own shadows.

On the other hand, if we take the case of our relation to an exotic architecture which is remote geographically, and therefore completely incommensurable with our own historically, such as that of a "primitive" society, then the implications are even more interesting. As Lévi-Strauss has said:

The paradox is irresoluble; the less one culture communicates with another, the less likely they are to be corrupted one by the other; but, on the other hand, the less likely it is, in such conditions, that the respective emissaries of these cultures

will be able to seize the richness and significance of their diversity.[36]

In other words, if it is the case that there exists no overlap at all between the architectural "fields of meaning" of our own society, and those of the "primitive" society in question, then what we can say that we perceive in their architecture will be nothing but a shallow (if diverting) reflection of our own. If, on the other hand (the more likely possibility nowadays), there is a partial overlay between the two "fields of meaning", then what we perceive of their architecture may indeed bear some relation to that society's own perception of it. However, in such circumstances, our threshold of conscious awareness of that architecture still does not coincide with that society's threshold. There will be a large area of meaning of which the society is conscious, but which we can only take for granted; there will be another area, which we will consciously perceive, but which they will take for granted. It is exactly this discrepancy which, in my view, prompts certain observers, such as Bernard Rudofsky, to extol the formal precocity of primitive architecture,[37] and others, such as Christopher Alexander, to savour its "well-adaptedness" and "unselfconsciousness".[38] One hopes the realisation that both of these characteristics are so largely a function of our own position as observers, that it will indicate how condescending it is of Alexander to attribute such "well-adaptedness" to an "unself-conscious design process".[39]

For that matter, while it is not possible here to examine Alexander's views in a general way, it is, I think, important to point out that semiological theory sees virtually all current versions of Functionalism, whether "organicist" like Alexander's, or not, as inadequate to explain or generate *any* social phenomenon. Since those social phenomena are socially representable structures of reality, they obviously "go far beyond any possible considerations of utility".[40] Indeed, although semiology nowhere yet includes a full-scale refutation of Functionalism, it does very strongly imply the kind of critique which Hannah Arendt has formulated. "The perplexity of utilitarianism", according to Arendt,

> … is that it gets caught in the unending chain of means and ends without ever arriving at some principle which could justify the category of means and ends, that is, of utility itself. The 'in order to' has become the content of the 'for the sake of'; in other words, utility established as meaning generates meaninglessness.[41]

Arendt's point is particularly important in my present context, for in continuing her argument, she then charged that utilitarian ideas had become so pervasive in the late eighteenth century as to affect even the thinking of Kant. His characterisation of the only objects that are not "for use", namely works of art, cannot, in her view, deny its origins in utilitarian thinking, since he described them as objects in which we "take pleasure without any interest". That charge has the most remarkable implications for architecture, for in the perspective of the subsequent century, it shows that the attitudes of "arts for art's sake", and "utilitarianism" are really two sides of the same coin. In the light of that revelation, we could conclude that the *Gesamtkünstler* and the life-conditioner do not only follow parallel paths, but in fact derive their design attitudes from the same philosophical premises.

But we must not be *too* surprised at this revelation. After all, to have understood that, we need not have turned to anthropology, communication theory and social philosophy. All we need to have done is to remember the eloquent statement (well within the normal scope of our discipline) by this century's greatest interpreter of "meaning in architecture", in defence of the ideas of Marsilio Ficino and Pico della Mirandola. What concerned Erwin Panofsky, was their conviction of the dignity of man, based on both the insistence of human values (rationality and freedom) and the acceptance of human limitations (fallibility and frailty); from this argued Panofsky, "two postulates result—responsibility and tolerance. Small wonder", he continued,

> … that this attitude has been attacked from two opposite camps whose common aversion to the ideas of responsibility and tolerance has recently aligned them in a common front. Entrenched in one of these camps are those who deny human values: the determinists… the authoritarians…. In the other camp are those who deny human limitations in favour of some sort of intellectual or political libertinism….[42]

Responsibility and tolerance. At the intersection of those two postulates lies the role of the architect who attempts to take the measure of *La Dimension Amoureuse*. In assuming that role, in designing *in* his fellows' experience, rather than above it, or outside it, such an architect will devise forms analogous to those of Lévi-Strauss' projected anthropology; forms, that is, which "correspond to a permanent possibility of man".[43] In short, that architect will *offer*, with neither the arrogance of the *Gesamtkünstler*, nor the indifference of the life-conditioner, "ideal" images of human existence, "ideal" frames for human action.

1 Barthes, Roland, *Essais critiques*, Paris: Editions du Seuil, 1964.

2 Germain Boffrand, quoted in Collins, Peter, *Changing Ideals in Modern Architecture*, London: Faber & Faber, 1965, p 174.

3 Saarinen, Eero, *Eero Saarinen on his Work*, Saarinen, A B ed, New Haven and London: Yale University Press, 1962, p 16.

4 Price, Cedric, "Life-conditioning", *Architectural Design*, vol 36, October, 1966, p 483.

5 Saarinen, *Eero Saarinen on his Work*, p 16. See also, Saarinen, Eero, *Progressive Architecture*, July 1965, pp 187–192.

6 Price, Cedric, "Potteries Thinkbelt", *Architectural Design*, vol 36, October, 1966, pp 484–497.

7 Venturi, Robert, *Complexity and Contradiction in Architecture*, New York: Museum of Modern Art, 1966, p 103.

8 *Life Magazine*, 29 April, 1966, pp 50–58; Welles, Chris, "How does it feel to live in total design", *Life Magazine*, 29 April, 1966, pp 59–60.

9 Barthes, *Essais critiques*. See also: Barthes, Roland, *Elements of Semiology*, London: Jonathan Cape, 1967; Gombrich, Ernst, *Art and Illusion*, London: Phaidon Press, 1962, and Gombrich, Ernst, *Meditations on a Hobby Horse*, London: Phaidon Press, 1963; Lévi-Strauss, Claude, *A World on the Wane*, London: Hutchinson, 1961; Lévi-Strauss, Claude, *La Pensée Sauvage*, Paris: Plon, 1962; Lévi-Strauss, Claude, *Structural Anthropology*, New York: Basic Books, 1963; McLuhan, Marshall, *Understanding Media*, New York: McGraw-Hill Paperbacks, 1966; Barthes is the best short introduction of the thought of Lévi-Strauss, *and* that of Peter Caws: "What is Structuralism", in *Partisan Review*, winter 1968, p 759.

10 Lévi-Strauss, Claude, "The Scope of Anthropology", *Structural Anthropology*, New York: Basic Books, 1963 p 16.

11 Barthes, *Eléments de sémiologie*, p 93.

12 Paul McCartney, quoted in the *International Times*, London, 29 January, 1967.

13 Readers of Gombrich's *Art and Illusion and Meditations on a Hobby Horse*, may have noticed the striking conceptual similarity between semiology's use of *langue* and *parole*, and Gombrich's use of "schema and correction", which he has derived from perception psychology. Then too, of course, Professor Gombrich has been influenced as much as the semiologists by the precepts of information theory.

Readers of Christian Norberg-Schulz's *Intentions in Architecture*, London: Allen & Unwin, 1963, will also recognise how the semiologists' use of information theory is similar to his own use of it, as well as of perception psychology.

14 Price, "Life-conditioning", p 483.

15 Jakobson, Roman, *"Aspects linguistique de la traduction"*, *Essais de linguistiques générale*, Paris: Editions de Minuit, 1963, p 81.

16 The phrase comes, of course, from Matthew Arnold's "The Function of Criticism at the Present Time", of 1864, but it is characteristic of a whole nine-teenth century tradition. Compare, for example, Ranke's description of the proper scope of historical studies, "to show only what really happened".

17 Saarinen, *Eero Saarinen on his Work*, p 16.

18 Merleau-Ponty, Maurice, *The Phenomenology of Perception*, London: Routledge and Kegan Paul, 1962, p 00.

19 Aldo van Eyck quoted in *Team 10 Primer*, Smithson, Alison ed, London: Standard Catalogue Co, p 40.

20 Colin Cherry, quoted by Gombrich in *Meditations on a Hobby Horse*, p 61.

21 Saussure, quoted by Barthes, "Communications no. 4", *Elements of Semiology*, p 115.

22 Roman, Jakobson, "Deux aspects du langage et deux types d'aphasie", *Essais de linguistiques générale*, Paris: Editions de Minuit, 1963, pp 43–67.

23 Carroll, Lewis, *Alice in Wonderland, and Through the Looking-Glass*, New York: New American Library, 1960, pp 186.

24 Perrault, Claude, *A Treatise on the Five Orders*, James, John trans., London, 1722, p ii.

25 Perrault, *A Treatise on the Five Orders*, p v.

26 Perrault, *A Treatise on the Five Orders*, p vi.

27 Perrault, *A Treatise on the Five Orders*, p xi.

28 Admittedly, not all members of this school have talked in terms of "beauty". But they have all taken a consistent attitude to what architecture "ought" to be, as opposed to what it "is" at any particular point in time (using "is" as "ought" in the manner of modern sociology).

29 Cassirer, Ernst, *The Philosophy of the Enlightenment*, Boston: Beacon Press, 1960, p 307.

30 Hume, David, *A Treatise of Human Nature*, 1738.

31 My information regarding Loudon's efforts I owe to George L Hersey, of the Department of Art at Yale University; that regarding Schinkel's, to Professor Christian Norberg-Schulz, of the State School of Architecture, Oslo, Norway.

32 The incident is described by Robin Middleton, in *Architectural Design*, July 1966, p 322.

33 Burroughs, William, *Dead Fingers Talk*, London: Tandem Books, 1966, p 197.

34 Wiener, Norbert, *Cybernetics*, Boston: MIT Press, 1965, p 50.

35 Eliot, T S, *The Sacred Wood*, London: Methuen, 1964, p 49.

36 Lévi-Strauss, *A World on the Wane*, p 45.

37 Rudofsky, Bernard, *Architecture without Architects*, New York: Museum of Modern Art, 1965.

38 Alexander, Christopher, *Notes on the Synthesis of Form*, Harvard University Press, 1964. See especially chapter three.

39 Alexander, *Notes on the Synthesis of Form*, p 32.

40 Caws, Peter, "What is Structuralism", in *Partisan Review*, winter 1968, p 80.

41 Arendt, Hannah, *The Human Condition*, New York: Doubleday Anchor Books, Garden City, 1959, p 135.

42 Panofsky, Erwin, "The History of Art as a Humanistic Discipline", *Meaning in the Visual Arts*, New York: Doubleday Anchor Books, 1955, p 2.

43 Lévi-Strauss, "The Scope of Anthropology", p 49.

The Dining Position: A Question of *Langue* and *Parole*, 1976

Having returned to Toronto in 1967, I continued to work on the dissertation, and obtained a teaching position at my home University of Toronto in the fall of 1968, owing to a helpful intercession by Aldo van Eyck, who was an admirer of the "Meaning in Architecture" project. "The Dining Position" was the first text I completed after commencing teaching at the University of Toronto. By this time, I had also become friends with Peter Eisenman, who had facilitated the publication of the American edition of *Meaning in Architecture*, and who was at the time in the process of setting up his soon to become famous Institute for Architecture and Urban Studies, along with its in-house journal *Oppositions*. Nothwithstanding his admiration for "Meaning", Eisenman was not ready to publish "The Dining Position", and it took several further years before it saw publication in *Dutch Forum*, the editor of which by that time was Herman Hertzberger.[1]

As is probably obvious from the text itself, "The Dining Position" was an effort on my part to bridge from the precepts of Structuralism to those of phenomenology. By this time, Joseph Rykwert's encouragement to me to read Maurice Merleau-Ponty had had its effect—the text is of course, among other things, an homage to Rykwert—and by this time also I had read Hannah Arendt, whose view of phenomenology is derived in turn, in a very complex fashion, from her own mentor, Martin Heidegger.

I begin with an account of an academic incident which is of no great importance in itself, but one which can illuminate a series of issues which I believe to be of considerable theoretical significance. During a review in an architectural studio, three critics became involved in a dispute, the intensity of which surprised them all, given the relatively modest nature of the issue which set it off.[2] A group of students had been engaged in the design of a "summer place" for 24 teenagers and three adults to holiday in the country for two weeks in August; the critical dispute concerned the question of what sort of dining facilities it would be most appropriate for the designer to provide there.

When the discussion began, student opinion was generally speaking split two ways: one group believing that one large table for everyone was the best idea; the other group equally convinced that a series of smaller, perhaps even variously sized tables was preferable. Critic A was new to this difference of opinion (which had existed in the studio for some time) and was not certain, on the face of it, that it would be wise for the group to accept that set of alternatives as an appropriate frame of reference for the discussion. He speculated initially whether any sort of arrangement of tables was really necessary—maybe it would be better if everybody just ate on the grass. But be that as it may (and the issue his question raises I shall return to) given these two alternatives, he took up a vigorous defence of the second. In fact, he even suggested that it might be crypto-fascist to have only one table for everybody, that such an arrangement called up a host of unpalatable connotations, that it was an all-too-likely symbol of an obsolete centralist model of social authority.

Given the same two alternatives, critics B and C thought that the single large table was more appropriate. Critic B imagined it as one possible communal focus for the entire summer place experience; as such, he thought the table would manifest in concrete terms an invaluable social legacy. For his part, critic C foresaw unnecessary and avoidable social nuances latent in the smaller tables idea. It seemed to him that arrangement had an inherent tendency to overdramatise the issue, for such a small but heterogeneous group, of who would or would not sit with whom. He thought the idea of the single large table offered a welcome anonymity in that respect.

Struck by the growing force of the disagreement, a student offered the suggestion of a series of tables specially designed so as to be easily combinable into one large one. That proposition, it seemed to critic C, would even more coyly play up the nuance he imagined as latent. At that point, critic B objected even more strenuously; he argued that even in such circumstances it was still quite conceivable that it would never occur to those present to combine the tables into one.

Now it seems to me that we may unfold from within this brief episode, a number of important implications for architecture of the structuralist concepts of *langue* and *parole*. The terms themselves derive from the turn-of-the-century theory of the pioneer French linguist, Ferdinand de Saussure, and they have recently taken on a renewed importance in the "structural" anthropology of Claude Lévi-Strauss, and in the "semiology", or comprehensive theory of signs, which have over the past few years been outlined by Roland Barthes and others.[3] In structuralist, or semiological terms, the *langue* of any social phenomenon is the pre-existent set of social elements and patterns within which any particular social gesture reveals its particularity. And the *parole* is precisely the particularity which thus is revealed. The *langue*, Barthes says, is both a "social institution and a system of values", and the *parole* an "individual act of selection and actualisation".[4]

If, in this perspective, we begin to explore the dispute with which I began, we may for instance point to the fact that both critics A and B took up their respective positions on the grounds that the proposed alternative dining arrangements embodied particular,

identifiable, social contents. Indeed, I am sure only a short period of reflections would be necessary on most of our parts, for us to imagine some of the kinds of social content that each of them had in mind, and on the basis of which each was arguing. For critic A the single large table idea called up connotations of bourgeois families dominated by authoritarian fathers, of regimented refectory meals in boarding schools, of all kinds of monolithic social groups, operating only within the restrictive patterns laid down by some central authority. For critic B, on the other hand, the single table idea evoked diverse and potent images of men's communality, ranging from the easy civility of the dinner-party, through such instances of profound interdependence as the barn-raising supper, right on up to the most exalted social forms of communality in Western culture: "Where two or three are gathered together in my name, there am I in the midst of them."[5] Both critics' critical judgments, I suggest, were reached in light of—not to say in the shadows of—such powerful recollections as these.

Now the fact that all of us can easily imagine these alternative social contents is the first matter that ought to give us pause. For it is not in any way self-evident that it should be so easy. Beyond that fact lies the further question why critics A and B should have been so convinced of their options as to prompt me to say each reached his judgment in the shadows of such recollections. In structuralist terms, we may say that in this instance a segment of the *langue* of the environment has been brought to conscious awareness. In other words a number of social elements and patterns, which would normally be just taken for granted, have explicitly surfaced in critical discussion. And it is precisely the institutionalisation Barthes describes, which enables us to so easily imagine those alternative contents, and which explains the depth of concern that arises in such discussion. Thus, in one sense of the term, we may say that the *langue* of the environment is the pre-existent set of such established patterns which is implicit in a given design situation. It comprises a loaded context within which a designer exercises choices; loaded in the sense that it establishes the relative social feasibility and potency of the various choices a designer might make. The *parole*, correspondingly, comprises precisely that set of feasible choices as established by the *langue*.

In proceedings this far, I have already referred to that part of our experience of the environment

which is "just taken for granted"; critic B, for his part, concluded his critique by raising the issue of what might not "occur to people" concerning the dining facilities they encountered upon arrival at the summer place. In short, by now we have also encountered the elementary proposition that architecture is a matter concerning human consciousness itself. Obviously, our experience of the environment, like our experience of anything else, has simultaneous conscious and unconscious aspects.

Less obvious perhaps, is the fact that psychologically speaking, we may describe our unconscious everyday experience of the environment of buildings and streets, not to mention tables, as comprising a set of gradually built-up organisational schemas.[6] In these terms, the *langue* of the environment comprises the unconscious set of schemas that we take socially for granted, and by means of which we make our way in the physical world. The *parole* is the smaller, more manageable day-to-day set of conscious options which we exercise in doing so.

It is in the light of considerations such as these that we may see why critic B's fear, of what may never occur to people, is so serious. If, for a moment, we adopt his point of view in the dispute, we can see that if it really were the case that the dining facilities had been so designed that it actually never occurred to the people there to make one large table, then it is clear that an entire social legacy would be irretrievably lost. Whether or not one approved of large tables, one would have to agree that the reality of the social world to which the campers belonged had suffered a kind of amputation.

To recognise that our consciousness of the built-form around us is as problematic as that, is to arrive at a phenomenological base for Structuralism, at the fact of our environmental "being-in-the-world".[7] Owing to the fact that the *langue* is relatively highly-developed, we are enabled to make our way in the environment with a certain ease and equanimity. To see the important truth of this seemingly circular claim one has only to ponder those environmental experiences which are edge-condition exceptions: in London, where I am writing, I think of the American tourists whom I so often see, suffering what we might call low-level environmental panic in simply attempting to navigate the London Underground system. We know of other experiences of the environment that are evidently beyond what can reasonably be described as edge conditions. These constitute large-scale culture shock, the result of which is an almost complete indifference. Lévi-Strauss cites the famous example of the Kwakiutl Indian whom Franz Boas sometimes invited to New York to serve him as informant, who was quite indifferent to the panorama of skyscrapers and of streets plowed and furrowed by cars. He reserved all his intellectual curiosity for the dwarfs, giants and bearded ladies who were exhibited in Times Square at the time, for automats, and for the brass balls decorating staircase banisters… "all these things", Lévi-Strauss tells us, "challenged his own culture, and it was that culture alone that he was seeking to recognise in certain aspects of ours".[8]

In short, we may say that it is precisely because the *langue* is so highly developed that in everyday experience we are able to take it so completely for granted. Moreover it is just this fact that it is normally taken for granted which renders plausible the assumption that no such institutionalised tendency exists in human affairs. But of course, in my present context, the same fact indicates how naive it would be of us to assume that in acting in the environment, we really are utterly free agents, whether it is a question of choosing, as men among men, how we will eat at tables, or rather one, as designers among men, of devising in advance those arrangements or dining that other men will encounter. We may even, in this respect, cite Marx's

famous observation, "Men make their own history. But they do not make it just as they please."[9] Tables, and arrangements of tables then, are neither platonic entities nor value-free data, but rather complex signs, which entail historically conditioned and socially potent tendencies to symbolise specific cultural contents.

There are of course those who will deny that these symbolic tendencies are anything more than epiphenomenal. They will be inclined to point knowingly to the fact that critics A and B took such different views of the likely social connotations of the alternative arrangements, and to suggest that such difference itself shows the whole discussion to be sheer sophistry. Generally speaking, this response nowadays follows from a philosophical stance we might call neo-positivist pragmatism. It rests upon the premise that if men would just be matter-of-fact and straightforward with each other, the things of the external world would be uniformly and consistently describable "as they in themselves really are".[10] It dismisses any "difference of interpretation" such as arose between critics A and B as either sophistical self-deception, or deliberate—and dishonest—mystification. Unable to come to terms with the fact of our phenomenological "being-in-the-world"; unable to accept that men will never know "the things themselves"; it cannot see that "differences of interpretation" in such matters may reveal quite different individual conceptions of a heterogeneous reality. Thus, when it is challenged to authenticate its own positivist-pragmatic conception of reality, when it is asked to prove that things really are what they seem on the face of it to be, then it has no choice but to fall back on a common-sense dogmatism.

The fact is, of course, that most of architecture's current neo-positivists are really just disillusioned determinists anyway. That is to say, they are the people who have yet to get over their disappointment at the failure of Heroic Period Modern Architecture to "save the world" single-handedly as it promised to do. After all, we have to remember that even Le Corbusier, who was far from being the most naive among the first generation moderns, was prepared to leave the impression in *Towards a New Architecture* that "architecture" and "revolution" could be seen as clear-cut social alternatives.[11] And now of course, when the messianic conviction of that generation has been so

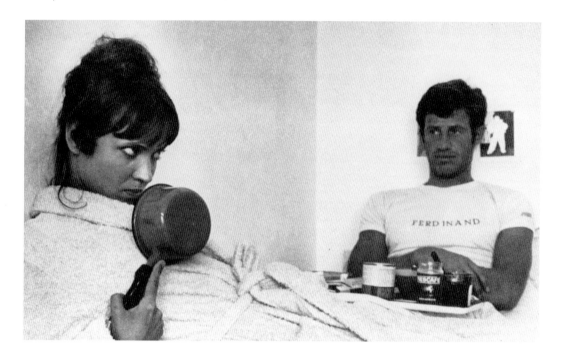

widely discredited and dissipated, there is as a reaction a pervasive skepticism as to the capacity of built form to exercise any social influence at all.

But this latter-day skepticism is just as misconceived as the messianic determinism which it is gradually supplanting. We may take a linguistic analogy. It would obviously be absurd to suppose that a verbal enquiry on my part will determine a response on your part.[12] But to say that it is absurd does not in any way suggest that my question will not have some ascertainable bearing on the response that you will make. Intuitively it is obvious that it will have some such bearing. And the important fact to note in our present context is that the precise way in which my question will influence your answer is only ascertainable in terms of the linguistic totality, that is to say the language which we are both using. For Saussure, who as I said above coined the terms, language was *langue* and as such a "social totality", and *parole* as an expressive tool available to each individual. In its turn, Structuralism sees the *langue* in this sense as the collective aspect of any social phenomenon, and the *parole* as the individual aspect.

Like a verbal enquiry, a design gesture is at one and the same time social and individual. It is the nexus of the designer's relation to the society within which he is working. At a conscious level, it both demonstrates a personal statement and at the same time announces a vision of a possible society. (To feel this at its fullest

force, think of the Utopian projects of Fourier, Garnier, or Le Corbusier.) But of course, over *dimostrazione*, as in such utopian schemes, still only forms part of such revelation. For like a doubly reflexive mirror, the design act also unconsciously betrays (to use C S Pierce's word) both the underlying structure of the thought of an epoch, and the intimate profile of an individual character.[13] Even in the brief discussion of the incident with which I began, I think it is possible to discern the outlines of just such reflexive revelation. One grasps already the conscious intentions of the various participants in the discussion. Beyond that, it seems to me, it is even possible to begin to sense the patterns of social life which they presuppose, the personal assumptions which underlie their expressed points of view.

It is by this line of reasoning that we encounter the problematical and profound contingency of architecture; a contingency which arises from the fact that—as the result of such acts architecture is so inescapably a social phenomenon. As designers, we face exactly the same human predicament as Lévi-Strauss' anthropologist:

We shall never know if the other into which we cannot, after all, dissolve, fashions from the elements of his existence a synthesis exactly super-imposable on that which we have worked out. But it is not necessary to go so far; all we need—and for this, inner

8. THE STORY OF FIDGETY PHILIP.

Let me see if Philip can
Be a little gentleman;
Let me see, if he is able
To sit still for once at table:
Thus Papa bade Phil behave;
And Mamma look'd very grave.
But fidgety Phil,
He won't sit still;
He wriggles
And giggles,
And then, I declare,
Swings backwards and forwards
And tilts up his chair,
Just like any rocking horse;—
"Philip! I am getting cross!"

understanding suffices—is that the synthesis, however approximate, arises from human experience. We must be sure of this, since we study men: and as we are ourselves men, we have that possibility.[14]

It is this fact that "we are ourselves men", which enables us to undertake design acts in the first place, yet which at the same time renders it impossible that we ever attain an utterly "detached objectivity" in doing so. It is, Lévi-Strauss warns us, in the "intersection of his subjectivities" that an observer exhibits "the nearest order of truth to which the sciences of man may aspire".[15] And the consequence of that is of course, that design acts are inescapably partisan.[16] Now this conclusion has the profoundest implications for the contemporary practice of architecture. For it suggests that there is no possibility of establishing a detached objective mode of design which carries no specific social connotations, which betrays no personal handwriting. That this is true is of considerable importance, in my view, for it is at odds with a number of the more influential tendencies in architectural thought since the eclipse of the theory of Heroic Period Modernism. These tendencies manifest themselves In the ideas of teachers (Serge Chermayeff) designers (Buckminster Fuller), theorists (Christopher Alexander, Bruce Archer), and

critics (Herbert Gans), all of whom have put forward arguments which presuppose not only that some such detached and objective professional stance is possible. They even imply (if not state) that it is desirable! In accordance with this tendency we see now around us the current trend towards increasingly 'scientific' research in "environmental design" as well as the entire international preoccupation with various forms of systematic design method.[17]

Yet, in the context I have outlined above, I think it is utterly clear that such techniques (and of course, like all techniques, they are also modes of thought) can never guarantee for design any greater a social 'objectivity' than which already follows from the fact that "we are ourselves men". The results of research in the social sciences and of systems analysis are more 'objective' than our own social observations, only insofar as social scientists and systems analysts confine themselves more rigorously than architects do, to treating their fellow men as 'objects'. "The trouble with modern theories of behaviourism", we ought in this respect to remember, "is not that they are wrong but that they could become true".[18] In other words, we will find no moral escape from the partisan contingency of our work, in a retreat behind the screen of scientific research, or of logically sophisticated design methodology.

Less obvious, but perhaps even more disturbing, is the fact that this same doomed and misconceived quest for detachment and objectivity can also be discerned in another currently influential and, philosophically speaking, not entirely unrelated body of ideas.

Consider the effort now being made by some architects to devise architectural forms which are less presumptuous and overbearing than those of establishment Modern architecture, forms which are more generalised and anonymous on the one hand, and more particularly responsive to personal modification on the other. Perhaps the most typical concrete result of such strategies has been a new conception of the environment which involves a radically sharpened demarcation between the permanent and the temporary, the fixed and the movable, the public and the private. In accordance with this body of ideas, it is the permanent, the fixed, and the public, generally speaking, which are intended to be generalised and anonymous; against which backdrop the temporary, the movable and the private are thereby (it is thought) enabled to be so particularly responsive to personal modification. Thus, this demarcation has to one side of it a tendency towards radical personalisation, and to the other side, radical depersonalisation of architectural form.

Radical personalisation involves an effort to render a larger proportion of the fabric of the environment than now exists fragmentary, and ephemeral, more like clothing to be consumed than like buildings to be inhabited in the traditional way. Thus arises the conception of the interchangeable, exchangeable, perhaps even throwaway, piece of individual environmental apparatus. Radical depersonalisation, on the other hand, involves a corresponding attempt to make more of the environment generalised to the point of being usable for almost any purpose; or if not that, then to

The pre-fabricated 'loft-space' school.

make more of it into anonymous servicing structure, capable of accommodating any of the clip-on ephemera which results from the corresponding drive towards radical personalisation. Thus we encounter the 'loft-space' solution to so many current architectural programmes, together with its philosophical consort, the service infra-structure, in its many various forms.

Now unlike the school of thought which focuses on more scientific environmental research and systematic methodology, this body of ideas does not usually entail a specific avowal of detachment and objectivity. On the contrary, it generally springs from an explicit and boldly normative social commitment.

Nevertheless, it seems to me that at the level of architectural strategy, there lies hidden a similar effort to elude the partisan contingency of the design act. Consider again the case of radical personalisation. As a general principle of design, it is meant to generate a wide range of highly manipulable environmental apparatus. Because of its variability and individual manipulability, such apparatus is deemed to be capable of neutralising the traditional architect-client relationship, capable of avoiding the specific and directive social implications carried by traditional architectural form. Now this argument has a certain plausibility, which derives from the fact that radical personalisation undoubtedly does increase the range of selective environmental options open to the individual. But this increase in no way really neutralises the designer-user relationship. It only generalises it, and generalisation of the relationship no more guarantees detachment and objectivity than the number of options available on a Chevrolet guarantees the detachment and objectivity of General Motors' relationship to me.

Radical depersonalisation, on the other hand, results in architectural form which is intended only minimally to impinge on its user's way of life in any case. But of course, insofar as it has, in these terms, to provide

the comprehensive framework which accommodates the heterogeneous paraphernalia characteristic of radical personalisation, such form is necessarily highly articulated, whether unobtrusively or not. And this means that it has profound (albeit, perhaps, unconscious) effects on ways of life. Accordingly it can no more guarantee detachment and objectivity than its polar opposite.

What is more, these two tendencies may, in terms of the argument of this paper, even be seen as an attack on the structure of *langue* and *parole* itself. When occurring independently, for instance, radical personalisation tends to promote a kind of haemorrhage of ephemeral manipulability, whereby the entire fabric of the environment is infinitely changeable into something else. And of course, in such circumstances, that part of our experience of the environment that can be "just taken for granted" is progressively reduced. That in its turn moans that our everyday capacity for coping with the physical world is jeopardised. Like the American tourists in the London Underground, like the Kwakiutl Indian in New York, we are perfectly capable of being progressively incapacitated by extreme environmental unpredictability. The social assumptions on which we perform the most routine of environmental actions could easily disintegrate to the point where for example just crossing the street would turn into a nightmare.

Taken all by itself, radical depersonalisation has even more obvious consequences. It simply promotes a progressive impoverishment of our consciousness of the world. So far as we would act in such an environment at all (and such an environment in no way invites us to), we would move more and more like indifferent robots, oblivious to the experience we are undergoing.

Most extraordinary of all is the fact that these two tendencies taken together give up an architectural analogue far more profound than any environment which now exists of the kind of one-dimensional world that

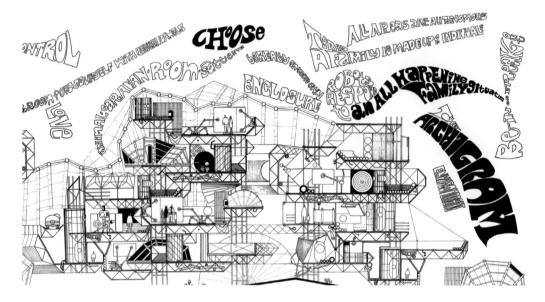

has been characterised by Herbert Marcuse. For they point towards an environment which fundamentally comprises only two conceptual layers, the first of which, the result of radical personalisation, is indeed open to our active and interested participation, but which possesses only a transient and ephemeral substantiality, and the second of which, following from radical depersonalisation, is indubitably substantial, but which is hardly at all accessible to our active consciousness. In short, the relationship of *langue* and *parole*—indeed, the very integrity of our experience of the world we live in—depends not upon a demarcation, but upon an intersection of the personal and the impersonal, the private and the public, the temporary and the permanent. As Hannah Arendt puts it:

> Only where things can be seen by many in a variety of aspects without changing their identity, so that those who are gathered around them know they see sameness in utter diversity, can worldly reality truly and reliably appear.[19]

Since it is the design act alone, so far as architects are concerned, which is responsible for the reification of that "worldly reality", we may conclude simply by repeating: unless it simply abolishes itself, the design act is inescapably partisan.[20] The truth is, of course, that these efforts to elude the social contingency of design are in any case completely misplaced. What is after all really desirable is not design which is less partisan, but rather design which is more responsible. Were he to emulate Lévi-Strauss' anthropologist, the architect would forsake the quest for detached objectivity; instead he would commit himself wholeheartedly to the "social totality" for which he was working; he would strive, in Lévi-Strauss' words: "to put himself in the place of the men living there, to understand the principle and pattern of their intentions".[21]

In this perspective, we may return again to the dispute with which I began, first to consider the question I set aside at that time, critic A's speculation whether any sort of arrangement of tables was really necessary. The issue his question raises is, of course, the intensely topical one of the appropriate limits of the architect's design intervention. Some architects today (including many of those whose positions I have characterised above) would read his enquiry as implying that the architect had no rightful business even considering whether the campers should eat at one large table or several smaller ones; as corroborating the popular view that any such preoccupation on an architect's part is presumptuous and unwarranted.

Yet if, as I have claimed, the integrity of our experience of the world depends upon an intersection of the personal and the impersonal, the private and the public, the movable and the permanent, then it follows that the architect may quite reasonably concern himself with such matters. Indeed, it will be impossible to "put himself in the place of the men living there" without doing so.

It is only our current mood of professional self-abasement that makes such a concern seem necessarily to constitute an attempt to pre-organise the entire dining activity of such a summer place. A more reasonable

view, it seems to me, is that putting himself in their place would reveal how hermetic such efforts at comprehensive pre-organisation usually are.[22]

To be sure, the men living there can always be expected to bring to a built setting more kinds of activity and paraphernalia than any designer can possibly anticipate in advance. The point is that their doing so reflects no discredit upon him, no more than his endeavouring as best he can to anticipate those activities reflects any discredit upon him either. We may even say that it is a kind of positive, partisan gesture on a designer's part which invites positive and reciprocal gestures in return. To be sure, it was far from being critic A's intention, in speculating about the possibility of a dining position without tables, to lend comfort to the advocates of a professional withdrawal from any such concerns. For he not only addressed himself vigorously to the consideration of the possible social contents of the two principal alternatives under discussion (the many tables and single table alternatives, to which I shall return); he was also ready to explore the possible contents of the 'no tables' alternative.

Clearly, the initial attraction of such an alternative would be the possibility of creating an informal and pluralist setting for dining, which imposed the least social pressures on the campers as individuals. But of course, even given the likelihood that dining without tables avoids some of the connotations of formal dining

at tables, we nevertheless have now to ponder what are, and how powerful are, the connotations of dining without them. What, we now have to ask ourselves, are the likely contents of an arrangement involving no tables at all? In asking such a question, it seems to me, we encounter another whole strand of social history, which includes such forms as the picnic, the Baroque *fete galante*, and which in its deepest implications even leads us back to the mythology of the Garden of Eden.

What are the social connotations of the picnic? I suggest that its most central structural characteristic ties in its deliberate transposition. That is to say, it is typically an indoor social occasion which has deliberately been transposed to an outdoor setting; it is typically a social occasion which involves a certain apparatus of dining (not just tables, but also chairs, dishes, cutlery, etc) which has deliberately been transposed so as to take place with the aid of only a minimum of that typical apparatus; following in turn from both of those, it is typically a social event for which foods have been deliberately transformed so as to be especially easy to serve and to eat.

In fact, so complex a sign is the picnic in our society, so deeply ingrained are its connotations, that it is even socially feasible to perform what I would call secondary, and inverse, transpositions without weakening the symbolic integrity of the picnic as such. For instance, it would obviously be possible in our society to conduct a social event which was understandable as a picnic indoors.

One way of doing so would be to abide rigorously by the second and third primary transpositions I cited above. Thus, even though it occurred indoors, such a "picnic" would involve no tables, or chairs, and would involve a minimum of serving apparatus; it might even involve some of the serving apparatus specifically associated with picnics, such as hampers, paper or plastic utensils, etc. Then too, it would have a menu made up of foods associated with picnics.

Alternatively, it would also be possible to conduct an event which was understandable as a picnic which involved almost all of the apparatus customarily associated with the most elaborate indoor meals, so long as it did indeed occur outdoors, and so long as it involved the appropriate kinds of foods. Think, in this respect, of the extraordinary picnics which emerge from limousines, and which are set upon the grass at Ascot.

But of course, even though I am making no claim here to give an exhaustive account of the picnic phenomenon,

I have to suggest that there is still more to a picnic than that. For the primary transpositions I have cited, and which in my view so typically characterise it, themselves possess a decipherable rationale. In its modern guise, the picnic may only embody that rationale unconsciously, but its historical antecedent, the *fete galante*, demonstrates it overtly. The transposition from indoors to outdoors, for example, carries within it a connotation of a larger social transposition from a mundane urbanity to a pastoral idyll. In addition, eschewing the customary apparatus of dining carries with it a connotation of a temporary exemption from social convention, in favour of some natural, and innocent abandon. In eighteenth-century terms, this last transposition was especially important, because the opposition between convention and abandon then pointed equally deafly in two separate directions. For a rationalist, it pointed to the orgy; for the believer, it pointed to the idyllic life in the Garden of Eden, before the Fall.

It is in the light of such considerations as these, I think, that we now have to ask what we think the "worldly reality" of the summer place ought to be. Do we think that summer place eating is appropriately reified in terms of a picnic? That question leads in turn to several further ones. Do we think that the paradisal connotations of a picnic, which typically lasts for a few hours, can feasibly be extended over the period of two weeks? Or, a larger question still: should summer place dining serve as a symbol of a recovered paradise in any case? Should it not serve instead as a symbolic microcosm (albeit refracted somehow) of the larger society outside, to which all of the campers belong, yet from which they are separated for the period of two weeks?

Then there is one last consideration. It would seem likely, given the reasons why it was proposed, that a summer place dining position based on the paradigm of the picnic would involve a much less elaborated physical setting than dining positions deriving from the other models discussed. In that case, one would have to ponder whether such a setting for dining, once created, would in fact establish for the people living there the frame of reference intended; or, indeed, for that matter, whether it would establish any identifiably worldly reality at all? If the setting failed to establish the frame of reference intended, then all the designer's efforts would be rendered pointless, and the setting's acquired significance fortuitous. If no frame of reference were established all, it would be the case that the social forms of eating together would have disintegrated altogether, and we would be faced with another instance of cultural amputation. It is my conclusion that the picnic paradigm is not appropriate to summer place dining—or at least not appropriate to the central experience of summer place dining. I am convinced that the number of people and the length of time involved inescapably make the summer place some sort of society. And that, in turn, of course, commits me to seeing the summer place dining arrangement as some form of communal focus.

But of course, in pursuing such an investigation this far, I have moved far beyond the discussion of the no tables alternative as it actually transpired during the student review in question. And I have still left unresolved the central dispute of that review and this paper, the choice between the single table and many tables dining alternatives. In light of the theoretical framework I have now elaborated, I would like to return to that central dispute.

As you recall, critic B saw the single table as a potent symbol of communality, while critic A feared its tendency to become a powerful manifestation of authoritarian centrality. It is important to note that critic B in no way intended to argue the merits of authoritarian centrality (this was clear from his opinions about sleeping arrangements at the summer place), nor did critic A deplore the phenomenon of commonality (one of his most favoured architectural images was of the skating rink at Rockefeller Center set within the standard Manhattan grid of public streets). By the time the discussion ended, it was evident that critic A acknowledged the potential of the single large table as a symbol of communality. It was just that for him, that potential was outweighed by its latent centralist and authoritarian tendencies. For his part critic B was prepared to risk the possible consequences of these admittedly latent tendencies, for the sake of the intense communal focus the single table offered. Their respective weightings of the situation are delineated in sharp relief if we consider their attitudes to the question of the relative particularity of possible dining arrangements. Critic B, for example, entertained a student's suggestion that the single table might have around it exactly the number of seats as there were campers at the summer place. Thus, while the table symbolised the group as a whole, the seats would represent the campers as individuals.[23] In contrast to this highly particular—and exclusive—form of communality, what attracted critic A to the Rockefeller Center skating rink was of course precisely its anonymous and non-particular communality. For his part, critic C had not considered the possibility of such a highly particular arrangement of seats. Not having done so, he was attracted to the large single

table alternative, as I said above, precisely because of the anonymity which it offered, compared to the many-tables alternative, in the context of such a small, but heterogeneous group.

Now I put forward quite early in the argument of this paper the proposition that tables and arrangements of tables are complex signs, which entail historically conditioned and socially potent tendencies to symbolise specific cultural contents. In tracing the logic of the above dispute in such detail, I would hope that I have succeeded in illustrating something of both the scope and the character of those signs' complexity. For it is precisely in the web of that complexity, after all, that the whole dispute ultimately lies. Moreover, it is only in a further exploration of that complexity that a resolution of the dispute, should any such resolution exist, may reasonably be sought. Up to now, within the general outlines of the argument, we have considered the themes of centrality and de-centrality, of particularity and anonymity but there are many other comparable themes which invite consideration. Regarding the single table alternative, for instance, it will obviously be of great importance to ascertain whether or not the table has a 'head' position. It will be of importance to ascertain whether there is likely to be another table of any sort elsewhere in the vicinity of the single dining table. It is almost self-evident that such matters will affect profoundly the single table's capacity for and tendency towards authoritarian centrality.[24]

In fact, several months after the dispute, following a reading of an earlier draft of this paper, critic A confirmed my view that further exploration of that complexity might uncover further resolutions to the difference of opinion. For he put forward a proposal which, as far as I can see, addresses itself interestingly, and precisely, to every issue raised. It is a proposal for a single table which, despite its marked singularity, nevertheless manifests exactly that anonymous character which he pointed to as so valuable in the case of the Rockefeller Center skating rink. It is, in short, a table which is also a street; it is a unitary entity, and a communal focus but it has no 'head' nor 'foot'; indeed, no hierarchical potential whatsoever.[25]

Nevertheless, the fact that this proposal so aptly meets the difficulties of this particular dispute should not be taken to suggest that every comparable architectural dilemma will have its own convenient resolution. I have already quoted Marx's view that we don't make history as we please.

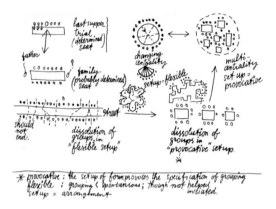

The sketches by Critic A, that he prepared after reading an early draft of this paper.

A part of the partisan character of the design act therefore depends upon an appropriate formal circumspection. It is perfectly conceivable that another comparable dilemma will have no such resolution. In such circumstances, should a designer proceed simply on the basis of his own wishful attraction towards a particular architectural configuration, all he will have done is to throw the responsibility of his own partisanship into doubt.

Yet if, as responsible designers, we do not have the possibility to make architecture "just as we please", it is still perfectly possible to devise built forms which, as Arendt says, can be seen "by many of a variety of aspects without changing their identity, so that those who are gathered around them know they see sameness in utter diversity". Indeed, if such circumspection as I have urged, is a negative consequence of an appropriate respect for the *langue* of architecture, then such a multivalent ideal architecture is surely the positive perspective which an understanding of the *langue* will open up. In our present context, for example, we may observe that the "worldly reality" of tables is indubitably enhanced, tables are nonetheless tables, if they are capable of being seen as settings for formal as well as for informal meals, it they can readily welcome few or many people around them, if they can serve as stages, or rostrums, of altars or biers…. That the form of the built world should be devised in such a way as to be capable of being seen in a "variety of aspects" in this way becomes an architectural analogy of the plurality of the human condition itself. The greater the range of possible individual perspectives upon a social built-fabric, the greater the possible richness of human action is possible within that built-fabric.

I said at the beginning of this paper that I would strive to demonstrate the broader importance of the dispute about the summer place timing position before my argument was concluded. For me, the importance of the structuralist concepts of *langue* and *parole* as they are employed in the growing disciplines of semiology, lies in their capacity for a deeper and more articulate illumination of the social and cultural consequence of built-form than has previously been possible.

I would hope that I have begun to indicate just how that needed illumination might occur. For there is no doubt in my mind that what is ultimately at stake is nothing less than that "worldly reality" which is the frame of all our being. And all our current professional self-deprecation, all our doubt about the social effectiveness of built-form notwithstanding, that "reality" is "related… to the human artefact, the fabrication of human hands, as well as to affairs which go on among those who inhabit the man-made world together." "To live together in the world" according to Arendt, "means essentially that a world of things is between those who have it in common, as a table is between those who sit around it; the world, like every in-between, relates and separates men at the same time."[26]

1 Earlier drafts of this paper have been read by a large and varied group of people, to all of whom I owe thanks. Notwithstanding some highly critical responses. I owe special thanks to Joseph Rykwert, Peter Prangnell, Herman Hertzberger, Peter Eisenman and Kenneth Frampton.

2 The critics were Herman Hertzberger, Peter Prangnell and myself.

3 Among the basic texts which I have consulted are the following: Saussure, Ferdinand de, *Cours de linguistiques générale*, Paris: Payot, 1965; Lévi-Strauss, Claude, *Structural Anthropology*, New York: Basic Books, 1963; Lévi-Strauss, Claude, "The Scope of Anthropology", London: Jonathan Cape, 1967; Lévi-Strauss, Claude, *The Savage Mind*, London: Weidenfeld and Nichcolson, 1968; Barthes, Roland, *Elements of Semiology*, London: Jonathan Cape, 1967.

4 Barthes, *Elements of Semiology*, pp 14–15.

5 The Gospel according to St Matthew, chapter 18, verse 20.

6 For an account of the conception of perceptual schemas applied to art history, see Gombrich, E H, *Art and Illusion*, London: Phaidon, 1962; and *Meditations on a Hobby Horse*, London: Phaidon, 1963.

7 The conception of "being-in-the-world" which is employed in this paper derives chiefly from Maurice Merleau-Ponty. The effort to 'marry' phenomenology to Structuralism, which I attempt here, is, I recognise, controversial, but I remain unconvinced of any incompatibility between the bodies of ideas which is truly fundamental.

8 Lévi-Strauss, "The Scope of Anthropology".

9 Marx, Karl, *The Eighteenth Brumaire of Louis Bonaparte*, Moscow: Progress Publishers, 1967.

10 The formulation and development of neo-positivist pragmatism is, by now, a familiar part of intellectual history. For my part, in this paper, I have relied particularly on the critique of Leszek Kolakowski.

11 Le Corbusier, *Towards a New Architecture*, London: The Architectural Press, 1948, p 250.

12 A failure to recognise that this is true is a basic flaw of behaviourist linguistic theory. For example, see Chomsky, Noam "Knowledge Of Language", *Times Literary Supplement*, 15 May, 1969.

13 Perhaps the most striking example of the "betrayal" of the underlying structure of an epoch of thought, is still Erwin Panofsky's *Gothic Architecture and Scholasticism*. The most interesting instance of a betrayed individual profile is Gustav Morelli's revolutionary nineteenth-century technique of identifying forged paintings through a meticulous comparison of brush-work technique in "incidental" background areas of real and forged works.

14 Lévi-Strauss, *The Scope of Anthropology*, p 14.

15 Lévi-Strauss, *The Scope of Anthropology*, p 15.

16 Upon reading an earlier draft of this paper, Peter Eisenman objected strenuously to this conclusion, arguing that "existentially speaking" design acts are ultimately of the same nature as any others, and therefore not partisan. In discussion of this, I agreed that there is, of course, a distinction between inadvertent, and deliberate, bias. And the discussion reminded me of a remark of Stanley Kauffman's, in scorn of certain highly politicised American documentary films of the late 1960s. "There is no such thing", conceded Kauffman, "as objectivity, but there is such a thing as objective intent". All this is true, and important. It even forms a major part of Hannah Arendt's arguments respecting "Lying in Politics" (see *Crises of the Republic*, San Diego CA: Harcourt, Brace Jovanovich, 1972). But except for explicitly excluding any interpretation of my position which would allow for deliberate deception, I think Eisenman's criticism is inapplicable.

17 I have not the space here to undertake a detailed critique of the views of these men, and I cannot even refer to an extant critique of Chermayeff's ideas. However, there is a brief criticism of Fuller's ideas

somewhat along these lines in Paul and Percival Goodman's *Communitas*, New York: Vintage Books, 1960, pp 76–82. The best comprehensive outline of the covert partiality of systems design *per se* is Robert Boguslaw's *The New Utopians*, New Jersey: Prentice-Hall Inc, Englewood Cliffs, 1965. For a witty attack on the concept of an objective participant-observer as described in Herbert Gans' *The Levittowners*, New York: Pantheon Books, 1967, see Friedenberg , Edgar Z review in *The New York Review of Books*, 23 May, 1968.

18 Arendt, Hannah, *The Human Condition*, New York: Doubleday Anchor, 1959, p 295.

19 Arendt, *The Human Condition*, pp 52–53.

20 In another paper, *"La Dimension Amoureuse"*, in *Meaning in Architecture*, edited by Charles Jencks and George Baird, London: Barrie and Rockliff, 1969, I have criticised certain architects' assumption of privileged positions *vis a vis* their fellow men. It is my view that owning up to the unavoidable partisanship of one's own position is a key part of forsaking such privileged positions. That is to say, in owning up to the partisanship of one's own position, one forsakes any claim to set the terms of one's relations to one's fellows in advance.

21 Lévi-Strauss, *The Savage Mind*, p 250.

22 For a fascinating early account of this problem, see Adolf Loos' essay "The Story of a Poor Rich Man" in Munz, Ludwig and Gustav Künstler *Adolf Loos: Pioneer of Modern Architecture*, New York: Praeger, 1966.

23 The student also suggested that if this kind of arrangement were adopted, should one camper be

absent from the meal, his seat would 'represent' his absence. Thus was proposed a secular metaphor of an ancient sacred tradition. In Christian theology, one sets a place at the table for the absent Christ at a Eucharistic supper, and in Judaism, such a place is set for the absent prophet Elijah, at the evening meal of the first night of Passover.

24 There are other matters affecting the table's ultimate significance which, even more obviously than those just mentioned, have to do with the physical setting within which it is placed. Obviously, with respect to a large social issue such as authoritarian centrality, other factors besides just the form of dining tables will come into play. In this, as in other respects, it is at the level of the "social totality" that the *langue* is ultimately operative. There is a part of the theoretical apparatus of semiology especially intended to deal with this matter of the setting of any element in the overall social field, involving what Barthes calls *"systeme"* and *"syntagme"*, but a consideration of this part of the apparatus would be beyond the scope of this paper.

25 Interestingly enough, a student had already formulated a summer place dining arrangement which met the terms of this proposal by critic A (Hertzberger). It was a long table which had supporting frameworks for a tent roof in the places of the 'head' and 'foot' of the table, thus ensuring the impossibility of anyone assuming those key social positions during a meal.

26 Arendt, *The Human Condition*, p 48.

A Critical Reflection on the Theory and Practice of Architectural Symbolism in the Work of Venturi, Rauch, and Scott Brown, and Their Colleagues, 1976

In 1976, I received a telephone call from Colin Rowe, who had been asked to step in and to reorganise a conference that was planned at Cornell University. It was to be the first event in honour of the Cornell student, Preston Thomas, who had been tragically killed in an automobile accident. As of the time of Rowe's call, three venerable architectural figures had already been asked to participate in the event, Edmund Bacon, Serge Chermayeff, and Nathaniel Owings. Thinking that the addition of some younger generation figures would enliven the event, Rowe added Michael Graves, Robert Stern and myself to the roster. My text on the Venturis and their colleagues was my contribution to the event. In 1993, there was a proposal to publish a collection of Preston Thomas Lectures delivered at Cornell over the years, so I wrote a 1993 introduction to the 1976 text. As it turned out, the collection never materialised. As a result, the text has not previously been published, but I think it has turned out to be prescient.

George Baird, September 2014

The text which follows is anomalous in several consequential respects. First of all, it was originally delivered as a more-or-less extemporaneous lecture, nearly 20 years ago, and was never developed or published until recently. Second, it was the only lecture early in the Preston Thomas series which was an account of architectural work other than that of the speaker. Thus it must sit somewhat awkwardly among documents in this compilation from the same early period of the series' history.

Finally, it concerns itself with a nexus of issues which I saw at the time leading from semiotics in architecture—as it was then understood—to what I tentatively characterised as the possibility of a theory of "decorum" in architecture. Given the disreputability which has since overtaken so-called "Postmodernism", and the intensity of current concerns with "authenticity", it seems to me that the theme of the text must appear anything but germane to current concerns in architecture, and in architectural theory.

In the circumstances, how to contextualise it for today? I have chosen to make modest editorial improvements to it, but not to attempt to reshape its basic argument, which appears to me now not only an underdeveloped one, but also one which reads as very much of its time. As for its anomalous status amongst its contemporaries, it will be interesting to see how it appears in the context of the critical/theoretical texts by younger figures which have typified Preston Thomas Lectures in more recent years.

There is of course, also the basic matter of its substantive concerns. In this respect, I find myself hoping that it may prove to have a value other than a purely historical one. To its credit, it does intimate the troubles for Postmodernism which most surely did follow it; insofar as architecture might once again be thought to be in search of a "social ground"—indeed a ground which might even be able to encompass architecture's further absorption into media—perhaps its "datedness" may prove no less damning to it as a piece of critical commentary of the 1970s, than it also currently does to the now so inappropriately undervalued efforts of the remarkable group of American architects around Robert Venturi which it took as the consequential object of critique, nearly two decades ago.

George Baird, March 1993

Since I intend among other things to be somewhat critical of certain developments in the evolving theories of Robert Venturi, John Rauch, Denise Scott Brown and their colleagues, it may be significant for me to begin by putting a few of my own theoretical cards on the table. I am, as my introducer explained, co-editor of *Meaning in Architecture*, a volume which followed the publication of Venturi's *Complexity and Contradiction in Architecture* in 1966 and which preceded the publication of *Learning from Las Vegas* in 1972. Indeed, in *Learning from Las Vegas*, Venturi, Scott Brown and Izenour were kind enough to acknowledge the two editors of *Meaning in Architecture*, Charles Jencks and myself, as influences on their developing ideas. I should point out also, that the situation is complicated further still by the fact that I find myself driven to conclude that, to the extent that the arguments of *Meaning in Architecture* did influence Venturi, Scott Brown and Izenour, that influence was an unfortunate one. Certainly there is no doubt in my mind that the arguments respecting symbolism which are so insistently pressed in *Learning from Las Vegas*, confuse the situation as much as they clarify it, particularly when compared with the arguments put forward earlier in *Complexity and Contradiction*. A comparison between the two books along these lines has, of course, already been made by Stuart Cohen in *Oppositions* 2, in an essay which is one of the best pieces yet to appear on Venturi, Scott Brown and their colleagues, and this paper proceeds quite directly from some of Cohen's arguments.

Be these criticisms as they may, a further reason why it is appropriate to address the topic of the work of Venturi, Rauch, Scott Brown and their colleagues, is that they are so undoubtedly a major theoretical influence on the generation of architects now starting to call itself "Postmodernist". What is more, it seems to me to be the case that—given the criticisms both of the clarity and of the utility of their theorising I will make—that influence itself must be seen to be both confused and confusing.

Yet the fact that I hold such critical views as these also doesn't alter the fact of my fascination with, and considerable regard for much of the current oeuvre of Venturi, Rauch, Scott Brown and their collaborators. Indeed, given that I am making these remarks in the presence of our moderator Colin Rowe—and that I have recently been rereading his "Character and Composition: or some Vicissitudes of Architectural Vocabulary in the Nineteenth Century", published in the same issue of *Oppositions* as Stuart Cohen's

Front facade of the Vanna Venturi House.

essay—it is probably apt for me to cite the compelling deployment of "character" and of "composition" in two of the products of the Venturi oeuvre—one which is already an architectural icon of our times, and the other of which may well soon be. These are the Vanna Venturi house of 1962, and the recently published Brant House of 1972. As architecture, I find them both utterly compelling, and their power must be seen as the first qualification of the sets of theoretical criticisms I am about to make of the theory of Venturi, Rauch, Scott Brown and their collaborators.

More specifically, I will endeavour to delineate points of confluence and diversion between the authors and myself, and between them and other commentators. Let me begin my argument in detail by quoting from the essay mentioned above, Stuart Cohen's "Physical Context, Cultural Context: Including It All", published in *Opposition* 2. Cohen began by characterising briefly the concept of "inclusivism" as it was associated with Venturi, Rauch, Scott Brown and their colleagues, as opposed to that of "exclusivism" which they characterised as typifying mainstream Modern architecture. The distinctions in question are of course, drawn from a book of my fellow speaker, Robert Stern, *New Directions in American Architecture*. Having recapitulated Stern's distinctions, Cohen went on:

Recently, inclusivism, as represented by Venturi's work, seems to have abandoned analysis of formal organisation as part of the critique. In *Learning from Las Vegas* by Robert Venturi, Denise Scott Brown and Steven Izenour, Modern architecture is criticised entirely on issues of symbolism. Buildings are "ducks" or "decorated sheds". Modern architecture, the argument goes, by abandoning the use of applied decoration, began to decorate its buildings by articulating building elements such as structure and mechanical systems. This has resulted in the tendency to grossly deform simple buildings to serve the purpose of decoration, thus turning the buildings themselves into decoration. For the purpose of Venturi's argument, it seems that decoration equals symbolism, for we are offered, the Long Island Duckling, a roadside building deformed into a symbol—the famous duck—where building equals symbol. What is suggested as an alternative is the simple, straightforward building, the shed to which decoration is applied—the "decorated shed" or building plus symbol. Through the continued citing of examples that only illustrate this issue, inclusivism now seems to deal almost entirely with architectural imagery, suggesting that this is to be taken as the sole dimension for evaluation.

The first Brant House of 1972.

This is unfortunate. The chosen forms and their sources may now be clear, but what is the intended relationship of these forms to formal structure and of formal structure to meaning? Up to now it has been clear what inclusive architecture was not, but now, with its emphasis even further removed from formal analysis, as in *Complexity and Contradiction*, it is unclear what the organisational strategies for the forms of an inclusive architecture might be.[1]

Now, it seems to me that Cohen is correct in lamenting the relative abandonment of formal analysis in favour of the dominant preoccupation with imagery which typifies *Learning from Las Vegas*. And I am convinced also of his claim that the plan organisation typical of the work of Venturi, Rauch, Scott Brown and their collaborators, is often formally highly sophisticated, despite their own recent protestations of interest only in imagery. Later in this paper, I shall have occasion to return to his argument and to the remarks he makes on Guild House. In fact, I shall argue—pursuing the argument he makes for what he calls contextualism—that a theory of architectural symbolism itself requires an underpinning in terms of formal structure. But this is to anticipate later stages of my argument. For the moment, to address the question of symbolism directly, I want to quote the—presumably—definitive passages on "ducks" and on "decorated sheds" from the introduction of Part II—that is to say the theoretical part—of *Learning from Las Vegas* itself. I quote again this time, from Venturi, Scott Brown and Izenour themselves:

We shall survey this contradiction in its two main manifestations.

1. Where the architectural systems of space, structure and programme are submerged and distorted by an overall symbolic form. This kind of building becoming sculpture, we call the duck, in honour of the duck-shaped drive-in, the Long Island Duckling, illustrated in *God's Own Junkyard*, by Peter Blake.

2. Where systems of space and structure are directly at the service of programme, and ornament is applied independently of them, this we call the decorated shed. The duck is the special building, that is a symbol; the decorated shed is the conventional shelter that applies symbols. We maintain that both kinds of architecture are valid—Chartres is a duck (although it is a decorated shed

The facade of Paul Rudolph's project for Crawford Manor.

as well), and the Palazzo Farnese is a decorated shed—but we think that the duck is (seldom) relevant today, although it pervades Modern architecture.[2]

Now, careful readers of *Learning from Las Vegas* will remember that the above passage, colloquial in tone, but moderate in orientation, is directly followed by a contentious comparison between two recent projects for Senior Citizens' housing buildings: Venturi and Rauch's own Guild House in Philadelphia and Paul Rudolph's Crawford Manor in New Haven. Guild House is, of course, for Venturi, Scott Brown and Izenour, a decorated shed and Crawford Manor is a duck. Following on through the book, one finds discussions titled: "Heroic and Original", or "Ugly and Original", or again "The Renaissance and the Decorated Shed", or again in Part III, an exposition of the Venturi's own work, which is called "Essays in the Ugly and Ordinary: Some Decorated Sheds".

Venturi, Scott Brown and Izenour may in the most general terms have conceded that both kinds of architecture—both ducks and decorated sheds—are valid, but the thrust of their argument doesn't seem to leave much room for ducks. Perhaps the pithiest summary of their feelings in the matter (if not of their theoretical position) is to be found in the interview between Venturi, and Scott Brown conducted by John Cook and Heinrich Klotz, and published in the book: *Conversations and Architects*. Here again I quote, this time from Venturi:

Boston City Hall is to me, a very good example of what's wrong. It's bombastic, I think. Boston City Hall is trying to do something through architecture that architecture can no longer do. In the past architecture could be monumental. It could denote civic monumentality in the city. Siena could have a Palazzo Publico, but not Boston. Philadelphia could do it well in the nineteenth century with its lovely monstrosity of a City Hall. The urban renewal people with their urban revival, traditional urban spaces are trying to return to Italian monumental urbanism. The urban renewal has tried to bring the city centre back via pure architecture and it has not succeeded, because this is not the era for grand architecture. Every age has its medium. The medium for now is not pure architecture. The Boston City Hall employs the formal vocabulary of late Le Corbusier. These pure Heroic forms were great as the tense manifestation of late genius in a Burgundian field for the monks. Not so for bureaucrats and citizens in a Bostonian piazza.

What the building should be is an ordinary loft building or a shed that will shelter and accommodate the bureaucratic processes that go on in the City Hall. Then you cover that shed with a great big sign that blinks "I am a Civic Monument", if that is what you want. In other words, for us the main impact must come from the media other than architecture. What I have just described for the City Hall is what we have called the decorated shed. Modern architects have maintained essentially that the impact comes from the expression of the process of designing and building. The image of the building is the resultant of structure and space and programme, and these all work harmoniously.

We don't agree with that. We think that these architectural elements can be contradictory to each another—that the outside might want to be different from the inside, for instance—and that the impact cannot come only from pure architecture. The history of architecture can tell us

Front elevation, Guild House.

that architecture always incorporated iconographic and symbolic meaning. The Gothic cathedral is a decorated shed to some extent, teeming with mixed-media messages. The image is not just architecture. In fact, there are contradictions resulting from a complex image: the facade of Amiens is not 'organically' related to the building behind it. Or rather, a disunity exists if you look at the building as pure architecture. But this is not only a building. It's also a billboard facing a place which broadcasts a message. The billboard functions more in front, the architecture more in back, up front, architecture alone wouldn't have had enough impact.[3]

In the colloquialism of conversation with Cook and Klotz, it seems to me that Venturi and Scott Brown have here elaborated the presuppositions that lie behind their attitude to symbolism—as they relate to the duck/decorated shed distinction—in a way which I want to take off from specifically. It is true, of course, that the preface to Part III of *Learning from Las Vegas*—a presentation of their own work—begins with a cautious disclaimer:

A building is a building and a theory is a theory, no artist should go all the way with his own philosophy, translating too literally his theory into his architecture, particularly into any one piece of architecture. That is too dry.[4]

But even this disclaimer hardly prepares one for the shock of the projects which follow, most specifically for the D'Agostino and Wike houses, which are described somewhat sheepishly, as I read it—as admitted "ducks". That is to say, certain of their own projects are called "ducks" right in *Learning from Las Vegas*. Evidently the disclaimer of tight relations of theory to practice is meant to permit the inclusion of these two exceptions to the general rule.

But no rationale of the exception is provided. We are simply left to ruminate on the implication that in some marginal way ducks, as well as decorated sheds, are valid in our time and that houses for the well-to-do can legitimately take the form of ducks, while city halls and offices cannot. Even allowing for a certain latitude of non-compatibility between theory and practice, I find this an unsatisfactory mode of argument. And my attitude in this respect is coloured by the fact that I admire the projects for the two houses called "ducks". Indeed, they look as interesting to me as the two houses which got built, with which I began—the Vanna Venturi House and the Brant House, both of which I suspect, by extension are also ducks. What is more; even though I agree with Venturi and Scott Brown that the Boston City Hall is an unsatisfying example of a public building for our own time, I don't agree with the line of criticism of which I have quoted.

Now the complex—and even partly contradictory—statements and suppositions combined here lead me to suggest the presence of a fundamental theoretical problem. Moreover, it seems to me that it is a problem that lies at the theoretical heart of the distinction between ducks and decorated sheds as it was initially formulated by Venturi, Scott Brown and Izenour. In my view the distinction rests on a theory of symbolism which is misconceived in the first place. In the section of *Learning from Las Vegas* which refers directly to the arguments of *Meaning in Architecture*, Venturi, Scott Brown and Izenour employ an argument concerning the inescapably representational character of any architecture to refute the hoary, hand-me-down theory of Modern architecture called Functionalism. They are of course, right to do this. One of my own chief purposes in writing in *Meaning in Architecture* also was to do precisely that.

But surely, in most current architectural discussions, the refutation of Functionalism is a theoretical *fait-accompli*. Certainly no one at this symposium is going to hear a defence of Functionalism; at least not from me, nor I suspect will they hear one from Graves or Stern or Rowe. And even if I am wrong in my estimate of the state of current opinion, Venturi, Scott Brown and Izenour ought not to have allowed themselves to permit an attack on Functionalism—in terms of symbolism—to lead them to make the problematic distinction they have done between ducks and decorated sheds. For, given their fascination with Pop and vernacular phenomena, this employment of symbolism against Functionalism was bound, in my opinion, to lead to an insupportable conclusion and ultimately even, in a very practical sense, to undermine their own preoccupations with explicit as opposed to implicit symbols.

To place these remarks in a broader intellectual context, let me set beside Venturi's remarks about the Boston City Hall, the by now quite famous quotation by Walter Benjamin:

Architecture has always represented a prototype of a work of art, the reception of which is consummated by a collectivity in a state of distraction.[5]

In short, I would argue, following from Benjamin's profound observation, that the most potent architectural symbolism is likely as not the least explicit symbolism. If one really were to erect an ordinary loft building or a shed to shelter and accommodate the bureaucratic processes that go on in a city hall and then to cover the shed with a sign that blinks, "I am a civic monument", then it seems to me, following Benjamin, one would have got it precisely backwards. The too, too explicit symbolism of the sign would, over time prove all too perishable, and the bureaucratic shed would itself come to comprise the ultimate vessel of implicit meaning.

I can make the same argument in another way. The practical effect of the idea of the "decorated shed" is to drive a conceptual wedge between the unconscious and the conscious aspects of our experience of architecture. To put it another way again, it is to polarise programmatic expediency on the one hand; and symbolic expression on the other. The result of such a polarisation—if applied at-large—would be a highly explicit, and therefore highly volatile symbolism up front in any given building's conception, behind which may well lie an utterly unmediated programmatic reality.

As I have intimated up to now, while I don't see the duck/decorated shed distinction as a deplorable theoretical idea in itself, I also don't think the work of Venturi, Rauch, Scott Brown and their collaborators reduces to that idea. Their intuition and their practice have never, as far as I can see, taken the extreme form of the polarisation suggested by my analysis of the idea of the decorated shed. Nevertheless, I can cite, I think, two instances from their work, of the volatile nature of architectural symbolism in the form of signs.

By now, I expect all of you will know the notorious "decoration" which Venturi saw fit to apply to the facade of the project for Guild House. I quote again:

The giant order (of the facade) of the building is topped by a flourish, an unconnected, symmetrical television antenna in gold anodised aluminium which is both an imitation of an abstract Lippold sculpture and a symbol for the elderly.[6]

Well, sometime after the opening of the building, the symbolic antenna came down. According to Venturi it was, "falling apart. The clients will not replace it, perhaps because they are Quakers."[7]

Then there is the sign which was intended to announce the Brant House:

> We plan a green sign like the standard expressway signs indicating 'The Brant House' where the driveway diverges from the central road.[8]

The handsome, recently published photos of the house, do not include the sign referred to. I am not surprised that it—either was not built, or—like the Guild House antenna—was removed. My surmise is that such explicit symbolic representations as the Guild House antenna and the Brant House sign, are too volatile to be able to be assimilated into any substantive conception of architectural meaning.

In fact, these two instances reminded me of the historical fact that when, in 1789, the French revolutionaries attacked the Medieval cathedrals which they saw as symbols of the Ancient Regime which had oppressed them, it was the tympani over the doors of the great buildings which they so consistently defaced. Following the analogy put forward by Venturi, Scott Brown, and Izenour themselves, one might note ironically that to the extent that the Medieval cathedral is a decorated shed, its most explicitly symbolic signs proved historically to be similarly volatile and similarly vulnerable as the exclusively symbolic signs on the front of Guild House and Brant House.

Then there is the other side of the coin, the unmediated programmatic reality which lies beneath the explicit symbolism of the shed's decoration. I think I detect traces of this unmediated reality showing through the conception of one of Venturi, Scott Brown and their collaborators' less elaborately decorated sheds: the recently completed Humanities Building for the State University of New York at Purchase. This is a building which—according to the architects—has only one "rhetorical" space, the high narrow gallery which forms part of the interior street linking all the lecture spaces. Save for this, the building is largely "dumb and ordinary", notwithstanding the evident formal associations with the late work of Alvar Aalto that show up in the plan. Indeed, in many of its parts, the Humanities Building seems to me to edge dangerously close to being dumb and ordinary (without quotation marks) and when this happens, of course, the result is that the architects lose control of the implicit symbolism of the building altogether.

To sum up this part of the argument, it seems to me that the practical implications of the theoretical polarisation represented by the idea of the "decorated shed" can—along the lines of the commentary I have just made—be discerned in the work of Venturi, Rauch, Scott Brown, and their collaborators. It seems to me that the idea is misconstrued, and that the discernible consequences of its implementation are unfortunate.

But this is not the end of the matter. By my interpretation—rather than theirs—their buildings and projects are by and large mostly "ducks", in any case. And I think it goes without saying—given my argument so far—that is all to the good that they are. However, if this is so, then where does my argument leave the critique of so-called "ducks"?

The answer to this, in my view, can also be elaborated in terms of a more ample theory of symbolism in architecture, than that which *Learning from Las Vegas* has provided, a symbolism which takes account of the whole range of levels of our experience of buildings; from the most conscious to the most unconscious; and from the most explicit to the most implicit; and which attempts to outline a corresponding account of the phenomena of formal structure within architecture, with which to interrelate all of the above. Given the admitted inconsistencies *within* their own theory, and between their theory and their practice, we should not, I think, be surprised to find imitations of possible theoretical alternatives elsewhere in the arguments of *Learning from Las Vegas* itself. Myself, I find two such imitations, both highly interesting ones. The first appears in an elaboration of the critique of the so-called "duck". Again I quote Venturi, Scott Brown and Izenour:

> When it cast out eclecticism, Modern architecture submerged symbolism. Instead it promoted expressionism, concentrating on the expression of architectural elements themselves: on the expression of structure and function. It suggested, through the image of the building, reformist-progressive social and industrial aims that it could seldom achieve in reality. By limiting itself to strident articulation of the pure architectural elements of space, structure, and programme. Modern architecture's expression has become a dry expressionism, empty and boring—and in the end, irresponsible. Ironically, the Modern architecture of today, while rejecting explicit symbolism and frivolous appliqué ornament, has distorted the whole building into one big ornament.

65. Neiman-Marcus building, Houston, Texas; Hellmuth, Obata, and Kassabaum

66. Neiman-Marcus building

Page excerpted from *Learning from Las Vegas*, showing sequence of photographs from La Tourette to Neiman-Marcus.

In substituting 'articulation' for decoration, it has become a duck.[9]

Now this is an argument which ought not to sound too strange at Cornell since it tends in many ways to complement, if not to parallel, the critique which Colin Rowe has made of Neo-Plasticism and its many progeny, within mainstream Modern architecture. The suppression of the phenomena of the relations of front and back, of top and bottom, of solid and void, and the literal organisation of all these instead, would, I think have been more strongly emphasised by Rowe, than it has been in the arguments of Venturi, Rauch, Scott Brown, and their collaborators. But the phenomenal vacuity Venturi, Scott Brown and Izenour's critique points to is the very same one, as I understand it, to which Rowe's also does.

The other intimation of the (subtler) theory of symbolism which I find in *Learning from Las Vegas* isn't an argument at all, it's merely a highly provocative and discriminating set of images. It's the set which begins with La Tourette, that "tense manifestation of late genius in Burgundian field" and ends with Hellmuth Obata & Kassabaum's Neiman-Marcus Store in suburban Houston. I think you know this sequential set of iconic images. Starting in Burgundy, it proceeds to New Haven and Boston, through Cornell and ends up in Houston.

Together, it seems to me, these two brilliant sets of observations of Venturi, Scott Brown and Izenour, do propound a devastatingly effective critique of mainstream Modernism's collapse into banality, and do point to a need for a new theoretical approach. But what is needed, is in my view, not a theory of decorated sheds. Rather, it is a theory which concerns itself at least in part with contemporary variants of the traditional concept of "decorum". What such a theory would do would be to structure the varying levels of explicit and implicit symbolism as I have discussed above, and to establish systems of propriety in relation to the employment of any particular architectural vocabulary.

Now, calling for the return of such a classical concept of decorum may seem even more contentious than the claims that Venturi, Scott Brown and Izenour have made that I have criticised, but I don't think it ought to be. To begin, I should state that I can only imagine the contemporary theory of decorum being formulated in the context of the (wary) attitude manifest in a familiar remark of Jean Cocteau: "Tact in audacity, consists in knowing how far too far you can go."[10]

The Lieb House in context.

Any modern theory of decorum would have to sustain that degree of ironic resonance. But of course, examples of contemporary decorum which are ironical *do* exist. Indeed the work of Venturi, Rauch, Scott Brown and their collaborators itself often can serve as a vehicle to illustrate such a theory. Stuart Cohen's contextual analysis of Guild House illustrates how it manifests whole sets of ironic urban relationships: the inversion of the typical form of front to back of the building, to close the open spaces of the housing behind, and to address the maximum number of units to the street; the distortion and modulations of scale of the windows to the two facades; the replication of locally employed building materials in a high art context and so on. All of these components of the building's contextual character manifest an "ironic decorum".

In another notable passage, Venturi, Scott Brown and Izenour themselves present an image of irony which Cocteau himself might well have appreciated. The passage in question concerns the Lieb House of 1967:

> It is a little house with big scale, different from the houses around but also like them. It tries not to make the plaster Madonna in the bird bath next door look silly and it stands up to, rather than ignores, the environment of utility poles.[11]

But the ultimate instance of audacious tact, at least by intention, is Venturi, Scott Brown and Izenour's effort to address the particular reality of Las Vegas by employing analytical mapping tools based on Nolli's neo-Classical maps of Rome.

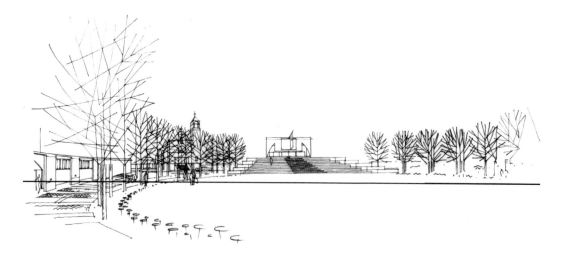

Perspective view of the project for a town hall for Canton, Ohio.

Now it seems to me that the logic of the argument I have developed thus far makes it clear that there can be no objection in principle to the focus on Las Vegas or to their employment of Nolli as a precedent for their spatial analysis. But while there can, I think, be no objection in principle, the mode of creative inquiry being used, is like any other, also subject to requirements for tangible and useful results. And surely it is a fact that, to date, the Venturi's specific and elaborate analyses of Las Vegas *à la* Nolli has had no clear, positive impact on their work—or on that of any other architect with which I am familiar.

Note that I am attempting here to stay clear of another argument concerning the legitimacy, or the lack thereof, of the controversial interest in Las Vegas in the first place, an argument which has recently caused a grave split between Denise Scott Brown and Kenneth Frampton. There is no doubt in my mind that in tackling Las Vegas, the Venturi's have got themselves in deeper, conceptually speaking, than their stance of non-judgementalism would safely take with them. But in elaborating this argument relating to the limitations of architectural symbolism, I want to confine myself to a consideration of the questions of decorum and of symbolism and not to become involved in any 'moral' or 'ethical' considerations of the appropriateness of the Las Vegas model.

So, let me conclude by commenting briefly on the audaciousness of the symbolic explorations in a number of specific instances of the work, of Venturi, Rauch,

Scott Brown, and their collaborators, with a view to testing out my proposition concerning decorum. Let me say before I do, that the range of architectural issues involved here, seems to me to be of a kind that can *only* be dealt with through a specifically intense consideration of symbolism in addition to that of formal structure.

Let me comment briefly in this respect, on a series of symbolic motifs in different projects from different periods of their oeuvre. The first is the flag which was deployed as part of the facade design for the scheme for a town hall in Canton, Ohio from 1965. This is the scheme in which the "enormous flat", to quote Venturi, "is perpendicular to the street so that it reads from up the street like a commercial sign".[12]

This is the symbolic image which has provoked Kenneth Frampton to launch his notable attack on Venturi, Rauch, and Scott Brown in his recent essay "America, 1960–1970: Notes on Urban Images and Theory".[13]

The Canton flag, it seems to me, is an image in the realm of the super explicit, an image; that is to say; like the Guild House television aerial, and the Brant House sign, which cannot realistically be expected to be incorporated into any substantive architectural conception, on account of its *too volatile* connotations. It is interesting to note in this connection that Venturi's own interest in the flag appears to spring from the famous Jasper Johns' painting of three flags superimposed. In *Complexity and Contradiction,* the Johns' painting is cited for the strange tension which is created by the three flags' superimposition, one upon the other.[14] The flag

Jasper Johns, *Three Flags*, 1953.

appeared only later to take on a significance more directly concerning its explicit, connotative, symbolic meaning.

It may be worth pointing out that Stuart Cohen has, in the piece I started from, outlined this shift of emphasis and of orientation in the work of Venturi, Rauch, Scott Brown, and their collaborators, from *Complexity and Contradiction,* on to *Learning from Las Vegas.* I find myself beginning to suppose, having completed this paper, that in fact perhaps that emphasis is now beginning to shift back. I have already stated that my view that the Venturi, Scott Brown and Izenour approach to Las Vegas has got them into deeper waters than they can cope with; that they need a more deliberately, and elaborately formulated conceptual apparatus with which to do what it is they have attempted, successfully. It seems to me that I can now see them retreating from some of the theoretical implications of that approach, in a way which might get them back on to what I would call the solider ground of *Complexity and Contradiction.* In that sense I think the fact that the flag started out being representational of a formal organisation device, and then in the middle period turns into an explicit symbol on its own, can perhaps itself stand for the clearest indication of

this shift of emphasis and, in my opinion, of the dangerous consequences which follow from it.

I have already spoken of the comparably explicit employment of the television aerial atop Guild House, a motif which I find equally problematic. It is of significance, I think, that Guild House also includes a minor motif at a much less explicit level of significance, but one which is instructively enough, much more successful on the plane of symbolic expression. This is the standard security fence surrounding the side garden which (inflects) centrally and symmetrically toward the main entrance. The fence imitates a pair of inverted flanking Palladian screen walls which complement the inverse relation of front to back of the whole complex, to which Stuart Cohen's article refers. It seems to me that this fence is a striking success of Venturi, Rauch, Scott Brown, and their collaborators. They may have even made it a potential addition to the vocabulary of Modern architecture. After all, it consists materially of the utterly banal standard security fence—surely one of the most ubiquitous and last considered real elements in all contemporary architecture. Such fences—in all traditional architectural photography—

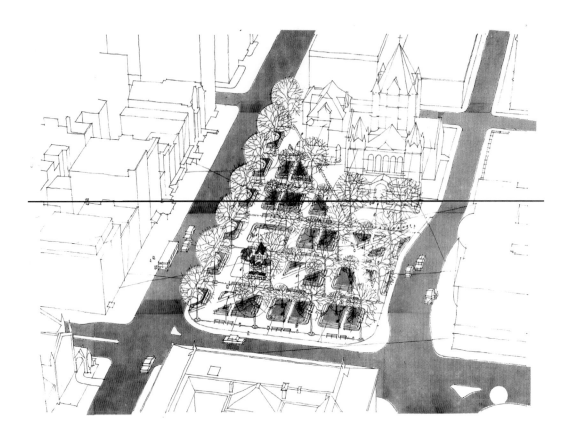

Bird's-eye view of the proposal for Copley Square.

are among the things that are almost always there—and almost never photographed. So, in that sense, in terms of a theory—a contextual theory relating to the array of building materials in the real world—incorporating into their conception this particular element, stands as one of the most ambitious, and successful instances of the effort towards "inclusiveness" that Venturi, Rauch, Scott Brown, and their collaborators have made.

In contrast to the motifs I've just reviewed, such as the flag and security fence, which play partial, secondary, roles within larger symbolic ensembles, there are others in the work of Venturi and his various collaborators which seem to play a fundamental role as primary organisers of the ideas of buildings. The first of these is miniaturisation, most strikingly represented by the miniature of H H Richardson's Trinity Church, as the pivot of Venturi and Rauch's 1966 submission to the competition for a new design for Copley Square in Boston. In this case, my response is more ambiguous than

it was in the case of the flag, which I think at a symbolic level failed, and the security fence, which in my opinion succeeded. In the end, I think the miniaturisation achieved here is too blatant to escape the charge of triteness, (especially when compared with the subtler interplays of large and small commonly characteristic of the entrances of Venturi buildings—and we can use Guild House as reasonable an instance of this as any other).

Then, more critical still than the Copley Square scheme, is the scheme for the restoration of Franklin Court in the historic sector of Philadelphia, a scheme in which the central motif is a frame outline standing in free space, symbolically representing the unreconstructable historic Franklin House. Here I am more sympathetic, since this is a brave attempt at the material realisation of a straightforward representation which has a basis in a historic reality. Yet the motif in the end still seems unconvincing, still too self-evident to escape a reading as merely picturesque. I find myself supposing in this case

View of Guild House with chain link fence.

General view of Franklin Court.

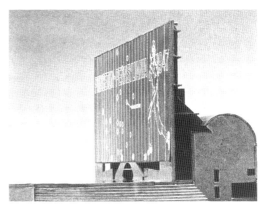

View of the model of the National Football Hall of Fame.

that the giant cowl forming the foci on the fragments of the original house's actual foundations might have formed a more plausible formal vehicle for a central symbolic motif than the house's line outline against the sky.

But lest it should seem that I think few—if any—of these explicit motifs succeed, let me point to the project from 1967, the National Football Hall of Fame, in which I think the symbolic relation of the giant projection screen to its supporting elements is more successfully resolved, even though it constitutes the explicit representational, symbolic image which sustains the entire building from. This is probably due to the number of mutually reinforcing readings of the

two elements which are possible, as contrasted with Copley Square and Franklin Court examples, in which the "miniature" on the one hand, and the "line against the sky" on the other, are readable as representational symbols on one level only.

Finally, I would like to point to another—only implicit—symbolism which is nevertheless highly recurrent in the oeuvre of Venturi, Rauch, Scott Brown, and their collaborators, and it is this one I am going to end with. It is particularly interesting to me because it has an anthropomorphic and anthropological significance richer than some of the ones I've talked about so far and because it is so recurrent in the recent various

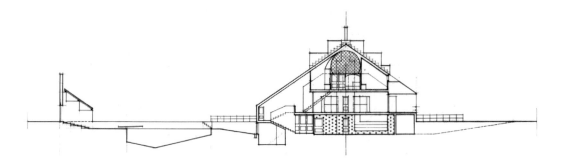

Cross-section drawing of the proposal for the D'Agostino house, showing the "upper room".

projects for houses. This is the "upper room", usually a bedroom, which occupies a central, even symmetrical position in the characteristic Venturi house section, from that for the Chestnut Hill house, right through to that for the Trubek House. The same room occurs also in the same location in the Brant House. Indeed, in the project for the D'Agostino House, the "upper room" in question is even proposed to be finished in wood in the manner of a Polish church. For me, these recurrent symbolic spaces in the Venturi Houses recall, quite compellingly the similarly intense centrally axial dining rooms of the early houses of Frank Lloyd Wright in Oak Park, with their fireplaces and their Biblical inscriptions. How extraordinary that none of this has heretofore been discussed!

What all this symbolic connotation—at what I would call the middle level of a possible symbolic theory of decorum—ultimately means for Venturi, Rauch, Scott Brown, and their collaborators, I don't propose to pursue at this point. But I think it can be said that a symbolic interpretation which can articulate such a preoccupation—which as far as I know, Venturi, Rauch, Scott Brown, and their collaborators have themselves, never discussed—will ultimately be inescapable. Indeed, I even hope that some such reconsideration of their theoretical stance respecting symbolism, on rather deeper and richer ground than the duck/decorated shed distinction such as the "upper room" so compellingly intimates might be possible, could even lead to a resolution of the political predicament in which they seem to have found themselves.

In perhaps the unhappiest passage in all of *Learning from Las Vegas*, Venturi, Scott Brown and Izenour make the following remark:

Although architects have not wished to recognise it, most architectural problems are of the expedient type. And the more architects become involved in social problems, the more this is true. In general, the world cannot wait for the architect to build his Utopia and in the main, the architect's concern ought not to be with what ought to be, but with what is and with how to help improve it now. This is a humbler role than the Modern Movement has wanted to accept, however it is an artistically more promising one.[15]

In light of the phenomenal potential of a richer symbolism in the work of Venturi, Rauch, Scott Brown, and his collaborators that which their own theory has so far embodied, this passage seems to me preposterously misconceived. Though its sincerity is beyond dispute, surely this passage gets the political commitment and the irony precisely the wrong way round. True, we know that the real world problems the architect characteristically faces are expedient; true, the world cannot wait for Utopia. But this is exactly the legitimate basis of the architect's preoccupation with what ought to be or at least with what could be. It is surely what could be that architecture, albeit ironically, ultimately ought symbolically to represent. And this suggests to me that the manifest imagination and talent exhibited by Venturi, Rauch, Scott Brown, and their collaborators, make this timidity of theirs—on the plane of theory—fundamentally misplaced.

1   Cohen, Stuart, "Physical Context/Cultural Context: Including It All", *Oppositions* 2, January 1974.

2   Venturi, Robert, Denise Scott Brown and Steven Izenour, "Some Definitions Using the Comparative Method", *Learning from Las Vegas*, Cambridge MA: MIT Press, 1972, p 64.

3   Venturi, Robert, Denise Scott Brown, in conversation with John Cook in Cook, John W and Heinrich Klotz, *Conversations with Architects*, Praegar Publishers, 1973, p 249.

4   Venturi, Robert, Denise Scott Brown and Steven Izenour, "Essay in The Ugly & Ordinary: Some Decorated Sheds", *Learning from Las Vegas*, Cambridge MA: MIT Press, 1972, p 111.

5   Benjamin, Walter, "The Work of Art in the Era of Mechanical Reproduction", *Illuminations*, New York: Harcourt, Brace & World, 1968, p 241.

6   Venturi, Scott Brown and Izenour, *Learning from Las Vegas*, p 68.

7   Venturi and Scott Brown, *Conversations with Architects*, p 262.

8   Venturi, Scott Brown and Izenour, *Conversations with Architects*, p 172.

9   Venturi, Scott Brown and Izenour, *Learning from Las Vegas*, p 72.

10 Jean Cocteau (quotation source not located).

11 Venturi, Scott Brown and Izenour, *Conversations with Architects*, p 172.

12 Venturi, Robert, *Complexity and Contradiction in Architecture*, New York: Museum of Modern Art, 1966, p 125.

13 Frampton, Kenneth, "American 1960–1970 Notes on Urban Images and Theory", *Casabella*, issue 359–360, 1971, p 24.

14 Venturi, Robert, *Complexity and Contradiction*, p 62.

15 Venturi, Scott Brown and Izenour, "Theory of Ugly and Ordinary and Related and Contrary Theories", *Learning from Las Vegas*, Cambridge MA: MIT Press, 1972, p 84.

Semiotics and Architecture, 1998

The last text in this grouping is from two decades later. In 1998, Oxford University Press published the first edition of its four volume *Encyclopedia of Aesthetics*. At the suggestion of Kenneth Frampton, Editor Michael Kelly invited me to prepare an entry on this topic. My very long retrospective view of this issue, but not so long text describing it, is my response to his invitation.

By the mid-1950s, confidence in the principles of Modernism in architecture had reached a point of crisis—if not for architectural practitioners at large, then certainly for its most thoughtful historians and critics. Mainstream Modernism's "Functionalist" design methods had come to seem prosaic, and its long-accepted aesthetics of abstraction increasingly vacuous. In historical retrospect, it is evident that there were two particular bodies of theory outside architecture to which revisionist thinkers predominantly turned at that time, to seek intellectual reinvigoration for their discipline. These were "operations research", on the one hand, and theories of "perception" and of "reception", on the other. By means of a retheorisation of 'functionalism' in architecture, "operations research" led eventually to what came to be known as "systematic design methodology". The various theories of "perception" and "reception", on the other hand, through an intensified consideration of architecture's audience, led to an effort to apply semiotics to architecture.

One key venue at which both of these lines of inquiry were explored early on was the Hochschule für Gestaltung in Ulm, founded as a sort of "new Bauhaus" in 1953. Not a school of architecture in the usual sense, the Ulm Hochschule combined industrial and building design with visual communication and information—encompassing press, films, broadcasting, television, and advertising. At Ulm, all these design disciplines were intended to be explored from the perspective of what one of the school's notable early pedagogues, Gui Bonsiepe, named "technological rationalism". Tomás Maldonado—another of the leading figures at Ulm—eventually concluded that "operations research" alone could not adequately address the significance of form in architecture; as a result, like many of his colleagues, he found himself exploring theories of perception and reception as well. One important source was Max Bense, whose approach to communications was first outlined in his *Aesthetica* of 1954, and another one was the early American semiotician, Charles Morris, whose works had first appeared in the 1930s. Kenneth Frampton observed, in an essay on the Ulm school, that "operation" and "communication" were the two poles that were to "play major roles in the evolution of Hochschule theory".[1] The school's commitment to technological rationalism meant that both these poles were being explored from a predominantly positivist philosophical vantage point.

The fact that this was so was not lost on an early visitor to Ulm, who was later to become one of the most committed critics of its "scientistic" intellectual orientation. This was Joseph Rykwert, whose 1958 lectures at the school eventually took the form of an essay (to be discussed later) titled "The Sitting Position: A Question of Method". Rykwert had already published the previous year an essay, "Meaning in Building", in which he lamented what he saw as the vulgar and banal consequences of a "preoccupation with rational criteria" for the design process, and called instead for architects to "acknowledge the emotional power of their work", insisting further that such an acknowledgment would depend on "investigations of a content, even of a referential content in architecture". In choosing to employ a term such as "referential content", Rykwert challenged the supposedly transparent abstract aesthetics of mainstream Modernism head-on, and opened the way to the explicit consideration of the semiological "signifier" and "signified" in architecture, which was to commence some years later. "The Sitting Position", moreover, emphasised the anthropological— as opposed to the functional—aspects even of such an "operational" discipline as ergonomics. (Both of Rykwert's prescient essays of the late 1950s were later compiled in a collection titled *The Necessity of Artifice*.)[2]

As it happens, the first publication of Rykwert's "Meaning" essay was in the Italian magazine *Zodiac*, no 6, and Italy became the home of the next notable series of efforts to apply semiotics to architecture. For example, in 1964, Giovanni Klaus Koenig published *Analisi del linguaggio architettonico,* the first extended text devoted explicitly to the study of the possible application of the models of semiotics to architecture along parallel lines to those that had been explored at Ulm.[3] (Appropriately enough, Koenig's text was preceded by an introduction by Maldonado.) In 1967, Koenig's book was followed by Renato de Fusco's *Archittetura come mass medium* of 1967—this being a text whose very title foregrounded what was coming to be known as "reception theory"—in particular, the influence of the celebrated Canadian media theorist Marshall McLuhan.[4] Then, in 1968, the rapidly evolving Italian perspective on semiotics was put into a definitively sharp focus with the publication of Umberto Eco's *La struttura assente*.[5] Eco's comprehensive text not only summarised the whole earlier history of the various intellectual strands that made up the theory of semiotics up to that date; it put into context the contributions of Koenig and de Fusco to a possible semiotics of architecture, and went on to set out the clearest, most detailed, and most broadly based application of such principles to architecture that had appeared up to that time. (Eco made a number of efforts to translate this text into English, but eventually abandoned the effort, instead folding its arguments into a later book, which he wrote in English, *A Theory of Semiotics*, and incorporating its architectural contents, translated into English, in a 1980 anthology discussed later in this essay.)[6]

In a stream of thinking parallel in many ways to that of the Ulm thinkers and the Italians, a group of French scholars had begun to make their own significant contribution to the emerging field. From 1954 to 1957 had appeared the now-famous series of *feuilletons* of Roland Barthes that were compiled in French under the title *Mythologies*.[7] The following year, Barthes' text was joined by the French edition of Claude Lévi-Strauss' equally influential *Structural Anthropology*.[8] Like most of the structuralist French texts of that period, both of these were more heavily dependent on their respective authors' debts to the linguistic theory of the Swiss pioneer Ferdinand de Saussure than on the work of either Charles Morris or Charles Sanders Pierce, even though the French scholars, like Eco, acknowledged the significant role played in the early development of semiotic theory by such figures. As a result of the rapid rise to prominence of Barthes' and Lévi-Strauss' typical methods of cultural interpretation, their works rapidly achieved considerable intellectual influence in an increasing number of nonliterary cultural fields—painting, photography, and cinema no less than architecture itself. With the French publication of Barthes' *Elements of Semiology* in 1964, this growing influence reached a definitive first culmination.[9]

Among the revisionist theoreticians of architecture who eagerly read Lévi-Strauss' and Barthes' arguments of the early 1960s was the present author, who was engaged during the mid-1960s in the preparation of a doctoral dissertation in architecture at University College London. The professor of architecture there at that time was Richard Llewellyn-Davies, and he had made his school a British centre of a revisionist architectural tendency known in those years in the English-speaking world as "systematic design methodology". Like their intellectual fellow travellers at the Ulm school, the British methodologists were engaged in an intellectual project intended to devise a new mode of designing that would possess the authority of science, and that would eschew any preoccupation with subjectivity, intuition, or myth.

It is difficult from the vantage point of three decades later to recall just how powerful this tendency appeared to be in the mid-1960s—especially in Britain, given how little influence it has managed to sustain in the years since. At the time, the advocates of this tendency bid fair to succeed in their project, at least insofar as they did manage to supplant the rapidly fading pieties of "orthodox" Modernism, in numerous schools of architecture throughout the world, especially those of the former British Empire. Probably the first culmination of their project of revisionism was the publication in 1964 of *Notes on the Synthesis of Form* by Christopher Alexander.[10] In this first of his many influential books, Alexander employed the concept of "fit" within the design process to devise a sort of utterly frictionless end point by which the ultimate appropriateness of any finally designed "form" could, as he saw it, be dispassionately assessed.

Revisionist theoreticians, who wished to see architecture regain a securer social role than mainstream Modernism had been able to achieve for it, but who also believed that such a role needed to be one that was not limited to "functionality"—even to the sophisticated new versions of functionality that the design methodologists were claiming to find in applications of architecture of "operations research"—found highly promising the potential alternative applications of semiotics, particularly in the structuralist semiotics associated which the French intellectual lineage stretching back to de Saussure.

Among the intellectual efforts to realise that promise was a 1967 issue of *ARENA*, the journal of the Architectural Association School of Architecture in London, England, edited by the present author and devoted to the theme "Meaning in Architecture". Among the texts included in this issue that have proved to have some historical influence were "Typology and Design Method" by Alan Colquhoun, "The Sitting Position: A Question of Method" by Rykwert (the first English-language publication of the essay that had been first published in Italian in 1965 in *Edilizia Moderna*), and "*La Dimension Amoureuse in Architecture*" by George Baird. Colquhoun's essay was one of the first attempts to challenge the methodologies that had been developed at Ulm and at University College London, and was even framed as an explicit reply to Maldonado, whom Colquhoun had met when they were simultaneously visiting faculty at Princeton University. Baird's "*La Dimension Amoureuse* in Architecture" was one of the first texts published in English to set out a systematic exposition of the Saussurean concepts of *langue* and *parole*, of the "signifier" and the "signified", and of "system" and "syntax", as they might be employed to interpret architecture as a social field of meaning. In 1968, the journal publication was followed by a book of the same title, edited by Charles Jencks and Baird, and substantially expanded to include a number of additional texts on related topics by authors such as Françoise Choay, Gillo Dorfles, Kenneth Frampton, and

Charles Jencks.[11] In subsequent years, the book *Meaning in Architecture* went on to play a role in the dissemination of Saussurean semiotics as applied to architecture, first in the English-speaking world, and then also in Spain and in France, where foreign-language editions appeared.

In 1972, it became possible for the first time to discern the impact of the project of semiotics in architecture on an already established generation of thinkers, for in that year a still controversial text was published that was much more directly oriented to the design of actual buildings than *Meaning in Architecture* had been, and was thereby more influential—at least in the English-speaking world. This was *Learning from Las Vegas,* by Robert Venturi, Denise Scott Brown, and Steven Izenour.[12] Of this trio of authors, Venturi had already made himself famous as the author of the seminal revisionist text of 1966 *Complexity and Contradiction in Architecture*—probably the single most important of the critiques of the principles of "orthodox Modern architecture", to use Venturi's sardonic term, that had preceded the historic application to architecture of the methods of semiotics.[13] But the *Las Vegas* text went much farther down a revisionist road than Venturi's earlier text had done. Where *Complexity* had mounted a formalist critique of the compositional principles of Modernism, *Las Vegas* went on to make a much more "sociological" and "populist" disparagement of Modernism, and the precepts of semiotics formed a supportive methodological backdrop to it. For that matter, the choice by Venturi and his co-authors of Las Vegas itself as the putative exemplar of an identifiably distinctive—and popular—American urbanism was deliberately polemical.

It is interesting to note that the authors of this inflammatory book cited arguments from *Meaning in Architecture,* in particular Colquhoun's increasingly influential essay "Typology and Design Method". Indeed, during the early 1970s, the concept of "type" that had been so compellingly employed by Colquhoun in his 1967 essay merged with a body of ideas that had been being developed in Europe during those same years, and that revolved around the paired concepts of building "typology" and urban "morphology". Associated in the first instance with an Italian architectural lineage from Ernesto Rogers to Saverio Muratori and Aldo Rossi, the body of ideas comprising "typology/morphology" established a conceptual relationship of architecture to urban form that, like semiotics, was deeply embedded in the "social".

Five years after Venturi's *Las Vegas* came what is still probably the most influential English-language text on semiotics in architecture, Jencks' *The Language of Post-Modern Architecture*.[14] Where *Meaning in Architecture* set out a theoretical apparatus for consideration, and *Las Vegas* oriented this apparatus to "popular culture", Jencks' book not only recapitulated and extended both of these intellectual trajectories, but it also went on to illustrate a number of actual built examples, and explicitly linked the analogy of "language" in architecture, based on semiotics, with the specific architectural tendency then coming to be known as "Postmodernism". For the next decade, the Postmodernist tendency rapidly took over the practice of architecture throughout the English-speaking world, now intellectually sanctioned by the apparatus of semiotics. In the United States, architects who became very prominent celebrities—such as Michael Graves, Charles Moore, and Robert A M Stern—all did so as perceived practitioners of the new Postmodernist style, and they in turn were followed in the world of more commercial architecture by practitioners in large corporate firms.

In 1980, a shift from popularising texts back to more scholarly ones occurred in the English-speaking world with the publication of a follow-up volume to *Meaning in Architecture,* edited by one of that book's co-editors, Jencks, this time joined by Geoffrey Broadbent and Richard Bunt. *Signs, Symbols and Architecture* brought together a revised version (and English translation) of the portion of Eco's *La struttura assente* that had been devoted to architecture, with various texts by other authors.[15] These included specific, detailed applications of semiological analysis to specific building elements (by Eco and Jencks, as well as by Mario Gandelsonas and David Morton), texts of a more sociological character (by Judith Blau and Maria Luisa Scalvini), and even certain expressions of skepticism in respect to the whole project of semiotics in architecture (by Xavier Rubert de Ventos and Bunt).

Historically speaking, the contribution to this book by Gandelsonas and Morton (a reprint of an essay that was first published in 1972) is particularly interesting, because it was devoted to semiological interpretations of the work of a number of American architects, including Peter Eisenman. Eisenman was soon to become part of a polemical backlash against the influence of semiotics in architecture. As of 1980, it was still politically possible for his work to be discussed in a volume of essays largely oriented to it affirmatively. It is true, of course, that at an earlier point in his career, Eisenman had been interested in a loose linguistic analogy with architecture, based on the concept of "deep structure" that had been framed by the American linguist Noam Chomsky. By 1980, Eisenman had abandoned the influence of Chomsky, but this did not prevent Gandelsonas and Morton from reprinting in that year an earlier text that discussed his work primarily in terms of its "syntactics".

As the 1980s proceeded, and as the populist and popular phenomenon of Postmodernism in architecture grew ever more ubiquitous throughout the world, it became increasingly uncommon to emphasise the "syntactic" aspects of the application of semiotics to architecture. Instead, the overwhelming bias of Postmodern architecture toward the "semantic" utterly overwhelmed mainstream architectural practice. At the same time, the parallel urban ideas that had been framed in Europe in relation to the concepts of "typology" and "morphology" similarly lost their former sharp focus. Worst of all, other related aspects of this bias became strikingly evident as well. Instances were, on the one hand, the increasingly reactionary polemics in favour of a historicist, populist urbanism propounded by Britain's Prince of Wales and, on the other, the newly systematic appropriation of the techniques of Postmodern architecture then being undertaken by the Disney Corporation for its proliferating theme parks.

An undercurrent of dissent also became increasingly visible among leading theorists and critics in those years. The increasingly 'scenographic' character of Postmodernist architecture—in both its historicist and its more commercial theme-park modes—precipitated stronger and stronger objections among its critics, who pointed to its increasingly evident loss of cultural authenticity. What is more, some of these identified the application of semiotics to architecture as a cause of the perceived undesirable direction of architecture that had become so widespread. Polemical counterattacks on Postmodernism—and at least implicitly on semiotics—grew increasingly vociferous in the late 1980s and early 1990s, and most of them derived from two distinct, but related, cultural/intellectual positions. The first was a resurgent architectural neo-avant-gardism, and Eisenman was a prominent representative of it. He had, of course, from the very beginning of his career had avant-gardist leanings, and the accommodationist political success of Postmodern architecture offended him. Its historicist iconography, its mainstream popularity, and

Architectural Theory Between Structuralism and Phenomenology

As I have already noted, it has been a theme of my writings across my career to attempt to bridge, theoretically speaking, between the precepts of structuralism, as derived from the writings of (early) Barthes, Lévi-Strauss, and de Saussure, and those of phenomenology as derived from Merleau-Ponty, Arendt, and, to a lesser extent, Heidegger.

As my text for the *Oxford Encyclopedia* makes clear, this interest of mine has from time to time placed me in the cross-fire between theoretical protagonists in architecture in the camps of Postmodernism and Rationalism on the one hand, and of Post-structuralism on the other. That having been said, it has always seemed to me that the dispute in question has been one that was more polemical than profound. In this regard, it has been a source of some intellectual comfort to me that such major figures as Lévi-Strauss and Bruno Latour have tended simply to side-step the whole quarrel.

The first and the last of the texts that follow are phenomenological, methodologically speaking, and the middle one more structuralist.

Alvar Aalto, 1970

While I was still in London, Robin Middleton took on the general editorship of a series of popular monographs about well-known Modern architects. The series was an extensive one, with each book in the series requiring an introductory interpretive essay to accompany a series of photographs of buildings by the specific architect in question, taken by the Japanese architectural photographer, Yukio Futagawa. Since Aalto was one of the only architects in the prospective series with whose work I was already familiar at that time, I agreed to take on the assignment in regard to his work. The resultant text remains a favourite of mine among my own texts, and it has been cited favourably to me by such diverse readers as Martin Filler and Kenneth Frampton.

Born in 1898, Alvar Aalto was 11 years younger than Le Corbusier, 12 years younger than Mies van der Rohe, and 15 years younger than Walter Gropius. This age discrepancy is of real historical importance, for it meant that Aalto was old enough in the 1920s to be deeply affected by the new architectural developments which were then taking place in Europe, yet young enough not to become an integral part of the powerful milieu which grew up around these three key figures in the history of twentieth-century architecture.

Aalto's real contemporaries include men like Marcel Breuer, yet he does not really belong among them either, not least because his work demonstrates a profundity and seriousness to which none of these architects attained. Aalto is then, a real historical anomaly.

It is perhaps because of this that there exists such a dearth of interpretive studies of his work. There are the works by Giedion, Neuenschwander, Gutheim, Flieg, and Venturi, but excluding magazine references, that is all. Furthermore none of these texts attempts any sustained interpretive analysis. This introduction is of necessity brief and far from filling the gap. All it claims to do is to take three

rather particular soundings of Aalto's as yet unexplored depth. These three soundings, which I have characterised as Balustrades, Ruins, and Politics, have been chosen partly just because they are so interesting and indicative of Aalto's style, and partly because they are somewhat remote from those aspects of his work which have already received some scant consideration.

Balustrades

There are parts of buildings we scarcely ever touch: roofs and chimneys, eaves and cornices. There are others, such as floors and steps with which we are in constant, unavoidable contact. In everyday terms, actually touching roofs and chimneys is such a remote possibility that it usually does not even occur to us that they are touchable. Touching floors and steps, on the other hand, we normally take for granted. In between these two extremes lies the area of conscious experience of our environment, and, in the environment of buildings, particularly those parts whose touch is neither so remote as never to occur to us, nor so constant as to be taken for granted. These parts include door-handles and push-bars, railings and balustrades.

Particular examples are door handles such as those of the National Pensions Institute in Helsinki or those of the Rautatalo Office Building in Helsinki (see opposite). These particular forms not only belong to the area of conscious experience described above; their touch is their most manifest characteristic. To be sure, any comprehensive attempt to understand them will also involve other considerations—ranging from the technics of door hardware to the formal organisation of facade design. However, in the case of Aalto, no analysis that begins from such considerations will finally account very adequately for the particular character of these forms, or for the intensely tactile quality which they embody. If they lead us to a central theme in Aalto's work then they do so most essentially through their touch.

Door handle at the National Pensions Institute, Helsinki.

Door handle at the Rautatalo Office building in Helsinki.

Touching a door-handle crystallises an experience for a moment, touching a railing extends it in time. Consider the railing on the flight of stairs leading to the council chamber in the town hall at Säynätsalo, or the ones on the staircases in the Otaniemi Institute of Technology (see p 80 top left and top right). Like Aalto's door-handles, these forms owe their typical cross-section to the shape of the human hand, and they make that debt palpably evident. But while a handle is usually grasped only for an instant, the extent of a railing can be traced with the hand as far as the railing goes. And Aalto's railings penetrate the space of his buildings very extensively. In the Säynätsalo town hall, a railing leads almost continuously from the public entry area up a flight of stairs, across each landing, to the furthest extent of public access to the council chamber. In the Otaniemi interior (see p 80 top right), it is possible to follow a railing past the foot of the stair with which it begins, around the side and rear of a stair-enclosing screen; or to follow another one from an upper level down one flight of steps, then along a wall and around a curved corner, before it descends again to another floor below.

The touch of these forms, of course, is as potent as that of the door handles. But this touch possesses

a further significance: all of these railings extend far beyond the physical limits of the steps which are their functional *raison d'étre;* in penetrating so pervasively the space of the buildings' interiors they form elaborate networks of touch. Thus the tactile quality of Aalto's railings, for all its importance, is still only the key to their further, and subtler role as basic cues to an understanding of the extent, character, and accessibility of space beyond that immediately visible.

But that is still not all there is to them. For in forming networks above and beyond their function as related to stairs, they take on something of the character of the walls and screens to which they are attached. It becomes just as possible to read them as typical wall or screen elements which happen to play a role in relation to flights of stairs, as it is to read them as stair elements which extend along adjacent walls and screens. This means in turn that they assume yet a third level of significance. For they become not just forms to touch with the hand, or even to follow with the hand, but also forms simply to pause by or lean against. Because of this, we experience them not just as tactile, but even as corporeal objects. In discovering that, we discover the ontological core of Aalto's work. These railings project the basic human image of Aaltoesque space. They offer to us both the enclosure and the disclosure of balustrades.

It is simplest to begin to illustrate this image by discussing first balustrades which are indisputably literal ones, such as that of the main staircase at the Teachers' University of Jyväskylä (see p 80 bottom left). This balustrade is, in the first instance, a simple vertical extension of the massive masonry wall which supports the steps themselves. It follows the steps' ascent

A view of the staircase to the Council Chamber at the town hall. at Säynätsalo.

The lobby of the auditorium at the Helsinki Institute of Technology at Otaniemi.

The Michelangelo staircase in the anteroom of the Laurentian Library, Florence, 1559–1571.

Stairhall near the foyer in the Pedagogical University at Jyväskylä.

through four floor levels, reflecting their gradient by its profile. An expansive landing occurs at each floor level, and the balustrade flattens out at each of them. From without, then, the balustrade rises from the floor like a cliff, and ends as a parapet. As for the flight of steps, it rises slowly from landing to landing, between the balustrade and the wall-screen, as though it were the face of the earth itself, fortuitously assuming a form which encouraged men to mount it.

What is more, in spite of the fact that it is a major public stair, the space its balustrade encloses does not project into the space of the room. It is, in this respect, the opposite of such traditional major staircases as that of Michelangelo in the anteroom of the Laurentian Library (see above), or that of Charles Garnier in the Paris Opera. In these cases, not only do the staircases project boldly into the space that contains them, even

View from the south of the main approach staircase to the Säynätsalo town hall.

The grassy ascent to the courtyard at the Säynätsalo town hall.

the individual steps which make up the stairs project from the space which is enclosed by the balustrades. Aalto's staircase, by contrast, quite distinctly recedes, between the balustrade to one side, and the wall-screen to the other. Each landing, behind its balustrade, is made into a potent enclosing and disclosing space, a space which is both haven and promontory, both shelter and stage.

This is the basic human image of Aaltoesque space—the space of the balustrade—and it is characteristic

of every Aalto stair. One will, for instance, also find it sustained in major stairs at the Säynätsalo town hall (see above) and at the Otaniemi Institute of Technology. Neither of these is as extended as the stair at Jyväskylä—the Otaniemi stair has only two landings, and at Säynätsalo there is only one. And both of them have balustrades whose profiles are rationalised to a rectilinear grid; thus neither balustrade reflects as precisely as that at Jyväskylä the gradient of the steps. Nevertheless all the constituent characteristics of the space of the balustrade are again present. In both cases, there is a wall to one side, a solid balustrade to the other. The space of the stair recedes between the two, and its surface again rises slowly as the surface of the earth itself might.

More interesting still, there are in Aalto's work a number of variants of the space of the balustrade, in which certain constituent elements of the space are not present, yet in which the image itself is nevertheless sustained. One of these can be seen at both the Säynätsalo town hall (see above left), and the Seinäjoki town hall. Here are stepped grassy ascents which, unlike the stairs described above, clearly do project volumetrically

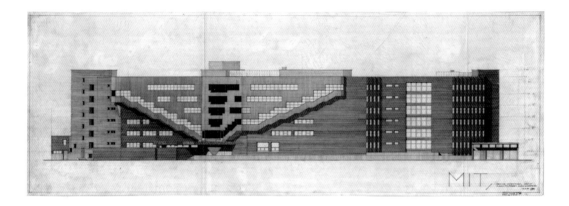

Drawing of an elevation of Baker House at MIT, showing the staircase slung off the side of the building.

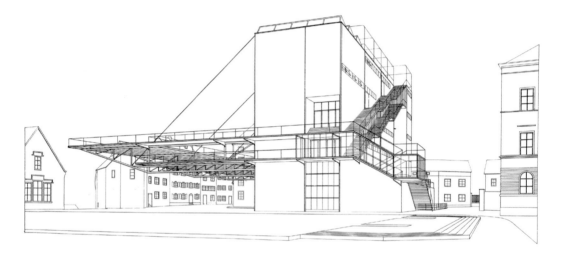

The staircase slung off the side of the Petershule project of 1927 by Hannes Meyer.

into the space which contains them. Yet if one anticipated element of the image (spatial recession) is absent, another one occurs even more intensely than in the examples cited above. Those stairs were only metaphors of the surface of the earth. These steps literally are that surface; as proof they even have grass and flowers growing on them.

To move to the opposite extreme, consider a variant which is in fact totally disconnected from the surface of the earth, the stair which descends the side of Baker House at Massachusetts Institute of Technology (see above). This would seem on the face of it to be a stair which dramatically 'floats', suspended above empty space, as does its celebrated Heroic Period predecessor, the stair which is slung off the side of Hannes Meyer's Peterschule project (see above).

But despite its obvious similarity to Meyer's, the Aalto stair clearly does not float. The connection to the surface of the earth is broken, but the sense of enclosure is heightened. Where the Meyer stair is clad in large sheets of glass, Aalto's is largely enclosed in solid material; where Meyer's is 'slung off' the side of the building, Aalto's is volumetrically incorporated into the mass of the building proper. The very pattern of glazing breaks the thrust of the ascent, and emphasises the repose of the landings.

A third variant occurs in the interiors of the Otaniemi Institute of Technology and the Wolfsburg Cultural Centre. These staircases relinquish neither the spatial recession nor the connection to the surface of the earth, but rather, the enclosing wall. Both of them descend from the open centres of spaces to the open centres of spaces one floor below. But in both

View of the sunken area in the library in the Wolfsburg Cultural Centre.

View of the sunken area in the library in the Pensions Institute.

View of the projecting balconies on employee housing at Sunila.

View of workers and employees housing in Sunila with more enclosing balconies.

A view of the Bauhaus building at the Dessau, showing the studio and dormitory building with the characteristic balconies projected off the face of the building.

View of more enclosing balconies on the apartment building at the Hansa-viertel in Berlin.

cases there are introduced enclosing screens, which play the role taken by the walls in the earlier examples. As before, the landings become the spatial foci of the stairs. Platforms to see from and to be seen upon, they offer nevertheless the enclosure characteristic of the space of the balustrade.

The image, moreover, is not confined to literal expression on staircases. As the basic human image of Aaltoesque space, it not surprisingly recurs in several other important contexts, for example, on every occasion involving the famous recessed well in the centre of a major space, first introduced in the library at Viipuri. The well reappears at Baker House, the National Pensions Institute, Helsinki, and the Wolfsburg Cultural Centre (see p 83). Literally speaking, it is always defined by the balustrade which surrounds it; metaphorically speaking, the relation of the upper to the lower floor level is always defined by the space of the balustrade. Like all of the landings described

The entrance to the Paimio Sanatorium.

above, the floor areas adjacent to the balustrades surrounding these wells in every case take on the typical character of haven and promontory, of shelter and stage.

Embodied in the railings which so extensively penetrate Aalto's interiors, the image predictably recurs wherever his wall surfaces are articulated at railing height. Thus all the tiles, thongs or battens which surround piers and columns in his buildings, such as at Jvyäskylä and Seinäjoki, are vestigial embodiments of the space of the balustrade. Even his balconies—at least his characteristic balconies—project its image. Compare the two types employed in the housing at the Sunila Cellulose complex. That illustrated in the adjacent image (see p 84 top left) projects the basic human image of Heroic Period Modernism, an image from which Aalto had not yet completely turned away. Like the Meyer staircase cited above, almost exactly like the balconies on Gropius' Bauhaus block at Dessau, these balconies project boldly forward into empty space, offering no enclosure at all, but rather, only a Heroic kind of disclosure. By contrast, the balconies illustrated in the following image (see p 84 bottom

right) point towards the image which was to become typical of Aalto. Like the quite late examples from the apartment buildings at Bremen and Berlin (see p 83 bottom right), these balconies already project the image of the space of the balustrade. Receding spatially between powerfully enclosing walls, they mark the beginning of Aalto's turning away from the Heroic psychology so characteristic of the major figures of the Modern Movement, by whom, up until then he had been so influenced.

Ruins

According to rumour, Aalto holds that his buildings will not be ready to be judged until they are 50 years old. There is no doubt that such a rumour is in many ways surprising; yet there certainly are features of his buildings which substantiate it. Indeed, in taking it up, we touch on his attitude to one of the most poignant issues in the whole history of Modern architecture—the awful, inescapably timebound character of built-form.

Recall any of the key buildings of the period during which Aalto began his career, the period we now call

A view of the House of Culture, Helsinki.

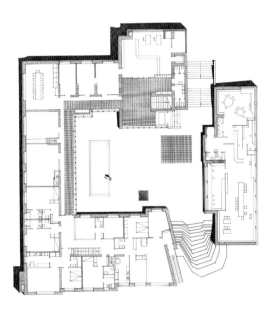

Plan of the "main level" of the town hall at Sayantsalo.

Heroic. Saturated with a sense of their own timelessness, those buildings were designed in such a way as to lead one to suppose that all history had ceased, that the elemental and eternal constants of built-form for all time had been discovered. For them, the whole future had been collapsed into a timeless present. Yet now we can only look back at them poignantly, can only concede their pathetic vulnerability. History has not ceased; not even time has ceased to pass, and the supposed elemental and eternal forms of the great buildings of the 1920s and 1930s are crumbling. With an irony whose full weight we still do not really appreciate, we refer to them as Heroic relics.

We also now know that the fiction of these buildings' timelessness could only be preserved under conditions of the most lavish, meticulous and constant maintenance. The buildings were often enough compared to boats; it turned out that it was the kind of care customarily extended to boats that they required for themselves.

It is only one more aspect of this irony, that perhaps the largest of buildings of the Heroic Period which has actually received the kind of care they all needed, should be one of Aalto's—and it, moreover, is one of the only two of his buildings that can reasonably be described as Heroic. This is, of course, the Paimio Sanatorium, whose

A view of the Vuoksenniska Church at Imatra.

A view of the town hall at Säynätsalo.

beautifully preserved state can easily be appreciated from photographs (see p 85), and even more easily when one considers at the same time the present state of such comparable buildings as Le Corbusier's Salvation Army building in Paris and Bijvoet and Duiker's 'Zonnestraal' Sanatorium near Utrecht. It is almost as though the narrow escape of the Paimio building (from the kind of neglect so many of its peers have suffered) had haunted Aalto ever since. For he subsequently moved further and further away from the conception of building-in-time which it represents, to another, quite different one, which seems almost deliberately intended to save his works from time's painful ravages. All his buildings after Paimio give the impression of having been aged in advance. The timelessness of the buildings of the Heroic Period might have proved utterly vulnerable, but the timelessness of buildings which were already ruins would surely prove less so. And if, as I suggest, all Aalto's buildings after Paimio are metaphors of ruins, then the point of the rumoured 50-year suspension of judgement also becomes clear. It would not be that by then the buildings had finally attained their ideal state; rather, by then their invulnerable timelessness would have become universally accepted, simply as a matter of course.

The most obvious evidence of Aalto's preoccupation with ruins is his attitude to materials. In the place of the concrete and stucco, steel and glass so characteristic of the buildings of the 1920s and 1930s, Aalto began increasingly frequently to use brick and stone and, eventually, tile, copper and marble; all of these are materials which, to the extent that they do show their age, do so far less dramatically, and far more predictably, than the newer ones. In the most characteristic of his works, he has ensured—to the extent that choice of

building materials can—that at least the worst shock resulting from the passage of time is successfully eluded.

But this is still just the surface of this preoccupation. Consider how frequently his buildings seem consciously to succumb in advance to extraordinary outgrowths of planting. The Säynätsalo town hall is organised around a courtyard overgrown with verdure (see p 81 bottom); even the interior gallery which surrounds the courtyard makes concessions to the advancing greenery. Vines begin to overtake walls of the Helsinki House of Culture (see p 86 top); plants have been set strategically in the interiors of the Vuoksenniska Church, the Cultural Centre at Wolfsburg, and the Enso-Gutzeit building in Helsinki. And significantly, in none of these cases do the built-form and the planting complement each other, as they typically do in comparable works of Frank Lloyd Wright. In Wright's case, the built-form and the planting together make up—indeed even celebrate—a metaphor of organic unity. It is one role of Wright's 'organic' building geometries to sustain that unity. Aalto's characteristic building geometries, on the other hand, are fragmented rather than organic. In his buildings, the built-form and the planting represent a fundamental and ironic antagonism. It is as though the final victory of nature over the vulnerable creations of mankind, had already been conceded in Aalto's works at their inception.

In its turn this characteristic outgrowth of planting forms part of a still larger theme of ruinousness. Aalto's buildings are most often strikingly rural in character, even when the purposes they serve seem indisputably urbane. Already at Sunila in 1936 (see p 84), the various elements of the complex (factory, communal facilities and housing) are disposed in such a way that each one remains a

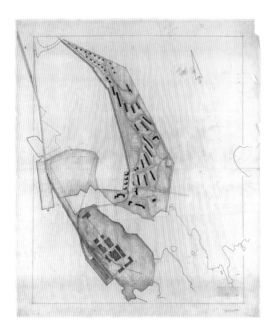

Site plan of the Cellulose Factory and related facilities in Sunila.

formally isolated incident in an overwhelmingly rural setting. Although a town hall is surely the most urbane of building types, Aalto's at Säynätsalo is quite calculatedly set in the midst of a bush (see p 87 top left); even the Cultural Centre located in the geographic centre of metropolitan Helsinki is set in its immediate context in such a way that its actual urban connections are minimised. Both the University at Jyväskylä and the Otaniemi Institute of Technology are unobtrusively set in forested sites; and the Vuoksenniska Church has been consciously separated from the other communal facilities in Aalto's town plan, to be set instead in the midst of a grove of trees (see p 87 top right).

At a more detailed scale, huge panes of glass are used in the foyer of the main assembly hall at Jyväskylä, to bring the forest into the interior (see p 89 top right), and a grassy, flower-bedecked ascent serves as an approach to the town hall in the civic centre complex at Seinäjoki (see p 89 top left), In all these cases it is implied that to establish unequivocal urban space of any real intensity would pose far too provocative a challenge to the ravages of time. Instead, the buildings are always set in natural contexts in such a way as to ensure a distinct, albeit ironic, dematerialisation of any urban space that might tend to crystallise there.

An important variant of the basic metaphor occurs. There are a few Aalto buildings whose contexts are so inescapably urban that the tactic of dematerialisation would not succeed. However, the metaphor of ruins is then frequently sustained by an alternative device—the ironic fragmentation of ostensibly rational building geometries. Take the case of the National Pensions Institute, Helsinki. An unquestionably urban building, it even presents a formal entry facade to an open urban space which exists in front of it (see p 90 top). Yet any further exploration of the form of the building as a whole only throws into greater and greater doubt the apparent urbanity of that facade. The opposite side of the building, for instance, faces the axis of a major public park of Helsinki; yet the building's only acknowledgement of this is an unutterably subtle recession at that facade's centre. And an approach to the complex from any other angle reveals only a highly fractured and formally inscrutable profile.

This same irony is developed to an even greater extreme in the Enso-Gutzeit building. On the face of it, it would seem to have as its most prominent facade the one which looks magisterially over the main harbour of Helsinki (see p 89 bottom left). But a closer approach reveals that the right-hand bay of that facade is void at street level, while the corresponding left-hand bay is not. Then too, the recessed pavilion on the roof extends to the far right-hand roof edge, and not to the left-hand one. This, in turn leads one to suppose that this facade must really be a side of the complex, and that the front facade is really the one that faces towards the town centre. Indeed, that facade proves to be perfectly symmetrical, with a formal arcade extending ceremonially across its entire ground floor. But this interpretation implies a formal axis running longitudinally through the volume of the building as a whole. And this interpretation founders in turn when one discovers that a large part of the third facade (a 'side' of the building, from this point of view) has its centre randomly eaten away (see plan on p 90 bottom). Thus two facades of this strange pavilion make large claims to be seen as its front, yet the volumetric integrity of the building as a whole is deliberately fragmented, in such a way as to make it impossible ever to resolve the ambiguity between the two alternatives. In each of these two most prominent urban complexes of Aalto's oeuvre, the urbanity inherent in the building situation is allowed to crystallise, only to be ironically undercut by the radical fragmentation of the volumetric integrity of the building form as a whole. The heroism of human intervention in the world may appear, but the metaphor of ruins casts its ironic shadow all the same.

View of the grassy ascent to the town hall complex at Seinäjoki.

A view of the entrance hall and foyer of the Pedagogical University at Jyväskylä.

Enso-Gutzeit corporation Headquarters, Helsinki.

Politics

At the zenith of their confidence in the 1920s, the major Modern architects and their apologists proclaimed with messianic fervour the beginning of an exhilarating new era. Illness and inhibition, social strife and obfuscation would end; in their place would arise a new spirit of vigorous good health, order and rationality. Briefly stated, the two key aspects of the Moderns' position were: first, a utopian social commitment; and second, a deep confidence in the efficacy of the newly rigorous—even scientific—rationality they proposed to apply to design.

The pervasive physical presence of light, sun and fresh air was sought in building designs and brandished in polemics, not only because the Moderns were so confident that they promoted good health, but also because they were such potent symbols of the new world which Modern architecture promised to bring into

being. As a building type, the tuberculosis sanatorium eventually became the single most convincing public symbol of the new architecture, because the actual medical treatment then recommended for tuberculosis (lots of light, sun and fresh air) coincided so exactly with the cultural metaphor of good health so central to the philosophy of Modern architecture. Quite naturally then, upon the completion of such a prominent example of the new "social architecture" as the Sanatorium at Paimio, Aalto assumed a place among the major Modern architects of the day.

No one at the time seems to have noticed that one problematical consequence of this whole development was to place the Modern architect in the role of doctor to society. Problematical, because it has put the whole subsequent history of Modern architecture in a political predicament from which it has yet to extricate itself fully. As doctor to society, the Modern architect assumed a role which, it was granted, might have incidental political implications, but which was not thought in any inherent sense to be a political role. Not at all. It was held that the social vision embodied in Modern architectural theory sprang from that theory's scientifically rational methodology, rather than from any political *parti pris*. By the same token, if that methodology seemed increasingly to require the Modern architect to undertake planning in a comprehensive fashion, even that was taken to show no proof of his special political significance. It was only the logical consequence of his 'scientific' methodology. After all, it was well known that 'scientific' success depended completely upon comprehensive control of experimental conditions.

Aerial view of the Pensions Institute Complex in Helsinki.

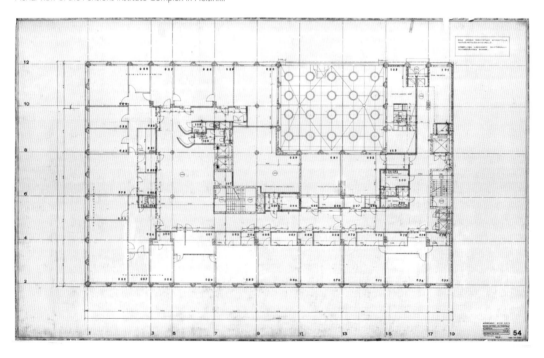

Plan of typical office floor of the Enso-Gutzeit Headquarters building.

The front facade of the Rautatalo Office building in Helsinki, showing the entrance to its interior atrium.

To be sure, no Modern architect was—or was likely to be—given the opportunity comprehensively to replan the whole world, as this argument, when taken to its logical conclusion, would clearly suggest. But this only meant that each took it as an obligation, when given a commission, to make the strongest possible symbolic statement out of it. The resultant projects would then serve as miniature symbolic paradigms of the total new world that could eventually be expected. Here again, Aalto proved to be in the vanguard of the movement. Paimio had with great success symbolised Modern architecture's role as a restorer of social health; in turn, the Sunila Cellulose complex was even more evidently a triumph of comprehensive planning (see site plan on p 88). Here were all rationally planned in advance not just a factory, but also administration, employees' and supervisors' housing, and various communal facilities; in short, a fully thought-out, healthy and orderly milieu to serve what Aalto calls "the little man".

In the end then, the careful non-politicality of Modern architecture proves to be no more-or-less than a benevolent paternalism. In comparison to the old, crowded and 'unhealthy' city to which it is set in conscious contrast, Sunila indeed offers a healthy and orderly milieu. But this utopian coin has another, and much less attractive, side. For its orderliness also symbolises at the same time, and with precisely equal force, an utterly hermetic petrification of a particular social status quo; housing here, playgrounds there; administrators here, workers there; and so on. In such paternalist utopias not only is destroyed the anonymous heterogeneity which is the essence of public life, but the very integrity of public space itself is compromised.

Moreover, even when, later in his career, Aalto began to build such giant complexes back inside the old city, he in no way moderated this tendency towards paradigmatic utopianism. Both the National Pensions Institute and the Enso-Gutzeit building in Helsinki are large quasi-private/quasi-governmental bureaucracies. And both buildings demonstrate their character as would-be internalised utopias, independent of the urban activity which in fact surrounds them. Among the welfare benefits which these bureaucracies provide for their employees are extensive communal facilities such as subsidised cafeterias. Thus the employees are encouraged to spend much of their time in the ersatz public space inside the paternalist bureaucracy, and less of it in the real public milieu outside. Moreover, Aalto has located such facilities in the complexes (typically on their upper floors) away from the points of effective public access—their street entrances. Not only, then, are the employees not encouraged to mingle in the real world outside; the people outside are actively discouraged from ever taking the space inside the buildings to be real public space.

But Aalto's political behaviour as an architect should not be seen as especially disreputable. The political predicament which these buildings demonstrate is not unique to Aalto; on the contrary, it is the Modern Movement as a whole, which has yet to extricate itself from the dilemma posed by assuming the role of doctor to society. What is more, there is even discernible in Aalto's work another theme—albeit a minor one, compared with this one, yet a distinct, and impressive one—which stands in direct opposition to it. Take the Rautatalo office building in Helsinki (see above). Its most distinct feature is precisely its generous and elaborate extension into its interior of the public space of the street. The entrance to the staircase which breaks the building's facade, and the interior court (with its public restaurant) to which it

View of interior atrium of the Rautatalo Office building in Helsinki.

leads, are among the most significant public spaces of downtown Helsinki.

Paradoxically, an even richer elaboration of public space is accomplished in the middle of the bush, in what is probably Aalto's masterpiece, the town hall at Säynätsalo. Predictably enough, given its function, the complex has as one public focal point (from both within and without) its council chamber. Less predictably however, it employs one of Aalto's characteristic networks of railings to give a subtle cue to the public accessibility of its various parts. Beyond that, there is the open gallery which serves so clearly as public access to the various departments of the local administration.

Finally, least predictable and most important is the fact that the entire complex is organised around an open, raised courtyard. Quite clearly a part of the street space of Säynätsalo, this courtyard nonetheless sits at the very heart of the town hall complex. If the symbol of elected authority—the council chamber—is one focus of the complex, then the symbol of public power—the courtyard—is another equally powerful one. "Let us say", with Aalto, "that a democratic meeting of these people—if they do these things—should be here in this piazza." It is a public space whose modest political dignity no other architect of his time has matched.

Rome and Modern Architecture: A Personal Reminiscence, 2000

Whatever one's view is of the quarrel between Structuralism and Post-structuralism, it remains the case that my own work moves relatively pragmatically back and forth between structuralist and phenomenological constructs. One obvious example of this is the following text on Rome and Modern architecture. It is the result of an invitation from Eric Haldenby, the former Director of the Waterloo School of Architecture, which was preparing a publication to commemorate the twentieth anniversary of its Rome programme.

By a curious fluke of personal circumstance, I was in my mid-40s before I had occasion to visit the city of Rome for the first time. London, Paris, even Berlin and Vienna: I had become familiar with all of these great European cities before I had any first hand experience of Rome.

I did not appreciate, until that fateful first visit some decade and a half ago, the extent to which my previous European urban experiences had shaped my expectations of the Eternal City. I am not an urban historian, but I knew that the urban forms of such cities as Paris, Berlin and Vienna—especially from the Baroque period forward—had been strongly influenced by Rome. Indeed, all of their planners, one way or another, took Rome as their urban model. What I hadn't realised was that the procedures of emulation followed by the builders of the northern European cities were so tenuous, and so qualified. Even though they had supposed themselves to be following the Roman model faithfully, the discrepancies in their emulations turned out to be at least as significant as the continuities. Their efforts—sometimes to be faithful, and sometimes even to improve on the original—showed the power of the *episteme* to subconsciously shape thought—even such instrumentalised thought as produces the design of cities.

During my first stroll through the centre of the city, I realised that the urban morphology of central Rome remains a Medieval one. Somehow, my subconscious had led me to suppose that since Rome's influence on the evolving urban form of the northern European cities was primarily a Baroque one, that Rome itself would look like a Baroque city. That the fabric of the city would instead comprise a Medieval tissue within which were embedded a host of Baroque monuments, came as a considerable surprise.

There was also the matter of the typical dimensional characteristics of this tissue: tight and intimate where I had expected them to be grand and expansive.

Wandering as a newcomer through a residential quarter in the centre of the city just after dusk, I was seeking the address of the apartment of my friend Lorenzo Pignatti. Imagine my surprise and my delight, on turning a corner in my ongoing quest for the apartment in question, to find myself in front of the Trevi fountain! Slowly I began to understand that the scale of central Rome has nothing in common with those northern cities I already knew. I realised that one could fit most of that central part of Rome that lies within the great curve of the Tiber within the single precinct of Paris that comprises the Tuileries and the Place de la Concorde. Before long, I also came to understand that this considerable difference of scale also had to do with the particular way in which the Baroque monuments were embedded in the fabric. As renovations of a pre-existing Medieval fabric, they are often less than fully freestanding objects. Sharing party walls with vernacular structures on one, two, or sometimes even three sides, they rely on the iconography of their principal facades, rather than on their discrete status as objects in space, to establish their relative eminence within the grain of the city.

In retrospect, one realises that the Baroque monuments of Rome are products of a world view that was in the process of being formulated concurrently with the creation of those monuments. In the case of the cities of northern Europe, a different set of intellectually generative circumstances pertain. There, the world view that generated the major built forms was socially and politically already in place prior to the construction of those forms. Thus, the Baroque monuments and urban spaces of Paris, Berlin and Vienna are results of a world view that had already been substantially framed. Unlike Rome, those cities exhibit characteristic urban situations which have far more of the characteristics of a *tabula rasa*. One must conclude that although the European Baroque indisputably emanates from Rome, it does not typify its urban fabric to the extent that it does in Paris, Berlin or Vienna.

Now with this talk of *epistemes* (Foucault) and world views (I have said everything except *Zeitgeist*) I bring into the centre of my commentary what that great shift in seventeenth-century thought brought into being: what we used to call the Age of Reason. When we proceed from the new ascendancy of reason in the seventeenth century to that of instrumentality in the eighteenth, we are well on the way to what we have come to call "Modernity".

I do not intend to reprise here the particular relationship of reason and instrumentality to that branch of Modernity that is Modern architecture.

But I am inclined to speculate as follows: first in respect to Modern architecture, and then in respect to Rome. It becomes increasingly difficult to think of Modern architecture *per se*, other than as a historical episode that is now ended. In earlier texts, such as "The Space of Appearance", I have argued that the relationship of Modern architecture to the nexus of reason and instrumentality now calls for its historical closure.

While Rome participated fully in the Baroque project of reason, Italy never followed its neighbours to the north in the later close linkage of reason to instrumentality. There is, after all, no Italian equivalent of Jeremy Bentham or Benjamin Franklin. Significantly, there is Giambattista Vico instead.

Rome's curiously limited role in the development of the project of reason and instrumentality that led to modernity, far from being a limitation, might now be thought to stand as a demonstration of intellectual independence pertinent to imagining how architecture might be reconceived now.

For example, following the orthodox trajectory that links reason to instrumentality to modernity, one might imagine a long historical trajectory linking a world view with built artefacts in the world, and see it stretching from a fascinating, problematic beginning at Versailles, to an equally fascinating, problematic ending at Brasilia.

It will not come as a surprise to any lover of Rome that I find this trajectory utterly architecturally alien to the Eternal City. If my hypothesis on the historical closure of Modernity in our time has any merit, and the ending at Brasilia is truly concluded, then I would suggest that we might well be ready again to learn some "lessons of Rome". After all, what principally attracted Le Corbusier, that complex intellectual chameleon, to the architecture of Rome, was the sheer phenomenological power of its plasticity, and of its palpable materiality. Its rationality was for him a secondary consideration, and its instrumentality no consideration at all.

If the hegemony of instrumentality wanes, and if our idea of the potential power and intensity of architecture comes to depend less on its dimensional scale, then it seems to me that intriguing new Roman possibilities may open up to us.

Another odd feature of my personal late arrival in the Eternal City may be relevant to this theme. The resistance of the 1920s generation of Roman architects to that Modern architecture that was being imported from the north, until it had been "Mediterraneanised", is by now a familiar historical fact. I have found myself fascinated by the unorthodoxy of Roman contributions to the canon of Modernism in architecture. For example, on being introduced to the built projects in Rome of Libera, or for that matter even the early Moretti, I found them to be highly sensuous material artefacts, rather than rational constructs in the world. My reading seems to me to have striking parallels with that of Le Corbusier's own reading of Michelangelo's San Pietro.

This reading also relates to my discovery of the intimate scale of the city. Late in my experience of Rome, I explored the EUR, that notorious urban precinct of the politically complicit 1930s. Yet even the EUR can hardly be seen as hegemonic in its urban scale, certainly not by the standards of Versailles or Brasilia. At its heart lies the poignantly beautiful Congress Hall of Libera, the great delicacy of which still moves me, and the particular design tenor of which powerfully evokes a comparison with the works of Alvar Aalto.

I do not propose to name Libera "Nordic" (perhaps I don't need to, since it is also well recognised by now, how "Italian" Aalto wished his buildings to be). But this observation suggests that we might now see the various revisionisms that typify Roman Modern architecture, as encompassing more than just "Mediterraneanism"—or for that matter, much more than just a propensity to make political accommodations. For the theoretical part of the argument I have been making here leads me to suppose that the Roman architects resisted all along that sad shrinking down of the scope of architecture's power that accompanied the problematic shift in the eighteenth century, from the ascendancy of reason, to that of instrumentality in human affairs.

If I am close to correct in this historico-theoretical speculation, then now that Modernity itself is a historical episode, many more lessons will be learned from the Rome that I have found—however late in my life—so disarming, and so engaging.

On the Phenomenology of Spatial Sequences: Frank Gehry's Disney Hall and Hans Scharoun's Berlin Philharmonic, 2012

This text is the result of an unexpected conjunction of visits relatively close together in time, to Walt Disney Concert Hall and to the Berlin Philharmonic. This pair of visits forced me to alter my view of the comparative relationship of the two buildings.

From the beginning of my writing career, I have tried to make my architectural criticism phenomenological. My first effort was in response to an invitation from Robin Middleton, many years ago in London England. Middleton had taken on the editorial assignment to commission introductory essays to folios of photographs by Yukio Futagawa of the works of a number of famous architects of that era. He asked me if I was interested

in taking on one—or perhaps more than one—of those assignments.

The only one of the famous figures in his list whose works I knew at all well was Alvar Aalto, and so it was that I agreed to write an essay for the 1970 Thames & Hudson monograph on the Finnish architect. I was fortunate, that at that time, there had as yet been very little critical interpretation of Aalto's oeuvre. The only insightful commentaries on Aalto that I was aware of then were brief ones Robert Venturi made from time to time in his *Complexity and Contradiction in Architecture* of 1966. Accordingly, in taking on the assignment, I was ploughing relatively fresh critical territory. And while there was no opportunity to look

Frank Gehry's Walt Disney Music Hall.

again at the buildings Aalto had designed for many parts of Finland, preparatory to writing the essay, it was the case that I had visited many of them some years previously, and already had fairly well developed opinions about them. In my short essay, I focused on three phenomenological themes in Aalto's work: Balustrades, Ruins, and Politics.

In retrospect, I would have to say that I was very lucky in this undertaking, in that my recollections of the buildings of Aalto I had visited some time previously proved precise enough to support the critical arguments I made in the essay. I have discovered over the years since, the startling extent to which buildings, when experienced "in the flesh", can differ from their published images. And of course, in recent decades, this prospective existential gap has only widened further, on account of the formidable technical adaptability of digital photography. I have had a recent experience in the critical judgment of a building that quite disconcerted me, and that has reinforced my commitment to a mode of criticism that is resolutely personal, first-hand, and experiential; in short: phenomenological.

I almost managed to visit Frank Gehry's Walt Disney Concert Hall on the day that it opened. As it happened,

I had a business appointment in downtown Los Angeles that day, and Gehry's administrative staff made a special arrangement for me to slip in and explore the building before the official opening later in the day. But alas, my business was as an expert witness in a lawsuit, and the lawyer for the opposing party that was "examining me for discovery", made sure that I missed my Disney Hall appointment. So it was several months later before I was once again in Los Angeles, and made a second effort to get to see the building (I was especially eager to see it, since I had already visited his Bilbao Museum, and was curious to compare the two). But even my second effort was only partially successful. All the performances scheduled during my stay in the city were sold out, so I was unable to attend one. I did join an organised daytime tour of the public areas of the building, and found myself quite impressed by the spatial drama and the exquisite workmanship of the detailing of the lobbies and lounges—detailing that I found very superior to that of the Bilbao building. More interesting still, I also found those spaces powerfully reminiscent of one of Aalto's own late works that I much admired: the Church at Imatra. But during my tour, I was not able to see the actual concert

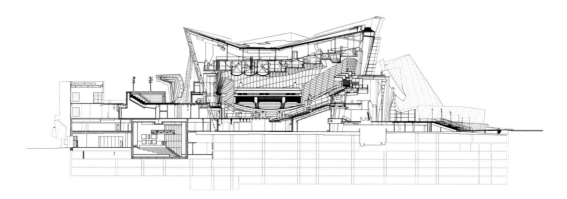

Frank Gehry's Walt Disney Concert Hall, cross-section.

hall, on account of Esa-Pekka Salonen's policy that building tour groups are not permitted to enter the hall at all, when not only performances, but even any sort of rehearsal activity is taking place there. Still, I was aware from published images and drawings of the hall that the ever-literate architectural aficionado Gehry had used Hans Scharoun's Philharmonic Hall in Berlin as a precedent for its overall configuration. And I had visited—indeed had attended a concert at—the Philharmonic a few years previously.

Some time later, I became involved in the preparation of an article for *Vanity Fair* magazine, whose editors decided to survey opinion among so-called "experts", as to the selection of the most important architectural works of the later part of the twentieth century. In my capacity as one of the magazine's roster, I decided that I knew Disney Hall well enough to include it on my list of nominees. It seemed to me that it represented a sort of summa of Gehry's late career.

Then again, later on still, I again found myself back in Los Angeles, and this time did manage to attend a concert in the hall. Having parked in the public garage beneath the hall, my wife and I shortly arrived at the first of Gehry's grand gestures at Disney, the dramatic and spacious atrium which collects all visitors from the parking garage, and leads them unusually graciously up to ground level. And this before we even reached the great sequence of lobby and foyer spaces that lead attendees to their seats! Once having arrived at the level of the quotidian entrance to the hall on Grand Avenue, we proceeded to the foot of the first set of escalators, where an attendant checked our tickets, and gave us quite specific instructions to proceed to a particular staircase. I remember being struck by the specificity of the instructions, but thought nothing in particular of it at the time. We crossed the great concourse, across the back of the hall, and ascended a grand stair up one level, at which point we were again directed to a particular staircase. Upon reaching it, we discovered that it was not an open stair overlooking the public foyer space—as the previous flight had been—but rather, a relatively small enclosed one leading us upward to a further, small enclosed lobby, off which a door led to a section of seating in which our seats were located. A few moments later, we found our seats, and for the first time had the opportunity to begin to appreciate the design features of the concert hall itself. It was clear that the way in which the seating surrounded the stage provided a spatial drama parallel to that of Scharoun's Berlin building. What is more, the great clerestory window behind the orchestra—a Gehry innovation not found in Berlin—lent a further drama to the void of the hall. Our seats were neither the most expensive ones in the Hall, nor were they the cheapest ones, but they provided excellent sightlines to the orchestra platform.

It was at roughly this point in our absorption of the features of the space that we were now in, that I realised the consequence of the specificity of the instructions we had been given on our way to our seats. Had we not followed them precisely, we would not have been able to reach our seats. At this point

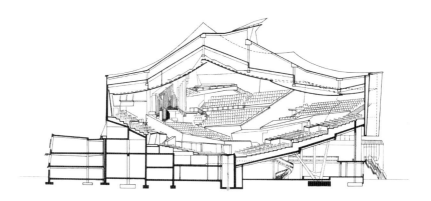

Bernhard Hans Scharoun's Berlin Philharmonic, cross-section.

I realised that while the configuration of the interior of Disney Hall does indeed reprise the so-called "vineyard" conception of the hall in Scharoun's Berlin building, the Gehry version of the "vineyard" is a qualified one. Subsequent examination of drawings of architectural sections of the two halls showed how this is so. In Berlin, the long axis of the hall is longer than that of the Los Angeles one. And its gradually upwardly sloping sections of "vineyard" seating rise only very gradually to the back wall. In the Los Angeles hall, the seating towards the back rises much more steeply. For example, the section of seating in which my wife and I were located was well above the level of the seating in the section in front of us. It is true that the section of seating we were in was not quite a "balcony"—there were, for example, no seats underneath it. But spatially and visually, it was more balcony-like that the equivalent areas of seating in Berlin. Moreover, we eventually discovered that there was another section of seating above and behind us that really was a "balcony". Accordingly, while our seats had excellent sightlines to the orchestra platform, it was not possible for us to take in visually the entire space of the hall in which we were members of the audience. Moreover, we could not move from our section of "vineyard seating" to the adjacent one, as we had readily been able to do in Berlin. This is another reason for the specificity of the instructions we received. The enclosed staircase we employed was the only one that gave access to the seats in our section of the hall. (From my recent examination of drawings of the building, it does appear that there was another stair that could have

given us access to our seats, but it was on the other side of the hall.)

When intermission arrived, it became apparent to us that the only way to the foyer was to retrace the path we had taken to get to our seats in the first place. Back to the small lobby, and down the enclosed staircase we went, eventually arriving out in the great spatial sequence of the lobbies and foyer at the north end of the complex. At the end of the intermission, we retraced our steps back up again. After the concert ended, as we drove back to our hotel, I found myself ruminating on the experiential implications of the circulation sequence that we had traversed four times during our evening at Disney Hall. At a minimum, it is clear that the compression of visitor experience in the enclosed staircase constrained the capacity of the spatial order of the building to serve as a potent social condenser for the audience as a whole. Too often one's sense of outreach, of overlook, and of audience participation was cut short. In short, an experiential disappointment, after the fact.

Then, as it happened, some months later, I had reason to return to Berlin, this time in the company of architectural colleagues who had not previously been there. Given that they hadn't, our itinerary necessarily included the major architectural monuments of the city, including, of course, Scharoun's Philharmonic. One of our company managed at short notice to obtain tickets for our entire group to a concert at which Daniel Barenboim would not only serve as guest conductor of the orchestra, but would also be guest soloist to

View of the interior of the hall of the Berlin Philharmonic.

painted. A far cry from the sumptuous metal and wood panelling of the public spaces of Disney Hall.

And then we began to ascend to our seats, making our way across mezzanine after mezzanine, and up flight after flight of stairs, until we arrived in the upper reaches of the Berlin version of the "vineyard". My first impressions on this second visit, following the one to Disney Hall, were telling. First of all, the Scharoun Hall feels much bigger (it is, in capacity, slightly bigger being approximately 2,500 seats as opposed to Disney's 2,265, but the perceptual difference is greater than this numerical one). Moreover, one has a sense of being able to see almost every other visitor in the hall from one's own seat. And subtle geometric differences in the configuration of the seating—for example, sections of seating on either side of the Los Angeles orchestra platform bow outwards toward it—result in the Berlin vineyard having a greater degree of spatial "concavity' than the Los Angeles one does. One's sense of the overall space of the hall is more psychologically unifying in Berlin than in Los Angeles. Despite the fact that it is actually larger than the Los Angeles hall, one could even say that this unifying quality makes it feel more intimate. And, of course, one can move from section to section of the seating, without having to exit the hall proper.

In the intermission at the Barenboim concert, we left our seats, and began the descent into the public foyers. And with this, all the pictorial drama I remembered from my first visit years before came back to me. Long downward vistas over tier after tier of concert-goers on mezzanines at different levels, some drinking champagne, others, in groups enjoying pre-ordered intermission meals at tables, and all of them basking in the palpable public pleasure of their spectacular, mutual visibility.

Eventually, the social excitement of the intermission died down, and we returned to our seats for the second half of the concert. At its conclusion, the audience gave Barenboim and the members of the orchestra a standing ovation. Barenboim departed from the stage, but after a few minutes of intense applause, returned, and sat down at the piano to play an encore. Having concluded it, he then left the stage again, and members of the orchestra began to follow him off stage. Some of the audience began to exit the hall, but a significant number of them refused to stop applauding (such is the passionate affection of Berliners for Barenboim). At a point when more-or-less half of the audience

play two Mozart piano concertos. Off we all went to the Philharmonic.

It was quite moving to visit the building again after an interval of several years. Between my two visits, for example, the exterior of the building had finally been clad in the red and yellow ceramic tiles that Scharoun had originally planned for it, but which he himself never saw completed. As we moved across the entrance foyer towards the stairs that led to our seats, I was reminded again that the basic sectional organisation of the building in Berlin is more different from that of Disney Hall than I had remembered. In Los Angeles, the public spaces of the lobbies and foyers are entirely disposed behind, and at the rear sides of the concert hall, whereas in Berlin, they are largely underneath the back two-thirds of it. Indeed, as one passes through the entrance lobby in Berlin, one gradually realises that the hall is overhead—in fact its underbelly quite palpably hovers over one's head. Like my colleagues of that evening seeing the building for the first time, I was struck once again by the modesty of its material palette: terrazzo flooring, and columns and soffits mostly of exposed, cast-in-place concrete, as often as not simply had exited the hall, and a substantial proportion of the still present half was moving through the aisles to the exits, Barenboim returned again to the stage, to the piano, and to the remaining small, but still very enthusiastic band of admirers. At this point, those of us still standing in the aisles on the way out of the hall simply reconfigured ourselves as a smaller audience in adjacent empty seats, and Barenboim played his second encore.

At this point, my recollection of the circulation route to our seats at Disney Hall returned to the forefront of my mind. I realised that the capacity of the Berlin hall to perform as a social condenser was significantly enhanced by the fact that all of the seating in the hall is interconnected; that the circulation routes leading to it are almost continuous, spatially interconnected with the mezzanines and lobbies, and that virtually all parts of the hall are visible from all other parts. The passionate Berliners, I came to realise, possessed a hall that not only accommodated their enthusiasm but actually intensified it. The Angelenos, on the other hand, not quite.

Two major buildings of the twentieth century by two great architects, with a surprising number of design features in common. Yet this after-the-fact, hands-on experience of mine demonstrated to me how significant the differences were, despite such extensive similarities. My experience of the two of them over the span of a year or so, made all too clear to me again, the importance of a phenomenological orientation to architectural criticism.

Urban Morphology and Building Typology

If the essays on Alvar Aalto, and on Walt Disney Concert Hall and the Berlin Philharmonic represent the strongest phenomenological pole of my thinking, then the first two following, both of which are relatively old, surely represent the strongest structuralist one.

Theory: Vacant Lots in Toronto, 1978

During the mid-1970s, I became increasingly interested in the architectural tendency that came to be known as European Rationalism—in its Italian mode even often called simply "the *Tendenza*". A French colleague teaching with me at the University of Toronto during those years—Marc Baraness—was a principal conduit to me of such ideas, having himself previously been a student of Bernard Huet. In 1977, with the enthusiastic support a group of thesis students at University of Toronto , I launched a year-long research investigation of the urban morphology and building typology of a precinct of my home city of Toronto. The text below was written to document that student work. It was also written in response to an invitation from Barton Myers to join him in the editorship of a special issue of *Design Quarterly*, the journal of the Walker Art Center in Minneapolis, an invitation I happily accepted. The text remains one of the few methodological investigations of its kind of North American urban form.

1 The City That Works?

In recent years, Toronto has begun to impinge on the American consciousness in an unprecedented way. Increasing numbers of outside observers have visited the city, and major American periodicals have labelled Toronto "the city that works", and "the last livable metropolis". For Torontonians, all this new attention must be seen to be somewhat problematic. First of all, they are simply unused to it. Up until the early 1960s, the city had little international image. Even inside Canada, its urban role was regarded as decidedly secondary to that of Montreal. But all of this is now changing, and Torontonians are having to cope with a reputation not previously possessed by their city.

The fact that Toronto's new reputation has been so hastily fabricated—and that it is largely the work of American outsiders—complicates the situation for her residents. A key component of her citizens' former provincialism was their seriously deficient historical sense of their own city. Hence, while they recognise its celebrated new 'livability' and value it highly, they have difficulty fully understanding it, and therefore fail to respond as thoughtfully as they should to international examination.

We may take two currently significant instances of this difficulty. Outside observers are usually quick to notice that Toronto has not suffered a so-called "race" problem. Unlike many American cities of its size, it has never become a battleground of racial hostility. But it now begins to be clear that Torontonians run the grave future risk of self-righteousness on the one hand, and bigotry on the other, in ascribing the 'livability' of their city to such a contingent historical phenomenon. At the least, it is dangerously complacent to suppose such a history ensures a livable future.

A second instance of this difficulty is Toronto's notable metropolitan system of government, the envy of innumerable representatives of beleaguered American inner cities. Toronto forms part of a politically powerful metropolitan municipality, along with five surrounding suburban boroughs. While the city and the five boroughs individually formulate policy and supply services, the Metropolitan Council coordinates policy, funds and services for the entire metropolitan area (3,000,000 total population). To a degree, Torontonians agree with the outside observers who admire the "metro" concept. They recognise that it has moderated the tendency towards drastic political cleavages

Aerial view of downtown Toronto. The "North Jarvis" precinct is shown in the block frame in the upper right.

between inner cities and their suburbs which is so common in American cities of Toronto's size. But here again, the external perception of success, and the circumstances of actual local politics sit awkwardly next to one another. In the eyes of many of the inhabitants of the inner city who have been politically active in recent years, the metro concept looks less attractive than it does to outsiders. For example, the Metropolitan Council is currently pressing for the extension of Toronto's existing network of expressways. Most particularly, it wishes to see completed two extensions which will cut right through the inner city to its core, and which

have been strongly opposed for at least five years by Toronto's City Council. Then, too, the Metropolitan Council advocates the gradual reduction of Toronto's intermediate-capacity transit mode, its historic network of streetcars, despite the city's strong pleas for the retention of this popular inner city municipal convenience.

Other significant splits between city and suburbs in Toronto could also be described, but no more than those cited above can they be said to contribute to a diminution of Toronto's bright new image. In the meantime, we Torontonians bask—albeit tentatively—in the unaccustomed glow of international admiration, quietly guarding our reservations about the accuracy of our admirers' perceptions of us, and trying at the same time to commence the important task of discovering what really has happened in the historical evolution of this city; what really are the structural patterns that have generated so apparently desirable a configuration of urban life. We have to hope that we will accomplish this task, before our dangerous, lingering naiveté invites exploitation, before our too-complacent 'success' brings on its own disintegration.

As might be expected, the history of the city's evolving architectural form is at this stage even less understood than is the history of its politics. Only very recently have younger generations of architects and architectural students begun to see the historical form of the city as having any relevance for their professional work.

At this early stage of our evolving understanding of the form of Toronto, it is difficult to cite strategic dates with which to mark its history; but most local observers would agree that 1954 was a crucial year, for it saw three major events; the formation of the metropolitan system of government; the opening of the city's—and the country's—first underground rapid transit line; and the adoption by City Council of a new zoning bylaw which was, for the first time, designed to foster downtown redevelopment, both commercial and residential. To be sure, Toronto's post-war development boom was already underway by that date, but previous to 1954, it consisted primarily of the extensive development of low-density suburbs at the urban periphery. Thus, as of that date, Toronto comprised basically three elements: a central business district which had been erected, for the most part, between 1870 and 1930; a vast series of residential neighbourhoods from the same period; and a newer series of suburban neighbourhoods from the post-war period. Of these three elements, only the first involved a scale of building which can be called high-density. And even that density was moderate and intermittent. The older inner city neighbourhoods, and the newer suburban ones, also lacked significant concentrations of density. In the case of the new suburban developments, this is hardly surprising, since neither in Toronto, nor anywhere else in North America at that time, was the idea of forming high-density nodes of development in the suburbs fashionable. Indeed, the whole attraction of the suburbs at that time consisted in large measure of a flight from the tighter configuration of downtown, in favour of a

putatively pastoral image of spaciousness (ranging from five to ten dwelling units per acre). But what is remarkable and unique about Toronto's historical evolution is the fact that throughout the first half of the twentieth century, Toronto's inner city residential neighbourhoods retained their nineteenth-century form. These neighbourhoods consisted of row upon row of two-to three-storey single family dwellings on individual lots, either detached, semi-detached, or in row house form (ranging from ten to 20 dwelling units per acre). To be sure, the expansion of the central business district (CBD) during that 50 year period saw the replacement of some of this housing by higher density structures, but these new buildings were almost invariably commercial. Surprisingly few higher density residential buildings were erected in the inner city before 1954.

In the years following the major events of 1954, this relatively stable pattern began to change drastically. In the suburbs, the increasing extension of the low-density pattern continued, but the highly structured planning conceptions of the metropolitan system also began to foster the formation of high-density mixed-use nodes of development—usually in relation to shopping centres—within the generally low-density suburban territory as a whole. Within the CBD, now linked to the new suburbs by expressway systems and rapid transit, redevelopment began to escalate in scale, culminating in the famous concentration of bank towers which now dominates Toronto's skyline.

Then, too, in the zone between these two, that of the older inner city neighbourhoods, significant redevelopment also began to occur after 1954. The edges of the CBD pressed further into these neighbourhoods as the scale of downtown commercial building escalated. Virtually anywhere within them that the new official plan permitted, new high-density residential redevelopment began to occur. The high-rise residential slab blocks which were becoming a familiar element at the new nodes of the suburban landscape also began to replace block after block of the older neighbourhood housing which had survived more-or-less intact up until this time.

For nearly a decade and a half following 1954, Toronto's citizens welcomed the new development boom uncritically. Having previously shared outsiders' opinions of their city as utterly unremarkable, they now saw almost every development as a manifestation of a new cosmopolitan, metropolitan sophistication. In the course of this boom, innumerable historical buildings were demolished; entire low-income neighbourhoods were razed in the name of slum clearance; eventually the city even began to assist in the assembly of large parcels of downtown and inner city property—for private redevelopment—in the name of what was by then known in planning circles as the desirable objective of "comprehensive planning".

Looking back over these events of recent history, I think it is true to say that the development boom might well have continued unchallenged into the 1970s were it not for the fact that the development industry became increasingly involved in a programme to redevelop the old inner city neighbourhoods on the same scale and in the same manner as it was redeveloping the CBD. I have already noted how stable these neighbourhoods had remained for half a century; in the 1950s and 1960s they continued to house representatives of all Toronto's social classes: low income groups to be sure, but also middle and upper ones who had never joined the flight to the suburbs to the extent that their American counterparts had. Indeed, to the degree that those neighbourhoods did become unfashionable for a part of the middle class in the 1950s, they were surprisingly quickly rediscovered as early as the mid-1960s by another part who began to see living in them, amid the new ethnic diversity of the city, as being part of the same new cosmopolitan sophistication that was backing the redevelopment boom.

Thus, when the continued escalation of the redevelopment boom began in the late 1960s to reach a scale that threatened the very existence of many of these neighbourhoods, political sentiment began to change significantly. Already in the 1968 municipal elections, a number of pro-development representatives went down in defeat, to be replaced by new citizen activists, who subsequently mounted a vigorous campaign against the development industry and the remaining pro-development majority of City Council. Four years of highly contentious municipal debate raged, and in 1972, a loose coalition of reformers discovered to their astonishment that they had gained a majority in that year's election. Since that time, the form of development has been a major continuing theme of political discussion in Toronto, with the development industry now on the defensive, and various factions among the reformers debating the degree to which the rules of redevelopment ought to be altered. At the centre of this discussion has been the formulation of the new Central Area Plan for the city, a plan which has been in preparation and under review from 1972 right

up to the present. (It now appears that by the time this issue of *DQ* is published it will finally be in effect.) While opinion regarding the merits of the plan is still divided, it is generally agreed that it accomplishes several things:

1. It virtually stops the old form of redevelopment of middle class inner city neighbourhoods.
2. It moderates, if not stops, the form of that redevelopment in inner city neighbourhoods adjacent to the CBD.
3. It requires most further redevelopment of the CBD itself to be in the form of mixed-use, including very substantial components of high-density residential development; and the former maximum allowable densities for commercial redevelopment alone having been substantially reduced.
4. It submits all redevelopment, of whatever kind, to new sets of urban design requirements which are intended to increase the compatibility of new development with the existing form of the city.

During the six years of discussion and formulation of this plan, close attention has also been given to redevelopment proposals being implemented during the 'interim' period. Indeed, such projects have, in large measure, been the guinea pigs for experimentation regarding the evolving principles of the new plan. Two of the most important of these have now reached completion: phase one of Eaton Centre, a commercial redevelopment in the CBD; and Sherbourne Lanes, a residential redevelopment in one of the low income inner city neighbourhoods.

Procedurally, the two projects have much in common. In both cases, earlier projects had been prepared under the old bylaw. Both earlier projects were opposed by citizens' groups, most particularly by historical preservationists who objected to the demolition of, or incompatibility with, important older structures on both projects' sites. Partly as a result of all this controversy, and partly because both projects required civic cooperation in order to proceed, the original projects were scrapped. In the case of Eaton Centre, the Cadillac Fairview Corporation brought in Zeidler Partnership to be design architects for a revised new proposal. In the case of Sherbourne Lanes, the city itself bought the property, and hired Diamond and Myers to prepare a new scheme. In both cases, radical redesign was undertaken. Subject to client pressures (in the case of Eaton Centre) and land economics established under

View of the Sherbourne Lanes project as completed.

Aerial view of a model of the Eaton Centre in context.

the old bylaw (in the case of Sherbourne Lanes), the newly appointed architects strove to meet the concerns which had been expressed by the preservationists, the citizen activists, and (in the case of Sherbourne Lanes) neighbouring residents.

Both phase one of Eaton Centre, and Sherbourne Lanes are now completed and occupied. The critical evaluation of these and many other new projects, of which they form the vanguard, constitutes a further Important stage in Toronto's historic discovery of itself.

II Evolving Methodologies

In 1974, my associates and I were invited, together with two other firms, to prepare a set of new urban design guidelines for Toronto. These guidelines were to be employed to evaluate projects submitted for consideration to City Council during the interim period preceding the formulation of a new Central Area Toronto Plan. At the same time, the guidelines were to indicate the direction which urban design requirements ought to take within the new plan itself.

Our concerns included: the retention of buildings of historic or architectural merit, conditions of micro-

climate in public areas, public views of major monuments and activities, the quality of street furniture and other similar questions.

In September 1974 we published the final edition of our report "Onbuildingdowntown" which has since gone on to become the most sought after consultants' document ever published by the city's Planning Board.[1] At the time of the preparation of the guidelines, our clients and our co-consultants shared a strong methodological attraction to design guidelines based on performance criteria. To them, this had the great appeal not only of transcending the grossness of the old zoning bylaw, but also of eliminating its arbitrariness. While we were not opposed to performance criteria *per se*, we were concerned about their lack of specificity relevant to architecture in Toronto. Therefore, while "Onbuildingdowntown" did successfully bring into more serious public view several major concerns of urban design, it failed to elicit a generic form of desirable architecture for Toronto at that particular time.

Our ongoing quest for a method which would disclose a generic form of architecture continued with a second report prepared for the City of Toronto Planning Board the following year, this one called "Built-Form Analysis".[2] In this case, our clients asked us to explore possible prototypical built-form configurations for the sorts of medium-to-high-density residential commercial building bonus towards which their policy studies were beginning to point.

In the case of "Built-Form Analysis", our historical interests had become sufficiently aroused that we attempted a very general historical typology of multiple residential building forms in the city, as a background to our work. At the same time, following the performance criteria approach of the earlier report, we attempted to formulate recommendations respecting conditions of dwelling amenity for residential buildings at varying densities, on various sized sites, in various neighbourhoods within the core area.

The results of this approach, like those of "Onbuildingdowntown", proved less than fully satisfactory to us. Within the limited time frame of our report, and within our limited understanding of the historical evolution of the built-form of the city, we proved incapable of coping with the wide variety of densities suggested, and sizes and shapes of sites worked on. Once again, in our view, we didn't succeed in devising a form of architecture for Toronto that could be considered to be generic.

By the time of the completion of "Built-Form Analysis", we had become aware of the urban conceptions of typology (building types), and morphology (urban structure) as they were being developed in Europe by such architects as Aldo Rossi and O M Ungers. Eventually, it began to seem that these conceptions, being more vigorous politically, intellectually and historically than those with which we had previously been working, might well prove a more effective means of establishing the elusive generic form that we were after. To be sure, we were aware that the conceptions of type and of urban morphology, as they had been employed in Europe, concerned themselves primarily with the reconsolidation of the historic cores of much older cities than Toronto. But Ungers had applied the technique in his submission to the Roosevelt Island competition, and Rem Koolhaas and Elia Zenghelis had employed them as one base for all of their theoretical work on Manhattan. Moreover, insofar as the principles of typology and methodology manifested a powerful historical orientation, they corresponded with our own growing suspicion that the roots of the generic form we were seeking would lie in the historical evolution of Toronto itself—the city whose urban architecture we were attempting to advance.

For these reasons, we undertook, from 1975 to 1977, an extensive investigation of the conceptions as they were being developed in Europe up to that time.[3]

In the summer of 1977, a group of 12 final-year students agreed to work with me on a study of North Jarvis—one of Toronto's inner city residential neighbourhoods that was slated for redevelopment.[4] Moreover, we agreed that the conceptions of typology and morphology as we understood them at that time, would form the basis of our work. Following this, we undertook an extensive, systematic documentation of the evolution of the precinct. After the documentation and analysis of the historical evolution of the neighbourhood were completed, each student prepared an individual thesis for a project within the precinct, based on an understanding of the principles which had been developed in the group investigation of the precinct's typology and morphology.

III Studies on North Jarvis

North Jarvis is a downtown residential neighbourhood in Toronto, adjacent to the Central Business District. It was selected as the vehicle for this urban investigation for a variety of reasons. First, it is a historic neighbourhood; its development began in the mid-nineteenth century. Second, it has sustained successive waves of redevelopment throughout its history, all significant enough to remain perceptible in its overall form today, yet none so all-encompassing as to negate the influence of any of the preceding ones. As a result of this complex—if fortuitous—historical layering, the precinct possesses extant examples of almost every form of residential building—both single family and multiple-that has ever been erected in Toronto. Thus it is still possible to discover there the occasional suburban villa of the 1850s, now surrounded by the row houses and apartment buildings of later periods. At the opposite extreme, North Jarvis also contains the notorious residential redevelopment project known as St Jamestown—a complex of high-rise/high-density residential slab blocks and point towers, that replaced several blocks of the former residential neighbourhood, and which in the late 1960s and early 1970s became the most striking symbol of the form of urban redevelopment Toronto's citizens finally decided they were against.

In addition to these historical and typological extremes of residential building, the precinct also accommodates a wide range of institutions, of them housed in the former mansions of the well-to-do who inhabited Jarvis Street at the turn of the century. Finally, around its north and west peripheries lies a whole series of mixed-use complexes, primarily oriented to the arterial roads that form its boundaries.

Obviously then, North Jarvis is a neighbourhood in transition. The heterogeneous—not to say jumbled—

Aerial view of the intersection of Sherbourne Street and Wellesley Street before the construction of the St Jamestown redevelopment project.

Aerial view of the intersection of Sherbourne Street and Wellesley Street, after the construction of the St Jamestown redevelopment project.

arrangement of existing buildings is not conclusively influenced by the urban form of any one period of its history, nor does it point clearly in the direction of any particular potential form. In short, the future built-form of North Jarvis will have to be invented.

The Morphology of North Jarvis

The investigation of the historical evolution of North Jarvis powerfully bore out the proposition that Toronto consists fundamentally of a grid on a lake. The original plan included only ten blocks, laid out in 1793 along the bay shore.

Subsequently, the grid was extended westward to Fort York, and northward to Lot Street, north of which the grid's limits can be seen in the 1842 city plan.

Above Lot Street lie the park lots, originally conceived as large suburban estates for the well-to-do, on which, it was thought at the time, urban development would not occur. For a brief time this pattern held. The 1842 plan shows the form of the estates, and beyond them, the still uncleared land of park lots in the centre of the area between Parliament Street to the east and Yonge Street to the west.

By mid-century, the pressures of urban growth and Toronto aristocracy's readiness to engage in land speculation led to the more-or-less total abandonment of this policy, and to the commencement of wholesale lot subdivision. The subdivision of the park lots between Yonge Street and Parliament (lots 3–18 inclusive) is the beginning of the precinct of North Jarvis, since the precinct as selected for investigation consists precisely of the northerly half of that series of lots.

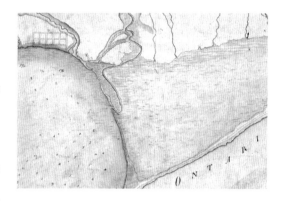

1793 Drawing of York Harbour, showing the original ten blocks of what would become the City of Toronto.

The fundamental basis of the morphology of the precinct is the original pattern of land division, and the park lot pattern still forms the first order morphology of North Jarvis.

Comparing the 1842 plan with today's plan, one can see how the next stage of division—that of the park lots into large suburban estate lots—constitutes the second order morphology. (See especially lot 4 on the 1842 map so strikingly divided into three long thin lots all fronting on Lot Street. Inevitably, one reads this as the subdivision of a family estate for heirs.) Following this, the third order morphology occurs, the division of the parcels yet again into small urban lots for sale. The beginning of this process can be discerned in the upper left-hand corner of the pattern of lot divisions as of 1848, and it can be read ever more clearly as the filling out of the third order pattern occurs right up to 1903.

1842 plan, showing the stage of development of the City of Toronto, as of that date.

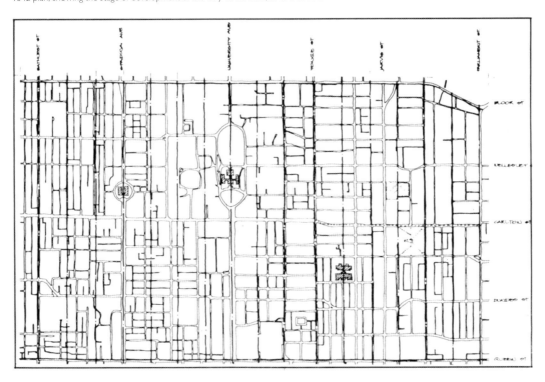

Drawing showing the contemporary street grid of midtown Toronto, laid over the original layout of the "Park Lots" between Queen Street and Bloor Street, between Parliament Street and Bathurst Street.

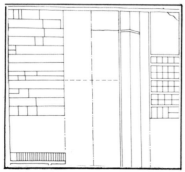

Lot Divisions, 1848

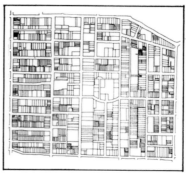

Lot Divisions, 1923

Lot Divisions, 1858

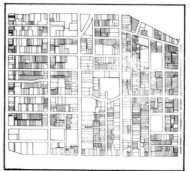

Lot Divisions, 1960

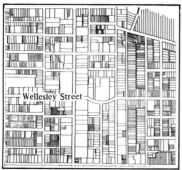

Lot Divisions, 1884

Lot Divisions, 1970

Lot Divisions, 1903

Lot Divisions, 1976

Built Context 1848

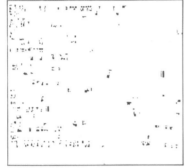

Built Context 1858

Built Context 1884

Built Context 1903

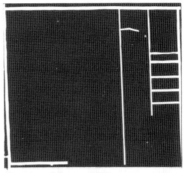

Streets and Lanes, 1848

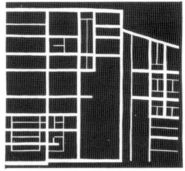

Streets and Lanes, 1858

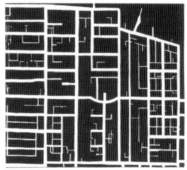

Streets and Lanes, 1903

Left: Sequence of drawings showing the evolution of the built form in the North Jarvis precinct, from 1848 to 1903, by means of figure-ground drawings.

Right: Sequence of drawings showing the evolution of the pattern of streets and lanes, from 1848 until 1903. Of course, the nineteenth-century lot division was related to a certain formal conception of a street, and like the lot division, the evolution of the streets and lanes can also be documented.

Opposite page: Sequence of drawings showing the evolution of the gradual pattern of land subdivision, and later on, of land assembly in the North Jarvis district, from 1848 until 1976.

If its overall subdivision into urban lots constitutes the third order morphology of the precinct, then, by the same token, the typical individual lot is the basis of Toronto's typology. For the typical lot has a characteristic shape—long and narrow; a characteristic width—usually not narrower than 20, nor wider than 50 feet; and a characteristic depth—usually between 100 and 150 feet. In addition, the typical lot has a street frontage with (sometimes) a lane frontage at the opposite end, and two side lot lines that normally abut to adjacent lots.

What is more, this typical parcel of property must be seen as having been conceived with a type of building—which it was presumed would sit on it—in mind. The characteristics of that building will be described in detail below; for the moment, it can be described simply, in relation to its lot, as long and narrow, front facing to the street, with service to the rear, and not less than two nor more than three-storeys high, excluding basement.

By 1903, the mature phase of the first generation of buildings in North Jarvis had been reached. As the lot division drawing of that date shows, the characteristic pattern of these typical lots has filled out most of the precinct. The major exceptions to this pattern occur along Jarvis Street and Wellesley Street, where the scale of the lots conceived for mansions exceeds their width and depth anywhere else. Indeed, so unique is Jarvis Street in the precinct—and in Toronto—that it is one of the few streets laid out down the centre of its park lot (compare the 1848 and 1858 lot division drawings to see this) having been conceived as a residential street of major civic prestige. In most other cases the most expedient conflation of park lot division *and* primary road access system was employed. The 1903 morphology holds with little change until the middle of the century.

By 1960, however, the beginning of a pattern—not of lot subdivision, but of land assembly—can be discerned. And the morphology, correspondingly, begins to shift. Between 1960 and 1970 this pattern of assembly accelerates, and between 1970 and 1976 it accelerates further.

The Typology of North Jarvis

Having explored thus far the morphology of North Jarvis, we may now turn to an examination of the building types which, up until 1903, constituted it. Here are some representative cases. First, a mansion on Wellesley Street. Second, a semi-detached pair

on Isabella Street. Third, a group of row houses on Monteith Street.

We have systematically documented all of these, in parallel fashion, taking pains to illustrate the principal floor plan on its lot, showing the relationship of that lot to adjacent lots, and any relationship of the building on its lot to buildings on lots abutting it. This documentation disclosed that despite differences of scale, all three of these nineteenth-century cases are typologically very similar. To show this, we need only consider the siting of these buildings on their lots, in relation to adjacent lots. First of all, the relation of front and back. All three are identical in this respect. Second, the differentiation of sides. In this case differences occur but they are systematically predictable. The mansion has differentiated sides, but since it is on the west side of a north–south street, the north side of the building is service/circulation oriented, and the south side deflects to accommodate a south side garden. In the case of the pair of semi-detached houses, on the north side of an east–west street, the sides are differentiated between the party wall and the open side, but are equivalent to one another. Only in the case of the row house does differentiation of sides vanish, for obvious reasons. Third, the relationship of public to private. In all three cases, the spatial order is such that the differentiation from public to private is progressively greater as one proceeds from street to rear of lot. (An examination of the interior spatial order would, in most cases, show the same to be the case as one proceeded upwards through the three typical stories of each building.) Fourth, the relationship of street to facade. Here again, despite the widely variable setback, an intermediate zone, however shallow, is established between the purely public space of the sidewalk, and the publicly evident facade of the dwelling. Even in the case of the row house, where overall dimensions are most constrained, this zone is established by recourse to a raised first floor level, and to a recessed entry. Such a summary doesn't exhaust the typological characteristics—even of the siting—of these buildings. And it does not go on to include any consideration of the interior spatial order of the buildings. However, it demonstrates the nature of the typology, illustrates the degree to which all three examples conform to the same type, and shows the relationship of the typology of buildings to the morphology of the precinct. To establish this clearly, as of the significant date of 1903, is of great importance, for it enables us to employ this set of mature relationships as bench marks against

Plan and Front Elevation of a Mansion, circa 1899

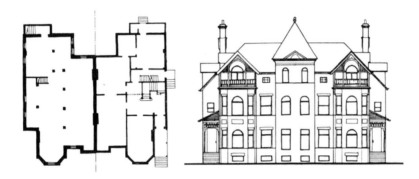

Plan and Front Elevation of a Semi-Detached Pair of Houses, circa 1890

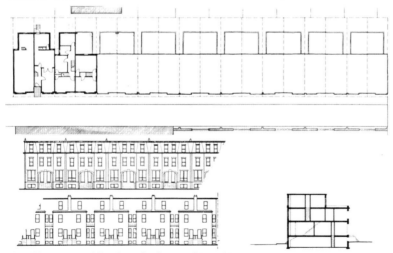

Plan, Elevation and Section of a Group of Row Houses, circa 1890

A sequence of drawings, documenting the characteristics of the building typology
of North Jarvis, over time (continues overleaf).

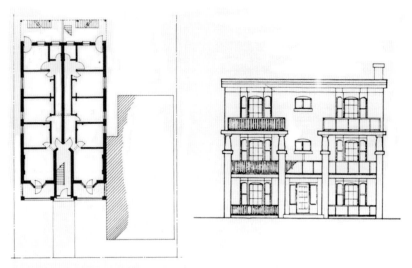

Plan and Elevation of a "Pullman Type" Apartment Building, 1911

Plan and Elevation of a 2-Unit-Per-Floor Apartment Building, 1920

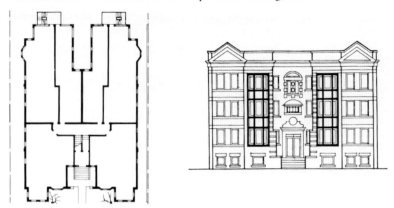

Plan and Elevation of a 6-Unit-Per-Floor Apartment Building, 1914

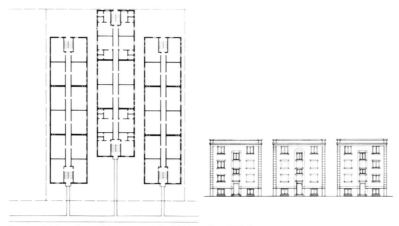

Plan and Elevation of Apartment Buildings, circa 1920

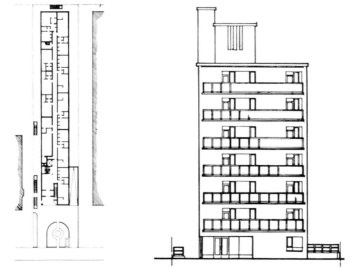

Plan and Elevation of an Apartment Building, 1954

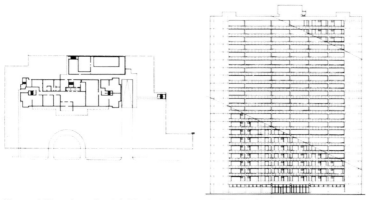

Plan and Elevation of a slab block Apartment Building, circa 1965

Historic postcard, showing Sherbourne Street around 1900. Note how the characteristic street form of North Jarvis, in its first generation maturity, is not primarily defined by the buildings on it, as would typically be the case in a nineteenth-century European city. Rather, the buildings in North Jarvis formed a generally recessive backdrop to the public space of the street, which is demarcated by the treed boulevard, the public pedestrian sidewalk, and by the systematic series of fences.

which to measure the typological and morphological transformations that occur in the twentieth century.

Interestingly enough, the first multiple residential buildings to be erected in the precinct, after the turn of the century, do not significantly vary from the type delineated above.

Here are some examples of an early Pullman-type apartment building, a two-unit-per floor and a six-unit-per floor building. Although, in the last case, conditions of dwelling amenity begin to deteriorate seriously, all three conform to the type characteristics of the nineteenth century buildings they replace. What is more, each of them occupies only a single or a double lot. Although they represent a second generation of buildings within the precinct, they do not precipitate a shift of morphology. Following the introduction of yet later buildings into the precinct, we still find basic adherence to the type characteristics and the morphology established by 1903. Here is an example of a group of three apartment buildings erected in the 1920s.

In this case, the three buildings sit on the lots of what were two nineteenth-century houses. And the ruthless and expedient introduction of the central double-loaded corridor and of minimum square footage units results in a grave deterioration of dwelling amenity relative to any of those indicated in this type sequence to date. Yet even here it is surprising to what degree the transformations of the type still conform to the extant morphology of the precinct.

Even jumping 30 years to an apartment building of the 1950s, we can still trace many similarities. Here, underground parking has been introduced, and elevator technology has facilitated an increase in height to nine-storeys. But the basic plan organisation of the building is similar to that of the 1920s building just examined. What is more, the erection of this building still entails no land assembly at all, for it simply replaces one Jarvis Street mansion on its long narrow lot. So the morphology, in a sense, remains unaltered.

In the 1960s and 1970s, however, changes of much greater significance in the typology and morphology begin to occur. With the advent of buildings such as the slab block shown here, most of the typological characteristics of buildings in the precinct change all at once. Relations of front and back, public and private are all obscured, and the definition of the street edge, independent of the building facade, disappears completely. At the same time, the scale of land assembly and the relationships of adjacency to existing neighbouring buildings are such that the morphology of the precinct is eroded as well. In the simplest terms, such buildings as the Isabella block imply in formal terms that their neighbours will simply disappear. By virtue of the presence of the new slab block, they are relegated to the position of fragments of a former, evidently doomed city.

It is interesting to note that the drastic alteration of typology and morphology which occurred in the 1960s and 1970s is not a function of density. The earliest multiple residential buildings of the twentieth century have a floor area ratio of 3–3.5, which is only slightly less than that of the contemporary slab blocks. The highest floor area ratios are those of the nine- to ten-storey buildings of the 1950s which rise as high as 4.5. Moreover, if it is true that these high-rise slab blocks, by virtue of their form, offer conditions of amenity superior to those of the buildings of the 1920s through the 1950s, it is not true that they surpass those of just after the turn of the century.

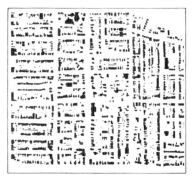

Built Context 1923

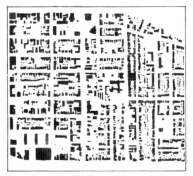

Built Context 1960

Built Context 1970

Built Context 1976

Sequence of figure-ground drawings showing the further evolution of built form in the North Jarvis district, from 1923 until 1976.

Twentieth Century Morphological Transformations

Having explored the drastic change to the typology of the precinct in the 1960s and 1970s, we can also trace the impact of the changes on the morphology, as shown in the following series of built context drawings from 1923–1976.

It is obvious, examining these drawings, how the coherent relations of public to private space, of street to block to public open space have all by now been radically dissolved. The buildings increasingly play the role of isolated monuments which do not engage, in any formal, visual or social way, with their surroundings. At the same time, the formal space of the street has also vanished. I have noted above how the nineteenth century built context of the precinct—two- to three-storey detached, semi-detached and row houses—was such that the primary definition of public space was a function of trees, boulevards, fences and shrubbery, rather than one of the buildings themselves. In the long transformation of the precinct between the turn of the century and the present, not only has the limited contribution of the buildings to that space been eroded, but all the primary defining elements are also gone, having successively been removed by generations of traffic engineers. There do not even exist any substitutions for these primary defining elements, such as one would find in New York or Chicago, where street-oriented apartment buildings have taken over some of the roles of public space definition which used to be played by the trees and fences.

In short, the impact of all the successive and cumulative transformations of the precinct in the twentieth century is as follows:

1. The process of lot division has been superseded to an ever-increasing degree by a new process of land assembly. A greater and greater proportion of the precinct's land is held in fewer and fewer hands.
2. The conditions of dwelling amenity, as against the coherence of the urban morphology, have, since the introduction of the first multiple residential buildings at the turn of the century, developed an increasingly problematical relationship to one another. The earliest multiple residential buildings—up to the First World War—offered reasonably high conditions of dwelling amenity in buildings which adhered fairly consistently to the nineteenth-century morphology of the precinct. The more speculative buildings of the next phase

continued to adhere—more-or-less—to the morphology, but the conditions of dwelling amenity which they offered dropped drastically. Following this, the buildings which have been erected since the 1950s have offered increasingly improved conditions of amenity—owing mostly to their greater height. But while these conditions—having primarily to do with outlook and privacy—have improved, the relationship of the buildings to the extant morphology has increasingly deteriorated.

3. As a corollary of the above, the consistency of typological relations from building to building has declined to a very serious degree. The general building orders which the newer buildings adopt are increasingly indifferent to those of their older neighbours. At the very least, this tends to erode the morphological coherence of the precinct as a whole. Sometimes, the newer buildings attain improved conditions of dwelling amenity for *themselves* at the cost of *reducing* that of their older neighbours. The net result of this obscuring of typological relations of building to building is that the remaining older buildings—the limited number that survive—instead of being enhanced by their new surroundings, appear increasingly vestigial, and hence, susceptible to eventual obliteration.

4. As a corollary, the obligations that, formally speaking, the individual buildings collectively paid to the public space of the street, have become gravely reduced. As a result, that space can be said to have disappeared.

Analysis of the historical evolution of North Jarvis among the students and discussion of its current state yielded a series of design objectives for the district that can be summarised as follows:

A Typological Objectives

1. To invent new building types which do not imply or require the necessity of further land assembly for their optimal implementation, and which possibly render feasible again the option of further lot division.

2. To invent new types which maintain the standards of dwelling amenity which have been attained by the recently erected multiple residential buildings, but do so in a fashion more consistent with the remaining older buildings in the precinct.

3. To invent new types whose essential characteristics are supple enough to mediate among the heterogeneous buildings that currently exist throughout the precinct, while simultaneously reinforcing the basic typology of the precinct's buildings over an extended historical period.

4. To establish what range of building densities can sustain the typology of the precinct.

B Morphological Objectives

1. To reconstitute a formally effective relationship of building to lot, to lane and to street.

2. To reconstitute the public space of the street itself.

3. To establish a new formal hierarchy of open space in the precinct: private garden, collective garden and public garden.

4. To reconstitute the formal relationship of street to park.

1 The consortium that prepared "Onbuildingdowntown", was: John Andrews International/Roger du Toit, Architects and Planners; George Baird Architects; General Urban System Corporation/Stephen McLaughlin. The members of the office of George Baird Architects who participated in the project were: George Baird, Robert Hill, Bruce Kuwabara, Donald McKay and John van Nostrand.

2 The members of the office of George Baird who prepared Built-Form Analysis were: George Baird, Donald Clinton, Bruce Kuwabara and Barry Sampson.

3 Among the many architects and theorists who assisted us in this inquiry, Rem Koolhaas, Rafael Moneo and O M Ungers were particularly helpful.

4 The students in the North Jarvis group were James Brown, John Chow, Paul Culpeper, Lev Danko, Paul Didur, David Fujiwara, Robert Hodgins, Carol Kleinfeldt, Roman Michalowicz, Kevin Smith and John Stephensons.

Studies on Urban Morphology in North America, 1988

The morphological and typological work on Toronto persuaded me that the urban parcel of land was a far more important element of urban form than it had ever been given credit for being—at least by architects or urban planners. I wrote this text to flesh out the implications of that conviction. An excerpt was published in French in *Morphologie urbaine et parcellaire* edited by Pierre Merlin, but this is the first publication of the complete text.

Part One: Urban Morphology and Urban Design: Distinct Historical Evolutions in Europe and in North America

In commencing such a report, one is obliged to state, right from the outset, that the concepts of urban morphology and typology have been far less significant, for the practices of architecture and urban design in North America, than they have been in recent years in Europe. Indeed, I am inclined to speculate that we in North America, in the past quarter century or so, have had as a set of tools at our disposal, the precepts of "urban design" instead of the European ones of urban morphology. In attempting to depict the evolution of the precepts of urban design during this period, one might draw a line from the publication of Edmund N Bacon's *Design of Cities* of 1967,[1] to Colin Rowe and Fred Koetter's *Collage City* of 1978.[2] Bacon's seminal work of the 1960s presented a whole series of major European examples of public spaces, from ancient times up to the present, together with an account of modern urban movement systems which, in his view, could be expected to lead to an anticipated new form of urban space in our own time.

In retrospect, one can easily see that Bacon's formal analyses of his historical examples, while sumptuously presented, were rather generalised and not particularly directive. Indeed, he acknowledged in his argument that he did not presume to foresee the form which the new urban spaces of our own time would take. Nevertheless, his own interest in urban design was heavily oriented towards activity as a generator, with the result that, when combined with his interests in simple geometries, his arguments inevitably led to an advocacy of what might be called "Baroque megastructures", a praiseworthy example of which, presented towards the end of his 1967 text, was the then under development proposal for the vast La Defence complex at the end of the "grand axe" in Paris. In its strong emphasis on orchestration of urban activity, Bacon's work can be seen to have led to a whole later series of process-oriented urban design methods, methods which can probably be said to have reached their zenith of influence during John Lindsay's mayoralty of New York City. Simple sets of spatial directives, coupled with "performance criteria" with

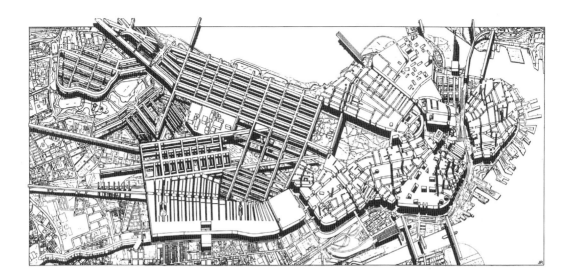

An example of the conceptual graphics developed by Mario Gandelsonas representing downtown Boston.

respect to such issues as sunlight and urban safety, become the emergent direction of this-major stream of urban design in the late 1960s and early 1970s, a direction that can be summarised as constituting "Urban Design as Public Policy"—this being the title of Jonathan Barnett's notable text which described the work of the period, and which was published in 1974.[3]

At the same time as this body of ideas was taking form, it is also true of course, that Colin Rowe was in the process of developing the much more specifically formal body of ideas which he eventually published, (together with his former student Koetter), in the 1978 book *Collage City*. In a sense, Rowe's book (much of the argument of which was familiar in advanced circles, long before the actual publication of the book) can be seen to have been a sort of urban companion to Robert Venturi's *Complexity and Contradiction in Architecture* of 1960.[4] The demolition job that Venturi's polemic did on mainstream 1960s architecture practice, Rowe's incisive criticisms did, in parallel, to mainstream mid-1960s urban design practice. But in its explicit interest in formal issues in urban design, Rowe's work was also enormously directive.

By introducing the extraordinarily powerful graphic technique of the figure-ground drawing, Rowe launched a revolution in the study of urban design in architecture schools across North America, a revolution which remains to this day of undiminished influence. At the same time Rowe's personal influence on a whole generation of architects now coming into their own as practitioners, makes his "contextualism" the most important theory of urban design currently operative in advanced architectural circles in North America today.

By now, there is even beginning to be evident a body of work by a younger generation, which re-examines the characteristic urban forms of North America, in the light of Rowe's pioneering work. My students' and my own work on Toronto from 1978, while largely the result of European influences, still bear the profound marks of Rowe's contextualist ideas and techniques.[5] Then too, one must point to the important efforts which have been made by North American scholars to rediscover the lost body of ideas having to do with "the pre-Modernist" planned suburb in England and in North America.[6] Robert Stern's 1981 text "The Anglo-American suburb", brings a valuable body of material of this kind together, even if it doesn't attempt a very extensive analysis of it. One of the most interesting recent morphological undertakings in North America with which I am familiar, is a series of studies which Mario Gandelsonas has pursued, during teaching visits in New York, Boston, Los Angeles, Chicago and Philadelphia.[7] Gandelsonas acknowledges a certain methodological debt to Rowe, and sees his studies as expanding the scale of analysis of urban form from the building and the precinct, to the formal order of the metropolis as a whole. In this sense, his studies take on a strongly European flavour, and they seem to me to be highly suggestive of the as yet untapped potential of morphological analyses to yield new formal understandings of the North American city. Still, Gandelsonas admits to a reluctance to theorise too extensively on his precocious urban graphics, preferring for the moment at least, simply to let the drawings speak for themselves. And to the best of my knowledge, the theorising his analyses so provocatively call for, is not being attempted elsewhere. Indeed, one is compelled to conclude that while Rowe's critique, and his successor's proposals have been profoundly influential; and while the victory of such ideas in important architectural schools across North America has been overwhelming, it nevertheless remains true that this body of ideas has had less influence to date in practice, than one would have expected.

My hypothesis is that the reason for this limitation of emphasis has to do with the fact that notwithstanding its formal sophistication and historical depth, Rowe's contextualism nevertheless shares with the body of urban ideas which it has so successfully discredited, one very problematic limitation. That is to say, while the "comprehensive redevelopment" of the 1960s failed to take adequate account of the ineluctable fact of the highly differentiated pattern of land ownership in any typical North American urban area, it is true that contextualism also fails to do so. As a result, contextualist urban design theory, when applied, has a disconcerting methodological tendency to treat urban texture somewhat like plasticine or cheese, to be carved into shapes suitable for the definition of positive urban spaces.

To be sure, the formal assurance with which these spaces are configured, represents a profound advance on the thinking of the previous generation. Still, the formal methods which generate those shapes fail to respond, as effectively as they should, to the imperatives of zoning, density, leasing and marketing.

What I have seen as a breakthrough in my own thinking in these matters, has been the realisation of the significance in urban theory of the phenomenon of the lot—or as Europeans have grown accustomed to calling it, the parcel. In the mid- to late-1970s, successive waves of information on the precepts of typology and morphology appeared in North America. Of particular influence on this author were the Roosevelt Island Competition proposals of O M Ungers and of Rem Koolhaas and Elia Zenghelis, as well as the theoretical writings of Christian Devillers and Rafael Moneo.[8] All of these proposals and texts made

the status of the lot fundamental to an understanding of the morphology of the city, be it European or North American. In the series of studies of a precinct of Toronto referred to above, I attempted to apply the principles of building typology and urban morphology, to the City of Toronto. These studies, together with subsequent reflections on them, have led me to a series of theoretical conclusions, in regard to urban morphology per se. These conclusions form the body of Part Two of this text.

Part Two: Four Theoretical Conclusions in Regard to Urban Morphology, Based on Efforts at Application, in North America

Fundamental to morphological studies potential, whatever the subject of analysis, is the historically applicable system of the division of land. This has led me—as it has many other students of the subject, to the key theoretical conclusion: THE LOT IS THE BASIS OF URBAN MORPHOLOGY.

This conclusion is, alas, one of those in the history of urbanism whose very self-evidence must have been responsible for its having—in theoretical circles— been so systematically avoided. No doubt a history of the philosophical and political biasses of precocious Modernism could be written, which would explicate the astonishing degree of suppression or avoidance of this elementary fact of urban form. For my own part, I have merely noted that common sense and ordinary architectural practice have never ceased to take into account the fundamental political reality that urban land is divided into parcels, and that the size and shape of the parcel on which any given new building is proposed to be erected, will have a major impact on the form which that building can be expected to take. Most precocious concepts of urban redevelopment on the other hand—at least from Tony Garnier's Cite Industrielle onwards—have striven to suppress acknowledgement of the realities of differentiated property ownership. From a political perspective, one is compelled to note that early Modernism characteristically preferred to see collectivist forms of land tenure as the wave of the future, viewing the extant differential patterns of ownership typical of existing cities, as temporary anomalies, which would eventually be superseded under new political arrangements. Through the 1920s and 1930s, these preferences of Modernism met with only limited political success, but the damage caused to numerous European cities during the Second World War opened the way for a whole new impetus to reorganised and simplified systems of land tenure, during the period of post-war reconstruction. Still, it is evident today that in the major cities of Western Europe at least, collectivised land tenure co-exists with adjoining patterns of differentiated ownership which remain very widespread.

But then, in one of the great cultural ironies of our period, the concepts of "comprehensive redevelopment" which were imported from Europe to North America in the post-war period, were eventually realised here by means of the large-scale urban redevelopment undertaken by private enterprise, beginning in the late 1950s and continuing right up until very recently.

An apt illustration of the "crisis of comprehensiveness" in relation to the extant pattern of differentiated land ownership, is Mies van der Rohe's Toronto Dominion Centre of the early 1960s in my home city. For this project, Mies conceived a classic series of pure cubic steel and glass objects, expected to sit on a simple granite plinth. But it turned out that his clients, powerful entrepreneurs though they were, proved incapable of assembling the entire city block which would have been required, in order for Mies' aesthetic urban conception to have taken shape in its pure form. As a result, the conception as-built, has to contend awkwardly with the existence of a series of historical buildings in one corner of the originally desired superblock. One of Mies' three objects, a Schinkelesque banking pavilion, sits nearby to an exposed rough-brick party wall of a building from the 1930s. The main tower of the complex has to its side a laneway giving access to a whole series of service entrances on the rear elevations of nineteenth-century warehouse buildings. Within the pre-Modernist building fabric of the block of course, neither the party wall nor the service entrances were open to public view. Only the cut in the fabric of the block caused by its partial assembly by Mies' clients, exposed these unseemly faces and Mies' concept was insufficiently supple, from an urban point of view, to respond positively to such problematic conditions of adjacency.

But this term "conditions of adjacency" already suggests that there is a greater significance to the concept of the lot, than my argument to date has recognised. For it implies that there is a natural affinity between a certain size and shape of lot, and a building type which, historically speaking, might have been

An aerial view of the Toronto Dominion Centre, looking southwest, as the second tower was approaching completion. At the lower left-hand side of the image can be seen the group of adjacent buildings facing Bay Street, that Toronto Dominion was unable to acquire.

expected to sit on it. To this I shall return. For the moment, I want only to underscore the profoundly important rediscovery of the fact that the lot is the fundamental module of urban development, from political, economic, legal, and (therefore) morphological points of view. Indeed, I believe that it is possible to state that it is this multifarious reality of the status of the lot which makes it so key a concept. For from it, one can commence efforts to understand urban growth from political, economic and legal points of view, each one of which will yield significant research conclusions in its own right, whilst sharing with architecture and urbanism a common conceptual base in the lot itself. Now that urban theory is beginning to recognise the key status of this concept, I believe one can hope that we will begin—finally—to understand the processes of urban development more realistically than mainstream Modernist theory, or for that matter, than many of its many recent critiques.

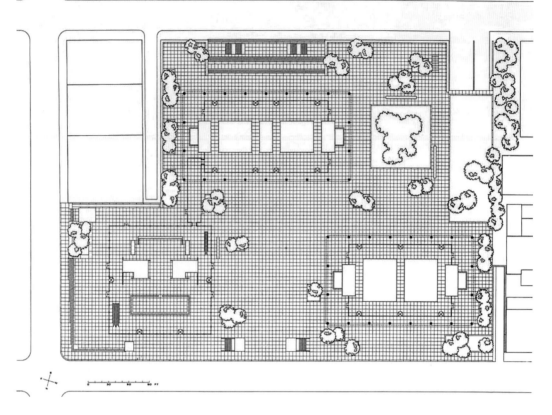

Site plan of the Toronto Dominion Centre as of the date of completion of the phase of the project designed by Mies van de Rohe. The unassembled properties are at the upper left.

Leaving the politics, economics, and legalities of systems of land division for further exploration by scholars in other disciplines, one returns to the particulars of architectural and urban discourse, to encounter what seems to me to be a second fundamental principle of urban morphology, which derives from the significance of the lot; that is: GIVEN ANY PARTICULAR TYPICAL SIZE AND SHAPE OF URBAN LOT, BUILDING AND ZONING BYLAWS APPLICABLE TO IT WILL ACT AS GENERATORS OF BUILDING TYPOLOGIES.

Viewed from an architectural perspective, the significance of the legal status of the lot yields expression in its size and shape. Similarly viewed, the significance of its economic status yields expression, by and large, in the quantity of floor space which it is legal and/or marketable to build on it. By the same token, the significance of its political status yields expression in the uses which it is permissible to accommodate on the lot. When combined with one another, and with considerations of public safety and amenity which form

substance of municipal bylaws, these various factors determine to a very high degree, the characteristic forms of buildings which can be expected to be erected on any lot of a 'typical' size and shape.

Now it is true, of course, that the same mainstream body of Modernist theory which saw differentiated land tenure as an irrelevance, and "comprehensive development" as the wave of the future, also deplored, by and large, the particularity of local building and zoning bylaws. Indeed, such frameworks of specific local legislation were commonly viewed as philistine impediments to the free play of the creative instincts of the designing architect. Hence, as often as not, the large-scale developments of the 1960s and 1970s discussed above, entailed the waiver of numerous local regulations which would, in the case of less ambitious projects have been applicable to a project on a given site.

But in light of the discoveries yielded by the precepts of morphology and typology it seems to me that even such cumbersome mechanisms of regulation of urban development as local bylaws can now, methodologically speaking, be seen as generators of typologies. Viewed politically or economically, of course, it is clear that such mechanisms of regulation are far from gratuitous. Still, the methodological perspective unfolding here would suggest that the precocious designer might well even be able to treat the framework of regulation as a form of "game theory" which arbitrarily determines the rules for the generation of new types. This would seem to me to open up a sophisticated new technique of incorporating the regulatory framework back into the architectural and urban theory of our own time.

In turn, if it can be seen that building typologies can be generated in such a fashion, then it seems to me that a third fundamental principle of such studies reasonably readily follows: REPEATABILITY OF FORMS IN A SYNCHRONIC DIMENSION IS A CHARACTERISTIC OF TYPOLOGIES.

The varied pragmatic forces which act as generators of building typologies—and I do not limit them only to building and zoning bylaws—tend to influence built forms proposed for similar sites in similar ways. As a result, there arises within any given area of jurisdiction a certain repeatability of types, which soon enough becomes recognisable, and which forms a key component of the characteristic urban morphology of the area in question. It has already been noted by many observers in this field how distinctly identifiable the component characteristics of the type can be. In my own work in Toronto we were, for example, readily able to identify such pairs of characteristics as front/back; public/private; sunny exposure/shaded exposure; servant/served. Very quickly we came to the conclusion that the "conditions of adjacency" between lots were crucial both to the formation of the types in the first instance, as well as to the process of substitution of one building by a succeeding one on the same lot over a long period of time. But this is to lead on to the last of the four theoretical conclusions of this paper: SUBSTITUTION OF FORMS WITHIN A TYPOLOGICALLY CONSISTENT EVOLUTION IS THE DIACHRONIC DIMENSION OF URBAN MORPHOLOGY.

If the repeatability of forms in the synchronic dimension amounts to a sort of constancy, against which is permuted what we might call the pluralist multiplicity of city fabric, within any given historical phase of urban development, then it is also true that substitution forms the diachronic dimension of the same morphology. It would appear that quite

radically different building forms can be substituted on the same lot over time, without damage to the morphology, so long as a sufficient number of the constituent rules of the typology are respected. Thus it becomes evident that the repeatability of types, when combined with their substitution, offers up a powerful model of urban morphology, in which the city can—in yet another new way—be read as a text, or perhaps even more readily (over time) as a cinematic collage. Repeatability produces limited sequences of conventional and identifiable elements in various transformations, instead of the unified overall ensembles we associate with mainstream Modernism. Substitution, on the other hand, on a lot-by-lot basis, complements repeatability so as to produce a legible, discrete, piece-by-piece image of historical evolution over time, within a given precinct, when it is viewed as a whole.

Part Three: Three Distinctive Characteristics Which Can be Expected to Form Key Parts of the Theory of Urban Morphology as it Applies to the North American City

I should think I have indicated clearly enough by now how morphological studies in North America (notwithstanding the work associated with Rowe and his successors) remain in their infancy. Yet I hope I have also succeeded in indicating how great I believe the potential of such studies can be. For it seems to me that they offer us a set of tools of unprecedented power with which first to understand the form of the North American city, and with which, then, as architects in practice, to begin to be able to deal more creatively and authoritatively with it. But I have to concede that three characteristics of such studies which can be expected to be truly distinct from European studies in this area, are ones which have already been well recognised by European observers—albeit not in the context of urban morphology itself. These characteristics are:

1 The urban land grid.
2 The tall building.
3 The suburb.

As far as I can tell, when it is once tackled systematically, the urban grid so characteristic of North American cities, will prove to be a crucial determining characteristic of their respective morphologies. Though this is not to say that all grids are alike, or that the impact of a grid *per se* is predictable. For enough work has been done already, to indicate that the various scales, proportions and consistencies of grids—both within any given North American city and in comparisons being made between different ones—have profoundly subtle influences on the particular morphologies which result. Both my own work on Toronto and Gandelsonas' on New York and Los Angeles are ample proof of this. But the fact remains that the detailed understanding of the various modes of impact of grids lies ahead of us. And I remain convinced that such understandings, once attained, will yield for us yet another set of those nuanced distinctions in theoretical discourse, which make Europe/North America comparisons so endlessly revelatory.

As for the tall building, this of course, has been a staple of Europe/North America theoretical distinctions, since the beginning of the century and Louis Sullivan. But here too, I believe we must be careful not to allow our familiarity with the issue in one theoretical context to blind us to its potential explanatory power in another one. For the possible sets of relationships of tall buildings to urban fabric generally are not exhausted in the precepts of CIAM. The whole series of vernacular developments in Manhattan following the 1916 zoning bylaw suggest one provocative possibility of understanding how the tall building itself can perfectly easily address itself to repeatability, to conditions of front and back, public and private, et cetera, not to mention to the profoundly important question of "conditions of adjacency".

In my view we can safely conclude in advance, that while the tall building, once incorporated into the body of such studies, will change their direction significantly, the results of the studies will be no less morphological—and no less revelatory—for the fact of their having been so changed. Indeed, the Manhattan skyscraper remains too unique a North American phenomenon for its analysis to settle all the crucial questions of urban form under review. The third of the three distinctive characteristics—the suburb—shows this clearly.

The suburb, of course, has for a long time been seen by European observers as the quintessence of North American exotica. And many critics—North American and European alike—have disparaged the suburbs as definite evidence of the fundamental non-urbanity of North America. But within the theoretical perspective opened up by the sorts of morphological studies now underway, I believe this dismissal will prove to have been too short-sighted. To be sure, it is clear that the customary methods of analysis of morphology—especially the ubiquitous reliance on the figure-ground drawing—will have to be modified, to cope successfully with the particular spatial characteristics of the suburb, which are determined at least as much by landscape elements, by highway engineering and by signs, as they are by built form itself. But there is nothing inherently unyielding to morphological analysis, in the suburb. Stern's 1981 compilation of ambitious examples begs for such analysis to begin in earnest. In fact, I would conclude that a fully fledged body of urban ideas which can indisputably be called "urban" and equally as indisputably be called "North American" still awaits the definitive commencement of such investigations.

1   Bacon, Edmund N, *Design of Cities*, New York: The Viking Press, 1957.

2   Rowe, Colin and Koetter Fred, *Collage City*, Cambridge MA: MIT Press, 1978.

3   Barnett, Jonathan, *Urban Design as Public Policy*, New York: Architectural Record Books, 1974.

4   Venturi, Robert, *Complexity and Contradiction in Architecture*, Museum of Modern Art, New York, 1966.

5   Myers, Barton, and George Baird, "Vacant Lottery'" *Design Quarterly*, no 108, Minneapolis: Walker Art Center, 1978.

6   Stern, Robert A M and John Montague Massengale, "The Anglo-American Suburb", *Architectural Design Profile, Architectural Design*, London, 1981.

7   Gandelsonas, Mario, unpublished documentation on morphological studies of various American cities, discussed with George Baird in 1985.

8   Ungers, O M, "Project for Roosevelt Island Competition" in *L'Architecture d'aujourd'hui*, no 186, August–September, 1976; Koolhaas, Rem and Elia Zenghelis, "Project for Roosevelt Island Competition", *L'Architecture d'aujourd'hui*, no 186, August–September, 1976; Devillers, Christian, "Typologie de l'habitat et morphologie urbane", *L'architecture d'aujourd'hui*, no 174, July–August 1974; Moneo, Rafael, "On Typology", *Oppositions* 13, Institute for Architecture and Urban Studies, New York, 1978.

Mutant Urbanity: Revisiting Las Vegas, 2004

Some 20 years after the morphological and typological work in Toronto, I found myself, while teaching at the Harvard Graduate School of Design, co-teaching a design studio with an urban design faculty colleague: Richard Marshall.[1] The studio in question focused on the supposedly notorious American city of Las Vegas. Following the completion of the studio, I concluded that the students in that studio produced some excellent and original analytical work on the contemporary urban form of Las Vegas, and I was prompted by that production of theirs to prepare a text about it.[2] The text below is the result. It has seemed to me that it is an urban analysis that completely supercedes the celebrated work of the 1970s of Venturi and Scott Brown, and I have been disappointed to see it have so little apparent effect.

In advanced architectural and urban design circles, the image of the city of Las Vegas has been largely defined by the revolutionary arguments of the 1972 publication, *Learning from Las Vegas* by Robert Venturi, Denise Scott Brown and Steven Izenour. Their discourse on "ducks" and "decorated sheds" had already up-ended conventional cultural opinion in regard to the urban form of the American city, taking putatively negative visual images from Peter Blake's polemical picture book of 1964, *God's Own Junkyard*, and representing them affirmatively. (Although it was written previously, the ducks and decorated sheds essay is included in *Learning from Las Vegas*.)

With the Las Vegas text proper, Venturi, Scott Brown and Izenour took the argument several steps further. They argued, for example, that the American—or, more precisely, the American commercial suburban streetscape was largely defined by signage, rather than by buildings. Similarly, they conceptualised the "large, low-ceilinged air-conditioned room"—the casino—that had no precedent in earlier typologies of architectural space. By such means, the Venturi team was able to significantly shift perceptions of American architecture and urban space, and to grant an unprecedented legitimacy to the specific architectural and urban forms of Las Vegas. And as a result, the distinctive architectural and urban forms of the controversial western American city have, over the past three decades, to a significant degree, entered mainstream American architectural and urban thought. But those three decades have now passed, and in the interval, Las Vegas itself has been changed in profound ways. Numerous observers have commented on these changes, yet to the best of my knowledge, no comprehensive reading of its present day architectural or urban form comparable in cogency or influence to that of the Venturi team has been attempted so far. This short essay is intended to begin such an attempt.

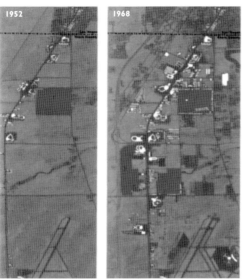

Figure-ground drawings of development on Las Vegas Boulevard at four key dates: 1952, 1968, 1982 and 2002. Note the continual expansion of scale, and intensification of construction between Sahara Avenue, the street running across all four of these drawings, close to the top (the boundary between the City of Las Vegas and Clark County, within which the strip is largely located) and McCarran Airport to the south. The depths of the development parcels also get greater and greater; the building masses fatter and fatter, and the so-called plinths of the casino-hotel complexes more and more extensive in plan.

The "Strip" and the "Boulevard"

In the context of Las Vegas, the term "strip" referred originally to the portion of the highway just outside the southerly limit of the city, where the first suburban casino-motels were constructed in the late 1940s. The term distinguished the location of these newer facilities from that of the more traditional casinos (which did not originally include accommodation) located 'downtown' on Fremont Street. Even today, the typological, geographic, political and economic tension between Fremont Street in the centre of the old city of Las Vegas, and the "Strip" outside in Clark County, continues to be a powerful one in the urbanised area of one million inhabitants that is now known as "the valley".

For the Venturis, the term "strip" carried such connotations as "auto-retail strip", "strip mall" etc and sure enough, the early forms of development on the Las Vegas strip followed this model. The typical casino-models of the early period were relatively low density, low-rise structures, set back from the street, usually not more than two-storeys high. Since they were strongly oriented to patrons arriving by car from Los Angeles (the closest major population centre), they provided ample areas for surface parking. As often as

not, the parking areas were located between the road itself and the front facade of the casino-motel building thereby definitively reinforcing the site planning strategy associated with the typical suburban "strip mall".

The more ambitious, or upscale casino-motels—Bugsy Siegel's famous "Flamingo" is a case in point—endeavoured, early on, to convey a certain "country-club" appearance. Thus the large and highly visible areas of parking in front of early casino-hotels were mitigated by efforts at patently luxurious landscaping, typically on a 'tropical' theme: hence, again the name of his casino: the "Flamingo". It then became necessary, to the extent that the areas of parking grew, and that the landscaping had the effect of screening the facade of the complex along with the parking, to reassert the presence of the casino-hotel, out at the edge of the street. To this end came the advent of the famous large-scale signs along the Strip, which eventually became one of the most significant world-wide utilisations of neon lighting technology. It is the constellation of such architectural and urban features as I have just enumerated, that was captured and codified by Venturi's 1972 urban analysis.

But of course, it is a fact that by that date, the classical suburban forms of development on the strip were already being superseded. The 1960s had

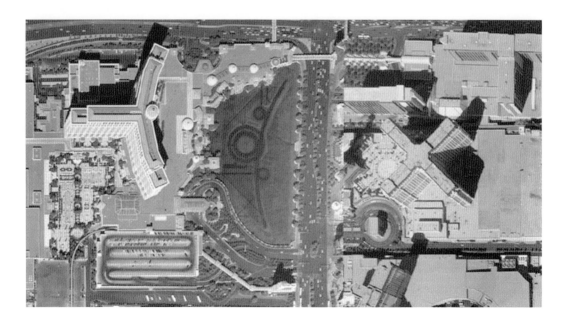

This illustration shows details of the relationship of the plinth of Bellagio to its hotel slab on the one hand, and to the water feature in its public forecourt on the other. Note also how the vehicular and the pedestrian entrance approach (visible to the lower left) makes its way slowly up to the main entrance of the complex, one level up from Las Vegas Boulevard.

already seen the creation of a new scale of hotel on the strip—examples being the Dunes, the Desert Inn and Caesar's Palace. Such buildings were still set back from the street, with at least some of their parking in front, but they were mid-rise as opposed to low-rise buildings, and their scale was such as to render surface parking in front insufficient to meet the demand of the volume of visitors being received. As a result, this generation of casino-hotels began to incorporate large-scale parking structures in addition to the traditional surface lots. What is more, these structures were typically and expediently located at the rear of the complexes they served.

Then too, this same generation of casino-hotels also expanded the entertainment function from the sort of lounge act associated with the "Rat Pack" of that era (Dean Martin, Frank Sinatra, Sammy Davis Jr, etc) to full-fledged theatrical performance necessitating large-scale auditoria. In turn, these large-scale performance spaces were added to the typical "strip" complex, which became a casino-hotel-entertainment complex. There had always been a nominal amount of retail activity associated with the casino-hotel-entertainment complex, but by the end of the 1980s, the retail component of a number of the major complexes had expanded dramatically. At the present time, Caesar's Palace, the

Aladdin and the Venetian all contain full-fledged shopping malls, in addition to their core programme components. By the same date, the phenomenon of "theming" had definitively begun to make a mark on Las Vegas, and the precedent of such theme parks as Disneyland began to profoundly influence the iconography of the architecture of the strip (as will be discussed in detail below).

Finally, the 1990s saw the formalisation of the full complement of building programmes in a comprehensive new building typology invented by the Las Vegas entrepreneur Steve Wynn. In Wynn's reconceptualisation of the typical casino complex, three key innovations were introduced: surface parking was entirely removed from the front of the building; pedestrian extensions of the retail malls were extended right out to the street edge public sidewalks, sometimes even with moving sidewalks; the new forecourts created by the removal of the surface parking and by the pedestrian extensions of retail out to the Boulevard were filled with extensive landscaping and with highly animated water features (all three of Wynn's original casino complexes, the Mirage, Treasure Island, and Bellagio follow this model).

Among other things, this reconceptualisation was based on the realisation that it no longer made business sense for each casino complex to attempt to hold its own hotel occupants isolated in their own complex.

A view of the contemporary, pedestrian-friendly version of Las Vegas Boulevard, just south of Flamingo Avenue.

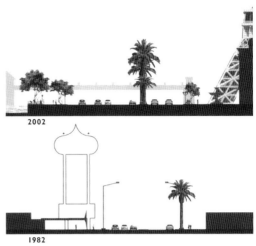

A view of one of the new public structures on Las Vegas Boulevard, incorporating escalators and elevators to provide easy access to the pedestrian street bridge over Las Vegas Boulevard at Flamingo Avenue.

Typical cross-sections through Las Vegas Boulevard at three different stages of its historic evolution. The lowest cross-section shows the early condition that existed in the 1940s and 1950s. In the middle is the classic condition described by the Venturi team in *Learning from Las Vegas*. Finally, the uppermost cross-section shows the current street condition in between Bellagio on the west side of the Boulevard, and the Paris on the east side. In the distance one of the new pedestrian bridges can be seen where the Boulevard crosses Flamingo Avenue.

Each casino complex could generate increased revenue, they realised, if it attracted guests of adjacent casino complexes, as well as their own.

With this, a fundamental social and physical transformation of the strip itself ensued. Visitors to Las Vegas began to move among the whole range of casino complexes located along Las Vegas Boulevard. In turn, the volumes of vehicular traffic being generated meant that it no longer made sense to encourage trips from complex to complex by car. Today, visitors are now discouraged from using their vehicles for local travel. Thus the Strip itself, or Las Vegas Boulevard as it (ironically) has been called all along, cannot in any sense be perceived any longer as an auto-retail strip; it now truly is a boulevard as the term has

traditionally been understood. For example, even with the incentives to visitors not to drive locally, Las Vegas Boulevard is heavily trafficked from noon until midnight. During this same period of time, on the busiest portion of the current strip (from Sands Avenue to Tropicana Avenue) a *passeggiata* of European character flows as throngs of visitors make their way from one casino, shopping mall and public attraction to the next. In the mid-1990s, Wynn even persuaded his fellow casino operators to pay the costs of relandscaping the median of the boulevard, to visually bind the whole ensemble into a more amenable urban whole.

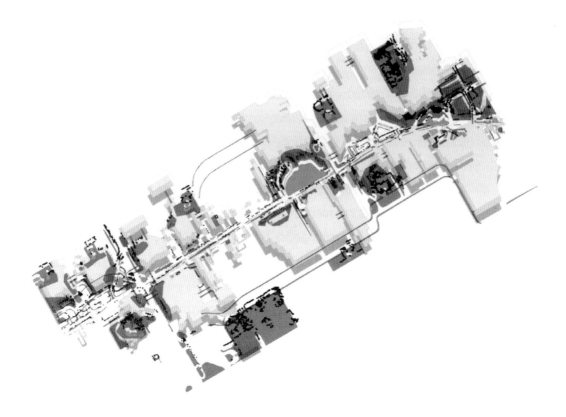

Axonometric drawing depicting the open space system linking the complex of casino-hotels between Tropicana Avenue (at the lower left) and Sands Avenue (at the upper right). Coded here are water features, plaza/forecourts, areas of lawn or low vegetation, and tree canopy. Also shown are the pedestrian bridges at the Tropicana Avenue and Flamingo Avenue intersections, as well as the route of the local tram/monorail on the west side of the Boulevard, and that of the new lengthier bridge connecting to the Convention Center.

New Discouragements to the Use of the Private Automobile, and the Advent of "Private" Public Transportation

I have already noted that visitors to the casino complexes on Las Vegas Boulevard are discouraged from using automobiles for local travel. The most palpable form of this discouragement is the traffic congestion on the Boulevard itself (permanent residents of Las Vegas make it a point to avoid driving on the Boulevard from late afternoon to late evening). But then there is the virtually limitless quantity of free parking available in the parking structures described above. There is even free valet parking at every major casino, to further encourage visitors not to drive locally (visitors are expected to tip the car valets who park their cars for them). As an unexpected consequence, a vibrant pedestrian culture now exists on Las Vegas Boulevard. Indeed, so dense is the pedestrian activity along it that further design innovations have been introduced. Where Las Vegas Boulevard crosses Flamingo Avenue and Tropicana Avenue (two of the busiest intersections) pedestrian street bridges have been constructed and paid for by casino operators, and pedestrian crossing at grade is discouraged. Encouragement to use the bridges is provided by outdoor escalators on all four corners of the intersections in question and elevators for wheelchair users are also provided. (Interestingly enough, the reconceptualisation of the casino complex represented by Wynn's Bellagio entails lifting the entire main level of the complex a storey up in the air, as a sort of *piano nobile* at that casino-complex. Vehicular dropoff thus occurs by a gently ascending driveway from the Boulevard to the front entrance of the hotel, and pedestrian routes from the hotel out to the Boulevard are already one storey up, at the level of the pedestrian street bridges. Most recently, two additional forms of 'public' transportation have been introduced. First, small-scale monorails or trams have now been introduced as a local connector between clusters of adjacent casino complexes (some

A view from the observation tower of the Stratosphere casino-hotel, located on Las Vegas Boulevard, just inside the city limit of Sahara Avenue. The view looks south down the axis of Paradise Road, on which the new monorail under construction is clearly visible. To the far right (just out of view), is Las Vegas Boulevard itself. In the right foreground is the back portion of the Sahara casino-hotel, and in the right background, the back portions of casino-hotels further south. The sprawling complex in the upper left is the Las Vegas Convention Center. Note how the new monorail bends in off Paradise Road to service it. Finally, in the intermediate distance (just above the Sahara casino-hotel, and across Paradise Road from the giant "Hilton" sign, are two new high-rise towers. Not parts of casino-hotels, these are residential condominium complexes, the first ones ever erected so close to the Strip. Thus is the architectural and urban programme of the Strip beginning to shift once again.

of them in affiliated ownerships). Finally, soon to be opened is a full-fledged large-scale monorail extending all the way from Tropicana Avenue (almost to McCarran Airport) at the south end of the strip, to Sahara Avenue (the boundary between Clark County and the City of Las Vegas) at the north end. Admittedly, the large-scale monorail is not located within the public space of Las Vegas Boulevard; it starts out in back of the large parking structures of the hotels on the east side of the Boulevard, and then makes its way up Paradise Avenue, an arterial road one block east of the strip, to the Sahara. Nonetheless, the new monorail will interconnect virtually all of the major casino complexes on the Boulevard, as well as two convention centres. Like the local small-scale monorails cited above, the large-scale model is also financed by the casino operators. Hence my term: "private public transportation".

The new monorail under construction on Paradise Road, one block east of Las Vegas Boulevard. In the distance, the observation tower of the Stratosphere casino-hotel.

A view of a portion of the shopping mall at the Venetian casino-hotel.

The Architectural Evolution of the Las Vegas Building-Type

Part 1: From Casino to Casino-Hotel, to Casino-Hotel-Entertainment Complex, to Casino-Hotel-Entertainment Complex-Shopping Mall, to Casino-Hotel-Entertainment Complex-Shopping Mall-Theme Park, to Casino-Hotel-Entertainment Complex Shopping Mall-Theme Park-Convention Centre

As I noted in my introduction, the early downtown casinos in Las Vegas were truly monofunctional facilities. They provided space for gambling, with only incidental supplemental programme elements such as bars and restaurants. One of the early programmatic innovations of the casinos located on the strip in Clark County was the addition of on-site accommodation. And so, the casino-motel was born. By the mid-1960s, the motel component had expanded to become a hotel. As I have also noted, by the end of the 1960s, the facilities for entertainment (bars, cocktail lounges, etc) had been dramatically expanded, and the emergent casino complexes began to include large auditoria for full-fledged theatrical performances. In the 1980s

and 1990s the established complement of uses was expanded again, this time to include retail shopping—often at the scale of a fully-fledged shopping mall. (Today, the retail mall that forms part of Caesar's Palace is one of the most profitable ones in the entire United States.) During the same period, components of the typical programme of a "theme park" also became part of Las Vegas mix. Amusement rides such as ferris wheels and other public attractions were added to the programme. Finally, some of the casino complexes on the strip now also include conference facilities large enough to accommodate national conventions, and these, together with the Las Vegas Convention Center on Paradise Avenue have made Las Vegas a top convention city in North America. Over the span of a half century then, a major new mixed-use building type has been devised in Las Vegas, and continues to evolve there.

Part 2: From Low-Scale Low-Rise, to Middle-Scale Mid-Rise, to Large-Scale High-Rise Hotel

The expansion of the number and size of the programmes accommodated in the typical Las Vegas casino complex has also transformed its architectural typology. As I have already noted, it started out as a low-rise complex (not exceeding two storeys), with surface parking in front and along its sides, and with nominal landscaping embellishing the edges (although more extensive landscaping was always present in the inner courtyards that were surrounded by the motel wings, and which accommodated swimming pools). And last but not least

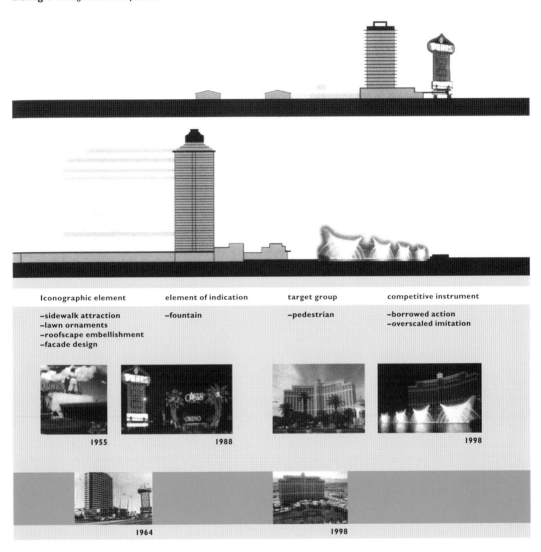

Iconographic element	element of indication	target group	competitive instrument
–sidewalk attraction –lawn ornaments –roofscape embellishment –facade design	–fountain	–pedestrian	–borrowed action –overscaled imitation

1955   1988   1998

1964   1998

This illustration shows the transformation of site planning of the typical casino-hotel, as in this case, the Dunes (shown in cross-section at the top of the illustration) is replaced by Bellagio (shown in cross-section just below the Dunes cross-section). Note the increase in the scale of the complex, the greatly increased street-setback, the provision of a major public attraction (the lake and fountain), as well as the plinth and the hotel slab in the by-now-typical configuration. Beneath the cross-sections are images analysing the iconographic components of both the earlier and the later design.

the famous, but now obsolete large-scale neon signs were located at street edge.

As I have also noted, by the 1960s, the original type had already escalated in scale, with the hotel component becoming a mid-rise one, surrounding an expanding plinth that accommodated all the public components of the growing casino complex programme and even though the traditional surface parking in front of the casino remained in place through this transformation, the sheer quantity of parking spaces required by this date meant that the large parking structure in the rear had already become necessary, and had joined the other essential constituent architectural components of the typical casino complex.

Here again, the specific transformation of the basic type that was introduced by Wynn in the 1990s merits

Caesar's Palace emergence of the themed hotel/casino

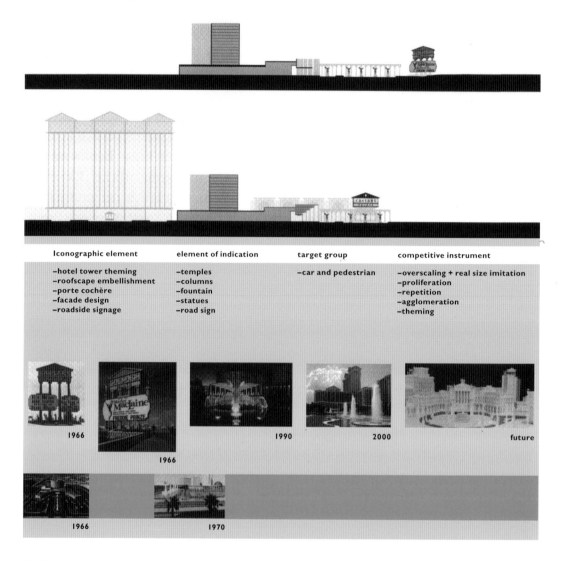

Iconographic element	element of indication	target group	competitive instrument
–hotel tower theming –roofscape embellishment –porte cochère –facade design –roadside signage	–temples –columns –fountain –statues –road sign	–car and pedestrian	–overscaling + real size imitation –proliferation –repetition –agglomeration –theming

This illustration depicts the transformation over time of the iconographic programme of Caesar's Palace. The uppermost cross-section shows the configuration of the complex as it existed in the 1960s. The cross-section beneath the upper one shows the same cross-section through the complex today. The images at the bottom of the illustration analyse the transformation from Modernist to Postmodernist iconography, over time.

special comment. First of all, Wynn never attempted to renovate or expand an existing structure on the strip. Instead, he has always opted for demolition, and for totally new construction. (Indeed, he belongs to a Las Vegas tradition that has made the demolition process a pubic spectacle: it has typically been accomplished by implosion, at night, with floodlights.) As a result, Wynn has been able to achieve his characteristic reconceptualisation of the casino complex unfettered by any constraints arising from

existing construction on the site. The key features of this reconceptualisation are as follows.

First of all, the entire complex is lifted one storey up off the ground level, producing a new at grade service level that is all but invisible to the public.

Second, all parking is removed from the front of the building, and the scale of and access to the parking structures at the rear are more structurally and functionally integrated into the complex as a whole.

Third, the entire built complex is moved back from the edge of the Boulevard. (In the case of Bellagio, which occupies the site of the former Dunes, such is the magnitude of this new setback from the street edge that the entire area of the footprint of the former hotel now falls within the area of what is now the water forecourt.)

Fourth, the scale of the entire complex is dramatically expanded (Wynn's Mirage was the first casino complex on the strip to contain 4,000 hotel rooms).

Fifth, the *piano nobile* described above is devised, and it accommodates all the publicly accessible components of the casino complex programme. This main public floor level sits on top of the 'invisible' lower level service floor concealed by landform and landscaping. Together, these two levels form the large plinth on top of which the hotel slab, or tower, is located. (Sometimes, the plinth also includes a retail mezzanine above the casino floor, as at New York New York.)

Sixth, the hotel component is located, roughly, at the centre of the plinth described above, typically taking the form of a Y with an elevator core at its intersection.

Seventh, pedestrian extensions from the retail facilities in the plinth are extended from the centre of the plinth right out to the public sidewalk along Las Vegas Boulevard: thus making the space in front of the main entrance to the complex a classical forecourt.

And finally, the resultant forecourt is lavishly landscaped, and includes a dramatic water feature which is actively programmed, so as to create a major public attraction for the throngs of pedestrians moving up and down Las Vegas Boulevard.

Part 3: Shifting Approaches to Architectural Iconography

Like the other components of the type, the architectural iconography of the Las Vegas casino complex has also shifted over time. The quasi-residential character of the early strip casino motels gradually gave way to an initial transformation that can almost be called "corporate". The major new complexes of the 1960s—the Dunes, the Desert Inn and Caesar's Palace, all exhibited a formal language not very different from the airport terminals and corporate headquarters of the same period. Interestingly enough, it is even possible to observe that during this period, the typical architectural vocabulary of the casino complex probably reached its highest level—at least by the conventional criteria of Modernist architectural judgement being applied at that time. The

expressionist populism of the signage at the time still stood in contrast to the (relative) Modernist sobriety of the architecture. (This was, of course, one of the reasons why the Venturi team chose to concentrate on the signs.)

But during the 1970s and 1980s, the influence of theme parks such as Disneyland began to impact Las Vegas. As a consequence, the corporate Modernism of the projects of the previous decade fell out of fashion. One of the most telling indicators of this shift in taste is the successive series of expansions and renovations of Caesar's Palace (the only one of the major hotels to have been so extensively expanded and renovated over time). With each successive modification, the complex grew ever more decorative, and its original Modernist facades were eventually entirely obliterated.

During the expansionist boom of the 1990s, a new iconographic programme was gradually codified. According to it the primary burden of iconographic communication is carried by the facade of the plinth of the complex, together with the landscape elements of the forecourt and even larger-scale signs out at the street edge than those of the Venturi era (they now combine LEDs and neon in complex ways). Surrounding this, the large-scale hotel slab or tower remains a relatively perfunctory functional programme element that does not participate in the iconographic programme.

Complexes from the early 1990s such as the Mirage, Treasure Island, and Aladdin's Palace all follow this pattern, and even such recent examples as Paris and the Venetian do not significantly depart from it. The chief innovation of these most recent examples has been to move the specific iconographic programme from a vaguely Disneyesque imaginary realm, towards a much more literal historical reproduction of major architectural monuments from other well-known urban tourist destinations—in the cases of Paris and the Venetian: literally Paris and Venice.

Finally, there are two interesting departures from the otherwise definitive 1990s typology: New York New York and Bellagio. And they depart in opposed directions. In the case of New York New York, the radical gesture has been to bring the slab of accommodation that is the hotel component of the complex into the iconographic programme, along with the plinth. Thus New York New York mutates the typical slab of accommodation, to produce the visual effect of a collaged skyline of more-or-less recognisable Manhattan skyscrapers. Research

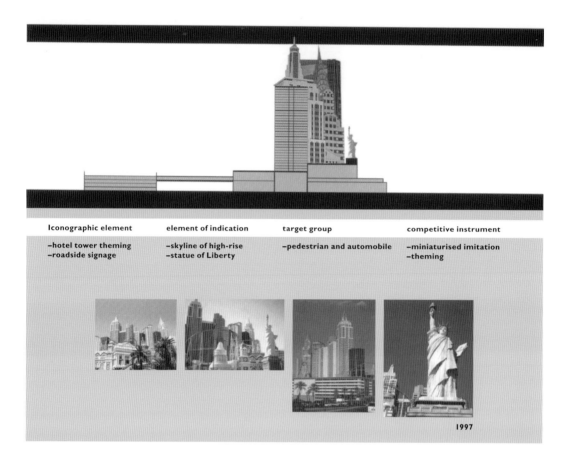

Iconographic element	element of indication	target group	competitive instrument
–hotel tower theming –roadside signage	–skyline of high-rise –statue of Liberty	–pedestrian and automobile	–miniaturised imitation –theming

1997

The distinctive relationship of building typology to iconography at New York New York is shown here. The upper cross-section shows the typical plinth and hotel slab relationship, with the parking structure behind. But one can also see here how the bent slab of the hotel accommodation component participates in the iconographic programme of the project. The images at the bottom of the illustration depict moments of this programme.

conducted by the Harvard Las Vegas studio students has indicated the means of achieving this effect, whilst still adhering closely to the norms of typical double-loaded slab blocks.

Basically the slab is bent, and slightly jogged back and forth along its length. The jogging which occurs in plan is extruded upwards, thus producing the appearance of one skyscraper juxtaposed against the next, in a long chain. Higher and lower towers alternate along the length of the overall jogging and bent slab, and vertical circulation shafts are located at the 'cores' of each of the alternating higher 'skyscrapers'. The whole complex slab sits on top of its plinth in terms that are entirely consistent with the basic type.

In the case of the last completed project of Steve Wynn, Bellagio, the iconographic approach is more subtle. As its name suggests, Bellagio is intended to evoke connotations of a luxury resort on a northern Italian lake. In this design, the plinth does, more-or-less, approximate the appearance of a village on the edge of Lake Como. In this case, like that of New York New York, the hotel slab rising above also participates in the iconographic programme of the complex. But unlike New York New York it does not do so through explicit mimesis. Rather, it presents a restrained, supportive backdrop to the picturesque complex below, consciously deferring pictorially to it. What is more, at the same time that it is iconographically

The Bellagio fountain illuminated at night.

This image shows details of the relationship of the plinth of Bellagio to its hotel slab on the one hand, and to the water feature in its public forecourt on the other. Portions of Caesar's Palace in its "postmodern" iconographic iteration can be seen in the distance, as can a glimpse of the Mirage casino hotel further to the north. Note also how the vehicular and the pedestrian entrance approach (visible to the lower left) makes its way slowly up to the main entrance to the complex, one level up from Las Vegas Boulevard.

reticent, the hotel slab also attempts a certain plastic and tectonic cohesiveness beyond seeking to be architecture, in a relatively traditional sense.

Wynn is now at work on the design and construction of a new casino hotel complex—this one on the site of the former Desert Inn. It is to be called Le Reve, and its advance notice declares that it will depart further from the type described above—even though Wynn himself is one of the key innovators within the local typological tradition. It will, according to reports, not be visually open to Las Vegas Boulevard at all, guarding its supposed allures described as non-themed. It is not entirely clear what the ramifications of this description are, in the context of the history of casino-hotel design in this setting. Still, it suggests at a minimum that the Disney influence on iconography in Las Vegas has peaked, and that an approach to appearance that is both more illusive and more allusive, is now under consideration there.

Conclusion

Clearly the Las Vegas that was theorised by Venturi, Scott Brown and Izenour no longer exists. The apotheosis of commercial suburbia that they canonised, has, over time, been replaced by something much more than urban. Indeed, it is my view that a certain "urbanity" can now, indisputably be seen to exist on the famous strip. To be sure, it is a mutant urbanity, which does not even come close to possessing all of the characteristics that have traditionally been associated with the term. For example, it does not yet encompass much of that key urban land use—housing—comprising instead almost purely commercial uses. Then too, up until now, Las Vegas Boulevard has remained a "Potemkin village", its putative urbanity rapidly petering out as one moves away from it, down any of the major avenues which cross it.

Nevertheless, it remains true that a fundamental transformation of the Boulevard has taken place and a large-scale interconnected mixed-use complex which is an almost fully unified urban megastructure has been created there. What is more, this mega-structural complex is dense and active throughout most of the day and night. Perhaps most significant of all, a vibrant pedestrian culture has been created in this most unlikely of middle-sized American cities, and this culture is deeply linked with a growing series of public transportation devices. As most knowledgeable observers of those middle-sized cities are aware, pedestrian life is withering away in many of them, as the progressive suburbanisation of middle American urban space continues. For a tourist urban destination such as Las Vegas to demonstrate to its typical middle American visitors, the pleasures of a pedestrian culture, is no small thing.

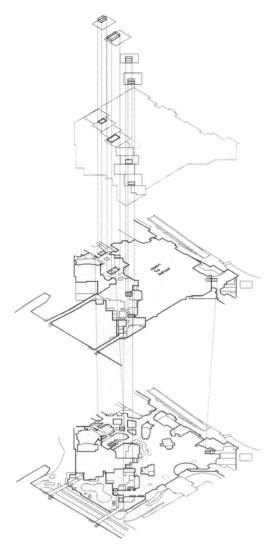

This is a view of the forecourt, public attraction, plinth and hotel slab at the Treasure Island casino-hotel. The vantage point for the view is the median of Las Vegas Boulevard, in front of the casino-hotel. In the close foreground, one sees the street sidewalk stepped up to produce a bleacher-like tiered platform to provide better viewing conditions for the stage "pirate battle" that recurs throughout the day and evening.

The characteristic architectural iconography of the casino-hotels along Las Vegas Boulevard shifted in the early 2000s. The shift was away from "theme park" type iconography to more literal historical reproduction. Shown here is a reproduction of a portion of the facade of Charles Garnier's design for the Paris Opera, here fronting the Paris casino hotel on Las Vegas Boulevard.

The typological relationship of building typology to iconography at the New York New York casino-hotel is shown here. Note how the jogs in the floor plate of the hotel produce the apparently individual skyscrapers, and how the elevator cores are co-ordinated with the typical hotel floor plans.

Admittedly, "Main Street", as a captive pedestrian venue, has been a key component of American theme parks since Disneyland itself was created in the mid-1960s. But while Las Vegas Boulevard has taken much of its inspiration from such theme parks, it is my view that it does not constitute one. There is no wall or fence enclosing the entire area as there always is at a theme park, and one does not pay to get in. What is more, rather than being inside, many of the largest-scale public attractions—the volcano at the Mirage, the fountain at the Bellagio, the pirate battle at Treasure Island—are all located within the space of the street, and thus allows viewing by the throngs of passers-by free of charge. Thus it seems to me that it is not preposterous to suppose that this extraordinary commercial megastructure may even be able to revive hopes of urbanity for those visitors from other American cities where it sadly continues to evaporate. The celebrated vision of the Venturi team, is thus in the process of being turned on its head, and one of the fountainheads of perceived 'excess' in popular American culture is helping to reconstitute a more traditional image of urban life— despite the breathless prognostications about it on the part of the dystopic contemporary design avant-garde.

Finally, there is one very recent development on the Las Vegas strip—one that has even astonished long-time observers of the city. This is the advent of high-rise, high-density housing, in close proximity to Las Vegas Boulevard. As I acknowledged above, that essential ingredient of a fully-fledged urbanity—high-density housing—did not yet exist there to any appreciable extent. But it is beginning to appear. In time, its growing presence as the newest ingredient of the astonishing Las Vegas Boulevard megastructure will cause the local urbanity to mutate once again. Local constituencies of residents will transform development politics and secondary land uses, and numerous other aspects of a traditional form of urbanity will begin to make themselves felt. Perhaps the current "Potemkin village" along the strip will begin to acquire some urban depth on either side. This is surely the next surprise to come in this most surprising of contemporary American cities.

1   Revisiting Las Vegas, Design Option Studio 2003, Harvard Graduate School of Design, co-taught with Richard Marshall, to whom all photography included in this essay in credited.

2   The students of the Revisiting Las Vegas Studio were Shangwen Chiu, Sandy Chung, Alexander Gill, Ross Hummel, Hyeseon Ju, Daniel Kraffczyk, Jeannette Kuo, Vicky Lam, Vivian Lee, Michelle Lin, Erwin Olson-Douglas, Seth Riseman, Jenny Stickles, Timothy Wong, Aaron Young and Xiaodi Zheng.

Thoughts on "Agency", "Utopia" and "Property" in Contemporary Architectural and Urban Theory, 2013

This text is the result of a diverse set of circumstances: first, an invitation I was unable to accept to write for another publication about Fredric Jameson; second, an interest in the work of the Japanese architectural firm Atelier Bow-Wow—especially their urban analysis of the urban form of Tokyo; and finally, a growing curiosity about the phenomenon of informal settlements in major metropolises around the world. This methodologically heterogeneous text could have been included in many of the sections of this collection of essays, but perhaps it can be seen as something of a synthesis of a number of my apparently diverse interests in urban form and in political theory, interests most extensively explored in my 1995 book, *The Space of Appearance.*

Fredric Jameson is the William A Lane Professor at Duke University, and the 2008 winner of the Holberg International Memorial Prize for his work analysing the relation between social formations and cultural forms.

When one considers that his own academic field is comparative literature, it has to be said that Jameson has had an unusually significant impact on architectural history and theory over the past few decades. Beginning with his now famous 1982 lecture at New York's Institute for Architecture and Urban Studies, "Architecture and the Critique of Ideology",[1] and continuing to the present day with commentaries on such figures as Peter Eisenman and Rem Koolhaas, Jameson's writings have influenced many historians and theorists in the architectural field, not least, such figures as Michael Hays of Harvard,[2] and Reinhold Martin of Columbia University.

I myself have not been part of the Jameson following. Indeed, when I was invited by Nadir Lahiji several years ago to contribute to an anthology of essays conceived as a tribute to Jameson, I came to realise that I had insufficient familiarity with his work to be able to do so in a timely fashion, and, as a result, did not participate in that publication project. Indeed, up until that time, based on my limited reading of texts of Jameson—

most of them ones explicitly referencing architecture in one fashion or another—I found myself first, puzzled, and subsequently, irritated, by the recurrent invocation of the concept of "Utopia", typically relatively late on in the development of Jameson's arguments in the respective texts in question, subsequent to his various iterations and explanations of the implacable grip of late capitalism on the world. Utopia tended to appear as a qualifying indication of the continuing presence, if not a readily accessible one—notwithstanding that grip—of a more hopeful, alternative political possibility.

But, in connection with his invitation to contribute to the next anthology he was assembling, Lahiji encouraged me to read a text of Jameson's that was earlier than any I had looked at up to that point, and that preceded his writings on architecture and urbanism. The text in question was "The Political Unconscious" from 1981.[3] Reading it significantly deepened my view of Jameson. I found it a magisterial—and to my mind an ecumenical—survey of literary theory from Joseph Conrad, through Claude Lévi-Strauss and Northrop Frye, to Paul Ricoeur—all this, admittedly, through the lens of Jameson's own Marxist frame of reference. Interestingly enough, in reading the book, I even learned something of the intellectual background of my Harvard colleague of long-standing, Michael Hays. I knew that Hays was an admirer of Jameson, but reading "The Political Unconscious" made clear to me the origin of Hays' distinctive reading of the concept of "ideology" as framed by the French Marxist philosopher Louis Althusser. For there, in a lengthy excursus by Jameson, was the articulation of precisely that conception of ideology that I had first learned at Harvard from Hays.[4]

In the conclusion to the same text, Jameson took it upon himself to spell out in much greater detail than I had seen elsewhere in his writings, the role of the concept of Utopia in his thinking. As he put it:

> Any Marxist analysis of culture… can no longer be content with its demystifying vocation to unmask and to demonstrate the ways in which a cultural artefact fulfils a specific ideological mission, in legitimating a given power structure, in perpetuating and reproducing the latter, and in generating specific forms of false consciousness (or ideology in the narrower sense). It must not cease to practice this essentially negative hermeneutic function (which Marxism is virtually the only current critical method to assume today) but must also seek

through and beyond this demonstration of the instrumental function of a given cultural object, to project its simultaneously utopian power as the symbolic affirmation of a specific historical and class form of collective unity.[5]

For Jameson:

> A Marxist negative hermeneutic, a Marxist practice of reading analysis proper, must in the practical work of reading and interpretation, be exercised simultaneously with a Marxist positive hermeneutic, or a decipherment of the utopian impulses of these same still ideological texts.[6]

In short, Jameson's complex construct of ideological critique is itself, quite Althusserian. One of the other implications of that, for his thinking, is that "active lucidity about ourselves", to use his terminology, is not possible, for the individual human subject. Accordingly, earlier in the same text, he took pains to dismiss the possibility of a:

> … vision of a moment in which the individual subject would be somehow fully conscious of his or her determination by class and would be able to square the circle of ideological conditioning by sheer lucidity and the taking of thought…. In the Marxian system, only a collective unity—whether that of a particular class, the proletariat, or of its "organ of consciousness"—the political party—can achieve this transparency; the individual subject is always positioned within the social totality….[7]

As this citation makes clear, at least as of 1981, Jameson's Marxism followed party lines rather strictly.

More recently, I came also to understand the—perhaps even greater—magnitude of the influence of Jameson on Reinhold Martin, historian and theorist at Columbia University. Martin recently published a collection of essays titled, significantly enough, *Utopia's Ghost: Architecture and Postmodernism, Again.* The collection includes a range of texts on various aspects of architecture over the past half-century, a number of which have been previously published. Among the best, in my view, are those devoted to an account of two head office projects for the American multi-national corporation Union Carbide; the first one on Park Avenue in downtown Manhattan (from 1960, and designed by Skidmore Owings and Merrill), and the second in the forested hills of suburban Connecticut (from 1982, and designed by Roche-Dinkeloo). These two are then compared and contrasted with the Union Carbide industrial facility in Bhopal, India, that leaked lethal fumes with catastrophic consequences for thousands of its workers and for surrounding residents in 1984.[8] Less compelling for me—and here I have to confess to an intellectual conflict of interest—was an essay on the effort of architectural theorists in the late 1960s and 1970s to employ a linguistic analogy to expand and reinvigorate techniques of analysis of architectural form in the social world, an effort in which I was an active participant, as the co-editor, with Charles Jencks, of the 1969 anthology *Meaning in Architecture*.[9]

But most significant for me, was my gradual realisation, as I worked my way through Martin's book, of the extent to which his critical method followed that of Jameson. It was not the form of "ideology critique" which was disconcerting. After all, Jameson, Hays, Martin and I all, to a greater or a lesser degree, belong to the intellectual tradition of the critical theory that had first been formulated in the 1920s by the revisionist Marxist Frankfurt School, including such figures as Theodor Adorno and Max Horkheimer. Indeed, reading Martin's text I realised how useful a Jamesonian model of such critique had been for him in previous books, as well as in the impressive account of the Union Carbide projects in this one. But in this text, Martin goes further, and takes over Jameson's argument for the necessity of retaining the construct of Utopia as well. Accordingly, he complains that "in architecture, as elsewhere, the active 'unthinking' of Utopia is among those practices that distinguish Postmodernism from Modernism."[10]

Indeed, Martin adopts Jameson's position that Postmodernism entails a near-universal proscription against utopian thought and speculation.[11]

And this stance of his leads him so far into Jamesonian negation that in the concluding chapter of the book, he is impelled to disparage a statement made by Mathias Ungers, Rem Koolhaas, Peter Riemann, Hans Kollhof and Arthur Ovaska, about their 1977 project for Cities within the City in Berlin. The statement of the authors of the project reads: "There is no need for a new Utopia, but rather to create a better reality."[12] This conclusion of theirs does not satisfy the all-too-Jamesonian critic Martin, and he reprimands them for it.

In short, Martin's adoption of Jameson's concept of Utopia places him in even greater debt to Jameson than Hays' reading of Jameson's concept of "ideology" does. Now Hays and Martin are respectively involved in two of the most influential doctoral programmes in architecture in North America. That one of the two of them—Martin—should rely so consequentially on Jameson's—in my view, problematic—concept of Utopia has given me concern.

It is time in this text for me to articulate this concern explicitly. Throughout much political theory from the nineteenth century all the way to the present, one finds reference to a political conception that lies mid-way between the grip of capital on consciousness on the one hand, and the version of Utopia as a posited alternative on the other. The political conception in question is human agency. As my citations from Jameson above make clear, his model of ideology, and his dismissal of the possibility of "lucidity" on the part of the individual human subject, do not leave much room for agency.

For my part, I derive my conception of agency from the political thought of Hannah Arendt, in whose writings it is given expression as "action". As she put it: "To act, in its most general sense, means to take an initiative… to set something in motion…" and "the fact that man is capable of action means that the unexpected can be expected of him, that he is able to perform what is infinitely improbable."[13]

But Arendt is not my sole source. In a 2011 issue of the *London Review of Books*, the Cambridge political scientist David Runciman referred to the "German social democrat Eduard Bernstein, who said at the end of the nineteenth century: 'The movement is everything; the ends are nothing'".

"Bernstein's remarks", said Runciman:

… were directed at his Marxist colleagues, who liked to explain how wonderful things would be after the revolution and made no attempt to organise for justice in the meantime. Bernstein thought that they were frightened of democracy because it was too messy, and as a result were squandering the chance to improve people's lives, preferring to wait for a future that would never arrive.[14]

Now it is beyond the scope of this text of mine to fully articulate the varied nuances of emphasis between different strands of revisionist Marxist theory in respect to agency, from the late nineteenth century to the present—most especially in the wake of the deliberations of the various protagonists of the Frankfurt School.

Still, it does seem to me that any intellectually adequate political/theoretical stance for our times must necessarily take greater, and more considered account of the phenomenon of "agency" than Jameson's ideology critique is able to do. Indeed, it is possible even to detect some notes of equivocation in Jameson's own writings in this regard. Notwithstanding the obduracy of the passages from "the Political Unconscious" that I have cited above, in his subsequent text "Architecture and the Critique of Ideology", he can be seen to ruminate in regard to the relative degrees of local political success attained by so-called "red communes", such as existed in the 1970s in certain Italian cities such as Bologna. In that text, he entertains the possibility that some promising manifestations of a new political order might even be possible in such "enclaves", within the overall hegemonic capitalist system. Action, then, might have been a conceivable possibility for the citizens of such communes. Jameson even concludes that essay with a conciliatory nod to political speculations of Henri Lefebvre and Antonio Gramsci that are considerably more open to consideration of "agency" than his own are.[15] But even here, he dismisses in a footnote "the idea that people will rebuild their own dwellings as they go along"—a dismissal that is very consequential, given the direction of the argument that this text of mine is about to take.[16]

For my part, I would say that it is not difficult to draw a line of intellectual lineage distinct from that of Jameson, this one from Bernstein to Rosa Luxemburg to Hannah Arendt. Indeed, it is interesting to note that Arendt herself had a mid-career change of heart in regard to the possibilities of "agency" in human affairs. In her magisterial survey of the late 1940s, *The Origins of Totalitarianism* she deduced that political action had been precluded in Nazi Germany and in the Stalinist Soviet Union—not, she thought, by economic hegemony as with Jameson—but rather by the sheer depth and comprehensiveness of political control of subject populations.[17] As a result of this conviction of hers, she was caught off-guard by the 1953 rebellion of workers against the Ulbricht regime in East Germany, and by the 1956 revolt against Soviet occupation in Hungary. In recognition of these unexpected developments, she shifted her intellectual position, and propounded a view of the potential of "action" in her next book: *The Human Condition* of 1958, which is significantly more optimistic than that expressed in the *The Origins of Totalitarianism*.

What is more, this Arendtian commentary of mine leads me in turn directly to the overall theme of this collection of essays, to a critique of the very idea of the possibility of a "post-political" condition for architecture in our time. In this regard, we may note how strenuously Arendt's interpreter Bonnie Honig has insisted that:

> Arendt's politics takes seriously Nietzche's claim that 'the will to a system is a lack of integrity', a claim that rests on the supposition that the contingent world is partly resistant to (never simply completed and enabled by) attempts to order it…. For Arendt, these spaces of worldly and contingent resistance to systematisation are the spaces of politics…. The mark of a true politics, for Arendt, is resistibility and a perpetual openness to the possibility of refounding…. Like Nietzche, she admires the agora, and seeks to protect it from closure, from domination by any one idea, truth, essence, individual or institution.[18]

And it is not at all difficult to hear the echo of such remarks in the insistence of Chantal Mouffe, expressed in her 1993 collection *The Return of the Political* that:

> … we have to see parliament not as the place where one accedes to truth, but as the place where it ought to be possible to reach agreement on a reasonable solution through argument and persuasion, while being aware that such agreement can never be definitive, but that it should always be open to challenge.[19]

And I do not doubt that Mouffe would acknowledge this conviction of hers to be an Arendtian one.

Nonetheless, it is my view that it is not even necessary to undertake such a comprehensive historical explanation, in order to be able to outline some of the problematic implications of such a relative indifference as Jameson's, to the phenomenon of agency in the fields of architecture and urban theory. To begin to do so, let me refer you to a recent publication by the former European Bureau Chief of the Toronto newspaper *The Globe and Mail*: Doug Saunders. Three years ago, Saunders published a book—it was the winner of the 2010–2011 Donner Prize for the best Canadian book on public affairs—and was cited in a *New York Times* review

An image showing a late stage of maturation of an Istanbul gecekondu when multi-storey apartment buildings have begun to be erected there.

as arguably the most important book on urban affairs since Jane Jacobs' *Death and Life of Great American Cities*. It is entitled *Arrival City*.[20] It is an account of the ongoing current migration of some five million persons per month from around the world, from their rural villages and agricultural settlements, to one of some 20 urban settlements that Saunders names "arrival" cities: major metropolises in a number of countries around the world. And upon their arrival there, of course, one of the frequent first actions of these people is to construct dwellings for themselves—as likely as not even on land over which they have no control. As Saunders points out, these settlements have had many names: "slums, favelas, bustees, bidonvilles, ashwaiyyat, shantytowns, kampongs, urban villages, gecekondular, and barrios". Notwithstanding the fact that many of these terms are pejorative ones, Saunders argues that the new neighbourhoods to which they refer, are instead, a triumph of contemporary social and political energy and optimism. They provide their inhabitants with new economic—and potential educational— opportunities, and they expand the economies of the larger urban conurbations of which they form a part. Through remittances, the new arrivals constitute a

major source of financial support for members of their families back home. For example, Saunders indicates in his book that rural Bangladesh receives almost $11 billion every year from overseas migrants and their descendants—this being a sum equivalent to all of Bangladesh's annual export earnings.

It is difficult to remember how recently it is that such informal settlements attained any kind of normative status in the world. Up until very recently, it was common for governments in countries in which they were being created, simply to raze them before their political status could be consolidated. Indeed, as often as not, the rhetoric of Heroic Period Modern architecture was invoked to legitimise such governmental destruction. Three important books were published in the 1970s to challenge such high-handed governmental activities, as well as the Modernist rhetoric that was then legitimating them, but they all seem to have been largely forgotten. They are *Architecture versus Housing* by Martin Pawley, from 1971; John Turner and Robert Fichter's *Freedom to Build* also from 1971, and Turner's own *Housing by People* from 1976.[21]

To be sure, not all of Saunders' arrival cities are characterised by the extensive presence of informal settlements. For example, Toronto is one of them, and the area of Toronto on which he focuses is Thorncliffe Park, an inner suburb comprising mostly existing mid and high-rise buildings which, over the years, have gradually come to be inhabited by new arrivals from South-East Asia.

Saunders goes on to acknowledge the fact that upon their arrival in the new city, the migrants are in need of assistance. Some of this comes from family members and friends who are already there, but governmental support is also important. Saunders goes to considerable lengths to evaluate the various governmental responses to the arrival of such migrants in their cities, and notes the wide range of successful and failed strategies in this regard. The successes are apparent in such arrival cities as Istanbul, Rio de Janeiro and Toronto, and unsuccessful ones in those such as Berlin and Paris. Not only are social support systems important, municipal infrastructures—water supply, sewers, electricity, movement systems—need to be incorporated into such settlements, after the fact.

One of the most important factors in the successful maturation of such settlements is security of tenure for their occupants. After all, most of the buildings there have been constructed with considerable effort by their occupants. Yet the occupants do not usually hold title in any form to the land on which they have constructed them—at least not in the first instance. In many of the settlements whose recent improvements have been deemed to produce social and political success, a key factor has been the establishment of a form of security of tenure—sometimes outright property ownership—and sometimes a lesser form of long-term security. It is, of course, precisely this security that encourages the residents of such districts to continue to make improvements to their homes. In the striking case of Istanbul, this has even led over time to a form of gentrification of some such areas, on the part of second and third generation inhabitants.

Now I would argue that one essential way to describe this phenomenon of migration and or urban resettlement, would be to call it as dramatic a manifestation of human "agency" that it is possible to imagine. These persons may not have succeeded in achieving a perfectly "active lucidity"—to use Jameson's term—in respect to the overall conditions of their existence. But they have surely succeeded in transforming their lives, as well as the lives of the members of their families, both those who have come with them to the "arrival city", as well as in the original

settlement back home, and, indeed, they have rebuilt their own dwellings as they have gone along.

But this is not the only aspect of this phenomenon that puts me in mind of historic tenets of political theory. After all, the fact that security of tenure for these persons is so important for their futures, puts me inevitably in mind again of Hannah Arendt, and of her lesson from the seventeenth-century British philosopher John Locke in regard to the key relationship of property ownership to citizenship. For Locke, property ownership was an essential premise of citizenship. For Arendt, not quite so, but she was all too aware of the profound Lockean implications of this relationship for citizenship, and therefore for "agency" as well. Linking Saunders' arguments to those of Arendt, we may point to the work of the South American economist Hernando de Soto, who has argued that a key tool needed by the rural-to-urban migrants of that continent to prosper in their new urban settings, is access to a secure form of title to their assets— primarily land—that would provide such long-term security of tenure for them.[22]

Let me now turn to another strand of the overall argument I am attempting to construct. In the history of Modern architecture in the first half of the twentieth century, we all know well enough the implicitly socialist orientation of the architectural projects and urban proposals of the Heroic Period of Modern architecture— at least in its dominant, northern European modality. And one of the most important—although rarely discussed— aspects of that socialist orientation, was the expectation of the radical reduction of the extent of private property in cities, and the control of most urban land—if not by the municipality, then at least by collective entities of various kinds: co-operatives, non-profit organisations, etc. It is only the most blatant example of this expectation that is evident in Le Corbusier's famous proposals for the rebuilding of Paris: the Plan Voisin, and the City for Three Million. A more subtle case, to my mind, is the view of architects Candilis-Josic-Woods—as late as 1964—that their competition entry for the rebuilding of part of war-damaged downtown Frankfurt, would prove to be implementable on account of their hope that the entire parcel of land on which the project was proposed to be located would be owned by the city. As Shadrach Woods put it:

Such a development, of course, would require some revision of existing laws governing public and private property, but the law is essentially reactive, and enough precedents exist to cover most of the cases involved here. Obviously the scheme would work best if it were all in public ownership.[23]

Now, despite the fact that such expectations on the part of contemporary architects in most of the world are now quite obsolete, one sees little acknowledgement of this reality in present day architectural and urban theory. Nor is there any of the separate, but perhaps even more important, question of the still relatively highly differentiated pattern of the ownership of urban land in much of our contemporary world.[24]

A recent visit to Japan prompted me to develop a growing interest in this matter of differentiated patterns of ownership of urban land. A Japanese architect colleague, Yoshiharu Tsukamoto has reported to me, that he has discovered, as part of his own urban research on the city of Tokyo, that there are some 1.8 million individual parcels of urban land, and that these parcels are owned by no fewer than 1.7 million private individuals or groups.[25] It is clear to me that this significant statistic explains a good deal about the urban form of Tokyo. In the book that made them famous as urban theorists: *Made in Tokyo*, for example, Tsukamoto and his partner Momoyo Kaijima (together with a colleague, Junzo Kuroda) carefully documented the Tokyo tradition of devising very complex mixed-use buildings, or mixed-use hybrids of buildings and infrastructure combined.[26] But in their more recent publication, *Pet Architecture*, they hiked the political and economic stakes of the debate further still, and documented an extensive series of very small buildings erected on very small parcels of land throughout Tokyo.[27]

Now there is no doubt in my mind that both these extraordinary and unique phenomena—the multi-use building complexes and the very small buildings on very small parcels—contribute substantially to the particular urban character of Tokyo. Indeed, arguments have been made that they even define the form of urban redevelopment, over time, in that city. For example, in his recent book *Emerging Architectural Territories in East Asian Cities*, Peter Rowe has argued that during his term of office, Prime Minister Koizumi saw this pattern of land ownership as an impediment to the—in his view—necessary modernisation of Tokyo's business districts.[28] As a consequence, Koizumi introduced policies at the political level of the national government to counter local municipal opposition, and

A small-scale "pencil building" in Kagurazaka, opposite the apartment we occupied on a visit to Tokyo.

to encourage such massively large-scale redevelopments in Tokyo as Shiodome, Roppongi Hills and Tokyo Midtown. As it happened, Shiodome and Tokyo Midtown were built on exceptionally large parcels that were already in unified ownership—some of them even public ownership. Accordingly, it was not difficult for the national government to facilitate their redevelopment. On the other hand, Rowe reports that the Mori Building Corporation had to deal with 600 different owners, in order to assemble the land for its Roppongi Hills project, and even then, had to agree to make some 400 out of the total 600, financial partners in the development project, in order to secure their cooperation in making their land available for it. It is my sense that Tsukamoto and Kaijima would see Roppongi Hills as problematically atypical for Tokyo, and that they continue to be more interested in the ongoing contemporary evolution of the fine grain of micro-development that more commonly typifies that city.[29] I show here two astonishing examples of this grain that I came upon myself in Tokyo. First is a so-called "pencil building" erected on a small parcel opposite the apartment we were staying in Kagurazaka. Second, is an even more remarkable one I

A larger-scale "pencil building" in Ginza.

discovered wandering around Ginza: a modern tower roughly 20 storeys high, sitting on a parcel of land that is roughly eight metres or 25 feet square.

Now I would speculate that the fine-grained pattern of land-ownership that still—notwithstanding Koizumi's interventions—largely typifies Tokyo is one that bears relation to the same political-economic circumstances that typify the successfully matured *favela*, as we have seen it evolve in other parts of the world. We have, for example, already seen that the *gecekondu* in Istanbul that has now reached a sufficient plateau of maturity that multi-storey apartments are beginning to be erected in it. In short, I would argue that "political agency" can, among other things, be seen to be manifest in the forms of urban development that are typical of cities with a highly differentiated pattern of ownership of land. Indeed, a Toronto land economist known for his strongly conservative political views once observed to me in conversation that emergent urban centres in the periphery of Toronto whose land holdings were broadly controlled by large development corporations tended to grow much more slowly, and in a much less urbane fashion, that those with more differentiated patterns of ownership of developable land. Two Toronto area examples demonstrate this.

In the first, Mississauga city centre, the very centre of the centre is the very large Square One shopping centre, occupying a vast territory accommodating only very low buildings and surface parking lots. The second case is North York city centre, an extensive stretch of high-density urban redevelopment along North Yonge Street in Toronto, encouraged over many years by the former Mayor, Mel Lastman. The latter case exhibits a far more urbane density of development than the former.

On the plane of political theory then, we might conclude that the pattern of differentiated ownership of land—in such cities as exhibit a high degree of it—constitutes a sort of "deep urban structure" that facilitates "agency" in respect to small-to-medium-scale historic urban transformation, gradually over time. Indeed, it is possible to see the comprehensive public ownership of urban land foreseen by the architecture and urban ideas of the Heroic Period, and the large-scale corporate control of large areas of urban land in the contemporary world—such as is increasingly typical in advanced contemporary cities—as two sides of the same problematic coin. In neither case does a real property 'market' exist. Only a relatively highly differentiated pattern of land ownership—such as in Tokyo—or at least long-term land tenure—can create that.

So I would argue then that from the *favelas* of the contemporary world to the centre of Tokyo, "agency" and the evolving forms of urban development that can be seen in both, are closely interrelated phenomena. What is more, they are phenomena that cannot, in my view, readily be captured by a Jamesonian schema that manifests little interest in them. And not only that, the neo-avant-garde that rose from the ashes of the Postmodernism that so troubles Reinhold Martin, tends to identify, as he also does, with the utopian aspirations of Heroic Period Modernism. As I have already pointed out, one of the key features of that Modernism was an assumption of the comprehensive availability of urban land for Modernist urban projects, and an indifference to the characteristic extant urban phenomenon of differentiated land ownership. The fact that this is such a basic premise of the period the avant-garde is so nostalgic about, has had a very curious and troubling consequence. Indeed, even though the neo-avant-garde has most typically behaved very apolitically, it has always been ready to make quite sweeping urban design gestures that ignore—or failing that, pretend to ignore—the circumstantial contemporary realities of differentiated ownership of urban land.

And not only that. At the same time that this is true, this neo-avant-garde's most successfully implemented projects have depended on the support of clients that are such large corporations as Reinhold Martin has frequently criticised, or hegemonic states, be they petro-states, or authoritarian ones. So it strikes me as more that a passing political irony that the absence of "agency" from Jameson's own thinking has contributed in a "trickle-down" fashion to the apolitical readiness of the neo-avant-garde to work with some of the most hegemonic political entities that exist in the contemporary world, in order to realise their projects. In this regard, it has taken an iconoclastic, renegade, sometime avantgardist like Rem Koolhaas to observe, as he did in his 2011 Cronocaos exhibition at the New Museum in New York City, that as compared with their Heroic Period predecessors, the participants in present-day architecture's star system "have traded power for celebrity".

In conclusion, I would like to refer back to the reference made by the *New York Times* reviewer of the Saunders book that compared it to Jane Jacobs' *Death and Life of Great American Cities*. For, of course, a few years after she published *Death and Life*, Jacobs and her family moved to Toronto, where she spent the rest of her career. This makes her a fellow Torontonian with Saunders himself. The first book Jacobs published after *Death and Life*, *The Economy of Cities*, was still written in New York.[30] But all the publications that followed—ones that were increasingly devoted to considerations of urban economics, reflected her experience of Toronto. Already, in *The Economy of Cities*, she had articulated her innovative ideas in regard to "import replacement" as the key generator of urban growth, as well as the idea that the formation of cities actually historically precedes that of agricultural hinterlands. But in her next book *Cities and the Wealth of Nations*, she went further still, and attempted to demonstrate that city regions—not nation states—were the actual drivers of regional economies throughout the world.[31] Later still, she grew interested in the benefits to be derived from the loosening of municipal regulatory frameworks, so as to facilitate local enterprise; all these later ideas were developed by her during her second career in Toronto.

It is interesting to note that it is not difficult to track analogies between a number of her arguments about urban form, and Saunders' ones about arrival cities. They share a conviction that cities are problems in organised complexity, as well as an interest in incremental—as opposed to wholesale—forms of development. Remember Jacob's fateful comparison in *Death and Life* between "gradual money" and "cataclysmic money", the first capable of generating much urban benefit, and the latter a great danger. This speculative comparison of mine has caused me to wonder whether I might be seeing a Toronto school of urban and economic thought coming into being. For it also has occurred to me in preparing this text, that one might add one more name to the list of Torontonians with consequential things to say in these matters. Naomi Klein has no particular interest in urban issues *per se*—let alone architectural ones. But her recent publication: *The Shock Doctrine: The Rise of Disaster Capitalism* spans much of the same recent historical period that Jameson's recent publications focusing on culture and politics have also done. Of course, *The Shock Doctrine* cannot be described methodologically as cultural critique. It reads more like a political detective story, in which we see unfold the development of international economic policy over the past half century: who exactly did what, where, when and how.[32]

Klein is not a Marxist. In *The Shock Doctrine*, she makes explicit her belief in a market economy. But she is clearly a formidable critic of late capitalism—especially of its international financial institutions. But her methodological preference, in the framing of historical description, is to identify individuals wielding economic power, and to track their fateful decision making over the period of her investigation. So she names the Chicago School economists led by Milton Friedman, who, in her view, have been responsible for so much of the gravely damaging neo-conservative economic policy of the past 35 years—not to mention of the series of dictatorships with whom they forged alliances, and the political crises in many other countries, that they exploited to implement those policies—whether the citizens of the countries in question were in favour of them or not. She also salutes the courage of the small number of individuals who resisted it—sometimes with unexpected success, such as the Prime Minister of Malaysia Mahathir Mohamad in 1997, and the President of Argentina, Nestor Kirchner in 2007, both of whom adamantly refused to obey dictates of the International Monetary Fund, when presented with them.

Such is the power of "agency" in the hands of individuals, even in the darkest episodes of contemporary history. In my opinion, it behooves we architects and urbanists to take much more active account of the profound potential implications of its actuality in our ongoing architectural and urban work.

1   Jameson, Fredric, "Architecture and the Critique of Ideology", Hays, K Michael ed, *Architecture Theory Since 1968*, Cambridge MA: MIT Press, 1998.

2   For an insightful account of the influence of Jameson on Hays, see Martin, Louis, "Fredric Jameson and Critical Architecture" in Lahiji, Nadir, *The Political Unconscious of Architecture,* Surrey: Ashgate Farnham, 2011.

3   Jameson, Fredric, *The Political Unconscious*, Cornell University Press, 1981.

4   According to Althusser, not only can "ideology" not be transcended or overcome by an individual subject to it, it even comprises a kind of world-view for that individual that—for better or for ill—enables him or her to make his or her way in the world. It is, in short, a rather phenomenological version of the idea of ideology that Althusser takes over from Marx.

5   Jameson, *The Political Unconscious*, p 291.

6   Jameson, *The Political Unconscious*, p 296.

7   Jameson, *The Political Unconscious*, p 283.

8   Martin, Reinhold, *Utopia's Ghost: Architecture and Postmodernism Again*, Minneapolis: University of Minnesota Press, 2010, pp 129–139.

9   Jencks, Charles and Baird, George eds, *Meaning in Architecture*, London: Barrie & Rockcliffe The Cresset Press, 1969.

10 Martin, *Utopia's Ghost*, p xiv.

11 Martin, *Utopia's Ghost*, p xxi.

12 Martin, *Utopia's Ghost*, p 174.

13 Arendt, Hannah, *The Human Condition*, New York: Doubleday Anchor Books, 1959, pp 157–158.

14 Runciman, David, "Socialism in One Country", *London Review of Books*, vol 33, no 15, 28 July 2011, p 12.

15 Jameson in Hays, *Architecture and The Critique of Idealogy*, pp 453 and 461.

16 Jameson in Hays, *Architecture and The Critique of Idealogy*, p 461.

17 Arendt, Hannah, *The Origins of Totalitarianism*, New York: Harcourt Brace Jovanovich, 1951.

18 Honig, Bonnie, *Political Theory and the Displacement of Politics*, Ithaca and London: Cornell University Press, 1993, p 116.

19 Mouffe, Chantal, *The Return of the Political*, London New York: Verso, 1993, p 130.

20 Saunders, Doug, *Arrival City*, New York: Pantheon, 2011.

21 These are Pawley, Martin, *Architecture Versus Housing*; New York and Washington: Praeger Publishers, 1971; Turner, John F C, and Robert Fichter, eds, *Freedom to Build*; New York: Macmillan Company, 1971; and Turner, John F C, *Housing by People*, London: Marion Boyars, 1976. In my own *The Space of Appearance*, of 1995, I flagged the importance of these early texts, but like them, my own argument has been largely ignored.

22 de Soto, Hernando, *The Mystery of Capital*, New York: Basic Books, 2000.

23 Woods, Shadrach, *The Man in the Street*, Harmondsworth: Penguin Books, 1975, pp 124–129.

24 There are some intriguing anomalies to be considered in this discussion. In London, England, for example, a substantial portion of the land of the West End is held by a number of aristocratic families, who rent it to residents on long-term leases: hence the term "leasehold tenure" so common there. Still, since the leases in question run as long as 99 years, they appear to offer significant security of tenure to their occupants. The case of Hong Kong—interestingly enough, a former British colony—is also food for thought. There, much of the land on Hong Kong Island is owned by the municipality, which leases it to occupants on a long-term basis. This is similar to an arrangement operative in Amsterdam, where the land leases run for 50 years.

25 Yoshiharu Tsukamoto and his partner Momoyo Kaijima in the Tokyo architectural practice Atelier Bow Wow are the only Japanese architects I am aware of who are equally as interested in the urban form of Tokyo, as they are in the particular architecture of the individual buildings that make it up. For example, see Fujimori, Terunobu, "The Origins of Atelier Bow Wow's Gaze" in Tsukamoto, Yoshiharu and Kaijima Momoyo, *Behaviorology*, Rizzoli: New York, 2010. Tsukamoto and Kaijima are also interesting for another feature of their publications: their commitment to deal with urban and architectural issues in a fashion which is assimilable by a lay audience.

26 Kaijima, Momoyo, Junzo Kuroda and Yoshiharu Tsukamoto, *Made in Tokyo*, Japan: Kajima Institute Publishing Company, 2001.

27 Tsukamoto, Yoshiharu, and Momoyo Kaijima, *Pet Architecture*, Amsterdam: World Photo Press, 2002.

28 Rowe, Peter G, *Emerging Architectural Territories in East Asian Cities*, Basel: Birkhauser, 2011, pp 116–129.

29 It is not insignificant, in my view, that Rem Koolhaas has mounted a such a strong attack on the Roppongi Hills project. See "Roppongi Hills" in *Content*, Koln: Taschen, 2004, pp 508–509.

30 Jacobs, Jane, *The Economy of Cities*, New York: Random House, 1969.

31 Jacobs, Jane, *Cites and the Wealth of Nations*, New York: Random House, 1984.

32 Klein, Naomi, *The Shock Doctrine: The Rise of Disaster Capitalism*, Toronto: Vintage Canada, 2008.

Critical Biography

Over the years, circumstances have prompted me to write about particular individuals who have made notable contributions to architecture, urbanism and theory in our time. The following section includes texts on four of them.

Part 1:
Rem Koolhaas, OMA, and some other Dutch Architects

In the early years following my 1967 return to Toronto, I made frequent trips back to London, not least to make regular guest appearances in the curriculum of the new Master's Programme in Architectural History and Theory that Joseph Rykwert had launched in the new Department of Art at the University of Essex. By this time, my friend Charles Jencks and his then-wife Pamela occupied a large apartment in Wimpole Street, and I became a regular beneficiary of their hospitality, as a house guest there.

During one of those visits, Jencks indicated to me that he wanted to introduce me to a new friend of his, a young Dutch student at the Architectural Association School, called Rem Koolhaas. On account of the arguments I had made in "*La Dimension Amoureuse*", Jencks looked forward with some anticipation to strenuous theoretical arguments between myself and Koolhaas. But despite the differences in our respective positions, such arguments never really materialised, and indeed, I became friends with both Koolhaas and his wife, Madelon Vriesendorp. So much so that on another, later trip to London, I found myself arriving there just as Koolhaas and his then OMA partners were putting the finishing touches to a special issue of the magazine *Architectural Design*, focusing on their practice. Koolhaas and the *AD* editor of the time, Haig Beck made a sudden—and spontaneous—invitation to me to make a contribution to the issue, even though it was about to go to press.

Les Extrêmes Qui se Touchent, 1977

I accepted the invitation, and literally overnight, composed this text. In response to my effort, Vriesendorp, over a second night, made the drawing of two athletes "eating oysters naked with boxing gloves" that accompanied it. Only later did I come to realise that the witty Vriesendorp drawing was actually of Koolhaas and me.

Notwithstanding the haste with which it was prepared—Peter Eisenman later told me that he would never accept such a risky, rapid writing assignment—the text has proven a rather durable one. Pier Vittorio Aureli, for example, has called it the most prescient of all the early texts on OMA. That having been said, it remains true that in my haste, and due to my shaky command of the French language, I mistakenly wrote for my title the phrase "*extremes qui se touchent*", as opposed to "*extremes qui touchent*" thus unintentionally evoking masturbation.

In my view, the work of OMA constitutes one of current architecture's most provocative revisionisms. To show this, one needs only to set OMA's position against two or three other important current tendencies. Colin Rowe, for example, has in his introduction to *Five Architects* conceded the contemporary irrelevance of the social programmes of Modern architecture, and pondered for us, with mixed feelings, the residue of forms—the "physique" without the "morale". OMA, on the other hand, argues instead that it is the forms that are moribund; and elaborates a new formal vocabulary around precisely those "social condensers" which once formed the core of Modern architecture's programme.

To take another important case, the current status of the reputation of Mies van der Rohe—surely, except for Ludwig Hilberseimer, today's least fashionable modern architect. Figures such as Van Eyck and Rykwert would deplore his influence—even Arthur Drexler, his earliest American promoter, now speaks of Charles Garnier! Yet OMA reasserts the pertinence of the work of Mies—and the grid, the curtain wall and the sheer plane surface all make their significant reappearance in OMA's work.

Or again, Robert Venturi's plea for a less ambitious, but more effacing Modern architecture than that practiced by his predecessors. To this, OMA responds by positing the continuing relevance of "visionary" projects.

By virtue of these oppositions alone, OMA's position must be regarded as significant. It is a highly complex revisionism, bringing together such a diverse set of heroes as the aforementioned Mies van der Rohe, together with Ivan Léonidov, Salvador Dalí, John Portman, Wallace Harrison and Norman Bel Geddes. What is more, it also involves, in a more intimate way, the concepts of OMA's sometime mentor/sometime collaborator, O M Ungers.

All of this produces an architecture of a nature which is, for today, quite astonishing. For it turns out to be visionary at the same time as it is implementable; surreal at the same time as it is commonsensical; puritanical at the same time as it is luxurious. And it possesses a 'revolutionary' character which lies precisely in its untypical—for a Modern architecture—loyalty to a historical tradition of the metropolis.

To be sure, the demeanour of *enfants terribles* plays a certain exorcist role in OMA's polemic. For example, insofar as it lauds Léonidov's Heroism, and

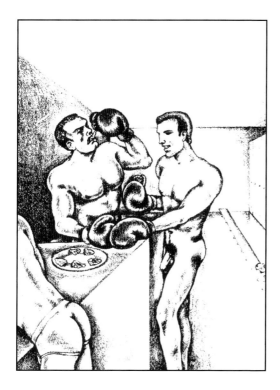

Cover image from *Architectural Design*, volume 47, no 5, showing Vriesendorp's drawing, *Oysters With Boxing Gloves, Naked*.

Modern architecture since the Heroic Period. Yet at the same time that all of this is true, the projects involve no *tours-de-force* of engineering, no "mile-high" skyscrapers, no transformations of extant urban patterns of public and private space. From time to time, buildings span streets (Hotel Sphinx) or bridges become buildings (Welfare Palace Hotel) in a fashion which would necessitate the entrepreneurial initiative of a Haussman or a Robert Moses, but save for these exceptional cases, these iridescent drawings depict eminently—if surprisingly—buildable buildings.

Second, an architecture which is surreal at the same time as it is commonsensical. In its most elaborate, and most voluptuous details, OMA's work indeed evokes a "secret life of buildings". Yet, following Art Deco precedents, such details tend to concern quite specifically the tops, bottoms and edges of buildings. The principal volumes in between these limits in most cases display a quite evidently "dumb and ordinary" neutrality which is not exceeded by that of Robert Venturi's Guild House or Brighton Beach competition entry. So commonsensical in fact are these forms, that it may be surmised how the projects if built, would be regarded as less exceptionable by the lay public, than they would be by informed architects.

Third, as architecture which is puritanical at the same time as it is luxurious. This is perhaps the most fascinating of OMA's polarities. On the face of it, the projects seem to offer up the most hedonistic of social possibilities—"eating oysters, naked, with boxing gloves" may serve as a definitive example. Yet it is significant to what degree the programmatic roles of OMA's social condensers are athletic and/or sublimating, rather than sedentary or gratificatory. Indeed, so true is this, that I find it difficult to see OMA's commitment to the metropolitan tradition revolving around flaneurs as originally conceived by Walter Benjamin. Rather, I see OMA's metropolitans, as they proceed serenely through architectural spaces of intense drama and luxury, as somewhat Corbusian Supermen, nonchalant and daring, but somewhat reserved, in their ongoing confrontation with metropolitan destiny.

Last, an architecture which is revolutionary at the same times as it is evolutionist. In its definitive commitment to the metropolis, OMA announces what must be seen as a clear *caesura* in the history of Modern architecture. For there is nowhere in the orthodox history even a leaning towards such a heretical sympathy. (Even OMA's hero, Léonidov, did not accept

spurns Le Corbusier's, the polemic relies for its impact on the relative unfamiliarity of the former, as opposed to the latter. Insofar as it raises to the level of heroes such contentious figures as Harrison and Portman, the OMA polemic, in large measure, strives merely to *épaler*—not this time *les bourgeois*—but rather, today's complacent arbiters of respectable taste. Insofar as it reveals for our astonishment "the secret life of buildings", it lastly demonstrates the iconic barrenness of most contemporary architectural debate.

But even allowing for a certain rhetorical tone—after all, Koolhaas has himself advised us of the methodological implications of the paranoid critical method—there remains for more serious, and more substantial examination, the fascinating set of conceptual polarities outlined above, manifested in the work Itself.

Let us take them in turn. First, an architecture which is visionary at the same time as it is implementable. OMA's work presents an image of the metropolis which is itself, indisputably visionary. Its luminous profiles and gleaming towers both represent an 'ideal' city. What is more, the projects propose the most elaborately disposed and equipped "social condensers" seen in congestion as the hallmark of modern urbanity.) But OMA has not only made an unprecedented commitment to the principle of the metropolis; it has also given urban form to that commitment, through its absorption in the matter of urban morphologies characteristic of, and appropriate to, the metropolis itself. (It is, of course, not possible to discuss morphologies without citing the name of Ungers, and I can only assume that this input to the work of OMA is Unger's major contribution—even to the projects in which he is not an active collaborator.) But of course, insofar as it is morphological in urban intention, OMA's work is necessarily evolutionist, since no morphological enterprise can proceed independently of a grasp of the generic form of any given urban entity. Hence, as a morphological commitment to the metropolis, the work of OMA is revolutionary and evolutionist at the same time.

As I have said, all these aspects of their work can be interpreted as a highly significant revisionism. Yet it remains to be seen, what the ongoing impact will be of OMA's polemic on OMA's production. For it is here that certain major reservations arise, for me, in respect to the possibility of sustaining all the polarities addressed. When they succeed, OMA's synthesisations of polarities manifest a liberating and exhilarating potential. We may take as dramatic, existential instances two of which—typically enough—are concerned with swimming. In the project for a house in Miami there is proposed the double diving board, from which one can choose either the salt water of the ocean, or the fresh water of the pool. In the Hotel Sphinx, the tower swimming pool extends at one point right to the edge of the building, so that it is possible, from the water, to savour the view of the metropolitan skyline beyond.

In these exuberant circumstances, the heroic optimism of OMA's vision is precisely crystallised. Yet there is a rhetorical counter-current to the work, in which the synthesis attempted remains unfulfilled. One may, for instance, cite the precedents of Electric Bathing, and Barrels of Love, in which the hedonistic gratifications are so automatistic in nature, and so unsublimated, as to be unconvincingly behaviourist. Or, alternatively, despite the relentlessly outward looking orientation of all the facilities of the Hotel Sphinx—to such a degree that the view itself risks absorption into the cycle of consumption. In this perspective, we may return to the Story of the Pool, which—swimming again—arises out of its own paradoxical polarity of swimming in a floating pool. In the heroic—if fortuitous—locomotion of the constructivist architect/ lifeguards, "hedonism" and "puritanical rigour"—to employ Koolhaas' own terms—really do converge, and the implications astonish. Yet in the rhetorical invocations of metropolitanism, these convergences are not always sustained, and spectres of legitimated kitsch, and soulless gratification re-emerge.

Still, if in all of the work of OMA, the paradoxical extremes of experience appropriated do not always touch, I, for one, am nevertheless prepared to wait. For, with such ambitious syntheses as are attempted here, it will be worth it.

OMA, Neo-Modern and Modernity, 2001

Over the next two decades, Koolhaas' and my own career trajectories diverged very substantially. He became one of the most famous and most influential architects and architectural thinkers in the world, while I devoted most of my time and effort to a more local career in Toronto. That having been said, after I joined the faculty of the Harvard Graduate School of Design in 1993, I thought that our relationship might start up again. But this did not happen. I only came to realise the depth of the estrangement that had evolved between us after a difficult joint public event at the GSD in 1995. I thought that he and I were going to have a public 'conversation', while he thought that I was going to 'interview' him, as part of a book launch for his new book: *S,M,L,XL*. In effect, that evening, our friendship was definitively ended in public view of some 600 architects, teachers and students.

That having been said, I was nonetheless later asked by Brendan Moran, one of the student editors of number 32 of the Yale Architectural Journal, if I would agree to a sort of long-distance interview on the topic of Koolhaas. I agreed to his proposal, and this text was the result. As one of the first texts to provide perspective on the early years of OMA, from the vantage point of Koolhaas' great later celebrity, the text attracted attention.

The following 'conversation' with George Baird was prompted by the editors' familiarity with two texts he wrote over 20 years apart. The first, "*Les Extrêmes Qui se Touchent*", appeared with Demetri Porphyrios' "Pandora's Box" in the May 1977 issue of *Architectural Design*, while the second, an encyclopaedia entry discussing the role of semiotics within late twentieth century architectural debates, was published in 1998.[1]

In conceiving of this issue of *Perspecta*, with its focus on the 1970s as a vital hinge between mid-century Modernism and the more contemporary resurfacing of some of its stylistic attributes, the work of OMA/Rem Koolhaas from the 1970s seemed to us not only nearly forgotten, but also noticeably under-valued. While in Baird's earlier essay, he claimed that OMA referenced and resuscitated aspects of mid-century Modernism at a moment that was apparently the nadir of its reputation in academic circles, in the later piece, he bemoaned what he saw as an ever-widening split between "the intelligentsia of the profession" and "its mainstream practitioners".

A certain confluence of these two contentions suggested that their author would likely have some insights into OMA/Koolhaas' work from the 1970s, and what it might mean regarding commercial/critical tensions as they have played out in architectural discourse since. Not only were we curious as to how his earlier observations had evolved over time, we were also interested in any new thoughts he might have on the connection of earlier events to contemporary production and debates. We thus sent him a number of questions circling around the topics of "neo-Modernism" and Modernity; what follows are those questions and his replies, edited into conversational form.

PERSPECTA 32 You wrote in your 1977 essay, "OMA constitutes one of current architecture's most provocative revisionisms." Would you characterise such a revisionist strategy as producing neo-Modernism? Can a particular achievement be historically attributed to neo-Modernism over other sorts of returns, specifically those associated with Postmodernism?

GEORGE BAIRD I feel compelled at the outset of this conversation to raise an issue that is at least terminological and perhaps even epistemological. You have employed the term "neo-Modernism" within the context of an issue invested in what you refer to in your editorial statement as "the resurfacing of mid-century Modernism that has been occurring over the past ten years."

It seems to me that these terms, and the distinctions you allow may exist between them, unavoidably raise the difficult question of "style". It might seem, for example, that you suppose, "the resurfacing of mid-century Modernism" to be primarily a stylistic development. On the other hand, you may see the possibility to read neo-Modernism as a cultural phenomenon that runs deeper than simple style. It is also not hard to imagine more wary observers than yourselves construing neo-Modernism primarily stylistically. It all depends on the propensity of any given commentator to see cultural products as primarily epiphenomena, or alternatively, as constructs deeply rooted in a complex history that are not exhausted through stylistic considerations.

For my own part, I am willing, for the sake of launching our conversation, to take your characterisation of neo-Modern as running deeper than style. And in that case, it seems to me that the OMA I described in 1977 *can* be said to produce a form of neo-Modernism. In a narrow sense, this would seem to be true in that so many of the OMA projects of that era were so explicitly "quotational" from earlier Modernist projects—much more than more recently published projects of the office. In this regard, it is interesting to note how efforts have been made, from time to time between the mid-1970s and now, by some members of the contemporary international architectural avant-garde—who see such quotational practices as inherently Postmodern—to challenge Koolhaas on this and to put his own avant-gardist credentials into question. But I also think my statement is true in a broad sense. For if we do agree that we see neo-Modernism as running deeper than style, then for me it will be appropriate to use the

term to describe OMA/Koolhaas' productive effort to gather up a number of strands from the earlier history of the great, ongoing project of Modernity.

Given the terminological/epistemological discussion just concluded, it is probably clear that for me, any answer to the second part of your question ("Can a particular achievement be historically attributed to neo-Modernism over other sorts of returns?") cannot be framed outside of a consideration of the relationship of architecture to what used to be known, before the philosophical critique mounted by Post-structuralism, as the "*Zeitgeist*"—or as we might now (following Foucault) call the *episteme* of our era. As you are no doubt aware, the nineteenth-century philosophical construct of the *Zeitgeist* has come to be seen as intellectually and morally unsustainable in recent times, on account of its unsupportable and unverifiable claims to omnipotence and its complicity in the acts of a variety of murderous ideologies. Efforts to replace it with a more intellectually supple and ethically accountable construct for explaining historical patterns have met with some recent success. Foucault's proffering of the concept of the *episteme* is one of them.

In our own field of architecture, Colin Rowe and Manfredo Tafuri are numbered among the contemporary theoreticians of architecture who have made compelling propositions intended to address the large, historical/theoretical question: what would be the features of an architecture that would be definitively appropriate to our era? Without presuming even to attempt to deal with such a large question here, let me simply table what are surely two of the likely dimensions of such an architecture. If we speak of social programme, for example, it is clear that we will not agree any longer with the declamatory 1930 statement of Karel Teige against Le Corbusier: "today we have no architectural solutions for churches, palaces, castles…".[2] But even if we would agree nowadays that Tiege's exclusionary stance went too far, surely we will agree nonetheless that we will not, today, have very many buildings with, for example, monumental flights of steps at their entrances or with separate zones for separate classes of users.

Or, alternatively, consider the matter of the material tectonics of building. In *The Space of Appearance*, I rehearsed an argument that would extend this kind of thinking to a consideration of contemporary building construction.[3] In that book, I conceded to an old argument of Robert Stern's that it is still possible nowadays to find skilled craftspeople to execute decorative plasterwork or stone carving, such as might have previously been employed on residential projects for the very wealthy. At the same time, I argued that one cannot proceed from this fact to suppose that there does not exist what I called a contemporary "political economy of construction" that determines what most, typical North American buildings will be built of nowadays. I am convinced that this economy will preclude most of these buildings (most of the time) from incorporating such decorative plasterwork or stone carving. I commended such architects as Frank Gehry and Dan Hoffman for their efforts to make the constraints of such an "economy" part of the conceptual content of the specific architectures they have invented. Thus, out of a broad combination of considerations such as these two I have just mentioned (programme and tectonics), it seems to me that it eventually may well be possible to determine roughly what the *episteme* of architecture in our time is, or, what it can be.

It is in this context that my concern about a merely "stylistic" reading of "neo-Modern" arises. After all, even if "Modernity", in the large, deep sense we used to know, is now historically behind us, it is not true that it has been historically superseded. As a result, I can say that whatever the differences of terminological emphasis between us may be, I have no difficulty in making the following statement: Even if the future of architecture does not belong to Koolhaas, or (as you later claim) "the New York Five or Deconstructivism", it certainty doesn't belong to the advocates of "the neo-Georgian, the neo-Palladian, the neo-Classical or the neo-vernacular".[4]

During the revisionist ferment of the 1970s it was not yet clear that would turn out to be the case. Many of the explorations that have since fallen definitively under the rubric of "Postmodernism" still looked at that time like potentially productive explorations within the expanded territory of Modernism. A notable example is Michael Graves' revisionist explorations beyond the post-Corbusian vocabulary that typified the early work of the entire New York Five group. By the mid-1980s, however, the overwhelming emphasis of Postmodernism on the semantic dimension of architectural form and on increasingly literal historical revivalisms drastically reduced its creative potential.

PERSPECTA 32 Considering the pronounced return over the last ten years of imagery associated with the 1950s, would you say that the resurfacing of mid-century Modernism now (which also might or might not constitute neo-Modernism) differs significantly from other forms of architectural revisionism that have occurred since 1945? And if so, have other kinds of neo-Modernism—such as the New York Five or Deconstructivism during the late 1980s—emerged in the 25 years, either proclaimed theoretically by its instigators or, in the manner of Koolhaas' Manhattanism, retroactively theorised by others? And are any of these capable of offering headway in what you described in 1998 as the split between intelligentsia and mainstream that has expanded during the 1990s?

GEORGE BAIRD Let me deal first with earlier cases, and then with more contemporary ones.

The first key case of revisionism that I would cite would be Charles and Ray Eames. For there is no doubt in my mind that they made an innovative connection between fabrication technologies imported from defence industries on the one hand and folk arts and vernaculars on the other. This provocative link significantly broadened the potential field of modern design in a strategic (and as far as I can tell) still insufficiently understood or appreciated way.

From the 1960s and 1970s, I would cite James Stirling and Robert Venturi. As far as I know, Stirling qualifies as the first neo-Modernist, since early on in his career he began to incorporate references to forms from the Modern architecture of the 1920s and 1930s. A well-known example is the Leicester Engineering Building, which included references to Constructivist worker's clubs in Moscow by Melnikov and the Johnson Wax Building in Milwaukee by Wright. While I have never heard Koolhaas talk about Stirling, it would be interesting to know if he would so quickly have fastened on Léonidov early in his own career if Stirling had not already made Melnikov a topic of interest among his peers. Interestingly enough, Stirling also had three other traits in common with Koolhaas: first, a personal propensity to act provocatively; second, a highly heterogeneous visual sensibility; and third, an extraordinarily inventive plastic capability.

But then there are differences that are just as important. To start with, Stirling's interests in earlier architectures were not limited to Modernism. He was as curious about Hawksmoor, Soane, and Butterfield as he was about Melnikov and Wright. Then too, for Stirling, programme was only one component of architecture that warranted consideration; he never

Leicester Engineering Building, England, by Stirling and Gowan, 1963.

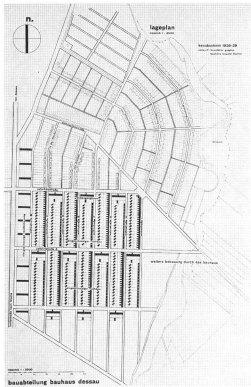

The site plan of the Torten Housing Estate at Dessau by Hannes Meyer, 1928–1930.

saw it as a primary driving force, as Koolhaas often does. Despite his similarly provocative persona, Stirling early on developed an aversion to polemics and to public theorising about architecture, an aversion that Koolhaas does not share.

As fellow revisionists, Venturi and Koolhaas share the intriguing distinction of having become well known as designers and as polemicists at one and the same time. But of course, Venturi, unlike Stirling, hardly qualifies as a neo-Modernist. To be sure, *Complexity and Contradiction in Architecture* includes references to high-Modern architecture as well as to Modernist vernaculars. So, also, do some of his most important buildings and projects, such as Guild House and the competition entry for Brighton Beach. But the only Modernist architects who receive sustained interpretation in his famous book are Aalto, Le Corbusier, and Moretti. And these three are easily outnumbered by Lutyens, Vanbrugh, Borromini, Guarini, Michelangelo, etc. Then too, programme—especially social programme—was seen by Venturi as a distraction for serious architects. Even though his

architectural revisionism manifested itself in a high-profile polemic—a "gentle manifesto", as he put it—his sensibility was much more that of an aloof observer than an activist.

In fact, Venturi's disappointing stance regarding the limits he saw on architecture's potential social power has the effect of throwing Koolhaas' obsessive preoccupation with "professional efficacy" into sharp relief. It is not for nothing that Robert Moses, Wallace Harrison, and John Portman are numbered among Koolhaas' American heroes, and it is their prodigious professional energy and impact on American society that so strongly attracts him to them. In fact, it is my view that this preoccupation with efficacy is a deeply important, though little discussed, aspect of Koolhaas' professional persona.

To turn now to more recent developments; here, too, it is not difficult to point to promising examples of architectural praxis that offer "head-way", though the New York Five and Deconstructivism do not, for me, lead the way.

I could speak instead, for example, of the work of Philippe Starck. Manifesting a sensibility that spans from the real to the surreal and from the vernacular to the rarefied, Starck also exhibits a remarkable loyalty to the traditions of 1968 and to the idea that design ambition and populist economy are not mutually exclusive concepts. Or take the case of Elizabeth Diller and Ricardo Scofidio, who have made a highly successful marriage of architecture and art installation and who have used video more effectively than any other contemporary architects I can think of. At the same time, this couple has also carried on more vigorously than any other current practitioners the fragile tectonic traditions of assembly associated with Carlo Scarpa, and they have paid a very modern homage to Scarpa's own intense curiosity as to the place of the human body in architecture.

Toyo Ito seems to me to have demonstrated an especially effective capacity to dematerialise architecture without losing control of its tectonically specific characteristics. This, it seems to me, distinguishes him among those of his peers who manifest strong interest in architecture's prospective digitisation.

But even this listing excludes innumerable interesting contemporary architects—I have recently been most engaged by publications of recent work from Spain—who continue to work productively within lineages of revisionist Modernism—or perhaps, as you would have it, the "neo-Modern".

PERSPECTA 32 In your 1977 *AD* piece on OMA, you suggested that Mies was "surely, except for Ludwig Hilberseimer, today's least fashionable architect", and continued, "OMA reasserts the pertinence of the work of Mies. The grid, the curtain wall, and the sheer plane surface all make their significant reappearance in OMA's work." Given his recent competition-winning design for a student centre at MIT that includes the renovation/expansion of a 1950s Mies building, this particular fixation would necessarily resurface in any serious evaluation of Koolhaas' sustained interests and achievements (if indeed it can ever be thought of as having gone away).[5]

What do you now see as being the special significance of Koolhaas' use—during his earlier production—of what can be viewed as historicist references to mid-century Modernism?

GEORGE BAIRD Is there a special significance to OMA/Koolhaas' use in the 1970s of references to mid-century Modernism? I think the answer to this question is yes. There are many reasons for this, which I will try to expand upon as we go along. To start with, however, I would simply note that a quick comparison between the era of the 1970s and that of the 1950s would demonstrate two very different climates of opinion. The later period—the period of Koolhaas' own formation—was one of acute professional doubts and self-questioning. The incapacitating shadow of the 1968 events still hung heavy over the profession. The earlier period, on the other hand, was one during which the sunny optimism of orthodox Modern architecture had not yet been called into question. What is more, it was also the period of Modern architecture's broadest social and cultural dissemination and of its greatest mainstream popularity.

Now while Koolhaas was indisputably both a product of, and a participant in the events of, the 1970s, there is no doubt that he has always been attracted to the kind of optimistic climate of opinion about architecture that typified the earlier period. What is more, a series of revisionist Modernisms had occurred in the intervening decades that were not attractive to Koolhaas (I am thinking here of various derivations of Brutalism, about which I'll say more later). Thus, from a number of points of view, it can be said that to make explicit references to the architecture of mid-century in the 1970s was a strategic polemical gesture.

PERSPECTA 32 Before we go on, let's clarify your primary characterisation of OMA's ideological strategy back in 1977. You said then that the most revealing aspect of the work was how it consciously attempted to be both contradictory and ambiguous. In your words, "[OMA's work] turns out to be visionary at the same time as it is implementable; surreal at the same time as it is commonsensical; puritanical at the same time as it is luxurious". Was OMA's penchant for employing a Miesian vocabulary during this period intrinsically more apt than the use of any other historical vocabulary for the sort of provocation embedded in their design strategy, with its predilection for being "contradictory and ambiguous?"

GEORGE BAIRD "Intrinsically" is perhaps overstated, but, again, I think the answer is yes. Two primary reasons are worth noting. First of all, to return for a moment to the 1960s era of Brutalism and of other architectural revisionisms, this was a period when

Mies was already out of fashion. The Postmodernist critique of Modernism's so-called "soullessness" still lay off in the future, but even so, leading architects of the 1960s were already looking for forms of plastic expression that left Miesian propriety behind. One could even say that Brutalism was a historical phase that Mies simply sat out.

Then, too, it cannot be denied that the powerful "reduction" that typifies Mies' formal method makes it especially suitable for "contradictory and ambiguous" purposes. Thus, in returning to a specifically Miesian Modernism, OMA/Koolhaas was able to snub the current vogue of Brutalism and at the same time was able to work with the absorptive voluptuousness of Mies' characteristic approach to surface.

PERSPECTA 32 Are curtain walls and sheer plane surfaces (of which we have recently seen a decisive comeback) more conducive to a have-it-both-ways position than other Modernist stylistic traits, say *pilotis*, *brises*, *soleils*, ramps, spirals, strip windows, marble veneer, and tension cables?

GEORGE BAIRD For the polemical purposes of early OMA/Koolhaas, yes, I think they proved to be so. It has to do with the shift between 1950s and 1960s emphases in the evolution of Modernism that I just referred to. For some of the motifs common then—*pilotis, brises, soleils*, and ramps particularly, or at least derivations of them—were prominent components of the ubiquitous Brutalist architecture of the 1960s. Remember the fateful Brutalism Sequence of images in Venturi, Scott Brown, and Izenour's *Learning from Las Vegas*: the deteriorating trajectory that leads from Le Corbusier's La Tourette Monastery through the Boston City Hall, ending with an HOK design for a Nieman-Marcus store in a suburban Texas shopping centre? This was the tendency that resulted in the creation of innumerable, egregiously assertive concrete buildings around the world. This description reminds me of a particular personal episode with Koolhaas that sharpens my point. He and I were being driven around Sydney, Australia together during a 1980 visit. Seeing a typical (but, up until that point, unfamiliar) example of the architectural tendency in question looming up on the horizon ahead of us, my sharp-tongued companion observed acerbically that it "looked like a dormitory for elephants".

In this climate of opinion, to return to the forms of the 1950s not only had a certain shock value (after

all, these were forms that were seen by conventional taste at that time as passé), but doing so also served to separate OMA/Koolhaas off from the by-then tired Modernist revisionism of Brutalism. Still, it is important to note that returning to the 1950s did not exclude all the other forms you include in your list of suggestions. In fact, many of them (spirals, strip windows, marble veneer, and tension cables—the ones that were already prominent in the vocabulary prior to the onset of Brutalism) do show up in the OMA oeuvre.

PERSPECTA 32 In your recent *Encyclopaedia* entry on semiotics and architecture, you attach much importance to the international emergence during the 1970s of typology and urban morphology as a basis for design methodologies that privilege the "social". One could conjecture that OMA/Koolhaas' own 1975 Roosevelt Island Housing Project is an important but neglected event within this moment. Do you see this as an exception in their work or an investigation more central to their project?

Furthermore, the rationalist and Miesian references in this project suggest unexamined complexities within the supposed "anti-Modernist" stance associated with both Rationalism and early Postmodernism. So then where does the OMA/Koolhaas 1970s work, with its mid-century 'quotation', sit in reference to the critique of Modernism as it unfolded during that decade?

GEORGE BAIRD Interestingly enough, I think the Roosevelt Island competition entry has to be seen as an integral part of the critique you mention. Surprising, as it may seem from the end of the millennium, the 1970s production of OMA/Koolhaas participated in the developing critique of Modernism at the same time that it revived certain strong Modernist themes (contradictory and ambiguous indeed!). A brief amplification of the climate of opinion of the 1970s will help to explain this. One of the consequences of the bifurcation referred to above has been the laying down of a sharp ideological demarcation line, and most activist architects have difficulty in resisting the strong pressure to declare allegiance to one faction or another. But the fact of the matter is that this line did not yet exist in the 1970s, and OMA/Koolhaas was one of many beneficiaries of the ideological confusion and promiscuity that reigned then. Influences, ideas, and formal devices were shared across a broader band of different architectural positions than has been possible more recently.

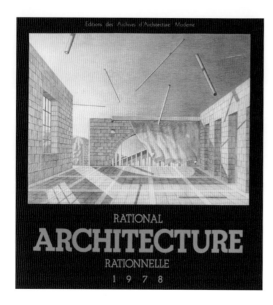

1978 cover of *Rationale Architecture*.

To demonstrate this, let me remind you of the notable publication *Rational Architecture* from 1978 (one year later than my *AD* article), assembled by Maurice Culot and Leon Krier. It included projects by OMA alongside those of the Krier brothers, Giorgio Grassi, and, most significantly of all, O M Ungers. Ungers, of course, had been Koolhaas' mentor and colleague during his unhappy Harkness Fellow's sojourn at Cornell University in the early 1970s. And in the early years, Ungers was even billed by Koolhaas as a participant in the collective practice of the Office for Metropolitan Architecture, all this, interestingly, despite Ungers' close ideological and professional associations with the Krier brothers, as well as with other European Rationalists.

These observations (as to the specific tenor of discourse about architecture in Europe at that time) have important implications for my response to your question. First, the rationalist interest I am ascribing to Koolhaas here is a mid-1970s European one, which is more stylistically neutral than the more explicit, postmodern North American one that overtook it some years later. Remember that Aldo Rossi saw Hannes Meyer as being as much of a precedent for Rationalism as Heinrich Tessenow. And by Koolhaas' lights, Mies himself would certainly qualify as one. The entire OMA/Koolhaas oeuvre during those years had a thorough going rationalist tenor to it. Thus I do not see the Roosevelt Island competition as being an exception,

as you suggest. Indeed, I see the prominence it is given in the series of projects illustrated in the same issue of *AD* as evidence of his estimate of its importance—an estimate, by the way, which I share. It is only a decade or so later (as part of the problematic "bifurcation") that Rationalism, especially its North American variant, came to seem irretrievably postmodern and that Koolhaas (for partly ideological and partly public relations reasons) eventually more-or-less consented to his appropriation into the canons of Deconstructivism.

Just to show how durable Koolhaas' ideological promiscuity has turned out to be, let me refer to its effects on a recent project of his; the well-known contribution to the Housing Complex In Fukuoka, Japan. This is a project that manifests all sorts of traditional urbanities that have gone entirely unrecognised, as far as I am aware. Has anyone, for example, noted how Koolhaas' Fukuoka project is a "mat building", in quite faithful emulation of Team 10 principles? Or that in the pairing of two masses around the main entrance to the project as a whole, the complex acts as a traditional urban gate? Or, for that matter, how its perimeter defers to the property line, in utterly traditional urban design terms? As far as I can tell from published photographs, the ensemble of buildings that makes up the Fukuoka project as a whole suffers from the insufficiently mediated conjunction of too many over-assertive architectural egos on a relatively small parcel of land. In such circumstances, Koolhaas' housing blocks have the exceptional—and in my view decisive—virtue of producing a small precinct of traditional urbanity, in what otherwise comprises a problematic field of self-aggrandising architectural objects. So it would seem to me, the author's rationalist inclinations have not left him, even at this late date in the expansion of his fame.

We agree OMA's method was from the beginning "contradictory and ambiguous" in any event. Given this, it is not difficult to see its production at a given moment in time as being more—or alternatively less—rationalist (or for that matter, deconstructivist) than it looks in retrospect.

PERSPECTA 32 Then do you see any direct connection between referencing the sleek surfaces of 1950s Modernism and employing a design strategy that showcases ideological contradiction? And does this strategy differ markedly from the formalist ambiguity of Venturi's earlier championing of double-functioning elements? Does it instead oscillate between seemingly conflicting scenarios?

Fukuoka Housing Complex, OMA, Japan, 1990.

GEORGE BAIRD My answer to this difficult question is: perhaps. But I am not sure. There is no doubt that there is a large gap between the overall professional approaches of Venturi and Koolhaas. Back in 1978, I already flagged Koolhaas' difference from Venturi's disparagement of explicit political commitments by architects. And it is also true that Koolhaas' professional stance has consistently demonstrated a robustness that differentiates him from the older American revisionist.

But whether there is a fundamental difference between "double-functioning elements" and an "active conceptual oscillation between seemingly conflicting scenarios" is another matter. It may be just that the latter operates on a larger architectural canvas than the former. Certainly it is my view that the ongoing cycle of architectural fashion has Venturi under an ideological cloud at the present time. And as a result, the brilliance—and the continuing pertinence—of the arguments of *Complexity and Contradiction* are at the present time seriously undervalued.

PERSPECTA 32 Let's look at some of these themes from a different angle. You claim in the *AD* article that "insofar as [the OMA polemic] raises to the level of

heroes… contentious figures,… [it] strives merely to *epater*—not this time *les bourgeois*—but rather, today's complacent arbiters of respectable taste." This comment suggests that quotation of the anonymous, commercial, or even sentimental aspects of some 1950s Modernism (such as the work of Morris Lapidus or, as you point out, Wallace Harrison) serves to encode a revisionism with possibly more radical potential than that associated with the 1970s Gray position. Can this quotation be seen as having a punk component and thus more extreme and challenging than that proposed by most other work during the 1970s?

Let us clarify what we mean by this: all quotation and revival tends to require a sophisticated familiarity with vocabularies in order to be read productively by viewers. However, the unique, shall we say *outré*, sub-version of currently 'acceptable' codes that one associates with Pop art and later punk sensibilities—and the ensuing communicative power it can afford the marginalised who instigate it—could be seen as bringing with it an activist call for the reconfiguring of accepted social structures. Is it reasonable to read this particular "subversion" into the work of OMA/Koolhaas from this period?

GEORGE BAIRD This is an issue in the oeuvre of OMA to which I have not previously given much consideration. On reflection, however, I am inclined to think that there is considerable truth in your speculation. In the beginning, there is no doubt that OMA's references of this sort were indeed intended to shock. Perhaps, in retrospect, some of them can also be seen at least to open the door to a consideration of the hitherto "marginalised".

Let me deal first with the intention to shock. To start with, remember how, in early slide presentations by Koolhaas on tour, representations of projects such as Exodus, or the Voluntary Prisoners of the Architecture were interspersed with occasional, unexplained sexual images. And some of this (by now vintage) 1970s pornography has even made it into the pages of *S,M,L,XL*.[6] Then too, your reference to Morris Lapidus has reminded me how a trajectory of populist imagery formed a strong theme in the work of OMA/Koolhaas from the late 1970s through the mid-1980s, following the 1977 issue of *AD* but preceding the fateful "bifurcation" discussed above.

We might cite an OMA project, which has not been much discussed—especially recently. It was an entry in a 1979 competition for a new residence for The Prime Minster of Ireland. The design's sinuous curves made strong associations with the work of such figures as Lapidus. By the early 1980s, the issue of "sentimental aspects of some 1950s Modernism" in the work (as you phrase it) was explicit enough to have become the subject of comment and controversy.

This matter arose in exchanges between Koolhaas and others at both the Charlottesville and Chicago conferences of 1982 and 1986 respectively. The exchanges began with Cesar Pelli and Jaquelin Robertson putting it to Koolhaas in Charlottesville that his historical references (they called them 1940s references—Miami Beach, palm trees, McDonald's arches, kidney-shaped swimming pools) manifested "nostalgia". Three years later in Chicago, Graves took up the term "nostalgic" again and used it in reference to a project that Koolhaas was presenting there. But this speculative attribution of a specific historical tone in his work prompted Koolhaas to close down the discourse, defiantly stonewalling as follows:

> If you define it that way, I would say that this project really has no longing for a better time or the memory of a better time. It is extremely and precisely ecstatic about this time, this year, this place, this moment, and nothing else.[7]

So we can see that too explicit an ascription of a historicising intention will not be countenanced, certainly not after the fateful "bifurcation" had already commenced (it is noteworthy that Leon Krier is present together with Koolhaas at both events, and the tone of the exchanges between them makes it clear that the collective publication of only five years earlier could no longer have occurred). By 1986 then, not only was the "bifurcation" well under way, but the modalities of shock available to Koolhaas had evidently begun to shift as well.

Leaving such polemics aside, let me return to the main thrust of your question: the matter of "subversion" and of any opening that can be seen in the work of OMA towards the "marginalised". Despite the tension of the exchanges in Charlottesville and Chicago, I find myself supposing that the opening to popular culture evident in the early projects does reveal a glimpse of an unspoken ethics in the works. I say unspoken, since there are a number of quite intense aversions deeply embedded in OMA's method and none of them runs deeper than the one against liberal do-goodery and the notorious "good intentions" commonly ascribed to orthodox Modern architecture.[8] As far as I can tell, a significant part of this aversion springs from that same preoccupation with "professional efficacy" that has prompted Koolhaas' admiration for Moses, Harrison and Portman. Far better, this approach to practice would seem to say, to be incorrect and yet efficacious, than to be correct but ineffectual.

Perhaps it can also be said that the other side of this ethical coin came into view during a fascinating episode in a recent exchange at the Harvard Graduate School of Design between Koolhaas and Andres Duany. The exchange had been set up as part of a symposium on The New Urbanism, and as far as I could tell, the expectation was that Duany would argue in favour of its practices, and that Koolhaas would attack them. To the surprise of most observers present Koolhaas largely declined to do so. Instead, he used the platform of the Harvard Graduate School of Design to mount an insistent and indignant challenge to Duany to use his influence as a now-prominent American practitioner to attack New York City's recent programme of gentrification of 42nd Street. Duany attempted to return the discussion to a consideration of New Urbanist principles and to their presumed debate. But Koolhaas would not be deflected. He shook his finger at Duany and chastised him for his (unethical?) failure to resist the obliteration by the political establishment of New York

City of the distinctive (can we also say "marginalised"?) subculture of hawking, hustling, petty crime, and pornography that typified 42nd Street until recently.[9]

PERSPECTA 32 Couldn't the particular subversion of OMA/Koolhaas work at this moment also be interpreted as a *sortie* targeting the values usually associated with historical knowledge, especially as it is privileged in the academy? Would this aspect of OMA's historicist resurfacing of mid-century modern stylistic elements further distinguish their project from that of the Whites and the Grays, contrasting with their apparent faith in symbolic content removed from contemporary professional conventions (ie, 1920s Modernism and Le Corbusier for the Whites, vernacular and classical imagery for the Grays)—and thus, by extension, challenging the Whites and the Grays firmly held belief in the power of the academy over the profession?

GEORGE BAIRD Does the OMA "subversion" distinguish them from the Whites and the Grays? Could they be seen as not sharing the other two groups' "firmly held belief in the power of the academy over the profession"? I think that there is truth to this speculation as well. Koolhaas' admiration for Portman, Harrison, and Moses all point to it, as does his complex regard for the un-famous Chinese architects who build so many more square feet of construction per year than their Western colleagues. Clinching evidence of such a possibility can also be seen in a little publicised report of a Koolhaas outburst at the 1994 ANY (Architecture New York) Conference in Montreal. Sitting among the members of the American avant-garde who have striven so assiduously over the years to co-opt him and listening to them express disdain for the complicit behaviour of most architects towards prevailing ideologies, Koolhaas lost patience and took on his colleagues head-on. "Why", he demanded to know, "is the only respectable position a critical one?" He continued:

> The problem with the prevailing discourse of architectural criticism is this inability to recognise that there is in the deepest motivations of architecture something that cannot be critical. Maybe some of our most interesting engagements are uncritical, emphatic engagements, which deal with the sometimes insane difficulty of an architectural project to deal with the incredible

accumulation of economic, cultural, political but also logistical issues.[10]

PERSPECTA 32 In the 1977 *AD* article, you claimed, "insofar as [OMA's work] reveals for our astonishment 'the secret life of buildings', it lastly demonstrates the iconic barrenness of most contemporary architectural debate." While by no means believing that today's climate is equally barren, we do share your feeling that OMA's sophisticated, early polemical efforts were not merely unimportant (forgive the pun) "academic" exercises. Furthermore—in a large part following your own observations—we see it as a vision containing unresolved antinomies that have yet to be given their historical due, containing diagrammatic schisms between utopian transformation and pragmatic expediency, between White autonomy and Gray heteronomy, between high art and lowbrow culture, and between elite design and mainstream practice.

So one last speculation: can the Gray position be seen to have evolved—over the quarter century since it was first codified as a sensibility (with ideological overtones)—so as nowadays to encompass a respectful, playful, and possibly even subversive neo-Modernism in addition to the neo-Georgian, the neo-Palladian, the neo-Classical, and the neo-vernaculars by which it has most often been recognised? If numerous instances of references to mid-century Modernism have occurred since the 1970s (and still more continue to occur), all of them would need to be evaluated in terms of different conceptual strategies: from the early efforts of OMA/Koolhaas to more recent work by figures such as those architects featured in our signature section. Wouldn't this continued viability imply practices of quotation—rather than merely being the schematic foundations of Gray Postmodernism—deserve to be treated all-around as a more complex proposition than they frequently have been?

To follow a line of reasoning that seems important for this issue of *Perspecta*, whether these practices are spearheaded by Louis Kahn or the more active commercial populisms of Robert Venturi/Denise Scott Brown, Charles Moore, and Robert A M Stern (all legacies connected to Yale who have hinged their theoretical and methodological strategies to certain "resurfacings" of the past), couldn't it be seen that a Gray position expanded by neo-Modernism points toward a more complex spectrum hidden in the binaries associated with 1970s American architectural debates? Might such a contention not only blur the line between the Whites' hermetic neo-Modernism and the Grays' mimetic Postmodernism but also reconfigure some of the important post-war developments leading up to the current moment? Perhaps a third historical position—resolutely professional and sympathetic to strategic quotation, yet dialectically encompassing White/Gray, autonomous withdrawal/pluralist cacophony, utopian optimism/commercial acceptance, and theory/practice-could be detected, lurking as a hidden historical thread that leads from the late 1940s to the late 1990s?

GEORGE BAIRD Interestingly enough, I find that I agree with this—for me—unexpected insight of yours as well. And I (let alone Koolhaas) would not have imagined that one could draw a parallel between the sensibilities of Venturi, Moore, and Stern on the one hand and of Koolhaas on the other. In fact, to the extent that I do agree, I would tend to draw the parallel much more closely with Venturi and Moore than I would with Stern, for a reason you have adduced in your earlier question about "punk" subversion. For I have always seen Stern's interest in popular culture as radically qualified by his especially strong "belief in the power of the academy over the profession".

But I think you are correct to see a connection between Venturi's interests in Pop art, Moore's interest in popular culture more generally, and Koolhaas' characteristically proto-punk manoeuvres. This observation has the effect of sharpening the distinction between the earlier, "quotational" Koolhaas, and the later—however reluctant—"fellow traveller" of Deconstructivism.

Still, this agreement between us notwithstanding, I return to your reference to a hypothetical "Gray position expanded by neo-Modernism" and to the sought-after "more complex spectrum". I do so in order to express a cautionary observation. It does not follow, for me, that such an expanded practice can be expected in and of itself to cause all relationships of ideology to tectonics to be happily evened out. To illustrate this, let me discuss the intriguing example of the evolution of the firm Kohn Pedersen Fox from the era of "high" Postmodernism to that of neo-Modernism. It came home to me as I found myself comparing one of their neo-Modernist skyscrapers from the 1990s (the IBM Headquarters Building in Montreal) with one of their more conventionally Postmodern 1980s ones (125 East 57th Street in New York City).

As one would expect, the 1980s project exhibited lots of local symmetries and classicising details. In the case of the later Montreal building, I found myself approaching it from a distance, savouring the drama of its almost constructivist tower and uppermost prow angling into the sky. But then, as I got closer to the base of the building, I noticed that a surprising number of the more local details of the skin and of its manner of abutting the ground were all too reminiscent of the earlier tower I had shortly before seen in New York. And these details, for me, carried awkwardly classicising elements forward into the ostensibly neo-Modernist project of a decade later.

To be sure, I understand that in a large office such as KPF, a certain number of cladding details for programmatically similar buildings are likely to be carried over from one project to another. And I don't even suggest that such a practice is necessarily cause for reproach. After all, if it was Miesian skins we were discussing, rather than those of KPF, we would be savouring the conceptual continuities that can be read from one project to another. No, it seems to me that the issue at stake here is the extent of the depth of reconceptualisation of the tectonics of building that proved feasible within such a firm, between the two projects in question. As an old-time semiotician, I am tempted to argue in this case that the deeply rooted *langue* of the KPF office has proved more tenacious than the more epiphenomenal shift of architectural styling that ensued between the 1980s and the 1990s at that particular firm.

So you will understand if I conclude by observing that the attainment of "a Gray position expanded by neo-Modernism" will not be a simple process, and that the sought after "more complex spectrum" will also not come so easily. All the same, I remain persuaded by your basic insights and believe that a surprising series of provocative linkages between heterogeneous figures from the late 1940s to the late 1990s really can be made. If this "hidden historical thread" leading from then until now really does exist, perhaps we should not be surprised that it has been sufficiently well hidden not to have been apparent even to the key protagonists to whom we have been ascribing its evolution. Perhaps this is one more testament to the power of the *episteme* in history.

1 *Architectural Design*, vol 47, May 1977, pp 326–327; "Semiotics and Architecture", *Encyclopaedia of Aesthetics*. Michael Kelly ed, Oxford: Oxford University Press, 1998, pp 271–275.

2 Teige, Karel, "Mundaneum", *Oppositions 4*, 1975, p 89.

3 Baird, George, "The Labor of Our Body and the Work of Our Hands", *The Space of Appearance*, Cambridge, MA: MIT Press, 1995.

4 Here Baird is referring in the second quote to the 1970s Gray Architects, using the editor's phrasing from a later question; the source of both references appear below.

5 It is, however, a fixation that has figured polemically in OMA's exhibition entries for both the 1980 Venice Biennale and the 1985 Milan Triennale. See the catalogue *Presence of the Past*, Venice: Edizione "La Biennale di Venezia", 1980, and Koolhaas, Rem and Bruce Mau, *S,M,L,XL*, New York: Monacelli Press, 1995, pp 46–61. See also Koolhaas' contribution to the Philip Johnson Festschrift Conference held in 1996, "Enabling Architecture", *Autonomy and Ideology: Positioning the Avant-Garde*, R E Somol ed, New York: Monacelli Press, 1997, pp 292–299.

6 Koolhaas and Mau, *S,M,L,XL*, p 14.

7 The two exchanges occur as follows: Pelli, Robertson and Koolhaas *The Charlottesville Tapes*, Jaquelin Robertson ed, New York: Rizzoli, 1983, pp 81–87; Graves and Koolhaas, *The Chicago Tapes*, Stanley Tigerman ed, New York: Rizzoli, 1987, p 168. Koolhaas' quoted retort is on the page 87 of the first book.

8 This is in the first instance a reference to a phrase that appeared in Colin Rowe's introduction to *Five Architects*, New York: MoMA, 1972. Rowe later went on to publish a book employing the same phrase in its title *The Architecture of Good Intentions: Towards a Possible Retrospect* (London, Academy Editions, 1994).

9 *Studio Works 7*, Harvard University Graduate School of Design, 2000, p 142.

10 Rem Koolhaas, quoted by Kapusta, Beth, *The Canadian Architect*, vol 39, August 1994, p 10.

Review of *Mart Stam's Trousers* by Crimson, with Michael Speaks and Gerard Hadders, 2001

After nearly a decade teaching at the Harvard Graduate School of Design, I had become a reasonably regular contributor to the *Harvard Design Magazine*, edited by Bill Saunders. The Mart Stam book attracted my attention on account of its provocative title, and of some of the contents, including an atypically straightforward contribution from Koolhaas himself. The following text was my response. Among other things, it triggered a thank you letter from the distinguished architectural historian at the Technical University of Delft, Max Risselada, who thought I had done something useful for Dutch architectural history with my review.

As an occasional contributor to this publication, I am from time to time invited to look over selections of recent books that have arrived at the magazine office, for possible review. A recent perusal of possibilities turned up the present collection of essays and photographs.

At first, I didn't think of myself as an appropriate reviewer, since I lack specialist knowledge of Dutch architecture, either historical or current. But the cover of the book caught—and held—my eye superimposing, as it does, the title *Mart Stam's Trousers* over a photograph of an apparently inscrutable urban street scene. This scene, as a reading of the book reveals, is a contemporary Dutch urban intervention: a "toleration zone for prostitution" specially designed and constructed in 1993–1994 by the planning department of Rotterdam. The superimposition of the name of the notable architect from the "Heroic Period of Modern architecture" over an image of such a distinctive product of contemporary Dutch social policy was, for me, already food for thought. It bespoke a frisky ambition on the part of the creators of the book (the Crimson Architectural Historians Group of Rotterdam, in particular Wouter Vanstiphout and Cassandra Wilkins, together with the American architectural theorist and critic Michael Speaks, and the designer/photographer Gerard Hadders). Out of curiosity I volunteered to take on *Mart Stam's Trousers*. The phrase that has given the book its title comes from one of the contributions, a 1996 'conversation' between the venerable English architect

Photograph on the cover of the 1965 issue of Architecture Design guest edited by Alison and Peter Smithson: *The Heroic Period of Modern Architecture* This is the photograph from which Mart Stam was removed graphically, except for a portion of his trousers.

and Team 10 member Peter Smithson and Crimson historian Vanstiphout. The focus of this conversation is Smithson's evolving view of Modern Dutch architecture—in particular as it was represented in the special issue of *Architectural Design* that Smithson guest edited in 1965 with his partner Alison Smithson, titled "The Heroic Period of Modern Architecture". Vanstiphout draws out Smithson on the logic of their inclusions and exclusions of Dutch material in the issue. And this leads, among other things, to a discussion of the archival photograph of Le Corbusier and Ludwig Mies van der Rohe that was used for the cover of the issue. Smithson tells Vanstiphout "the famous story" that the photograph in question originally also included Stam, but that he was later "edited out", it would seem, on account of his failure to accrue historical status as a titan of Modernism comparable to the other two. Smithson proposes to Vanstiphout that it remains possible, on close examination, to still see, in the photograph, a glimpse of Stam's trousers. Smithson's anecdote points to one of the key themes of the collection, as I read it: the process of construction of the master narrative of the history of Modern architecture—in particular of Dutch Modern architecture—as it has

been framed, often enough, by outside observers. And so the case in point: having been deemed by the constructors of that narrative to have been only a supporting historical player, Stam forfeited the possibility of appearing together with Le Corbusier and Mies on the cover of *AD*.

Interestingly enough, this intriguing anecdote is not the only illumination of this theme evident in the conversation. As the trousers story suggests, Smithson not only exposes the procedures of the construction of the narrative, but also participates in them as well. That this is so becomes more apparent still as Vanstiphout presses him on the evolution of his attitude to Modern Dutch architecture: to projects included in the 1965 *Architectural Design* generally as well to the Rietveld-Schroder house specifically.

Smithson had already described this last in a 1954 article as "the only truly canonical (modern) building in Northern Europe", by this epithet ranking it dramatically above virtually everything else produced in Holland during the period.[1] Under Vanstiphout's sustained questioning however, Smithson backs off his early declaration somewhat: "I don't think I would make those claims now. Time really alters one's perspective." But of course, by 1996, the formation of the narrative in question had already become definitive, and Smithson's reconsideration at this stage was too late to spare two or three generations of Dutch architects the anxiety of living with such canonical inclusions and exclusions.

A more personal experience of the impact of this narrative on the Dutch appears in an exchange also documented in the book, a collection of correspondence between J J P Oud and Philip Johnson, between 1931 and 1955, compiled by Dolf Broekhuizen. In this case, through the exchange of correspondence alone, we witness the Dutch architect seeing himself being edited out of the narrative over time. This occurs, first, as the negative reception of his 1942 design for the Shell building in The Hague sets in, and then proceeds further as the Museum of Modern Art in New York conceives a 1952 exhibition on de Stijl in which Oud is was relegated to a secondary rank.

I have for some time had the impression that architectural discourse in The Netherlands exhibits an unusual but characteristic tone, both personal and somewhat shrill. At least as far back as Aldo van Eyck's notorious RIBA lecture, "Rats, Posts and Other Pests", the *ad hominem* polemic has seemed all too typical.[2]

First off, then, *Mart Stam's Trousers* has caused me to ponder how it must feel for architects in such an intense local culture as the Dutch to confront these recurring edicts of influential outsiders in respect to their own history. And I wonder whether this may be a contributing factor to this curious intellectual and political shrillness.

Of course, it is not simply a matter of observing the influence of these outsiders as they shape the unfolding historical narrative of Modernism. What seems to be equally disconcerting is the continuing influence on the ongoing formation of the country's architectural culture. This influence and its effects seem to me to constitute the second key theme of the book. Certainly, as the topics of the varied contributions to *Trousers* move closer to the present day, the tone becomes ever more brittle. Even that of the redoubtable Rem Koolhaas, "How Modern Is Dutch Architecture?" from 1998, betrays such a tone. Then, following Koolhaas, Matthijs Bouw and Wouter Vanstiphout's interview with Carel Weeber, "Raw Power/No Fun", and Bouw and Joost Meuwissen's concluding essay, "Disneyland with Euthanasia: The Vicissitudes of the New Welfare State", successively intensify it.

To take Koolhaas first: his edginess is already apparent in his dissent from the canonical view of the Rietveld-Schroder house posited by Smithson and his Dutch colleagues in Team 10. Despite its fame, Koolhaas confesses that he cannot help viewing the house as a "seventeenth century genre piece". Then, picking up polemical momentum, he proceeds to mount an overall critique of Dutch architecture from the Heroic Period of the 1920s and 1930s right up to the present. As he sums it up:

> Dutch architecture is like playing a piano of which only the right half of the keyboard works. In Holland, grandeur and architecture have, it seems, been unhitched for all time, and it is the Dutch architect who is first to applaud this move, living as he does in a straightjacket of self-effacement.

Or, more tellingly still, as he puts it in one of his characteristic double ironies:

> In this country, the cowardice of resolve is pitted against the recklessness of a kind of Nietzschean frivolity. This is what makes me most hesitant about the nature of Dutch Modernism.

But Koolhaas' edgy "hesitation" pales in comparison to the world-weariness manifest in Bouw and Vanstiphout's interview with Carel Weeber. A figure of influence in The Netherlands, but not as well known abroad as many of his contemporaries, Weeber is presented by his Crimson interlocutors as a kind of historical "other" to Aldo van Eyck on the Dutch architectural scene since the 1960s. Where van Eyck was humanist, Weeber was realist; where van Eyck was for small-scale interventions, Weeber accepted the reality of large-scale urban gestures and of state institutions; where van Eyck still believed in the redemptive power of architecture, Weeber did not. As he insists, "I cannot fantasise happiness". To be sure, Weeber's interviewers acknowledge the widespread unpopularity of Weeber's projects. As they put it, he "made the buildings that everybody liked to hate".

But even a taste for *realpolitik* doesn't adequately prepare one for Weeber's responses to Vanstiphout's inquiries. For example, here he comments on the students who occupy a housing complex he has designed, and on their attitude to collective spaces in such buildings:

> Elite and other vermin. As you can see, all that is collective is out. They don't want it. I have done it in the past in Delft, with the student housing on the university campus, but it doesn't work. The laundromat is all that is collective.

And again, to a question regarding the relationship of his designs to the larger urban context, he comments as follows about his approach to architectural expression:

> You mustn't forget that with a few exceptions, all I have done is housing.... Starting with the Peperklip [the nickname of one of his projects], I told them: "Guys, you are covering up the problem. This is what housing is!".... I call them tenements. We were not allowed to use that word. My main point was that I wanted to show the housing corporations what kind of clients they really are. I don't mind what they are but they shouldn't make the buildings look like quasi-luxury condos. In my commissions, I have astutely tried to express what the project is about—be it a train station, a prison, or a housing project.

And once more, in the last words of the interview, he remarks on the Heroic Period of Dutch Modernism that forms the substratum of the book: "I'm not really interested in Modern architecture. I don't find Duiker very interesting."

To be sure, it is possible to read between the lines, and to intuit an effort on the part of Bouw and Vanstiphout to propose a distinct cultural lineage in Dutch architecture of van Eyck, within which Weeber would find his appropriate place: "Oud, Dudok, Maaskant, van den Broek, Weeber, Koolhaas maybe." But they make their proposal tentatively, and Weeber himself responds that their proposed list is "not very strong".

The concluding text, "Disneyland with Euthanasia", begins as a broad polemical over-view of the present cultural and political situation of architecture in The Netherlands.

As the title suggests, it also seeks to broaden the frame of reference of the discussion to encompass the governmental structure of patronage—or "welfare" as they call it—which supports and shapes architecture there. Anecdotal, impudent, and partisan, Bouw and Meuwissen adopt a tone that is the sourest of the entire book. On the recent evolution of Dutch economic policy, for example, they observe:

Socialism became realised as the better market economy. If the former version of the welfare state had night school (ie social improvement) at its core, today's version has the shopping mall.

Amplifying their assessment of the impact of this shift, they go on to observe:

A market was created for everything, and everything became a possible market. There are markets for sex, for crime, for drugs (called coffee shops), for death (called euthanasia), for money (called subsidies), for nostalgia (called history), and for architecture (called Rem Koolhaas).

For that matter, they see the cultural condition they depict as extending historically still further back:

State-enforced humanism and the persistent myth of the Dutch architect as its helpful friend have since the 1920s created generation upon generation of architects that will not do anything to distort the harmony. Within the well-established framework of dos and don'ts (quite a lot of don'ts), their sole purpose in practice seems to be to generate dumb little differences, little things which can be called "individual" without too many ideas or too much depth.

But if Bouw and Meuwissen hold the efforts of the older generation in contempt, they are not very impressed with those of the rebellious younger one either. Citing "what the firm MVRDV calls the 'architectural one-liner'", they remark:

The young architects frantically search for that particular component within the programmatic requirements, building codes, or urbanistic conditions that they can extrapolate and enlarge in order to give reason and meaning to their designs.

All in all, this is a daunting burden of scorn for a pair of architects to carry. To be sure, in the concluding paragraphs of their text, Bouw and Meuwissen seek to rehearse a constructive hypothesis for Dutch architecture. It is one that takes off from Koolhaas' well-known "paranoia", as well as from—surprisingly enough—the (not so well-known) psychological analyses of two academic protégés of van Eyck: Peter Gonggrijp and Michel Polak. This hypothesis is intended to generate what they call a "graceful empiricism". But coming so near the end of their argument—not to mention of the whole book—this hypothesis is too late and too little to displace the otherwise pervasive tone of contempt.

I noted at the beginning my lack of specialised knowledge of Dutch architecture. But I do have an ongoing interest in the question of how any specific architectural culture situates itself within the larger society to which it belongs. And my ruminations thus far on the complex relations between insiders and outsiders in the formation of the master narrative of Dutch Modernism lead me to conclude that for all its gradually escalating shrillness of tone, *Mart Stam's Trousers* does suggest an intriguing historical hypothesis in respect to this issue.

It would run roughly as follows: Modern Dutch architecture has historically held an especially highly integrated place in Dutch society. From Berlage to Oud, all the way to the *Mart Stam's Trousers* generation, architectural innovation and social policy have been much more closely interrelated than they would be in such countries as Italy or the United States. To see this, just think successively of Berlage's Amsterdam South, Oud's Kiefhoek, Brinkman's Spangen, even Mart Stam's project at the Weissenhofseidlung of 1927, or his Drive-in Flats in Amsterdam of 1936 (and I would even go so far as to include Herman Hertzberger's Diagoon Housing in Delft of 1969–1970). All of these projects are tangible physical products of Dutch social policy and at the same time icons of modern Dutch architecture. (Even Koolhaas' favourite Dutch avant-gardist, Cornelius van Eesteren, spent most of his professional career as a planner of new housing settlements.)

Then consider for a moment the comparative case of the United States: to be as integrated as that of The Netherlands, the broad social and political discourse about architecture and urbanism would—if the commentaries of Mart Stam's Trousers are to be believed—require that the founders of the New Urbanism, the National Home Builders Association, the policy makers of HUD, and the editorial boards of ANY and Assemblage publicly justify their intellectual positions to each other, on a more-or-less weekly basis.

If you can imagine the ideological tension such an ongoing confrontation would engender, then imagine further how destabilising it would be if such a situation were to be overtaken by the political events of May 1968, with their dramatic undermining of the hitherto established institutions of architecture and urbanism. And then, if that were not startling enough, imagine further still that in these combined historical circumstances, the then-acknowledged intellectual leader of the architectural profession—in The Netherlands at the time, Aldo van Eyck—should indulge increasingly in public vituperation and jeremiads.

Then, as if all this were not enough, imagine that in the wake of this deeply disconcerting series of historical turns of events, two subsequent ones were to transpire. First, that the Dutch architect in recent times to have achieved world-wide fame outside his homeland—Koolhaas—should, despite his many strengths, prove temperamentally incapable of performing a constructive role as an exemplar for his many professional followers; and second, that a newly revisionist Social Democratic government should choose to restructure the system of economic support that had sustained the relationship of architecture to society in The Netherlands for most of the previous century. I am beginning to suspect that, in The Netherlands, the combination of these various historical circumstances has worked to dramatically unravel such consensus as had underpinned architectural practice for a half-century or so. Is it possible that the unravelling of the consensus has, over time, led also to

the episodes of brittle mutual professional contempt on the part of leading Dutch practitioners and critics, such as is evident in so many of the pages of Mart Stam's Trousers?

So many of the pages, I say, because this tone does not, in the end, typify the entire book. Three contributions are especially notable departures: Ed Taverne's essay, which takes its title from Smithson's problematic phrase, "The Only Truly Canonical Building in Northern Europe"; Michael Speaks' commentary on Alessandro Mendini's (and collaborators') Groningen Museum; and most significant of all, Gerard Hadders' remarkable series of photographs of a provocatively broad range of Dutch buildings spanning the twentieth century. For his part, Taverne attempts, in a measured way, to deconstruct the various mythologies that have built up around the Rietveld-Schroder house, and in relation to its conceptual and ideological place in the history of de Stijl. Without any polemic that I can discern, he dismantles supposition after historical supposition, and claim after ideological claim, producing an exhilarating recreation of an actual historical episode in all its specific contingency. Reading his account, one gets a compelling sense of the circumstantial relationships of personalities, institutions, and historical situations within which the famous house was created. In turn, Michael Speaks makes a partisan, but to my mind intriguingly upbeat plea for critical reconsideration of the project for the Groningen Museum that Alessandro Mendini executed between 1988 and 1994, together with his designated collaborators, Team 4 and Coop Himmelb(l)au. Speaks argues first that the architectural world has yet fully to accept and understand the implications of Robert Venturi's concept of architecture as a practice based not upon "space" but upon "communication". He then claims that Mendini has succeeded, at Groningen, to build on this insight of Venturi's to create anew, nonessentialist architecture as a productive "art of framing" of human activities.

Yet interesting as each is, neither Taverne's nor Speaks' commentary lingers in my memory the way Hadders' photographs do. Groups of them are included in between virtually all the texts of the book. Other than a series of inscrutable overall titles ("Protect Me from What I Want", "Door to Door", "It Takes a Village", etc) and brief identifying credits, they are presented without comment. They encompass everything from "canonical" works (the inevitable Rietveld-Schroder house, Bijvoet and Duiker's Zonnestraal Sanatorium, etc) to Team 10 icons (van den Broek and Bakema's Lijnbaan Shopping Centre, van Eyck's Orphanage, etc) to fashionable contemporary projects (Koolhaas' Kunsthal and MVRDV's Villa VPRO, etc) to Modern Movement restorations (J J P Oud's De Kiefhoek housing estate and his site hut from the 1923 Wytze Patijn, etc) to public works installations (images of the Rotterdam planning department's "toleration zone for prostitution" both begin and end the series). What is more, the majority of these projects are photographed in a consistently considered manner difficult to capture in words. Hadders has succeeded in evading the immaculate perfection of current professional architectural photography. At the same time, he eschews any tone of "scene of the crime" exposé. Contemplative but nonetheless highly alert, ruminative at the same time that they are historically self-aware, his views of secondary facades of famous buildings (Oud's Shell headquarters), of densely occupied buildings that have usually been photographed only when empty (Villa VPRO and the Lijnbaan), and of somewhat desolate architectural icons (van Eyck's Orphanage) cumulatively succeed in producing an interpretation that dispels much of the brittleness of the texts. They even succeed in contextualising a troubling series of projects by urban designers such as Ashok Bhalotra and architects such as Sjoerd Soeters (described by two of *Trousers* contributors as "the most amoral of architects").

Indeed, Hadders' images even caused me to imagine the possibility of constructing a newly unified reading of Dutch architecture that would begin far from the ideological wars that so frequently preoccupy *Mart Stam's Trousers*. My hunch is that this reading would commence in the region of a sociology of ordinariness, such as one would associate with the writings of such figures as Henri Lefebvre, Michel de Certeau, or Pierre Bourdieu, none of whom is even mentioned in this book. From this beginning, it might be possible to go on to construct a new "groundedness" for architecture, such as is evident, to my eye, in Hadders' photographs of some of the works depicted. In the first instance, it seems to me, one would look to his images of well-known works by Brinkman, Oud, van den Broek, and Bakema, as well

as to the remarkable but less well known "Warehouse Building" in Rotterdam, by Maaskant and van Tijen from 1949–1951. Beyond that, the new reading could even extend to a recontextualisation of insistently rhetorical contemporary projects such as those of Koolhaas, van Berkel and Bos, and Mendini and collaborators, revealing in them both greater depth and breadth than their too visible avant-gardism often suggests. Could one then, in turn, contemplate the possibility to go on from this to reconstruct a mythology of Dutch architecture for the future? Maybe; one hopes so. To be sure, such a reconstruction would have to be supple enough to come to terms with such matters as the troubled legacy of van Eyck: the moral leader of the older generation who sadly, in his later years, lost control of his public behaviour. This is not a task to which many of the contributors to *Mart Stam's Trousers* appear to be well suited.[3] (In his typically contrarian wisdom, Koolhaas here uniquely acknowledges that "van Eyck is the only Dutch architect who has dared to appeal to that status of myth".)

For that matter, the reconstruction in question would need also to address Koolhaas' other, equally contrarian insistence that "there should be an ideological response to the sudden disappearance of socialism, which in almost all cases has latently nourished and provided the justification for our Modern architecture, whether we are open about it or not". Hadders' meticulous, measured photographic project seems to me to open the door to such possibilities. It is in this sense that he has made the most productive conceptual contribution to *Mart Stam's Trousers*. His work recalls the haunting question with which Colin Rowe ended his famous introduction to *Five Architects* back in 1972: "Can an architecture which professes an objective of continuous experiment ever become congruous with the ideal of an architecture which is to be popular, intelligible and profound?"

If at some indeterminate time in the future, the answer to this poignant question of Rowe's should turn out to be "yes", then maybe we should turn again to the Dutch. After all the ideological turmoil they have endured these last 30 years, architects and laymen alike, they surely deserve to be the first to know.

1   Smithson, Peter, guest ed, "Modern Architecture in Holland", *Architectural Design* 8, 1954.

2   van Eyck, Aldo, "What Is and What Isn't Architecture: Apropos of Rats, Posts and Other Pests", *Lam: International* 28, 1981.

3   Admittedly, Bouw and Meuwissen do touch on the role of van Eyck's academic protégés, Gonggrijp and Polak; but Bouw and Meuwissen do not, as far as I can see, demonstrate any decisive influence of Gonggrijp and Polak's somewhat specialised researches on architecture in The Netherlands today.

An Open Letter to Rem Koolhaas, 2007

By the turn of the year 2000, notwithstanding the estrangement between Koolhaas and myself, it was clear to me that he had become the most influential architectural thinker in the world. As my last contribution to the curriculum of the GSD, I decided to offer a graduate seminar with the title "Carefully Reading Koolhaas". For three years, the seminar was a very popular one, and it enabled me to focus my thinking on his later writings sufficiently clearly as to enable me to write the "Open Letter". As a courtesy, I sent it to him soliciting comment before it appeared, but received no response.

Dear Rem,

Before our recent encounter in Montreal, it had been many years since you and I had spent time together. The prior occasion was the very public 'conversation' in the auditorium of Harvard's GSD, convened in connection with the publication of S,M,L,XL.

As far as I could tell, you didn't enjoy that "conversation" any more than I did. Indeed, the event led me to conclude that I had ceased to be a productive interlocutor with you, somehow being simultaneously too close to you and too far away from you to be able to precipitate fruitful dialogue. What is more, sometime after the event, I learned from a mutual colleague that you thought the view of your thinking I outlined in the text I published in Perspecta 32 was accurate only up until 1990, at which point you claimed to have undertaken a major change of direction.

Given such circumstances, I largely abandoned my efforts to keep up with you. It seemed that my earlier insights into the beginning of your career no longer held any relevance to your theoretical position—indeed, to the extent that I continued to pay any attention to your statements, I have to say that they made me uneasy. For example, I found the trajectory of your published polemics from "Atlanta" to "Bigness" too tendentious and to complicit in the evident "flows of global capital" to be intellectually or ethically defensible. It was as though that long-standing obsession of yours with sheer professional "efficacy"—which I had attempted to articulate in my Perspecta text—had finally unmoored you altogether from the stubbornly independent integrity I associated with your early career.

But of course your fame and influence with students of architecture nonetheless kept growing, and I found myself continuing to encounter second-hand versions of striking statements you had made on many topics in innumerable architectural academic settings. What is more, not only were these statements usually very challenging ones (what else would one expect?) but sometimes even—at least to my ear—contradictory. So a puzzled curiosity about your thinking began to grow again in my mind.

Then came the publication of Bob Somol and Sarah Whiting's "Doppler Effect" text in Perspecta 33, with its arguments for a newly "projective" architecture to replace the "critical" architecture that, in their view, had by then run its historical course. And of course, there you were in their text, presented as a prominent exemplar of the "projective" architecture they were advocating. I had already noted with some interest how you had declined to align yourself with Joan Ockman's arguments for a "new pragmatism" in architecture. I began to suspect that you might not be all that comfortable in the role of an exemplar of the "projective" either.

In a fall 2004/winter 2005 *Harvard Design Magazine* text entitled "Criticality and Its Discontents", I responded that, like Manfredo Tafuri and Dave Hickey—two other theorists cited in "Doppler Effect"—you held a much more complex position in regard to the "critical" than the authors of that text had allowed.

Then, as it happens, two circumstances converged in a way that led me to think I should take another, closer look at your theoretical writings. First, my "Criticality" text precipitated much more public discussion and response than I had anticipated and, second, Toshiko Mori invited me to hold post-GSD-retirement theory seminars at Harvard. The result was a series of classes entitled "Carefully Reading Koolhaas" that I conducted there between 2005 and 2007. Given your prominence in the world of contemporary architecture, it is probably not surprising that the seminar attracted an intellectually impressive group of students.

Our method was simple: we read the texts that we deemed to be among your most important, and we attempted to identify within them consequential continuities and discontinuities, relationships (where they could be perceived) between texts and design proposals and, last but not least, evidence of any major shifts of position on your part, declared or undeclared. (I continued to be sensitive to your claim that my *Perspecta* account was valid only until 1990.)

One of our first discoveries was that your position did change around 1990, and you have yourself acknowledged this in an ironic *mea culpa* in "How Modern is Dutch Architecture?". Indeed, the trajectory from the first version of "Atlanta", 1987, to the final one, 1994, demonstrates this. And the fact that, in addition to that final version, two other key texts, "The Generic City" and "Bigness", were also published in 1994 reinforces the significance of this period in your turning away from the neo-Modernism of the 1980s in a search for a form of architecture and urbanism that would—as you saw it—be more original and transformative.

Then too, our seminar's examination of this same trajectory brought home to us again the central importance in your thinking of the need to undertake the difficult task of understanding the actual phenomena of the contemporary world before adopting an intellectual or moral judgment about their legitimacy or desirability. One example of this "task of understanding" that we followed with interest was your enumeration of the key features of "bigness" that you had first discovered in John Portman's projects in Atlanta, and then found in many other parts of the contemporary world, especially Asia:

1. The ensemble of autonomous parts brought together in a circumstantial whole.
2. The operative necessity of the use of the elevator.
3. The end of the role of the facade as a register of internal programmatic organisation.
4. The establishment of the urban impact of building independently of architectural quality.
5. And, last but not least, the notable directive "Fuck context".

And we could not deny that we found this characterisation of a historic new building type as compelling as your admirers around the world did.

Yet upon close reading of the 1994 texts, we found that our view of your position in this matter was not altogether straightforward: we had difficulty reconciling your injunction to understand phenomena before judging them with the application of these same design principles to those projects that you yourself have authored. It seemed apparent that from the Zeebrugge Ferry Terminal to the Zentrum fur Kunst und Medientechnologie in Karlsruhe to the Trés Grandé Bibliotheque—perhaps even to CCTV—the principles of "bigness" were being more-or-less adopted and exemplified by OMA. We could even understand that the first three of the five principles you had enumerated could be considered to be non-judgmentally applicable both to projects in the world that you have analysed and to those you have designed.

But the last two principles seemed to us more problematic. Were we really intended to imagine that OMA's own "big" projects were meant to demonstrate "architectural quality" only secondarily? This did not seem to us likely, nor did it seem to be the case for the projects as designed. It seemed to us instead that in this regard we needed to distinguish between this principle of "bigness" as an identified contemporary vernacular condition in the world and an enhanced one operative in the analogous work of OMA. And then, of course, when we got to "Fuck context", the situation was more complex still, since it was hard in this case to see the new position of OMA as ambiguous, insofar as the question addressed in the firm's work did not seem to be as distanced from the vernacular version of "Fuck context" as the principle respecting architectural quality did. To this extent, then, it seemed that the distinction between understanding and judging was not entirely clear after all, even in your own hands.

Then there was the fact that "bigness" did not appear to be the only primary theoretical framework for design being employed by OMA over the years. As I saw it, a whole series of "mat" or—to use the term you seem to prefer—"carpet" projects also loomed large in the oeuvre. To be sure, many of these—Parc de la Villette, the plan for Melun-Sénart, Nexus Housing in Fukuoka—are early projects, but it has been interesting to me to see you return to the formal tropes of "mats" and "bands" in your recent proposals for preservation in Beijing. The "barcode of preservation", as you call it in "Found in Translation" evokes compelling echoes of the bands of your proposal for the Parc de la Villette two and a half decades ago. (And is it not noteworthy that, unlike the megabuildings typified by "bigness", buildings that are "mats" or "carpets" do not tend so strongly to isolate themselves from their surroundings but rather bind heterogeneous urban phenomena sociably together?)

This having been said, our group was unable to find the "mat" or "carpet" projects theorised in your writings to nearly the same extent that the projects exemplifying "bigness" were. And, not only that, we were not even able to determine what relationship (if any) these two typologies have to one another in your thinking overall—let alone how much importance the "mat" still holds for you.

But if such ambiguities as these lingered in our minds over the span of our sessions, we found another one easier to deal with. This is your supposed propensity for contradiction. Take the case of the conclusions of two of your texts written in the same year: "The Generic City" and "Whatever Happened to Urbanism?". The former ends with the statement: "The city is no longer", and the latter with "More than ever, the city is all we have". It would be possible to cite many other examples of such contradiction. Indeed, we came to the conclusion that two of your major texts—"The Generic City" in S,M,L,XL and "Junkspace" in content—have to be seen as a dialectical pair. They deal with many of the same contemporary urban phenomena, but do so in such very different tones of voice that the latter text reads almost as a refutation of the former.

In fact I, at least, concluded that the explanation is something like this: your pleasure in the construction of rhetorical prose exceeds your commitment to the descriptive accuracy of the phenomena under examination. (Should I see this as evidence of the one-time movie scriptwriter at work?) After all, it is surely a fact that your authorial skill with rhetoric surpasses that of any other current writer in our field. Examples abound. To take only two: the piano with only half a keyboard in "How Modern is Dutch Architecture?" and the summations of Derrida ("We cannot be Whole"), Baudrillard ("We cannot be Real") and Virilio ("We cannot be There") in "Whatever Happened to Urbanism?" These never fail to dazzle me.

I speculate that your method of writing is one in which you are as influenced by the momentum of the prose gradually appearing on the paper or computer screen as much as the prose appearing there is influenced by you, its author. In this sense, I have concluded, your prose has to be seen to have much in common with improvisational jazz or rap. Its tone and momentum are as important as its semantic content. So I suppose that the opposed claims about the city that end the two major texts are not so much definite statements of position as they are provisional constructs of exhortation, both to yourself and to others.

Yet while I think these observations on your rhetoric and prose are sound, it is also my view that they do not exhaust the significance of a careful comparison between "The Generic City" and "Junkspace", for the first of these texts surely falls into the category of one of your bold efforts to understand contemporary phenomena before judging them. Its (relatively) measured tone and its systematic sequences of description seem meant to present us with a compelling and plausible depiction of a hitherto unconsidered urban reality. And, for me, the argument is quite successful in achieving these aims.

"Junkspace", on the other hand, is neither measured in tone nor systematic—indeed, in our seminar, we came to call it a "rant". Despite the commonality of subject material between the two texts, the tone could not be more different. Where "The Generic City" seeks to be dispassionate and detached, "Junkspace" is unrelievedly intense and personal. Where "The Generic City" is observant, realist (and perhaps even a little stoic) in its sober confrontation with contemporary urban reality, "Junkspace" is bitter and disillusioned. To me, it is as though there came a moment for you when you could no longer sustain the studied, measured equipoise that had hitherto characterised your interpretations of generic modernity. That poise was shattered, and a much less guarded, much more intimate side of you was revealed. Indeed, so distinct, so unique and so atypically self-revelatory among your writings is "Junkspace" that it is still not clear to me why you published it or what ultimate place it will occupy in your critical oeuvre. What does seem clear to me about it is that it is surely evidence of another significant shift in your thinking after that in the early 1990s you have described so much more explicitly. But more on that later.

For the moment, having so insistently emphasised the differences between the two texts, I want now to comment on the fascinating extent of their commonalities, for I have come to believe that they are both remarkable commentaries on the profound extent of the reification of reality (as the Frankfurt School would have it) in the contemporary world. Not only that, one of the key ambitions of your own theorising has been to identify that reification, and in your design production, to avoid it, presenting instead a new reality that is, as far as possible, unmediated.

Clearly, one of the aspects of the "generic" that attracted you in the first place is its indifference to blatantly expressed modes of iconic reference. Your comparisons of Paris and London (the former supposedly too explicitly symbolic of itself; the latter agreeably indifferent—as you see it—to its urban self-image); your mocking of "historic" urban districts in "Lipservice"; your scorn of contemporary models of "theming"—all these are instances of a deep and acute aversion to varied contemporary modes of preconstituted reality.

Yet even if these corrupted modes of contemporary experience are to be set aside, "Junkspace" seems to say that it turns out that the procedures of modernisation that have produced the generic city are also problematic. "Junkspace" claims that the result is the "residue", the "fallout", or the "meltdown" of the procedures of modernisation. For you, in your dystopic mode of authorship, this state of affairs is characterised by "impaired vision", "limited expectations" and "reduced earnestness".

In fact, I can see that my growing confidence in my interpretation of the parallelism of the two seemingly opposed texts was strongly reinforced in a poignant moment in your discussion in Montreal with Peter Eisenman and Phyllis Lambert. Demurring at a number of your colleagues' observations on contemporary urban reality and attempting to counter them with references to a number of intriguing contemporary developments in Asia, you disarmingly, ironically, diffidently asked aloud, "Dare I use the word 'authenticity'?"

Dare you indeed! To be sure, the fateful word does not show up in either "The Generic City" or "Junkspace", and you are, of course, right to be cautious about employing it, since its polemical use—as Theodor Adorno pointed out long ago—is so especially susceptible to corruption. Still, it seems to me that a search for forms of architecture and urbanism that resist overly explicit iconicity and that seek to embody an unmediated new vision could hardly be more important for architects today.

In Montreal you also reiterated your dismay at the effect of the star system on our profession and argued that in opposition to its current architectural effects, OMA was returning to an exploration of the potential of the generic—this time not in urbanism but in architectural form itself. Is it possible that the "mat" itself might rekindle your curiosity?

These various recent developments also persuade me that I am right to discern a further significant change of direction in your recent thinking. As I argued in my "Criticality" text, while you are from time to time conflicted about it, you have not abandoned the "critical" dimension of architecture at all. Indeed, I have come to understand, I think, that in your (heroic) efforts to revive the professional efficacy of architects, while at the same time urging the maintenance of their rigorous critical independence of action, your own polemic struggle has to be seen as being at the point of its greatest conceptual stress. While I have from time to time been troubled by what seemed to me a too strong argument on one or the other side of this contest in your own psyche, I have now come to understand and appreciate the remarkable feat of reconciliation you are attempting.

So I can say that making this recent effort to read you again carefully and having had the opportunity to meet again with you in Montreal have been most gratifying for me.

Yours, in old affection and admiration,

George Baird

Part 2: Ignasi de Solà-Morales

I first met Ignasi de Solà-Morales at a conference on Mies van der Rohe that Detlef Mertins organised in Toronto in 1992. While his and my views of Mies were not co-incident ones, it was already clear to me then that he was a formidable critical intelligence. During the years I taught at Harvard, he was an occasional visitor, and our friendship, as well as my admiration for him, continued to grow. So, when, in 1997, Cynthia Davidson published a selection of his writings in her *Writing Architecture* series of books, I was eager to read it and to review it. Among the admirers of the review was Solà-Morales himself, who wrote to me afterward, to tell me that I had "cut through the very sinews of his thought".

Review of *Differences: Topographies of Contemporary Architecture*, 1997

This slender volume is a collection of essays by the noted Barcelona architect, theorist, and critic Ignasi de Solà-Morales. The essays were published between 1987 and 1993 in various books and publications, and focus on such topics as "Mies van der Rohe and Minimalism", "Architecture and Existentialism", "Weak Architecture", "Place: Permanence or Production", and "High Tech: Functionalism or Rhetoric". Such a list will give the prospective reader a sense of what to expect.

But in the first sentence of his introduction, Solà-Morales guardedly allows that the book seeks to be "more than a mere collection of published articles". "Guardedly", I say, since the author claims he has "found it impossible", in selecting the texts and in writing an introduction, "to construct a systematic discourse". But he does state:

> In some sense, this book should be understood… as a *flexible manifesto*, for it relies upon the modern tradition of the manifesto in its aim to provoke, but it does not subscribe to the totalising singularity that often motivated these Modernist proclamations.

And he goes on to give an account of the philosophical influences that have led him to his critical methodology. Principally there are two: Post-structuralism, as represented by Gilles Deleuze—particularly his *Différence et Répétition* of 1968—and phenomenology, as it has descended through a continental lineage from Husserl to Heidegger to Merleau-Ponty.

Now Solà-Morales is well aware of the unexpectedness of this combination of influences, and Sarah Whiting, in her astute editor's introduction to the book, takes pains to outline the logic of its formation. For me this distinctive and complex intellectual point of departure certainly does yield a number of valuable results in Solà-Morales' subsequent arguments. For instance, it enables him to develop a compelling new interpretation of architectural developments of the 1950s. Among the many examples is Solà-Morales' refreshing view of Mies van der Rohe, who he insists cannot be seen as having been influenced by Classicism. Instead, he argues, "Mies' work is developed not out of images but out of materials—materials in the strongest sense of the word; that is, the matter from which objects are constructed."

Using a conception of the work of art taken from Deleuze and Guattari—"a block of sensations"—Solà-Morales characterises Mies' architecture as "a consolidated, permanent block for the production of sensations", which he then likens to works of such American Minimalist artists as Donald Judd and Dan Flavin. Then, relying on a phenomenological characterisation of Minimalism taken from Rosalind

Krauss, he underscores what he sees as a neglected phenomenological thread in Mies' own thought, deriving from such intellectual contemporaries as Romano Guardini and Paul Ludwig Landsberg, "whose influence on him seems beyond doubt". And as a result of this distinctive reading, Solà-Morales is able to conclude:

> The Miesian project in architecture is inscribed within a wider ethical project in which the architect's contribution to society is made precisely by means of the transparency, economy, and obviousness of his architectural proposals.

Another example of the author's highly original reading of the 1950s has to do with the influence of existentialism on revisionist architectural thinking. Via the contributions to debates in CIAM and Team 10 made by, among others, Aldo van Eyck and J Antoni Coderch, Solà-Morales argues that "the change that existentialism introduced into European and American architecture in the 1950s was far more radical than was then realised."

This insight propels him to a number of distinctive readings of events during that decade and since. In his first chapter, for example, he argues that the deterioration of the existing rapport between architects and critics which occurred during that decade was related to the emergence of the "individualistic, decentered thought of existentialism". What is more, he sees this development as having set the stage for the more sweeping condemnations of architecture of the late 1960s, which he names "radical critique". In the chapter "Architecture and Existentialism", Solà-Morales outlines what he sees as an important shift of ways of thinking that began with revisionist sentiments inside CIAM in the late 1940s, and continued with the emergence of such radical groups as the Situationists in the late 1950s and 1960s. In a provocative essay entitled "Place: Permanence or Production", he develops an extended historical account of what he sees as the invidious consequences of one strand of existentialist thinking focusing on the shift from "space" to "place" as a basic schema of contemporary architectural thought. Here, Solà-Morales argues that "the idea of place as the cultivation and maintenance of the essential and the profound, of a *genius loci*, is no longer credible in an age of agnosticism; it becomes reactionary". Instead, he concludes that "place is, rather, a conjectural foundation, a ritual of and in time, capable of fixing a point of particular intensity in the universal chaos of our metropolitan civilisation".

The same point of departure, it seems to me, also enables him to frame intriguing characterisations of groups of contemporary architects. In his first chapter, for example, he sets out an account of two groups, one from the 1950s and another from the late 1980s and early 1990s, each of which he sees as illustrative of the tenor of their respective periods. From the 1950s he cites projects by Mies van der Rohe, Louis Kahn, Alvar Aalto, J Antoni Coderch, and Ignazio Gardella. These are then set in juxtaposition with a recent group by Tadao Ando, Jacques Herzog and Pierre de Meuron, Frank Gehry, Juan Navarro Baldeweg, and Álvaro Siza.

As Solà-Morales sees it, "one common concern manifests itself in all five of the works from the 1950s: not only to adapt the form to the clear definition of a programme, but to make the functional programme underpin the building's form." As he puts it: "They form an architecture born out of abstraction that sought, in the particularity of each programme, a ground for its formal justification." By contrast, he observes that:

> Today's built message seems to communicate itself in a far more mediated fashion. Relying on the notion of character and the mediation of images—derived above all from sculpture and the visual arts—today's built form is deployed by Jungian archetypes: the elementary silhouette of the house as natural notion; the skin as enveloping any monumental, public, significant space; basic geometries as references to the congenital, the essential; and materials as a return to the source.

Then, developing his argument, he observes:

> Our concern here is not with the use of stylistic codes that render a building recognisable as a particular instance of a common language, but with the search, in each case and for each work, for the presence and the manifestation that are inherently proper to it.

And he continues:

> The uncertainty with which Modern architecture broached the question of the formal definition of the object was met, during the crisis of the 1950s, with the pantheistic response of the dissolution of the object in the landscape.

Of the recent work, by contrast, he argues, "today's landscape hardly constitutes a background into which the architectural object might be thought of as inserting, or integrating, or diffusing itself." Rather, he says, "contemporary architectures make their appearance, *ex abrupto* taking us by surprise". And this combination of circumstances leads him to conclude:

> The 1950s pantheistic fusion with the landscape and today's isolated stupor of the object both serve to demonstrate that the architectural object no longer establishes a stable and hierarchical relationship between itself and its surroundings.

A provocative—and as far as I can tell—unique critical observation.

Finally—and perhaps for me most brilliantly Solà-Morales' point of departure leads him to make an affirmative (but of course subtle) case for two architectural ideas which he sees as currently being in great disrepute: "decoration" and "monumentality". The argument in question occurs within the essay "Weak Architecture", in which he assesses the impact on architecture of the ideas of the Italian philosopher Gianni Vattimo, to whom we owe the concept of "weak thought". To take the case of decoration first, Solà-Morales argues that it has the potential:

> … even to lend itself, in Walter' Benjamin's terms, to a reading that is not attentive but distracted, and which thus offers itself to us as something that enhances and embellishes reality, making it more tolerable, without presuming to impose itself, to be central, to claim for itself that deference demanded by totality.

And then, paraphrasing an argument from Heidegger's essay "Art and Space", Solà-Morales observes:

> The decorative is not of necessity a condition of trivialisation of the vulgar, but simply constitutes a recognition of the fact that for the work of art—sculpture or architecture—an acceptance of a certain weakness, and thus of relegation to a secondary position, may possibly be the condition of its greatest elegance and, ultimately, its greatest significance and import.

As for monumentality, he observes that

The monumentality of weak architecture is not continuous with the monuments of the classical age in either geometric or ideological value, but only in what remains within the present context of that condition of the root term *monitu*; that is to say, of recollection.

Or again:

> The idea of monument I want to bring in here is that which we might find in an architectonic object: for all its being an opening, a window on a more intense reality, at the same time its representation is produced as a vestige, as the tremulous clangor of the bell that reverberates after it has ceased to ring; as that which is constituted as pure residuum, as recollection.

These theoretical speculations strike me as distinct and provocative. And they offer an interesting promise of the possibility of a deep reformulation of the social role of architecture. Such, then, are among the many insights that in my view already make this little book valuable.

But before concluding, I want to return to the matter of Solà-Morales' unusual intellectual formation and to a feature I have alluded to, but not focused on—his interest in contemporary art and contemporary art theory. In my remarks on his original critical view of Mies van der Rohe, I noted that an analogy with Minimalist sculpture—particularly with the work of Judd and Flavin—was pivotal for him. But it turns out that this is so not just in relation to his view of Mies. For arguments revolving around what he sees as the intensely phenomenological orientation of Minimalism—particularly its American variety—mark many of his most compelling arguments.

A particularly important instance of this can be found in the essay "Difference and Limit: Individualism in Contemporary Architecture". For here Solà-Morales remarks:

> Just as there is a Minimalist art that defines itself precisely by its proximity to the limit, there is also an architecture capable of risking itself in a venturing toward the degree zero of geometrical and spatial conformation. In the laconic architectures of Herzog and de Meuron, in the reductionism of Souto de Moura or Juan Navarro Baldeweg, in the controlled gestuality of Garces and Soria,

in the strict monumentality of Francesco Venezia or Roberto Collova, we discover a refounding of architecture as far removed from modern efficacy as from postmodern historical memory.... In the same way that a piece by Dan Flavin or Donald Judd is lacking in references... these architectures also make themselves present, in the first instance, through the strict materiality of their volumes and materials. Further signification derives from the tension present in these material structures, in which some vibration is always inscribed, some slight gesture, an almost casual distortion, the fracturing of some geometry. In short, by the experience that the form cannot be reduced to a zero point and that the signification, not existing in the void, instead becomes intense at the moment when it is granted only a liminal space, a minimal appearance.

It seems to me that in making so intense and committed an argument, Solà-Morales must be seen to be going beyond the level of generalisation which is elsewhere typical of his critical method. I have, for example, already quoted him to the effect that certain works of the 1950s and of the 1990s can be similarly seen "no longer to establish a stable relationship between themselves and [their] surroundings". In another reference—this one to work by Siza, Ando, and Gehry—he remarks: "I believe we find in all three the full and eloquent resonance of the condition of contemporary culture."

Now it would seem on the face of it that this critical observation is a commendatory one even if this is not so clear in the case of the previous comment. But in the essay on "Place", a remark occurs which puts even this provisional conclusion in doubt. For there, Solà-Morales observes that "it is in the philosophy of negation and nihilism that contemporary culture recognises itself".

In short, I observe that much of the time Solà-Morales employs his quite subtle techniques of critical analysis to attempt to determine to what extent works of architecture succeed in reflecting appropriately the historic tenor of their times, even if, one suspects, this tenor is not, in his ultimate opinion, all that much to be admired. But sometimes—and it seems to me more consequential times—he goes beyond this to attempt to assess works in a critical context which not only takes account of, but also presumes to challenge, the tenor of the times within which those works were created.

And this suggests to me that there lies deep in Solà-Morales' body of critical writings—even as they are represented in a modest selection such as this—a not quite explicit, but more engaged critical position of the author. One senses this increased intensity of engagement in his discussions of "the limit"; one feels it again in his commentaries on the influences of Guardini and Landsberg on Mies van der Rohe particularly since one of these figures, Landsberg, was closely associated with the Catholic philosopher of the "personalist" movement, Emmanuel Mounier, by whom Solà-Morales was strongly influenced as a young man.

In his concluding essay on the practice of criticism itself, Solà-Morales makes the wry observation:

Oh, that there were a discipline of architecture! If there were only a knowledge, not craft-based and empirical but general and logically transferable, then the insecurities of those working on the practical side would be deliciously alleviated.

He is prepared to allow that there once were such times, but no longer:

Architecture was, in these times, an exquisite material labour capable of producing beautiful results; it was not a global discourse addressing the great questions filling individual consciences with uncertainty.

Well, we know—not least due to the efforts of such as Solà-Morales—that architecture is such a discourse nowadays, and that new intellectual techniques are required with which to shape it. Of course, Solà-Morales knows this too, admitting that the possibility of developing such techniques, while on the one hand a "vain hope", is also a "necessity".

On the next-to-last page of his book, there is a passage that I read as a challenge to himself. "It is possible to construct an internal discourse based on experience and actual practice, but avoiding the purely autobiographical. The contemporary discourse by architects on architecture has not yet reached that level of critical judgment, that holistic cultural confrontation."

It seems to me that among the limited number of figures in our field who are equipped to initiate such a confrontation is Solà-Morales himself. I for one hope that he will take up the challenge he has here so eloquently laid down.

Part 3:
Colin Rowe

As I have already noted, I first met Colin Rowe in connection with the 1976 inaugural Preston Thomas Lectures at Cornell University. But I did not develop a strong relationship with him until much later. He did accept an invitation from me to deliver a public lecture in Toronto in the late 1970s, but until 1995, that was all.

Oppositions in the Thought of Colin Rowe, 1997

That year, a precocious Italian graduate student called Paolo Conrad Bercah arrived at the GSD, and soon announced to me that he wanted me to serve as advisor for his MArch II thesis. I agreed to do so, and the two of us worked together for a term on his development of a textual fable about architectural relations between Europe and North America that I have described elsewhere as lying somewhere between Adolf Loos and Rem Koolhaas. While we were working together, Conrad Bercah asked me if I could arrange an introduction to Colin Rowe. I wrote to Rowe to ask him if he would be willing to meet the young Italian, and since my book *The Space of Appearance* had just come out, and since among other things, it commented on Rowe, I included a copy of the book with my letter.

Rowe agreed to meet Conrad Bercah, and also wrote back to tell me how much he had enjoyed *The Space of Appearance*. Thus began an intermittent long distance conversation between us. Then, in 1996, I discovered that he had recommended that I be invited to serve as one of the keynote speakers at the *Festschrift* that Cornell was organising in his honour. The text below was my keynote address.

The ironies of a European revolution which, perhaps, tragically failed to make it, do not comprise the most gratifying of spectacles. When these are compounded with the further ironies of trans-Atlantic architectural interchange and their physical results, in America, Europe and elsewhere, we find ourselves confronted with an evidence—an adulteration of meaning, principle and form which is far from easy to neglect. The impeccably good intentions of Modern architecture, its genuine ideals of social service, above all, the poetry with which, so often, it has invested random twentieth-century happenings may all conspire to inhibit doubts as to its present condition, to encourage a suppression of the obvious; but conspire as they may, and however reluctantly we recognise it, the product of Modern architecture, compared with its performance, still established the base line for any responsible contemporary production.... We are here, once more, in the area where the physique and the morale of Modern architecture, its flesh and its word, are again, not coincident; and it is when we recognise that neither morale nor physique, neither word nor flesh was ever consistent with each other, that we might reasonably approach the architects whose work is here presented.

These well-known passages from Colin Rowe's 1972 introduction to *Five Architects* fascinated me when I first read them and have continued to do so since. Indeed, they stood at the centre of the challenge I faced in preparing part of the argument for a recent book of mine: to come to terms with Rowe's presence as a contemporary theorist of architecture.

Let us look at some of the passage's distinctive stylistic features. First of all there is the startling psychological momentum. Reading them, it is as though we are going to be led, if by nothing else but this momentum, to conclusions we will find it impossible to resist. And this is the case, despite the paradox that in this essay of Rowe's (as in certain others of his that I will discuss below), the momentum in question does not lead very directly to its ostensible subject—the work of the New York Five—but instead, to a somewhat different one that, in its turn, casts back an ambiguous, if revealing, light.

Then there is the recurrent employment of complex oppositions, a feature so ubiquitous in Rowe's writings as to have given this essay its title: "trans-Atlantic architectural interchange", "what was anticipated and what has been delivered", "physique" and "morale", "flesh" and "word", and so on. Such are the apparent building blocks of Rowe's argument. Finally—and this feature is not one I would call typical—there is the poignancy of the text. We seldom see Rowe referring to the "impeccably" good intentions of Modern architecture or to its "genuine" ideals of social service. Likewise, rarely has he characterised it as "one of the great hopes of the world".[1]

I have long suspected that Rowe's intellectual stance was, at its base, more political than his characteristically elliptical public demeanour toward politics would lead us to suppose. This said, not until recently have I made any systematic attempt to come to grips with the overall shape of his characteristic modes of thought. Only when invited to speak at the 1996 *Festschrift* in Rowe's honour, did I decide to do so. Like most other observers of my generation, I had long admired his works from a distance. Unlike many of the participants in the *Festschrift*, I had never been either a student or an academic colleague of his. Indeed, although I lived in London from 1964 to1967, I only met Rowe, to the best of my recollection, in New York in 1974 at a conference at which we were both speakers. As a result of this relative distance from him, I had come to know his work but fitfully, and episodically, over an extended period of time.

I cannot recall, for example, when I first read the famous "Mathematics" and "Mannerism" essays of 1947 and 1950, although it must have been in London; I seem to recollect during that same period looking up and being fascinated by his "*La Tourette*" and "Transparency" essays of 1961 and 1963.[2] And while unsure of the precise date, I certainly remember as a highlight of a late 1970s lecture series at the University of Toronto, a version of "The Provocative Facade: Frontality and *Contrapposto*", a lecture that, it turns out, was a staple of the Rowe repertoire during those years.[3]

Now all these essays embody what could uncontroversially be characterised as the work of the "formalist" Colin Rowe. And it is clear enough that the formalist Rowe is a formidable figure who has altered our ways of thinking about architecture in our era. So thoroughgoing has been Rowe's influence in this respect that he has effectively appropriated to himself large parts of the formalist discourse of pedagogy that is available to us today. Peter Eisenman, for example, has remarked to the effect that when one is engaged in the teaching of Corbusian formal systems in architectural studios nowadays, it is almost impossible—even for the likes of Eisenman—to distinguish Colin Rowe's reading of those systems from Le Corbusier's own. Given this, it should be no surprise that observers from Eisenman to Sanford Kwinter tend to see the formalist Rowe as the definitive Rowe.[4]

Yet, for me, the matter is not so clear-cut. If Formalism really were the beginning and end of it, then the urgency that underpins the introduction to *Five Architects* would not be so palpable. If Rowe's mode of thinking were this unambiguous, then it would also be true that the strangely exorcising tenor of his recent book *The Architecture of Good Intentions* would make no sense.[5] It is my hunch that as important as the famous, virtuoso formalist analyses are, they are not for their author—nor should they be for his readers—the end of the matter. Rather, I'm inclined to speculate, they have been intended to sit inside a larger intellectual and historical project of Rowe's that is not only still incomplete but also not completable.

What, we may ask, is this larger project? Believe that it has to do with determining the feasibility of framing an affirmative reply to the poignant question Rowe asked at the end of his *Five Architects* introduction. That is to say, "can an architecture which professes an objective of continuous experiment ever become congruous with the ideal of an architecture which is to be popular, intelligible and profound?"[6] Moreover, I'm inclined to think that the intellectual and psychological effort Rowe has made to bring this larger project to fruition—and thus to answer the deeply difficult question he had posed to himself—can be considered through further examination of certain conceptual techniques identifiable in his writings over a relatively long span of time.

First, of course, there is in his penchant for complex, reciprocal oppositions. I have cited a number of such oppositions as they appear in the *Five Architects* introduction, but other, larger, more general ones manifest themselves elsewhere throughout his writings. "Europe/America", "high art/low art", and "Modernism/anti-Modernism" are key instances that we should examine more closely.

In the first place, it is a truism to speak of Rowe's "trans-Atlanticism". For it is, at least, a basic fact of his biography. But this phenomenon runs much deeper in his work than this simple biographical fact. Surely it suffuses his entire critical and historical position. For a provocative hint of it, consider this remark from his 1958 review of Henry-Russell Hitchcock's then recently published *Architecture: Nineteenth and Twentieth Centuries*:

> One of the most eminent American critics of contemporary architecture, Professor Hitchcock is able to survey the European scene with a certain trans-Atlantic calm while he can also approach the American picture with the degree of cosmopolitan detachment.[7]

For a deeper suggestion of the power of this opposition, consider this eloquent passage from Rowe's "Lockhart, Texas" essay written in 1955–1956 and published in 1957:

> Often in the sharp light and the vacant landscape of the West, architectural detail will seem to achieve an almost archaic clarity, so the most tawdry saloon or incrusted false facade may acquire portentous distinction, while whole towns founded no earlier than the 1860s can exude an Italian evidence of age. For these reasons, for the sympathetic traveller Utah will evoke memories of Tuscany, Virginia City, Nevada, will appear to be a nineteenth-century Urbino, while such mining cities as Leadville, Colorado, Carson City, Nevada, or Globe, Arizona, will seem as

unquestionably as Gubbio or Siena to have always occupied the land.[8]

"Cosmopolitan detachment" indeed! Then there is the manner in which Rowe's trans-Atlanticism facilitates the dazzling, speculative comparisons he often makes. One powerful set occurs in his 1958 review of Frank Lloyd Wright's *A Testament*. Here, for example, is a pair of passages comparing Wright with Edwin Lutyens:

> Both were gifted. Both from careful backgrounds. Both inherited certain traditions in common. And though they were separated by the spiritual gulf which intervenes between Surrey and Wisconsin, for a time at least their performances ran in parallel.[9]

Still, continues Rowe,

> Although Lutyens and Wright for a brief period were superficially close, it was only a matter of time before the great cleavage began to appear…. Wright—the *anima naturaliter classica*, to borrow from Henry-Russell Hitchcock—had already by the 1890s in his designs for the Milwaukee public library, and the Blossom House, Chicago, anticipated those classicising tendencies which were later to provide the English architect with his stock in trade. American prescience and Celtic quickness had forced to the surface and had overcome certain issues.
>
> In addition, Wright married no Lady Emily Lytton. He inherited by proxy no viceregal splendours. No effulgence like that of the Raj was to divert his course. No British Knebworth lay, like an instructive shadow across his career. For Americans of his generation and attainments, a move into public life was far from easy; and the sense of exclusion from a political society which had already nurtured a Henry Adams seems in Wright's generation to have contributed a peculiar brilliancy to intellectual life. The possibility of identifying with government, never hard for an Englishman and facilitated for Lutyens by his connections, issued in England as approximate determinations of form, as empirical working procedures. But the impossibility of identifying with government seems to have sponsored in the United States a vein of introspection and an aesthetic culture which could never be satisfied with less than a final statement. And that's what the English architect, as he achieves prominence, can become: more and

more that the mouthpiece of government; more and more like the mannered representative of the English system in all its supposedly august presence. These are the potentialities or privileges of which the American is largely deprived. And in the case of Lutyens and Wright, we are finally awarded the ironical commentary of Lutyens in England painfully suppressing his bohemianism, becoming an agent of an exclusive dream of imperium, while his wife— more certain of her position—cultivates her taste for Krishnamurti and other philosophical manifestations; and of Wright in America, strenuously maintaining a personal rebellion, assuming both Lady Emily's interest in Orientalia *and* her husband's architectural activity, going out to meet the most varied experience with nothing to uphold but principle. And taken side-by-side, the Imperial Hotel, Tokyo, and the Viceroy's house, New Delhi, complete the illumination of the point.[10]

Or again, from the same essay, startlingly acute comparison of H H Richardson with Richard Norman Shaw and Charles Garnier:

American by birth, English by sympathy, French by training, Richardson in his short career towers above all possible rivals. By his side Norman Shaw becomes a clever watercolourist.

Richardson reduces the splendidly endowed Charles Garnier to the status of a meretricious decorator. And it was the inheritance of a French rationalism, transmitted through him by the Laboustes, which above all else, permitted the sudden conversion of the picturesque house from a popular formula into a spatial explosion. Richardson introduced logic. He had acquired the Parisian rigor; he had compounded it with the passion of a Butterfield; and he had made it a operative via his most personal ability, both to control the profile of the local episode and to soften the edges of the total mass. With him the cultivation of the arbitrary seemed always to be propelled by internal necessity; the whimsies so dear to the nineteenth century always to be proliferated by principle; and the plan became something like the music of an opera of which the integrated libretto comprised the details.[11]

In *Good Intentions*, Rowe returns to the matter of the relationship of French and American architecture in the late nineteenth century. In the passage below, he comments on illustrations included in Viollet-le-Duc's *Dictionnaire raisonné de l'architecture* of 1868 and on their possible influence in America:

There are, for instance, a couple of houses, alpine or semi-Germanic—and one wonders did these ever exist? But, as exemplars of Vincent Scully's Stick Style, how quickly these two became domesticated in the United States. Then a Romanesque house perhaps from Provence, with a flat facade and heroic but stumpy arch which, in its American metamorphosis, was shortly to become a property of Richardson's and, after him, part of the repertory of Sullivan and Wright. And we can end with a house which, very likely, is supposed to be in Normandy and probably in Rouen. A half-timbered house with unknown infill, this might be seen as leading up to William Le Baron Jenney's truly superb First Leiter building of 1879; but all the same, Jenney's building had almost been anticipated by the facade of a Paris apartment house, cast-iron frame and brick infill, which Daly had published in 1878. However, since Richardson's long demolished Marshall Field Store of 1883–1887 can be considered intrinsically a grandiose and commercialised version of Henri Labrouste's Bibliotheque, should this curious little incident of a French priority be all that surprising?[12]

I know of no other architectural commentator than Rowe who could've written these astonishing sentences, who could frame such spectacular and revelatory trans-Atlantic comparisons.

The opposition of high and low art is both more elusive and more ambiguous. But it is certainly a key theme of the "Lockhart, Texas" essay. Consider some of Rowe's summary observations on the buildings he has been describing in Lockhart as well as those of other western American towns:

These buildings are scarcely inhabited by either taste or culture, were improvised apparently without thought, seem to be the embodiment of a popular architectural consciousness, and present themselves to the eyes of the present day as the final and the comprehensive monuments of a heroic age.[13]

Or again:

> They are structures which personally one finds deeply satisfactory; yet, with any conviction, one cannot attribute to the designer a developed or a conscious aesthetic intention, and certainly not the intention to produce the results of which one is most deeply appreciative.[14]

We find, then, already here a reference to the concept of "the popular" that is to resurface so poignantly at the conclusion of the introduction to *Five Architects*, as well as indisputable evidence of Rowe's readiness to take certain manifestations of the vernacular very seriously indeed. In a later essay, similar issues are discussed more elusively and more ambiguously still. I refer here to Rowe's controversial essay "Robert Venturi and the Yale Mathematics Building" of 1970. In the very first paragraph of this text, Rowe touches upon such matters—and he does so, significantly enough, with a reference not to the design for the Mathematics Building, but to the argument of Venturi's famous *Complexity and Contradiction in Architecture* of 1966.[15] Venturi, Rowe remarks, "has written a book which discloses to him to be something of a mandarin; he has designed a number of buildings which suggest something equally elitist; and because he admires paradox, he also professes a feeling for the commonplace."[16] Having begun in this manner, Rowe moves on, in the process assuming the tone of voice that was to make this essay so controversial in the first place and shifting his consideration of the matter of the vernacular from the "deeply appreciative" stance of "Lockhart, Texas" to one both sceptical and volatile:

> For the Yale Mathematics Building [Venturi] has made a project of which he says that the 'image is ordinary' and 'the substance is ordinary', and though there should be nothing wrong or remarkable about that, still, if a genuine commonplace is indeed to arise in Hillhouse Avenue, then what should there really be talk about? And why should criticism be solicited? Because surely, if the Mathematics Building is to be what it is said to be, then it will be no more than the equivalent of any old Main Street job and though, as such, it might afford casual gratification (native genius in anonymous architecture?), presumably it could, quite well, be unprovided with critical notice.[17]

Rowe then proceeds to lay out a relatively detailed account of what he sees as the strengths and weaknesses of Venturi's arguments in *Complexity and Contradiction*. And in doing so, he makes certain observations that lead us back to the present theme:

> Venturi finds it hard to accept the dated naivete of that body of ideas which still circulates as Modern architecture's apologetic; and, though he does not say as much, one suspects that he would be just as prone to condemn the Bauhaus ideal of a *total architecture* as being something dangerously Wagnerian. That is, while he is appalled by simplistic explanations and aspirations… he would prefer to insist upon the usefulness of a dichotomy between 'high' and 'low' culture, between 'fine' and 'crude' art, and upon the complete normality of a two-way commerce between the 'polite' and the 'vulgar'.[18]

But having posited the "usefulness" of the dichotomy and having introduced the model of "two-way commerce", Rowe nevertheless finds Venturi's ways of addressing them problematic:

> Venturi shuttles between an esoteric ideal—the game of the learned reference and the calculated footnote—and a would-be esoteric and populist one. Hence his preoccupation with ambiguity, whether of meaning of form, Honky-tonk and Caserta, Frank Furness and Hawksmoor, Parisien *hotels particuliers* and the Cappella Sforza, small town America and McKim, Mead and White; anything which can be ironically considered or is itself ironical has been absorbed if not always digested, and Venturi has then felt amazingly free to play with these discrete elements as though they were ingredients of a collage. We paste on an allusion to the Villa Aldobrandini; we make clear, *to the happy few*, our infatuation with the William Low House at Bristol, Rhode Island; we make commentary upon Stupinigi, Pavlovsk, Howard Johnson's, or Route 66; and then we syncopate the mix.[19]

Or again:

> And, if the notion of the 'ordinary'… begins thus to acquire some specific meaning, we might now

also notice how the world of Venturi's images is without homogeneity, how it seems to be rifted, how there here seems to be signified a world of ancient culture—aristocratic and primarily European—which is juxtaposed alongside a world of imminent culture, an incipient modern world which is, primarily, American.

Rowe continues:

This cleavage, I think, should be evident to anyone who is not hopelessly prejudiced either in favour of Venturi or against him; and it would seem to be important, for it allows Venturi the best of all possible worlds. He can be simultaneously the Jamesian American in Europe, indisputably more refined (and less Marxian) than any European could ever be, and a Whitmanesque type in the United States.[20]

By now, my own collage of quotations has begun to make a number of provisional generalisations possible. First of all, these various passages make apparent how the opposition "high art/ low art" is, for Rowe, an even more complex one thing than that of "Europe/America"—and this is true, I think, although the references to Venturi also make it clear how, for him, these two oppositions are in a number of important senses interconnected. It also becomes evident that Rowe imagines these conceptual oppositions ideally informing and enriching one another—in a "two-way commerce" to use his words—and that he sees the possibility of their doing so to be the result of the efficacious employment of the medium of irony; even if he has found Venturi's attempts in this regard insufficient.

But at least as apparent as these provisional generalisations is the deepest and most complex of all Rowe's oppositions, that between Modernism and anti-Modernism. A common perception in architecture nowadays—and one by which, in the preparation of this essay, I discovered myself to have been significantly influenced—is that Colin Rowe, when all is said and done, is an opponent of Modernism. Of course, the extent of this perception is not altogether surprising. And it would be quite easy to find corroboration for it in his own writings. We might, for a start, cite the imaginary "obituary" for Modern architecture that Rowe included in his Cubitt lecture of 1979. It begins:

We may ascribe her death (Modern architecture is surely a she) to the ingenuousness of her temperament. Displaying an extraordinary addiction to towers and completely unconstructed spaces, when young she possessed a high and romantically honourable idea of life and her excess of sensibility could only lead to later chagrin.[21]

The same passage concludes:

Not surprising, therefore, should be Modern architecture's agitated and long decline; but, though this death was to be expected, it is greatly to be regretted and the extinction of this once pristine creature… has been desperately sad to witness. But, a late nineteenth-century character and never fully knowing it, she addressed herself to a moral condition of permanent rapture, to an ecstatic condition which could only endanger her frail physique, and, to repeat, excessive sensibility abused by inadequate experience, motivated by quasi-religious sentiment not well understood and complicated by the presence of physics envy, *Zeitgeist* worship, object fixation and stradaphobia must be considered the greatest factors contributing to the demise.[22]

To be sure, even this obituary gives numerous indications of equivocation on Rowe's part: "greatly to be regretted", "desperately sad to witness," and so on. Later in the same essay, he even makes a plea for the "survival" of Modernism, albeit within the context of what he calls the "revival" of the city that has been so damaged by it. But, of course, even here, he concludes that such survival is never to be considered if the architect continues to insist that all buildings should be considered works of architecture; that all buildings grow from the inside out; that all design should be total; and that the architect is the messiah of the future.[23]

In "The Vanished City, or Rowe Reflects", written in 1984, his disillusionment with Modernism is ever more complete:

The limpid and beautiful future which the reformation of the city was all about has not exactly been inaugurated; and correspondingly, the mood is now more disingenuous than the style of 1920 to 1960 would have been able to accept. Suddenly we have all become cynics. No longer a pure and a revolutionary idea, as simply a fact of life Modern architecture is increasingly revealed to have been a very shabby and less than intelligent affair.[24]

Still, these devastating commentaries notwithstanding, my recent readings have convinced me that the Modernism/anti-Modernism opposition in Rowe's work remains ambiguous. One does not have to be a Shakespearean scholar to detect a significant quantity of "protesting too much" in the anti-Modernism of the argument of The Architecture of Good Intentions. Moreover, I'm inclined to see Rowe's predictable disparagement of the Zeitgeist, at certain recognisably structural moments of contemporary theoretical discourse, as symptomatic of deeply unresolved concerns in his position. Given the intensity of his disillusionment, then, can illuminating evidence be found in the writings, taken as a whole, of a Rowe who had ever been a true—or at least 'truer'—believer?

I think the answer to this question is yes. In my view, Rowe gives himself away in a preface to a very early text, republished in As I Was Saying, claiming in the wisdom of hindsight to be "mildly shocked by" his own early, "naive Hegelianism". The text in question is a rather negative review he wrote in 1952 for The Art Bulletin of Talbot Hamlin's Forms and Functions of Twentieth-Century Architecture. And it contains a passage that is as attractively straightforward a commendation of the principles of Modernism as was his 1957 one of the vernacular buildings of Lockhart. Rowe remarked at the time on Hamlin's critical method:

Mr Hamlin's unwillingness to involve himself in historical judgement is linked with his unwillingness to investigate the specific unity of principles which animates the architecture of the twentieth century. In the last analysis, the intuitive recognition that at the moment of creation, only a limited range of possibilities can claim a real legitimacy. It is the positive statement of what, for a given occasion, is historically significant that causes the manifestations of Le Corbusier and Gropius still to survive as the classic statements of Modern architecture's aims. Here, where creative tension is at its highest, the animating unity of principles is scrupulously observed. Here instinctively and without any thought of style, but by means of a positive position with regard to history, style is formed. Like all style, it is dynamic

and perpetually evolved, but it is not the 'stylishness' of particular buildings or designers. It is rather, the super-rational expression, the abstraction of preoccupations which are organic to our society.[25]

Here we have, then, evidence of a period of Rowe's more-or-less straightforward belief in the principles of Modernism "before the fall" (to employ an intellectual schema that his own Good Intentions would later designate as "eschatological"). From the perspective of the late 1990s, we can see how Rowe would wish to disavow at least some of the tenor of this youthful commentary. I would probably even be ready to see some of it as "naively Hegelian" myself. This having been conceded, it is nevertheless impossible to proceed straightforwardly from this interim conclusion to the further one that the pro-modern early Rowe notwithstanding, the late Rowe is consistently anti-modern. To demonstrate this, we need only to return to the introduction to Five Architects: while its tone is surely elegiac, it cannot in any way be perceived as dismissive or rejecting of Modernism. As I already said, for me, its poignant affirmations are among the most powerful moments in all of Rowe's writings.

And if this is not complicated enough, in reviewing the writings as a whole, we are required also to take account of a fascinating and confounding text that Rowe published in exactly the same year as the controversial Cubitt lecture: his introduction to the publication in English of Rob Krier's Urban Space. Given the criticisms of Modernism that typified the Cubitt lecture, given Krier's broad sympathy with this line of criticism, given the fact that Rowe had been invited by Krier to write such an introduction, we might think we know what to expect. In fact, we get no further disparagements of Modernism. Instead, we are plunged precipitously into a rather startling commentary on the problematic political and critical success of architecttura razionale circa 1979. Ponder the following passage from this document:

With the nitty-gritty of the Welfare State and the appalling bureaucratic details of pseudo-Capitalist administration we will have nothing to do; instead we will simplify, abstract, and project to the degree of extravagance a highly restricted, private, and not very hospitable version of what the good society might be assumed to be. We will give a nod to Kaufman; we will give three muted cheers for the Stalin Allee; we will adore the manifesto pieces of Boullée; we will (mostly) ignore the built work of Soane; instead we will unroll a few hundred yards of neutral Adolph Loos facade, build a lot of little towers and stand around on top of a quantity of Ledoux Villas, wave quietly but not too exuberantly to Louis Khan (congratulations on the Trenton Bath House), insinuate a reference to the metaphysic of Giorgio de Chirico, display a conversance with Léonidov, become highly enthusiastic about the more evocative aspects of Art Deco, exhibit the intimidation of curtains waving in the wind, and then, gently warm up the ensuing goulash in the *pastoso* of Morandi.[26]

A few pages further on we encounter the following passage, one that speaks to the durable tendency within the tradition of Modernism of a certain youthful—and sometimes destructive—rebelliousness:

So it was an important idea—and a dangerous one; and, like many important—and dangerous—ideas, it has become fossilised and survives as no more than unexamined and tedious tradition; let us rather be potential than productive; let us be dynamic rather introspective; let us prefer animation to reflection; let us condemn the unjust sophistications and special moral codes of established society; since Rousseau's noble savage… is almost the same as Peter Pan… then, in order to make a *tabula rasa*, in order to disclose a primitive house and to engender a future society—redeemed, and of renewed aboriginal purity—let us proceed to mock, to injure, and to destroy the existing.[27]

Here now what Rowe has to say about this tendency:

The fiesta of destruction (one imagines broken bottles on New Year's Eve in Naples) which has continued since the Enlightenment surely deserves to be applauded. For the most part it has been exhilarating; also it has resulted in previously undreamed of blessings; and as one attempts to imagine the condition of provincial society, circa 1770, in almost any small city in the world, then one can only say: Thank God for the ventilations which, over the last two hundred years, have been made![28]

And this praise of Modernism's means and of its effects does not end here. For Rowe continues:

If the advocates of *archittetura razionale*… are able to make a highly apt critique of Modern architecture's urbanistic failure and if this is of immense value, it does not automatically follow that *all* of the physical achievements of Modern architecture are to be condemned and we are entirely obliged to return to a simplified and innocent world, *à la* Laugier, a species of antediluvian (and Marxist) *belle epoque*, reminiscent more of Knossos than of New York, in which strangely deserted piazzas, seemingly prepared for not yet to be anticipated rituals, in the meantime support a somewhat scanty population of mildly desperate hippies.

Indeed, it may be a rather curious commentary upon a contemporary failure of nerve that a merely abbreviated reconstitution of the nineteenth-century city, enticingly equipped with surrealistic overtones, is now so widely received as the most pregnant and potential of disclosures. For, though such a reconstruction is in many ways what is required, there are still inhibitions about the tricking out of Beaux-Arts plans, with new primitive facades… and there are still reserves of feeling (oddly futurist and strangely technophile?) which will operate to prevent any such, immediate dispensation.[29]

With such compelling appeals to the political and technological traditions of Modernism, Rowe makes clear just how reciprocal and complex his feelings really are; indeed I see these passages as representing the quintessence of the ambiguity I wish to ascribe to him in respect to the deep Modernist/anti-Modernist themes in his work.

But there is one last feature of this particular text of Rowe's that is also, in my view, structural to it: a feature common also to two other texts already cited, the essay on Venturi and the Yale Mathematics Building and the introduction to *Five Architects*. This is Rowe's curiously insistent avoidance of directly facing the ostensible subject of a text that he has been commissioned to prepare.

In the case of the Venturi essay, for example, Rowe was asked to prepare a commentary on Venturi's winning submission to the competition for the design of a new building for the mathematics department at Yale. And while the text he produces does eventually include one, it is preceded by an assessment of Venturi's theoretical position that is so extensive—and so sceptical—as to completely colour our reading of the assessment of the building that follows. In the case of the *Five Architects* introduction, the surprise is that Rowe barely discusses the work. Rather, the introduction is dedicated to the elegy for Modernism examined in some detail above. And in the case of the introduction to Krier's book, a rather perfunctory discussion of the architect's work does indeed appear, but only after the extended and rather critical commentary on *architettura razionale*.

Now it would seem reasonable to ask, in the broadest possible sense, what is going on here? On the face of it, we would appear to be dealing with a thinker who has quite revelatory observations on the significance of various modes of trans-Atlantic architectural communication and influence over a couple of centuries, and who avows a very pregnant idea of the possibility of a productive two-way commerce between high art and low. Yet the same figure appears, after long reflection on the matter, to be unable to come to a final position in the weighty matter of the long-term viability of the principles of Modernism in architecture— even to the point of publishing two texts in the same year that exhibit quite opposed temperamental perspectives in this respect. And not only that, the same figure demonstrates a propensity, which appears to be structural, to avoid directly addressing the central matters at hand, in a series of at least three commissioned texts spread over a decade in the middle of his career.

In the dilemma I have found myself facing in attempting to come to terms with these issues in the work of Rowe, I have been reminded of the startling remark Hannah Arendt makes in *The Human Condition* in respect to the work of Karl Marx: "fundamental and flagrant contradictions rarely occur in second-rate writers; in the work of the great authors, they lead to the very centre of their work".[30] Could it be that the contradictions, ambiguities, and paradoxes I have been identifying in Rowe might lead to the very centre of *his* work? To start with, and to focus on the commissioned essays, an early clue may be found in the introduction to the Krier book. For in his opening sentence, Rowe refers to "the jungle-like politics of architectural self-advertisement".[31] I suspect that his aversion to self-advertisement inclines him to evade the expected form of a commissioned text; in other words, whoever asks Colin Rowe to contribute to a publication that is, in the first instance, an honorific one is likely to get in response something different from what was requested. Thus the convenors of the Yale Mathematics Building Competition asked for

a commentary on the winning design, and received instead of critical essay on Venturi's architectural ideas. The New York Five asked for an introduction to their work, and received instead an essay on precisely that cultural production on which their work depended deeply, but which it had in many profound ways left behind. And Rob Krier, having sought an introductory commentary on his work, received instead a text on the limitations of Rationalism and on its profound dept to Modernism.

Building on this initial reading in terms of architectural politics and diplomacy, let me further suggest that it is a structural inclination of Rowe's always to decline to accept the proffered—or even the implicit or assumed— intellectual frame of reference of any particular discussion. Instead, he cannot resist the urge to read the situation in question "against the grain", as it were, and to recast the frame of reference for its discussion in larger, and far less familiar, terms. And given that this inclination seems an instinctive, almost involuntary one, it is in retrospect not surprising that, on some occasions, his contrarianism comes across as perverse or as diplomatically inappropriate.

But the converse benefit of this propensity on Rowe's part is the powerful and unexpected widening of the terms of discourse about architecture in our time: this is its surprisingly frequent result. Even if the Venturi essay has not altered our overall ways of thinking about the possibilities today of American architecture, it certainly has sharpened our view of the capabilities and historical significance of Venturi himself. And there is no doubt in my mind that the astonishing essay of 1972 in *Five Architects* recast the terms of our view of architecture's future, in fundamentally important ways. Even the Krier introduction—leaving aside its virtuoso polemical imagery—has had the refreshing effect of de-ideologising, to some degree, the typically tiresome debates about urbanism of the past decade and a half.

And this leads me back to the matter of the "larger project" I imputed to Rowe near the beginning of this essay. For it was, as I argued, an attempt by him to answer the question of whether or not "an architecture which professes an objective of continuous experiment [can] ever become congruous with the ideal of an architecture which is to be popular, intelligible and profound."

In light of the consideration given to the characteristic oppositions that have so preoccupied Rowe over his career, in light of the complex range of social, political, and cultural questions these oppositions have brought into play, it is now apparent how heroic a project we are actually considering here. For within the broad historical and cultural canvas on which the discourse Rowe has established is now proceeding, it is clear that the objective of "continuous experiment" to which he has referred puts deeply into question the very ideals of "popularity, intelligibility and profundity" that he has also propounded—however desirable either he or any of the rest of us may see both this objective and these ideals to be. To be sure, I do not mean to propose that Rowe has failed to make any progress towards this goal. The revelatory, cross-cultural, and cross-disciplinary comparisons he has demonstrated between Europe and America; the two-way commerce between high and low art that he has so touchingly exemplified; and the great contest of Modernism and anti-Modernism that now seems to me the hallmark of his sensibility, all these have significantly shaped contemporary views of the possibilities open to us at the present time.

What is more, much as I know that Rowe grows quickly impatient with discourses in contemporary cultural theory, his temperamental inclination always to look at any particular issue both close up and from afar and to address questions that—on the face of it—appear ideological "from the side" sits quite easily within the context of circumspection about *alteritas* that distinguishes all the best in Post-structuralist cultural theory. But, of course, at the same time that these observations suggest that Rowe's characteristic ways of thinking and addressing controversies make him more contemporary than he might think—Rowe being somewhat "poststructural" in much the same way that the famous character of Moliere's has been speaking prose all his life without knowing it—they also suggest how it is that the larger project I have ascribed to him will surely remain incomplete.

For Post-structuralism, too, has abandoned the concept of the *Zeitgeist*, but in its ongoing efforts to come seriously to terms with the nature of reality, it has instead formulated alternative theoretical constructions with which to make sense of the trajectories of historical events. One that is appropriate to cite here is that of the *episteme* as formulated in the work of Michael Foucault. Through the idea of the *episteme*, Foucault attempted to frame those key historical forms of thought that can, through careful deconstruction, be seen to generate both the potentials and the limitations of thinking in a particular historical period, while simultaneously

eschewing the teleological momentum that, in earlier periods, would have been ascribed by its advocates to the *Zeitgeist*. It is my view that Rowe's efforts to recast the terms of architectural discourse in our time, powerful and provocative though they have been, will ultimately run up against the sheer limits of the possibility of thought in our time. That is to say, before the relations of "continuous experiment" in architecture to "popularity, intelligibility and profundity" can be adequately reframed, transformations more extensive than any our current theorising can encompass will have to occur. In this regard, we can even quote the younger Rowe against the Rowe who is with us today. For as he said in his review of Talbot Hamlin, a review whose "naive Hegelianism" he now disavows, "at the moment of creation, only a limited range of possibilities can claim a real legitimacy".

Let us consider an instance of an "excluded possibility" of this kind that has already arisen in the discussion. In "Lockhart, Texas", Rowe refers to the towns buildings as "the embodiment of a popular architectural consciousness", even though, "one cannot attribute to the designer a developed, or a conscious aesthetic intention". And the argument of his essay presents such buildings for consideration in a very affirmative way. Then, too, in his Cubitt lecture, he argues that Modernism's survival is not to be considered if, among other things, "the architect continues to insist that all buildings should be considered works of architecture". Between the two comments, Rowe would seem—at least implicitly—to be calling for a definitive reinstatement of the once-potent historical distinction between buildings that are works of architecture and those that are not.

Yet I would argue that as architects and as teachers nowadays, we no longer have available to us any conceptual means of making such a distinction. We know Adolf Loos' famous remark about the tomb and the monument being architecture and the house not being so, but this view of his has yet to yield any tangible results in practice in our century. Indeed, I am inclined to think that it is precisely the unprecedently high level of self-consciousness about cultural theory and praxes today that makes it even less possible for us now than it was for Loos a century ago to make such a distinction. It would be—to cite Arendt's words in another context—"like trying to step on our own shadows".

Such, then, is the potency and relative invisibility and intractability of the historical facts that Rowe's theorising has brought into play. And so, too, is it that the larger project of the later career of Colin Rowe will remain unfinished. The hoped-for congruity of "continuous experiment" with the ideals of "popularity, intelligibility, and profundity", it seems to me, will only become manifest of future terms that are impossible for today's observers to discern.

This said, in the Post-structuralist era to which I have just involuntarily appropriated my subject, it is also true that "complete projects" are intellectually and ethically suspect in any event. Indeed, we owe it to writers from Jorge Luis Borges to Italo Calvino to have so sharply delineated the contemporary concept of the limits of the thinkable, a concept that will need to be invoked in the undertaking of any definitive future assessment of Rowe's intellectual accomplishment.

I want to conclude with a short biographical speculation. For I found myself, along the way, intrigued by Rowe's temperamental preferences, in regard to historical personalities. Readers familiar with his work and personal taste will, I think, readily agree that it is unlikely he would have any enthusiasm to attend a dinner party with say, Walter Gropius or Tony Garnier. But I believe I have identified a pair of historical figures within Rowe's texts who can be seen as true soul mates for him: the politician and the political writer Edmund Burke and the architectural critic and journalist César Daly.

Both appear more than once in Rowe's writings, particularly in *The Architecture of Good Intentions*. And both are portrayed in uncustomarily congenial prose. But there is even more to it than this. For the Anglo-Irish Burke was definitely marked by a complex, dual, socio-political loyalty. The Anglo-Irish-French Daly, famously, made his *Revue generale de l'architecture* a truly international magazine. As Rowe remarks in *Good Intentions*:

Daly was… driven to continue and, gradually, to find consolation for what he felt that the French had not achieved in what he felt sure that the Americans would bring about. Thus, in an article of 1886… he presents specimens of American domestic architecture and expresses his admiration. Unable to associate himself with *confreres* who condemn the architectural eccentricities of the

United States, he continues that, although these exist, they are to be associated with boldness and daring of composition, an audacity of *parti-pris*, a sense of comfort and internal luxury which announce a vigorous bud about to blossom and which, pretty soon, will shine with a brilliant light. After 47 years as editor of the *Revue*, these are almost Daly's last words; and he concludes his article with the surprisingly *sportif* exhortation, almost as though he felt himself, age seventy-five, to be a cheerleader: "Bravo l'Amerique. Go ahead. Hurrah!" It is a pity that Daly could not have been transported to the New England of the 1880s.[32]

Well, some three-quarters of a century later, Colin Rowe was transported—if not to New England, then to Texas and upstate New York—and we have ever since been the beneficiaries of his particular trans-Atlantic sensibility.

With Burke, the analogies seem more intellectual than biographical. But Burke was criticised by his contemporaries for his deeply equivocal attitude to the revolution in France, much as Rowe has been for his own stance *vis a vis* architectural Modernism. And, as with Rowe among his theorist peers today, Burke appeared to many of his fellow politicians as unreliable—unwilling to accept party discipline, too eager to preserve independence of mind—and thus, in the end, as politically naive. Viewing the England of his time from the perspective of his native Ireland, he felt compelled to temper his generalised political views by the particularity of exterior circumstance; ostensibly a conservative in the Britain of his era, he nevertheless gave great intellectual and moral succour to the critics of industrialisation who belonged to the next generation. Perhaps most remarkable of all, while a member of Parliament, he took it upon himself to address at Westminster the welfare of the aboriginal populations of pre-revolutionary America.

In the ambition of the intellectual endeavours, in their breadth of vision, in their curiosity as to the state of things in territories afar, in their commitment to particulars, and in their magnanimity and congeniality, Burke and Daly are for Rowe happy historical companions.[33]

1   Rowe, Collin, introduction to Five Architects, Oxford: Oxford University Press, p 3.

2   All four of these famous essays—"The Mathematics of the Ideal Villa", "Mannerism and Modern Architecture", "La Tourette", and "Transparency: Literal and Phenomenal" (this last written in 1955–1956 with Robert Slutsky)—are reprinted in Rowe, Colin, *The Mathematics of the Ideal Villa and Other Essays,* Cambridge, MA: MIT press, 1976.

3   Rowe, Colin, *As I Was Saying: Recollections and Miscellaneous Essays*, 3 vols, Cambridge, MA: MIT press, 1976.

4   Eisenman's remark was made personally to the author. Kwinter's view on this matter is evident in the text of his contribution to the special issue on Rowe of *Any*: "Who's Afraid of Formalism?", *Any* 7–8, p 65.

5   Rowe, Colin, *The Architecture of Good Intentions: Towards a Possible Retrospect*, London: Academy Editions, 1994.

6   Rowe, Introduction to *Five Architects*, p 7.

7   Rowe, *As I Was Saying*, p 179. Reading this characterisation, I find myself supposing that the then-young Rowe and the older Hitchcock must have found each other's temperament quite engaging.

8   Rowe, *As I Was Saying*, p 56. The original publication of this essay gave Rowe and John Hejduk as joint authors. Rowe here claims that Hejduk acted as photographer and he is the author of the text. The issue of authorship, however, remains controversial.

9   Rowe, *As I Was Saying*, p 169.

10 Rowe, *As I Was Saying*, pp 171–172.

11 Rowe, *As I Was Saying*, p 171.

12 Rowe, *The Architecture of Good Intentions*, p 99.

13 Rowe, *As I Was Saying*, p 56.

14 Rowe, *As I Was Saying*, p 70.

15 Venturi, Robert, *Complexity and Contradiction in Architecture,* New York: Museum of Modern Art, 1966.

16 Rowe, *As I Was Saying*, p 280.

17 Rowe, *As I Was Saying*, p 83.

18 Rowe, *As I Was Saying*, p 83.

19 Rowe, *As I Was Saying*, p 87.

20 Rowe, *As I Was Saying*, p 90.

21 Rowe, *As I Was Saying*, p 154.

22 Rowe, *As I Was Saying*, p 155.

23 Rowe, *As I Was Saying*, p 208.

24 Rowe, *As I Was Saying*, p 241.

25 Rowe, *As I Was Saying*, p 119.

26 Rowe, *As I Was Saying*, p 258.

27 Rowe, *As I Was Saying*, p 262.

28 Rowe, *As I Was Saying*, p 262.

29 Rowe, *As I Was Saying*, pp 263–264. I cannot help but note that the provocations of a Rob Krier appear to be such as to elicit belated futurist and technophile inclinations in Rowe's psyche.

30 Arendt, Hannah, *The Human Condition,* Garden City: Doubleday Anchor, 1959, p 90. Anyone familiar with my previous work will not be surprised when I say that when confronted with apparent paradoxes of the sort just outlined, I often turn to this intellectual figure who has had such a marked influence on the formation of my thought.

31 Rowe, *As I Was Saying*, p 257.

32 Rowe, The Architecture of Good Intentions, p 96.

33 This text is one of a series of essays I am currently preparing on the thought of a number of the leading architectural theorists/historians of our era. It was first presented to an audience that included its subject, as the Festschrift in his honour convened at Cornell University, 26–28 April 1996. At the conclusion of the presentation, I asked Rowe what he had made of it. In particular, I was curious to know what he had made of the dinner party I had hypothesised. He allowed that it was, in fact, an aptly framed one, complaining only that I had left out one obvious additional guest: Benjamin Disraeli. Now Disraeli was not a figure with whom I had any great prior familiarity, but since the occasion of the *Festschrift*, I have come to understand the appropriateness for Rowe of his inclusion in such an event as I had imagined. Like Burke and Daly, Disraeli had the distinctive habit of conducting himself among his contemporaries simultaneously as an insider and as an outsider. What is more, he achieved the remarkable political objective in the Great Britain of his era of uniting the urban working class and the aristocratic landed gentry, thus forging a coalition for the Tory party that succeeded in defeating the Gladstone liberals who represented the ascendant urban merchant class. Then, too he succeeded equally brilliantly in his lifetime in playing off against each other his retrospective identities as an Englishman and as a Jew. For an informative commentary on the last aspect of his personality, see Hannah Arendt, "The Potent Wizard", in *The Origins of Totalitarianism*, New York: Harcourt Brace Jovanovich, 1968, pp 68–79.

The Work, Teaching and Contemporary Influence of Colin Rowe: A 1999 Status Report, 1999

By 1999 Paolo Conrad Bercah had returned to Italy, and that year I learned that he had persuaded Guido Canella, the Dean of the School at the Milan Polytechnic, to invite me there to deliver a lecture on Colin Rowe. In particular, the Milanese wanted me to focus on Rowe's urban ideas, and his book *Collage City*, co-authored with Fred Koetter. The text of my lecture was published in *Zodiac*, of which Canella was at the time the editor.

Three years ago, I delivered a lecture on Colin Rowe at a Cornell University *Festschrift* in his honour. Published in *Assemblage* as "Oppositions in the Thought of Colin Rowe", this led to an invitation to speak further on Rowe, this time at the Milan Polytechnic, and focussing on his work and his teaching.[1] This text is a revised version of the Milan lecture.

Preparing the Cornell lecture, I made a close reading of a range of Rowe's texts from all periods in his career. But I avoided dealing directly with one of them: *Collage City*.[2] My reasons for this were varied. First, my intentions for the Cornell lecture were substantially honorific, and I was aware that *Collage City* was not among his most admired works. Indeed, I knew that it was largely on account of it that he had recently been relegated by the American architectural avant-garde to the position of reactionary apologist for Postmodernism. In the neo-Modernist critical climate of the 1990s architectural academy in the United States, this has resulted in a noticeable decline in his critical reputation.

My admiration of Rowe was in any event based on other texts, and the three volume set of his previously unpublished essays had just appeared for me to mine for my purposes.[3] Thus I was easily able to develop my *Festschrift* piece while sidestepping the hot political potato of *Collage City*. Instead, I focussed on what I saw as the ambiguous—not to say dialectical—

Site plan of the Unité d'Habitation of Le Corbusier in Marseilles, rhetorically contrasted with the colonnade of the Palazzo degli Uffizi, Florence.

View of Sant'Agnese in the Piazza Navona.

aspects of his typical critical method, as I cited them in a series of other references across the whole span of his writing career. Starting out with a citation of a famous passage from his 1972 introduction to *Five Architects*, I argued that Rowe's stance was, when all was said and done, more political, and less purely formal, than was then supposed.[4] In the end, I was satisfied that I had succeeded in shifting to some degree the general view of Rowe as it existed in the American architectural academy, a year or so ago. Then came the invitation from Milan, with the specific request that I focus on Rowe's work and teaching. Given this specific mandate, it seemed to me that I was obliged to address the controversial text that I had thus far avoided, since it stood as the putative main summary of his pedagogical intentions for urban design, and of the legacy of his now legendary graduate studio at Cornell. Approaching *Collage City* from this perspective has been a disconcerting experience. For, despite its reputation, it turns out that it is not particularly didactic in respect to formal strategies in urban design. Instead—and perhaps more surprisingly—it is highly political in its intentions, perhaps the most consciously political effort of Rowe's entire writing career. Finally, it is an atypical piece of prose of its author, exhibiting a notable loss of momentum particularly in its mid-to-later sections.

Let us begin by noting the curious dearth of substantive urban design advice in this ostensible summa of Rowe's urban design pedagogy. The book has only five chapters.

The first is devoted to an account of the influence of the concept of Utopia on the formation of the ideology of Modernism in architecture, and the second to the consequences of the gradual loss of confidence in that ideology, after the Second World War. Only in chapter three do we arrive at: "Crisis of the Object: Predicament of Texture". And even here, where one would have expected the argument to turn didactic, we are presented with a prose structure which, is instead, primarily analytical and critical. To be sure, Le Corbusier's Unité d'Habitation is compared in some urbanistic detail with the Uffizi of Vasari, as is his entry for the competition for the Palace of the Soviets with that of Auguste Perret. But while it is illustrated, Rowe's fond example of Gunnar Asplund's 1922 scheme for the Royal Chancellery in Stockholm passes without any sustained explication—none in the main text, and none in the illustration captions either. Sant'Agnese in Piazza Navona is cited as an instance of a building which successfully mediates between object and texture, and Le Pautre's Hotel de Beauvais is contrasted with Le Corbusier's Villa Savoye, to demonstrate concepts of free planning which are externally, as opposed to internally generated, respectively. The Monica Lunga extension of the Quirinale in Rome is cited as a successful example of a building,

Site plan of August Perret's entry to the Palace of the Soviets Competition in Moscow.

Le Corbusier's entry to the 1931 competition for a design for a new Palace of the Soviets in Moscow.

which is both a space occupier and a space definer, as well as being an urban mediator between street and garden. The chapter concludes with the summary statement: "Ultimately, and in terms of figure-ground, the debate which is here postulated between solid and void is a debate between two models and succinctly, these may be typified as acropolis and forum."[5]

In chapter four "Collision City and the Politics of 'Bricolage'", the established emphasis of the argument becomes sharper still. Rowe tables the idea of the garden as criticism of the city, and cites Versailles and the Villa Adriana as two contrasting models of this idea. But it quickly becomes apparent that the operative contrast under consideration is not primarily a formal, but again, an intellectual one. At this point, the discussion quickly shifts to ideas derived from Isaiah Berlin, Karl Popper, and Claude Lévi-Strauss. To be sure, here too, architectural and urban references are made, and they include Le Corbusier, Christopher Alexander, Team 10, and Luigi Moretti (not to mention short comparative discussions of morphological urban features of Rome, London, Los Angeles and Houston). But the central thrust of the argument doesn't concern formal aspects of city building.

Finally, we come to the last chapter of the text: "Collage City and the Reconquest of Time". Probably the most sustained urbanistic discussion here is of the nineteenth-century urban projects in the Munich

of Ludwig I and Leo von Klenze, which Rowe tables as an ideal instance of the "city as museum". But that is all. To be sure, the book is furnished with an epilogue titled "*Excursus*", an "abridged list of stimulants, a-temporal and necessarily transcultural, as possible *objets trouvés* in the urbanistic collage". Here are briefly illustrated several of Rowe's favourite memorable streets, set pieces, splendid public terraces, ambiguous and composite buildings, nostalgia producing instruments, and so on. But these too, are provided only with brief commentaries.

In short, notwithstanding both its expectations and its title, *Collage City* is not primarily a pedagogical book of urban design methodologies. And despite the misnomer, what it is instead, is a brave—even uncharacteristic—if (in my view) unsuccessful effort by its author to rationalise his view of the politics of architecture. Thus the account of the tradition of Utopia that Rowe sees underpinning early Modernism; thus too his characterisations of the bifurcations that followed the dissipation of Modernism's original moral force after the Second World War: townscape versus scientific design method; Superstudio ironic minimalism versus Disneyland sentimentality; and so on. And it is, of course, in aid of this project of political rationalisation for architecture that Rowe turns to Berlin, Popper, and Lévi-Strauss. From Berlin he borrows the well-known categorisation of historical personalities that distinguishes "hedgehogs" from "foxes".[6] From Popper, he appropriates the famous political criticisms of

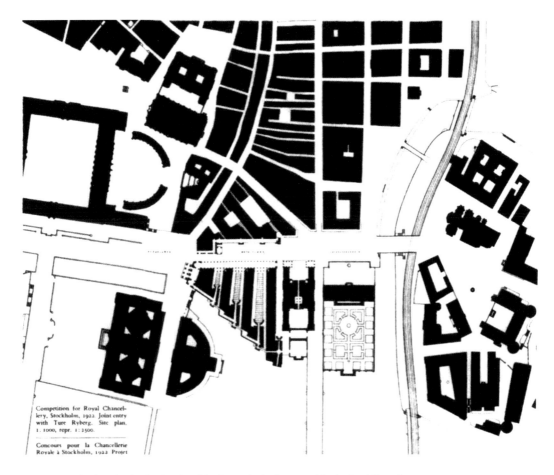

Competition for Royal Chancellery, Stockholm, 1922. Joint entry with Ture Ryberg. Site plan. 1 : 1000, repr. 1 : 2500.

Concours pour la Chancellerie Royale à Stockholm, 1922. Projet

Figure-ground drawings showing the site plan of the Gunnar Asplund's proposal for the Royal Chancellery.

"scientism", "historical determinism" and the "closed society".[7] And from Lévi-Strauss, he borrows the concept of "bricolage".[8] Together these intellectual constructs lead him to a conclusion: "It is suggested that a collage approach, an approach in which objects are conscripted or seduced from out of their context, is—at the present day—the only way of dealing with the ultimate problems of, either or both, Utopia and tradition."[9] Again:

> Proposing an order of release through the media of both Utopia and tradition, through the city as museum, through collage as both exhibit and scaffold, through the dubieties and duplicities of law, through the precariousness of fact and the eel-like slipperiness of meaning, through the complete absence of simple certainty, is also to propose a situation… in which the demands of activist utopia have receded, in which the time bomb of historical determinism is at least defused, in which

the requirements of composite time have become finally established, and in which that strange idea, the eternal present, becomes "effectively reinstated alongside its equally strange competitors".[10]

Now even if one roughly assents to this conclusion, it has to be said that it has not been presented with anything like the momentum that typifies the best of Rowe's prose (think again of the riveting introduction to *Five Architects*) or of his characteristic modes of formal analysis (think of the famous essay "The Provocative Facade").[11] And then there are the citations of Isaiah Berlin and Karl Popper.

I cannot but think that it is a combination of these features of *Collage City* that have invited its dismissal as the work of a reactionary. After all, notwithstanding its elegant civility, Berlin's liberalism is now widely seen to be notoriously passive. And Karl Popper's deference to extreme conservatives such as F A von

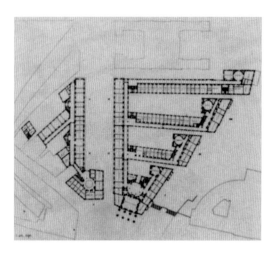

Plan drawing for Gunnar Asplund's proposal for the Swedish Royal Chancellery of 1922.

Hadrian's Villa, plan after Luigi Canina.

Hayek has significantly compromised his intellectual legacy. No wonder then, in the ideological polarised world of theoretical discourse about architecture in the United States after 1978, that *Collage City* got the reaction it did. For my part, I am more troubled by the insufficiencies of Rowe's argument than I am by his problematic political references. Indeed, viewing the text from the perspective of 1999, it is surprisingly easy to see how these political optics could have been avoided. After all, Rowe's book begins with quotations from Santayana and Pascal, which speak to the "constructedness" of social reality. Surely a proto-post-structuralist beginning. And what if he had relied, for his critique of "historical determinism", on Jean-François Lyotard, rather than Karl Popper? Then too, do "the eel-like slipperiness of meaning" and the "complete absence of simple certainty" not have much in common with what we now know as "undecidability"? Such questions leave me with a sense that the politics of *Collage City* have gotten something of a bum rap.

But what of the insufficiencies of his argument? Let me cite three particularly important ones. First is the puzzling absence of any adequate account of the status of the "type" from his urban theory, both formally and politically. Second is a conceptual problem concerning the status of "hypotheses" which lies at the heart of Popper's political philosophy, and which Rowe *de facto* imports into his urban theory. Finally, there is the intriguing matter of Rowe's insufficiently theorised view of the "profession" of architecture. Let us take them in turn. During the latter

part of Rowe's career as a theorist of what we now know as "contextualism" there was being developed in Europe, at the hands of the Rationalists and others, a parallel body of urban ideas known under the name "typology/morphology". Architects from Carlo Aymonino to Aldo Rossi to the Krier brothers made significant contributions to this body of ideas.[12] While Rowe's contextualism can be seen to have much in common with what the Europeans called urban morphology, his theory never developed a comparable concept to "typology". This is, in my view, a shortcoming, which has had problematic consequences in the practice of his protégés. Interestingly enough, an early part of the argument of *Collage City* disparages early Modernists for naively assuming the abolition of private outdoor space, in the development of their new visions of the modern city. Yet its author seems never to have become curious about the fact that the whole basis of the urban analysis of his European peers lay in the relationship of building typology to urban, morphology; that is to say, precisely in the boundaries of the individual building "parcel" that were determined by the system of differentiated private ownership of land. To be sure, the analytical comparison of the Hotel de Beauvais to the Villa Savoye (cited above) is a more-or-less typological one. But comparatively speaking, this aspect of Rowe's urban theory is very undeveloped, and the evident availability

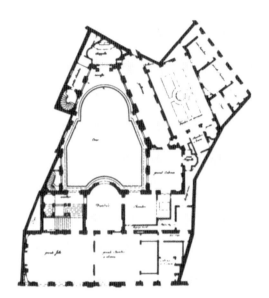

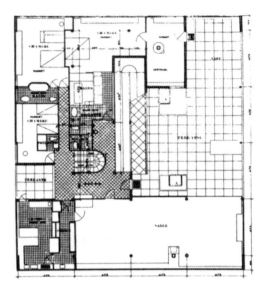

Plan drawing of Le Pautre's Hotel de Beauvais.   Contrasted plan drawing of the Villa Savoye of Le Corbusier.

of the relevant European texts from the mid-1970s onward, makes this inexplicable.

Now the Popper problem. As it happens, Popper was not only a political philosopher, but also a philosopher of science. And it was in that capacity, that he wrote the famous books: *The Logic of Scientific Discovery* and *Conjectures and Refutations*.[13] What is more, the conclusions that made these texts notable were anti-empiricist ones. In short, Popper argued that the conventional view that scientific theories came to be accepted as "true" as a result of empirical "verification" was logical nonsense. Rather than theories to be verified inductively, argued Popper, what science offered instead were "hypotheses": available for subsequent "refutation" deductively. What is more, in the interval following their formulation, prior to any decisive refutation, the criterion, which distinguished stronger from weaker hypotheses, was simply explanatory power.

In his political philosophy, Popper (perhaps as a result of his dangerous personal exposure to totalitarianism?) never seems to have absorbed the implications of his own radical epistemological conclusion in the philosophy of science. In *The Poverty of Historicism*, he advocated a politics, which was self-consciously "incremental", rather than comprehensive in its ambitions, even though in his own philosophy of science, such "incrementalism" would have been absurd.[14] While it was, of course, for him the case that scientific hypotheses are supposed to be set up

in such a way as to facilitate subsequent refutation, there was nothing in his argument that suggested that the hypothesis should be deliberately incremental in the first place. On the contrary, hypotheses which have a greater explanatory power for him, took precedence (albeit only provisionally) over those which had less. Somehow, the intimidations of totalitarianism (and the influence of such as von Hayek?) caused him to fail to see the gap between the radical philosophy of science that was his own creation, and the conservative politics he adopted. To his credit, Rowe admits to some discomfort with the adamancy of Popper's conservatism, but this does not prevent his influence from exacerbating the problematic passivity of Rowe's own political argument.

Finally, the matter of Rowe's insufficiently theorised view of the profession of architecture, or to put it another way, the "problem of manifesto". This encompasses a set of localised arguments in various places in Rowe's writings, which seem to me to have a powerful latent interrelationship, yet which never quite conjoin one another. Let us begin with a passage from *Collage City*, which cites the contribution to the political potency of Modern architecture made by the combination of "the gentler forces of the liberal tradition and the romantic directives of a fledgling avant-gardism".[15]

Set that next to his long-standing conviction that not all buildings should be thought of as architecture.

Plan of the Colonnade of the Palazzo degli Uffizi.

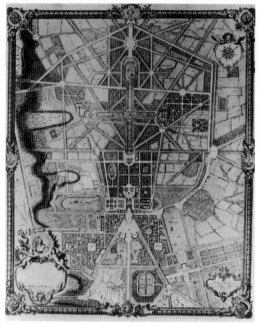

Plan of Versailles.

Evident in *Collage City*, this opinion recurs in numerous locations in his writings—usually as an aside.

Yet while Rowe clearly wishes us to grasp the consequence and durability of this cultural distinction, these do not for him, authorise untrammelled professional demeanour on the part of architects. In this regard, ponder the following passages on James Stirling, and on John Hejduk and Peter Eisenman. First, an encomium of Stirling, who:

> ... has never professed to be anything more than an architect preoccupied with [the job]. Stirling has declined to assume any public role as either theorist or critic. He is careful to avoid involuted verbal formulae. He never talks about infrastructure, superstructure, syntactical structure, semantics or semiotics. He has no desire to utter extravagant pronouncements.[16]

Compare this with his harsh account of two projects for the Cannaregio of Venice, by John Hejduk and Peter Eisenman, projects which he claims:

> ... serve to illustrate the extremely tenuous connections between architecture and some of the manifesto/demonstrations which are made on its behalf. A parade of false naivete and an uncalled for advertisement of cerebrality, neither of these projects approaches Cannaregio as an intrinsic part of Venice; and in both of them make the pretence of intellectual anguish, then, possibly, they may both be interpreted as attempts to rape poetry without going through the labour of encouraging talent to make love to reason.[17]

On the face of it, these various commentaries cannot be made to add up. If it is so that one of the strengths of Modernism lay in its alliance of liberal tradition and an avant-garde, and only some buildings are to be thought of as architecture, then would this combination of circumstances not seem to authorise a consciously theorised praxis? So why such an insistent commendation of Stirling's refusal to theorise, and so harsh an attack on Hejduk's and Eisenman's doing so? For that matter, what can we consider Rowe's own body of writings to be, if not a theorised praxis?

I don't think Rowe has thought this issue through. Yet the frequency with which the architecture/building opposition occurs in his writings, and the sheer intemperance of the passage on Hejduk and Eisenman suggest it holds a deep urgency for him. I suspect that what these varied passages ultimately point to, is a need for an explicit theory of professional and cultural *decorum* for architects. And the absence of such a theory within the argument of the unexpectedly political *Collage City* is another contributor to its own, ultimate inconclusiveness. Worse still, it leaves the strategic relationship within Modernism, between the "liberal tradition" and "avant-gardism" gravely open to contemporary manipulation by a self-declared neo-avant-garde.

View of the Quirinale and Monica Lunga.

My colleague K Michael Hays has argued that the body of urbanistic ideas cited (but not systematically expounded by Rowe in *Collage City* was already relatively familiar among the *cognoscenti*, well before the publication of the book back in 1978.[18] To the extent that this is so, then the relationship of the book and the influence of Rowe's ideas on American architecture and urbanism, must be seen to be discontinuous in any event. And given my own ambivalent view of the book, this is probably just as well. Let me offer here a few speculations on its possible influence. Exactly where would one most definitively locate it?

I recently heard Richard Meier summarise the work of his career to date, and it occurred to me at the time that it might be in his oeuvre that one could do so. After all, Meier is one of the five architects Rowe has written about, and his mature work has remained surprisingly faithful to many of the principles which launched it. The same, white, post-Corbusian material palette that typified his contribution to *Five Architects* has remained more-or-less constant ever since. And the supple dexterity with which Meier has deployed a characteristically post-Corbusian formal language to execute an astonishingly diverse range of projects over the years seems to epitomise a tectonic canon readily identifiable with Rowe. What is more, Meier has gone further, and demonstrated a remarkable

ability to rehearse a whole series of Rowian formal procedures. Building after building of his has exemplified the discourses of overlapping and colliding grids, and of one version after another of "the long thin building". Yet while he is clearly an eminent practitioner within a Rowian lineage, for me Meier nonetheless fails to serve as a definitive exemplar of his mentor's methods. For example, his works are surprisingly rarely bounded by those circumstantial conditions Rowe finds so engaging. In his oeuvre as a whole, one finds too many objects, and not enough texture. And it is perhaps significant that since the publication of his introduction to *Five Architects* a quarter century ago. Rowe has had relatively little to say about Meier. In the essay I cited above in which he is critical of Hejduk and Eisenman, he does comment on Meier's Douglas House, but in fact, he is critical of it as well. And surely it is not a coincidence that the *summa magna* of Meier's career to date, the Getty Center in Los Angeles, must be seen, in the context of *Collage City* not as a "forum" which would corroborate Rowe's argument, but instead, as an "acropolis", which Rowe's argument instead sees as all too typical of object-fixated Modernism.

But if Meier does not quite work, then what about another of his protégés—one who was also the co-author of *Collage City*, Fred Koetter. Taken as a whole,

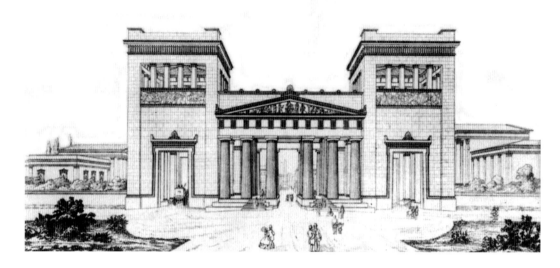

View of Leo von Klenze's Propylaea, Munich, 1846–1860.

the oeuvre of Koetter, executed in collaboration with his partner Susie Kim is far more urbanistic, and far more straightforwardly "contextual" than Meier's. And yet, insofar as we wish to speak in terms of intellectual and formal lineage and of demonstrations of pedagogical principles, the situation is not clear-cut here either. For unlike Meier, Koetter/Kim have moved away from the characteristically post-Corbusian language of architecture, in the direction of something far more normative, far more classicising. One senses, somehow, that Rowe finds the consistency of Koetter/Kim's move away from Le Corbusier's language as unsatisfying as Meier's fidelity to it. He has never said as much, but he has consented to write an introduction to a recently published collection of projects by Koetter/Kim, within which one can read between the lines. He observes:

> If, among architects, one might make a rough distinction between exponents of the plan and exponents of the vertical surface, I am compelled to think that Fred must surely be classified as a highly accomplished exponant of the plan. Not that the vertical surface is a negligible affair with him, but I do think that it takes a secondary place.[19]

Compare this passage with the one on Stirling where, with greater candour, Rowe owns up to a reservation he holds about the Stuttgart Landesmuseum:

Face, except for Le Corbusier from time to time, was never a preoccupation of Modern architecture…. Nor, today, in spite of all protestations to the contrary, does the exhibition of a *prime face*, of a face both opaque and revealing appear to be among the propensities of the various attitudes which fashionably may be considered Postmodern or alternatively to be ascribable to *la tendenza*. And so, perhaps I judge both Stirling and Stuttgart by impossibly private and too fastidious standards?

Rowe concludes: "All the same, I think not…."[20] Thus I conclude that Rowe's characterisation of Koetter's capabilities betrays a greater disappointment that the passage about Koetter by itself permits one to discern. But this leads us inevitably to a consideration of the sole contemporary whose work Rowe has described with more-or-less unreserved enthusiasm: Stirling himself. As a result, one would be inclined to nominate his as the definitive contemporary manifesto of Rowe's thinking. But this doesn't really work either, since Stirling hardly qualifies as a protégé of Rowe's having being more of a peer from the very beginning of their long-standing friendship. Problematically enough, one additional figure remains to be discussed in this sequence of failed nominations, and that is Peter Eisenman. For in many ways, Eisenman fills the bill of protégé much more successfully that any of the other

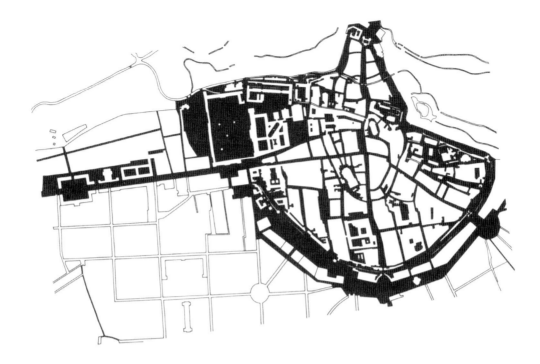

Munich, circa 1840, figure-ground plan.

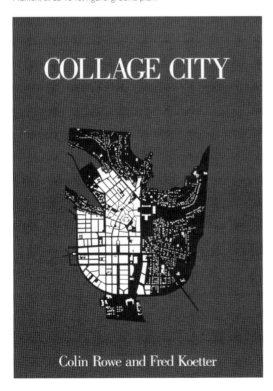

COLLAGE CITY

Colin Rowe and Fred Koetter

The cover of Rowe and Koetter's *Collage City*.

figures just discussed. Indisputably Rowe's student, both at Cornell and at Cambridge; an unsurpassed master of Rowe's formal and pedagogical procedures; Eisenman is also pre-eminent among the protégés in his grasp of, and response to Rowe's broad cultural/ theoretical project, as opposed to simply his formal one.

But alas, he is also the ultimate betrayer of it. The extraordinary rapport between them over a quarter century notwithstanding; the shared epiphany of Terragni notwithstanding; Eisenman's brilliant Cambridge dissertation for Rowe on Aalto, Le Corbusier, Terrangni and Wright notwithstanding; Eisenman has in recent years become a principal enemy of the cultural/theoretical project of the figure who was once his mentor. By now, utterly committed to the project of an ascendant neo-avant-garde Eisenman has moved so far from the political construct of architecture Rowe attempted to promulgate in *Collage City*, as to have become in may ways its critical target. And if this polemical reality is only implicit in the text of *Collage City*, it has become quite explicit in the passages of Rowe's introduction to the oeuvre of Koetter/Kim, where Rowe's insistently exasperated references to "the *Zeitgeist* boys" can only be to Eisenman and his own group of protégés and allies.

To conclude then, I find myself in the curious position of supposing that at the present time, Rowe's influence in the leading circles of American architecture is seriously confounded. And thus I end up seeing *Collage City* combining an intellectual fallibility of its author, together with a broad streak of political/cultural bad luck on his part.

Still, the powerful ability Rowe has demonstrated elsewhere suggests to me that the eclipse his critical reputation is currently suffering will not be long-lasting. One looks to a younger generation of architects and scholars to rediscover him, unhampered by the complexities of personal lineages that have so coloured the protégé nominations I have considered above. What is more, I predict that this rediscovery will not commence with his urban theory at all. Instead, what his new interpreters will encounter, and will find themselves spellbound by, is that enduring ability of his to cause us to look at—and to see—specific buildings in precise, revelatory, and unprecedented ways. I could cite here excerpts from his amazing commentaries on Richardson and Labrouste, on Le Corbusier and Terragni; passages which give concrete tangibility to relationships of tectonic plasticity to vision that would otherwise remain inaccessible to language. But instead, let me close with a passage discussing Stirling's employment of the diagonal corner, on the tower of the Engineering building at Leicester University:

An immensely absorbing and provocative corner which is altogether the best of Stirling until Stuttgart is appropriately unveiled. For this corner of Leicester will reward a long—very long—regard. It belongs to Viollet-le-Duc. It also belongs to the best English and American nineteenth-century traditions. It is both difficult and great. It is rough-tough and delicately gentle. It carries the memories of both William Butterfield and Frank Furness. Though scarcely to be analysed (do the words exist?), almost acrobatically, it is alert and intelligent.[21]

In my Cornell lecture, I observed that Rowe's characteristic discourse from time to time took us to what we might nowadays, in the wake of such writers, as Jorge Luis Borges and Italo Calvino, characterise as "the limits of the thinkable". Rereading this rather typical piece of Rowe's dazzling analytical prose. I was stunned to find him interrupting himself to ask: "Do the words exist?" Can it be that this incomparable master of analytical description of buildings in our time has encountered here the limits of the linguistically expressible?

Here, surely, will the critical reassessment of Colin Rowe begin.

1   Baird, George, "Oppositions in the Thought of Colin Rowe", in *Assemblage*, no 33, Cambridge, MA, August 1997, pp 22–35.

2   Rowe, Colin and Fred Koetter, *Collage City*, Cambridge, MA: MIT Press, 1978.

3   Rowe, Colin, *As I was Saying: Recollections and Miscellaneous Essays*, three vols, Cambridge, MA: MIT Press, 1995.

4   Rowe, Colin, *Introduction to Five Architects: Eisenman, Graves, Gwathmey, Hejduk, Meier*, New York: Wittenborn, 1972.

5   Rowe and Koetter, *Collage City*, p 83.

6   Rowe and Koetter, *Collage City*, p 91.

7   Rowe and Koetter, *Collage City*, p 95.

8   Rowe and Koetter, *Collage City*, p 102

9   Rowe and Koetter, *Collage City*, p 144.

10 Rowe and Koetter, *Collage City*, p 147.

11 Rowe, Colin, "The Provocative Facade: Frontality and *Contrapposti*", in *As I was Saying: Recollections and Miscellaneous Essays,* 3 vols, Cambridge, Mass: MIT Press, 1995, p 171.

12 For a useful summary of this material (and particularly of its influence on French thinkers), see the section entitled "The Quest for Urban Architecture" in Cohen, JL, "The Italophiles at Work", in Hays, KM, *Architecture Theory Since 1968*, Cambridge, MA: MIT Press, 1998, p. 511.

13 Popper, Karl, *The Logic of Scientific Discovery*, London: Routlege, 1959 and *Conjectures and Refutations*, London: Routlege, 1962.

14 Popper, Karl. *The Poverty of Historicism*, London: Routlege, 1957.

15 Rowe and Koetter, *Collage City*, p 31.

16 Rowe, Colin, *Introduction to James Stirling: Buildings and Projects*, New York: Rizzoli, 1984, p 27.

17 Rowe, Colin, "Ideas, Talent, Poetics: A Problem of Manifesto", in *As I was Saying: Recollections and Miscellaneous Essays*, 3 vols, Cambridge, MA: MIT Press, 1995.

18 See his introduction to the excerpt from *Collage City*, which is included in Hays, KM, *Architecture Theory Since 1968*, p 88.

19 Rowe, Colin, essay in *Koetter Kim & Associates: Time Place*, New York: Rizzoli, 1997, p 11.

20 Rowe, Colin, *Introduction to James Stirling Buildings and Projects*, p 23.

21 Rowe, Colin, *Introduction to James Stirling Buildings and Projects*, p 26.

Part 4:
Joseph Rykwert

Of all the intellectual friendships that began during my years in London in the 1960s, the one that has proven the deepest has been with Joseph Rykwert. It was he who encouraged me to read Merleau-Ponty, it was he who secured me my first teaching position—teaching art and architectural history to furniture and industrial design students at the Royal College of Art, where he was, at the time, the Librarian. So it is not surprising that when the University of Pennsylvania organised a *Festschrift* for him in 1996, that I was among the invited speakers.

When it subsequently became apparent that there would also be a publication including many of the contributions to the event, I decided that I would attempt to write something about Rykwert, not just something influenced by him. Given his formidable learning, this proved a daunting task. But he himself liked the idea of my doing so, and facilitated my effort. The text below is the result. I see it as very provisional, likely to be superseded by more expert future scholarship. But for the moment, it is all there is. Françoise Choay, for example—a friend of Rykwert's of long standing—told me that I had shown her a Rykwert she had not previously known.

"A Promise as Well as a Memory": Notes Towards an Intellectual Biography of Joseph Rykwert, 2002

It is not easy to identify precisely the place of Joseph Rykwert in the international architectural academy. It is difficult even to compare him with such contemporaries and friends as John Hejduk and Colin Rowe (both recently deceased), who have taken up ideological positions in architecture and pedagogical methods in its academy that are sufficiently familiar to be recognisable even in the hands of their many protégés. The analogy that Rykwert made between buildings and the human body, which underpins the chapters in the collection of essays about him entitled *Body and Building* is undoubtedly a powerful one.[1] Nonetheless, one would be hard pressed to identify a Rykwert 'school' in contemporary architecture, let alone a Rykwert 'style', such as one can do with the approaches to design that have been associated with Rowe and Hejduk at the Cornell University and Cooper Union Schools of Architecture, respectively, over the past two or three decades.

If there is an intellectual method to be characterised as "Rykwertian", it will be one that is neither as definitively articulated nor as readily transmissible as those of such figures as Hejduk and Rowe. It is probably symptomatic of this lack of ready transmissibility of his ideas, moreover, that he has been criticised for intellectual obscurantism. In a 1973 review of *On Adam's House in Paradise*, for example, Kenneth Frampton concluded that the chief problem with the book was the author's "failure to make himself clear". Contemporary architecture students often see him as an esoteric, acquired academic taste: a highly literate and historically knowledgeable figure, but not a promulgator of design ideas that will influence them as Rowe and Hejduk have done.

This view of him is, of course, a popular one, but it seems to me that it is also pragmatically and professionally narrow, not to say intellectually uninquisitive. Even on its own terms, it fails to take account of certain notable manifestations of and responses to the ongoing Rykwert project—for example, how it is that a scholar whose career has been largely spent in the field of architecture should be held in such high regard outside that field. The long list of distinguished intellectuals who have followed his career with interest includes the Nobel Prize winner Elias Canetti (an important mentor for the young Rykwert) and the social philosopher and historian of ideas Ivan Illich (a close intellectual collaborator and admirer in recent years).[2]

This popular view also fails to explain how Rykwert should have developed—despite his putative failure to establish an identifiable school in contemporary architecture—a following of students of such variety and intellectual distinction as he has done.[3] Finally, and perhaps most surprising, this sometime "populist" view curiously fails to take account of the long-standing second career of this alleged esotericist as a "reviewer of furniture and fashion" in architectural and other journals. This last failure is perhaps the most curious of all, since Rykwert's second career has involved him in polemical controversy on surprisingly frequent occasions, even with architects, critics, and historians who have also been friends.

An examination of a collection of Rykwert's essays, *The Necessity of Artifice*, makes evident this little-recognised feature of his activities: two of the texts included were rejected by the sponsors who had requested them in the first place! In attempting to get beyond the conventional, esotericist characterisation of Rykwert, it will be useful to examine a few of these essays more closely, beginning with the essay from the mid-1950s with which Rykwert chose to open *The Necessity of Artifice*, "Meaning in Building". It was initially commissioned by Eugen Gomringer for an anniversary issue of the *Basler Nachrichten* to commemorate the 45th birthday of the design organisation the Schweizer Werkbund. Given that he was unsympathetic to the Minimalist, Neofunctionalist policy of Güte Form that typified both the Werkbund and the new Hochschule für Gestaltung at Ulm at that time, Rykwert was doubtful as to the suitability of his views for such a publication, and said so when Gomringer extended the invitation to him. But Gomringer insisted, and so Rykwert went ahead and prepared his text, attacking what he saw as architects' undue "preoccupation with rational criteria" for the design process. He argued that there was instead an acute need for them to "acknowledge the emotional power of their work", and he insisted that

such acknowledgment led to "investigation of a content, even of a referential content in architecture".[4] As Rykwert had suspected, these observations proved too inflammatory to be included in the commemorative publication being planned, and the essay was rejected, seeing publication instead in the Italian journal *Zodiac* in 1957.

Then, some two decades later, there is the essay on a Tate Gallery retrospective of the works of two European artists, Yves Klein and Piero Manzoni: "Two Dimensional Art for Two-Dimensional Man". It was written in 1974 for *Domus*, the Italian magazine to which Rykwert was a regular contributor for a decade. In this case, one suspects that Rykwert's status as a sort of London correspondent for the Italian magazine contributed to the controversy that eventually ensued, given that this status might have led his Milanese editors to fail to anticipate the intensity of what he had to say on this particular topic. Be that as it may, the dismayed editors at *Domus* eventually refused to publish his essay. It appeared only in 1975 in another Italian journal, *Casabella*.

Distancing himself at the outset from the art world phenomenon he characterised as "full-scale canonisation", Rykwert launched a comprehensive attack on the exhibition, summing it up as a "sad and squalid affair". Sketching a brief critical account of the careers of the two neo-avant-gardists to whom the show was devoted, Rykwert concluded that when all was said and done, both were only vacuous reprises of the original Duchampian avant-garde of the early twentieth century:

> There are many ways forward from the zero that was reached 50 years ago: the understanding that everything is art is perhaps the most important of them. Klein and Manzoni worked against such an understanding. In the present climate, I cannot accept the operating of the art-market in the interest of exhibitionist personalities, however charismatic, as an entertaining and harmless diversion. It is a camouflage for the sinister forces which degrade the quality of our lives, and to tolerate it means that you accept the alibi of the despoilers of our visual environment.[5]

The editors at *Domus* declined to publish Rykwert's review, even though they had supported him through another polemical controversy only a few months before. This was the occasion of the publication of his review of the 15th Triennale in Milan in January 1974.

This text publication embroiled Rykwert in a controversy with two of his Italian friends, the architect Aldo Rossi and the historian Manfredo Tafuri. Rossi responded to Rykwert's challenge with a sardonic reference to "servile academics and reviewers of furniture and fashion". For his part, Tafuri objected to having been quoted by Rykwert second- as opposed to first-hand.

Although it escaped the fate of editorial rejection, this text is surely among the most impassioned polemics that Rykwert ever published. "Like an ageing primadonna", he began, "every time the Triennale reappears, it seems a farewell; every Triennale, we are told by its critics, is so much worse than the others, that it must surely be the last."[6] From this initial assault, he then went on to describe the ongoing deterioration that he saw as having typified a number of recent Triennales. The 13th he saw as problematically cynical, and the 14th, held in 1968, as ending in "the squalor of defeat". But for him, even these, in their respective unsatisfactorinesses, were only precursors of the "waste of talent and resources of a Triennale like the present one", which he could only describe as "unbearable".

The reviewer of furniture and fashion struggled to find some components of the exhibition to admire, including a series of reconstructions of Mackintosh chairs and selections of studio pottery and jewellery. But in between these, and looming over everything else exhibited—at least for Rykwert—was the architectural presentation of the work of the Italian Neorationalists or, to use Massimo Scolari's term, "the *Tendenza*". Here I quote Rykwert on the movement in question:

It has been coming for some time, of course. Its theoretical basis, however, was formulated recently. Manfredo Tafuri, from his splendidly isolated monastery of the Tolentini in Venice, proclaimed the death of architecture. Some time later, he modified his opinion. Aldo Rossi's competition scheme for the cemetery at Modena was another focus: a rigid arrangement of elementary geometries which still dominates the panorama (literally) in this exhibition. The conjunction was not accidental. Rossi, who heads the team which has organised the most important part of this exhibition, that concerned with 'rational' architecture and the building and the city, has often and loudly proclaimed the independence, the abstraction of architecture from all ideology, and from any 'redemptive' role. His is a 'pure' architecture, form without Utopia

which at best achieves a sublime uselessness. These are Tafuri's words, his apologia for Rossi: "We will always prefer, to any mystifying attempt at decking architecture in ideological dress, the sincerity of him who has the courage to speak of its silent and irrelevant purity."

Responding to Tafuri, Rykwert concluded, "So that's it then. Architecture may stay alive as long as she stays dumb. Dumb and beautiful maybe, but dumb."

Later in the same text, Rykwert returned to Rossi's ideas in an intriguing way, this time attacking his views on the role of function in architecture, particularly in certain ancient Roman buildings. He began by quoting Rossi:

Indifference to functional considerations is proper to architecture: the transformation of antique buildings… is its sufficient proof. [This indifference] has the force of a law…. Transformation of amphitheaters (Arles, Coliseum, Lucca) before the transformation of the (Roman) cities, means that the greatest architectural precision—in this case that of the monument—offers the greatest functional liberty potentially.

To this, Rykwert responded:

Here is as monstrous a *petitio principii* as one could wish to find. Has Aldo Rossi only looked at ancient buildings in Canina's engravings? Has he ever thought how they were used? Or that "the architecture of the Romans was from first to last, an art of shaping space around ritual" (and I quote the most brilliant interpreter of Roman architecture of recent times, Frank E Brown). Does he not remember from his childhood, the procession of lights and incense at the reading of the gospel? Does he not realise that he was looking at the perpetuation of a Roman civil law-court's ceremonial over 2,500 years, or thereabouts? The buildings of which he speaks, the amphitheatres, theatres, sanctuaries, baths, cannot be understood as "types" in the way he uses the word at all. They are not void forms, repeated in and out of different contexts. They are living forms, elaborated over centuries of use, and polished by it as are the pebbles in a stream.[7]

It seems to me that a few interim conclusions follow reasonably directly from the juxtaposition of these polemical controversies that Rykwert launched. First, it is surely not surprising that both Rossi and Tafuri were taken aback at the intensity of Rykwert's attack on them (even if, for reasons I will demonstrate, it is quite consistent with the basic premises of his moral and intellectual position). Second, this collection of controversies surely makes it just as evident that the familiar characterisation of Rykwert as an esotericist and an obscurantist is too easy, based as it is on a reading of his works that both ignores his journalism and fails to see the manifold ways in which his "reviews of furniture and fashion", and the more complex arguments of his books, are in fact conceptually interrelated.

Moreover, another conclusion—one that logically precedes the two just cited also follows—is this: a closer examination of the relationship of these three journalistic polemics may enable us to grasp some of these more complex contemporary implications of Rykwert's larger intellectual project.

To start with, we may observe that Rykwert would, in the late 1950s, oppose the "Rationalist Neofunctionalism" of the Ulm School and the Schweizer Werkbund; this (from the perspective of 2001) may not appear surprising, given the current unfashionableness of such ideas. But this observation has to be qualified by an acknowledgment of the widespread acceptance in those years of such ideas and of Rykwert's bravery in declaring his dissent at that time—before the broad-based revival of interests in symbolism and in "referential content" in architecture that he called for did in fact arise a decade later.

By comparison, his 1974 refusal to participate in the art world "canonisation" of Yves Klein and Piero Manzoni continues to look somewhat tendentious now, even if these particular artists are not currently seen as among the strongest representatives of neo-avant-gardism, which remains a subject of considerable intellectual interest and admiration. That he would launch such a vigorous attack on neo-avant-gardism only a few years after the one on Neofunctionalism is further food for preliminary thought. While it might be thought that his aversion to so many Modern architects' "preoccupation with rational criteria" for the design process would make him an ally of artistic neo-avant-gardism, Rykwert rejected both of these tendencies. It seems to me that an awareness of this complex, dual refusal is an early pointer in the direction of a deeper, fuller reading of his oeuvre.

Let us now turn to the most passionate, and (still today) the most controversial of these polemics: that against the Italian Rationalist architectural movement that came to be known as "the *Tendenza*", as it presented itself at the 1974 Milan Triennale. In this case, Rykwert is least in concurrence with contemporary opinion, since the conception of typology that underpinned Rossi's characterisation of the antique buildings he cited—particularly his provocative argument for a comprehensive, transhistorical disengagement of function from architectural form—continues to be a central component of the broad antifunctionalist theoretical consensus now widely accepted in advanced architectural circles. Just as Rykwert's early opposition to 1950s Neofunctionalism does not look at all out of step today, so his opposition to the *Tendenza's* antifunctionalist conception of typology most assuredly does. Let us take a closer look at what was at stake in this apparently paradoxical dissent.

There are, after all, several premises of the rationalist and Rykwertian positions in architecture that are held in common. Like the Rationalists, Rykwert has opposed the long trajectory of architectural theory in the twentieth century that has turned old-fashioned first-generation Modernist "Functionalism" first into "operations research" and then eventually into the purely economic "cost-benefit analyses" that typify contemporary development pro-formas. He is equally as dismayed as the Rationalists at the powerful, parallel tendency of much architectural production in recent decades to evolve into a widespread system of consumer-oriented imagery that is increasingly difficult to distinguish from that of advertising. Indeed, if we were to add to this list of concurrences the specific subset of the second tendency, which has seen certain formal approaches to architectural design during this same period appropriated by governments and power elites for explicitly political purposes of institutional representation, then I think we could be said to have summarised a number of the key premises of the *Tendenza* that would have inclined a more sympathetic observer than Rykwert to have endorsed the provocative statement of Tafuri to which he instead took such dramatic exception. After all, would not many of us read Tafuri's objection to "the decking of architecture in ideological dress" and his corresponding argument in favour of its "silent and irrelevant purity" as being cogent consequences of the powerful set of premises I have just summarised? And if this is so, then it means that in attempting to come to a deeper understanding of what was at issue in this particular polemic of Rykwert, we need to move to another plane of the discourse in question.

It seems to me that his key concerns with the project of the Rationalists do not stem so much from their basic intellectual position as from their rhetorical cultural demeanour. For example, Tafuri's inclination to deliver architectural and political edicts clearly irritated Rykwert—hence his aversion to the Italian's putative "splendid isolation" and his "proclamations". Deeper still, Rykwert was obviously unable to accept that the *Tendenza's* objection to the same dimensions of Enlightenment rationality that troubled him, led it to adopt an overall cultural stance of ironical self-reflexivity. He might have been able to go so far as to accept the idea of an architecture that was abstracted from any "redemptive" role, but once it became apparent that one of the consequences of this abstraction was that its purity would be "irrelevant", then Rykwert was bound to object. As troubled by the architectural self-reflexivity of the *Tendenza* as he was by the artistic one of Klein and Manzoni, Rykwert balked.

It seems to me also that it was this concern that caused him to refuse to accept Rossi's characterisation of Roman buildings, notwithstanding the widespread influence that characterisation has had. It is surely not insignificant that the authority Rykwert chose to cite to buttress his refutation of Rossi was "the most brilliant interpreter of Roman architecture of recent times" (the American classical scholar Frank E Brown) or that the citation in question unequivocally eschewed irony and self-reflexivity, insisting, instead that the "architecture of the Romans was from first to last, an art of shaping space around ritual". It is equally interesting in this regard that in pursuing his critique of Rossi's conception of typology, Rykwert went directly on to amplify the conception of ritual he found so important in the writings of Brown—and the absence of which was so troubling for him in the work of the *Tendenza*. Surely it is in a Brownian perspective that we are meant to read Rykwert's impassioned observation on the long acculturation of form over time that sees buildings being "polished… as are the pebbles in a stream". Finally, Rykwert was as troubled by the declamatory representational character of the projects of the *Tendenza* as he was by the polemical rhetoric of its intellectual promoters—hence, I think, his acute unease with the "rigid arrangement of elementary geometries", which typified the project of Aldo

Rossi for the Modena Cemetery, another focus of the exhibition.

If we look again at the emergent set of temperamental and intellectual aversions that appear thus far to typify the stance of the reviewer of furniture and fashion, we can already see that they begin to form a coherent pattern. Provisionally, I summarise them as follows: undoubtedly opposed to the positivist idea of function as a comprehensive measure of the worth of the things of the world, Rykwert is nevertheless troubled by any idea of the ultimate "uselessness" of architecture. Deeply committed to the necessity of "referential content" in architecture and design, he is at the same time wary of modalities of discourse that proceed onward from the idea of "reference" toward ironical self-reflexivity, be those discourses either avant-gardist or "rationalist". Intrigued by the original Duchampian idea that "everything is art", he is prepared to concur that nothing can be ruled out as potential raw material for art, but he is especially engaged by forms of artistic expression that eschew any preoccupation with the individual artistic signature and are instead "'elaborated' by centuries of use".

A significant clue to the development of this distinctive constellation of convictions can be found in the acknowledgments that appear at the beginning of the 1982 collection of Rykwert's writings, *The Necessity of Artifice*. The "two most important" of the debts that he considered himself to have incurred in his intellectual career up to that point were "to Rudolf Wittkower and Sigfried Giedion, whose wayward pupil I count myself."[8] To begin my account of this biographical trajectory, it is appropriate to ponder the intellectual obligation implied by the term "wayward pupil". There is no doubt that one of the pivotal episodes in Rykwert's intellectual formation occurred during the early 1950s, in connection with a review of Giedion's *Mechanization Takes Command* that he was then preparing for *Burlington Magazine*. That this is so is evident (among other ways) in the fact that when the 1954 review was reprinted in *Rassegna* 25 in 1986, it was accompanied by an introductory commentary by Rykwert himself. A part of it reads as follows:

When *Mechanization Takes Command* first appeared in 1948/9 copies were hard to come by in post-war Great Britain. Benedict Nicolson, editor of the *Burlington Magazine*… obtained a copy, and knowing of my enthusiasm for Giedion's writing, asked me to review it…. I was an untried reviewer, and grateful to Nicolson for the confidence. It seemed to me however, that more than a mere book-review was required: sniping at Giedion had already begun, and hostility to him seemed to me to be based on a misunderstanding of his enterprise. I therefore asked if I could do an assessment of the book in the body of Giedion's work. Nicolson readily assented. Being young and insecure, I even bothered Giedion himself; in the autumn of 1952 I visited him in Doldertal, handed him my article and asked him to read it.[9]

Giedion demurred, and proposed instead that Rykwert read it aloud, to Giedion as well as to his wife, Carola, who had joined them. Rykwert nervously complied and began to read, coming eventually to a paragraph in which he commented on the distinctive intellectual method that he saw Giedion having employed in his earlier book, *Spätbarocker und Romantischer Klassisismus,* 1922. Giedion responded to this part of Rykwert's commentary with particular enthusiasm, since it had the effect, as he remarked at the time, of liberating him from the legacy of his own intellectual mentor, Heinrich Wölfflin. The passage from Rykwert's review that so gratified Giedion reads as follows:

Spätbarocker und Romantischer Klassisismus was written as a doctoral thesis in Wölfflin's school, and in it the method of contrasts and of the autonomy of works of art is used, not for the refinement of connoisseurship, but almost as a weapon against itself. Giedion is concerned to demonstrate that Neoclassicism which had hitherto been considered by historians—if at all—as a style, was actually a blanket term to cover two divergent tendencies: the end of the Baroque era, and the first two decades of the Romantic movement. So that in his first work, by following Wölfflin's method Giedion inverted the achievement of Burckhardt. Where Burckhardt had demonstrated the internal unity of an epoch that had been studied fragmentally, Giedion demonstrated this internal cleavage in a period which had been accorded an apparent unity.

In amplifying his view of this methodological breakthrough as it appeared in Giedion's *Mechanization,* Rykwert argued that it was achieved, not by conjuring up a string of generalisations from the familiar facts out of the usual text-books, but by a method which

existed already in a somewhat more primitive form in *Space Time and Architecture*; that of fixing on an apparently insignificant section of the field (keys and locks, for instance) and demonstrating in the treatment of an entirely fresh case-history the process which, allowing for differences, operates also in the rest of the field: a method which is as different from the scissors-and-paste kind of historical writing as a Picasso collage is from a Victorian scrapbook.[10]

It would appear evident from Rykwert's depiction of Giedion's method, Giedion's gratified recognition of its identification, and Rykwert's having chosen, some three decades later, to depict in such considerable detail the episode in which this occurred that a key moment in his intellectual formation had occurred.

I have concluded that such an approach is central also to Rykwert's own methodology. Moreover, one can even see encapsulated in his commentary on Giedion how his own early career comprised a series of efforts to develop a method of historical interpretation of the things of the world that would be as compelling and as revelatory as Giedion's had been in its explorations of the "apparently insignificant".

These early encounters with Giedion's thought are later paralleled in a 1967 review Rykwert wrote on Giedion's late, and very controversial, two-volume publication, *The Eternal Present* (1962, 1964). Here again we find Rykwert noting Giedion's preoccupation with the "profound changes that were taking place beneath" the surface of Neoclassicism and with "the meanings below the surface ornament". In another passage in the same pair of reviews, we find him focusing on Giedion's method in *Mechanization*. According to Rykwert, Giedion succeeded in conceptualising a historical account of the furnishings of a room, the mechanical services of a house, and so on; he even follows the transformation in treating seriously the matter of bathing. But to Giedion the compact bathroom is only the atrophied, individual descendant of a great social institution. The Roman and the Islamic baths are perhaps familiar enough, but Giedion dwells on the function of the bath in societies which are both technically primitive and stuck with unfavourable climates, like the Scandinavian and North Russian peasants. He considers the Medieval bath and its relation to Reformation moralising, its banishment to the well-provided home, its elaboration within a tiny scale through the development of the American hotel, and finally its part in the prefabricated service core.[11]

Here, surely, we find evidence of an intellectual and methodological lineage that links Rykwert not only to his mentor Giedion, but also to his student Robin Evans. For can we not recognise in Rykwert's characterisation of Giedion's account of the "atrophied, individual descendant of a great social institution" a striking precursor of Evans' account of the sad historical emergence of functional zoning and "circulation" in domestic architecture, as he depicted it in his much-admired essay, "Figures, Doors, Passages"—a text viewed until now as an apparently purely Foucauldian one.[12]

Prior to Rykwert's fateful early encounter with Giedion, his long and wide-ranging intellectual search began when, still a secondary school student, he attended lectures by Rudolf Wittkower on "the Classical Tradition". Indeed, Wittkower proved to be a durable interest for Rykwert, for when he made a stormy departure from the Architectural Association in London some years later in 1947, he turned instead to two Wittkower seminars at the Warburg Institute—the first on the topography of Rome and the second on Raphael's Stanza. In retrospect, it would appear that Wittkower provided the young Rykwert with an early realisation of the renewed intellectual potential of interpretative procedures in architectural history, even prior to the publication of his precedent breaking *Architectural Principles in the Age of Humanism* in 1949.

But such was Rykwert's characteristically restless methodological inquisitiveness that the encounter with Wittkower proved to be only one of an ongoing series. By 1949, for example, Rykwert had already met Giedion and soon complemented Wittkower's distinctive historical approach with Giedion's much more anthropological one. Yet this still does not complete my account of the wide-ranging intellectual search of the young Rykwert. For example, in the years immediately after the end of the Second World War, he spent considerable time at the Gower Street premises of the Student Christian Movement (SCM), then a centre of intellectual activity for young thinkers who saw themselves as on the left politically but wished to dissociate themselves from a communism that increasingly was intellectually discredited. Rykwert met a number of individuals there who became long-standing friends, among them Elias Canetti. Older than Rykwert, Canetti had already published *Auto-da-Fé* in the late 1930s and was working at the time on *Crowds and Power*. Other strong influences from the SCM period are the philosopher Alasdair MacIntyre, the anthropologist

Fritz Steiner, and the psychoanalyst Franz Elkisch.[13] In response to them, Rykwert not only deepened his already established interest in anthropology but also expanded it to take on that precocious modality of contemporary discourse, psychoanalysis.

A last distinct strain of contemporary thought that came to interest Rykwert was phenomenological philosophy. In 1957–1958 he was an academic visitor to the Hochschule für Gestaltung in Ulm. It was there that he wrote the now well-known essay "The Sitting Position: A Question of Method", which launched his modern analogy between buildings and the human body.[14] During his stay in Ulm, Rykwert became friends with the philosopher and sociologist Hanno Kesting (besides himself, the only other "nonrationalist" on the faculty at the time). As a result of Kesting's encouragement, Rykwert extended his reading in this area from Gabriel Marcel and Jean-Paul Sartre, with whose works he already had some familiarity, to Maurice Merleau-Ponty.

As the 1950s were drawing to a close, Rykwert's intellectual formation thus took on the colouration that is now recognisable as definitive. During those key years, an increased unification of his complex set of interests occurred. In a telling comment, Rykwert has observed that he was provoked by Canetti around this time to read Arnold van Gennep's *Rites of Passage*, just as Canetti was himself completing the manuscript of *Crowds and Power*. In a sense both deep and broad, this led Rykwert to understand that the distinctive approach he had been seeking could be to read architecture as a field of meaning.

During this period of his mature formation, Rykwert grew increasingly dissatisfied with the tenor of discussion of architecture then proceeding in London. Particularly disturbing to him was "the Picturesque Tradition", which was being promulgated during those years by a group of writers associated with *The Architectural Review*. Troubled enough by the shallowness of this tendency as it applied to British subject material, Rykwert was more disturbed when its protagonists took on Italian urban form as a topic. By this time he had become a serious Italophile, and his anthropological interests had provoked him to try to understand the ancient origins of Italian urban form. He had been surprised in this regard to discover that the most up-to-date study on the subject remained Fustel de Coulanges' *The Ancient City* from 1864.

In 1963 Rykwert's dissatisfaction with current English discourse coalesced with his growing Italophilia and the maturation of his own intellect. The result was the first version of the now-famous text, "The Idea of a Town", published that year as a special issue of *Forum*, the Dutch architectural magazine edited by Aldo van Eyck.

Continuing the critique of Functionalism that had been at the heart of the essay "Meaning in Building", "The Idea of a Town" moved the argument to the plane of urbanism. Opposed to the shallow pictorialism of the picturesque tradition, Rykwert sought to identify the fundamental anthropological and psychological underpinnings of all urban form, ancient and contemporary. He noted in his first paragraph:

> Very occasionally a new town is created. We are then treated to a display of embarrassment on the part of authority and planners who seem incapable of thinking of the new town as a totality, as a pattern which carries a meaning other than commonplaces of zoning… or circulation. To consider it, as the ancients did, a symbolic pattern seems utterly alien and pointless. If we think of anything as 'symbolic', it is of an object or action that can be taken in at a glance.[15]

Following this polemical opening, Rykwert went on to explore in detail the principles that, as far as he had been able to deduce, had underpinned the overall design of many ancient, and particularly Roman, towns, using as a key part of his evidence documentation from diverse sources on town foundation rituals. Presaging the dispute he was later to have with Tafuri and Rossi, he remarked on the origins of the foundation rite itself:

> I am not at all sure that anything so complex and at the same time so hoary and vigorous can be traced back to two or three clearly identifiable sources; it is surely a syncretic phenomenon, made up of bits originating in different parts of the world—the whole thing growing through many centuries and altering in flavour and emphasis as the context of religious ideas in general changed and developed.[16]

The idea of such "a syncretic phenomenon—growing through many centuries and altering in flavour and emphasis" is surely closely related to the image of Roman architecture he framed in 1974 in opposition to Rossi. This conception of the power of cultural forms, so strongly associated with long duration, multiple authorship, and evolutional transformation,

had clearly become early on a central part of Rykwert's distinctive historiography.

The editorial sponsor of the original publication of "The Idea of a Town" was Rykwert's friend and ally, van Eyck. One of the key figures in the revisionist Modernist architectural movement Team 10, van Eyck was far and away the most intellectual, the most anthropological, the most poetic member of the group. He was also among the earliest of Rykwert's admirers to sense the potential created by the combination of anthropology and contemporary psychology evinced in his work. Historical anthropology though it may be, "The Idea of a Town" also served as a contemporary rallying cry for van Eyck. In his introduction to the special issue of *Forum*, he noted:

> If we, today, are unable to read the entire universe and its meaning off our civic institutions as the Romans did—loss or gain—we still need to be at home in it; to interiorise it, refashion it in our own image—each for himself this time. To discover that we are no longer Romans, and yet Romans still is no small thing![17]

Commenting on Rykwert's conclusion, van Eyck saluted the combination of anthropological and psychoanalytic methods of interpretation that had appealed to him so much, and he pointed directly to Rykwert's recurrent and potent analogy of buildings with persons:

> As we read the closing paragraphs, the 'ground of certainty' which our time can still neither find nor face—call it shifting centre or lost home—momentarily reveals its whereabouts. "It is no longer likely that we shall find this ground in the world the cosmologists are continuously reshaping round us, and so we must look for it" Rykwert concludes, "inside ourselves, in the constitution and structure of the human person."[18]

With the publication of "The Idea of a Town", Rykwert launched the mature approach that was to typify his entire oeuvre from then on. Indeed, he recently remarked to me that the argument of his more recent work, *The Dancing Column*, 1996, is, among other things, a response to the implicit question about cosmology he had posed to himself at the end of the earlier work.

While I will not discuss that text, in timely celebration of which the *Festschrift* in his honour was convened, I will conclude with a series of observations on the two major texts that Rykwert published in the years between: *On Adam's House in Paradise*, 1972 and *The First Moderns*, 1980. In doing so, I strive to elucidate the ways they manifest the characteristic historiographical methods I have attributed to him thus far.

On Adam's House in Paradise, like "The Idea of a Town", was first published on mainland Europe rather than in Rykwert's home base, Britain, by a sponsor who was also a personal friend. The place of publication was Milan, and the friend was Roberto Calasso, the editorial director of Adelphi, to whom, together with his wife, *Adam's House* was dedicated. Even as late as 1972, British intellectuals evidently still did not take Rykwert as seriously as continental ones did. Then too, this Milanese episode is a direct extension of his long relationship with Italy. Even his first encounter with Sigfried Giedion in 1949 had an Italian venue, the Eighth Meeting of the International Congress of Modern Architecture, being held in Bergamo. At this same event, he also made the acquaintance of the young Italian architect who was to become a lifelong friend, Vittorio Gregotti.

Rykwert saw the English architectural scene as typically looking to Scandinavia for inspiration. He looked instead to Italy. Having worked for two years in the London offices of Fry Drew and Partners, and Richard Sheppard, he found himself more interested in the work of Persico and Pagano, Figini and Pollini, Gardella, Albini and BBPR, than he was in that of his London employers and their local contemporaries. Together with John Turner (with whom he had travelled to Bergamo in 1949), he even contemplated in those years a joint project to write a book on modern Italian architecture. So admiring was he of Ernesto Rogers that he even hoped to write for Rogers' magazine, *Casabella*. He did, in fact, eventually meet Rogers, but despite his admiration and his own journalistic inclinations, he never struck a chord with Rogers sufficiently strong to be invited to write for him. Unexpectedly, he did strike such a chord with Giò Ponti. As a result, he became the correspondent for *Domus*, where his two controversial texts from 1974 and 1975 were published. Rykwert's interests in Italy and anthropology also led him to spend the summers of 1962 and 1963 working in Rome with Frank E Brown on his archaeological studies of the Forum. Indeed, it was on one of these trips to Rome

that he attended a dinner party that happened to be attended also by Roberto Calasso.

The intellectual bond forged between the revisionist Londoner and the Italian who went on to write *The Ruin of Kasch*, 1994, was evidently a powerful one, for clearly, the two shared a number of intellectual inclinations. Among these are a skepticism with regard to the supposed cultural superiority of Modernity as a project, as compared with its European historical predecessors, a keen curiosity as to the revelatory potential of comparisons of historical and literary phenomena from non-European cultures, and a disinclination to privilege any one art form—or, for that matter, any one form of knowledge—over any other.

On Adam's House in Paradise begins with a provocative quotation from René Daumal: "In order to return to the source, one is obliged to travel upstream."[19] Faithfully following this injunction, Rykwert took as his theme the curiously insistent and morally compelling idea of the origin of architecture. He explained first the extent to which such an apparently anachronistic idea has preoccupied some of the most notable of twentieth-century architects and then traced the complex lineage of the idea back through the centuries to antiquity.

Documenting the surprising hold this idea has had on such notable figures as Le Corbusier, Adolf Loos, and Frank Lloyd Wright, Rykwert then demonstrated how each had considered the idea within a frame of reference derived (consciously or not) from debates that had taken place among European historians of the preceding generation, including the German historian and theorist Gottfried Semper and his most assiduous critic, Alois Riegl. Working his way back from Riegl and Semper through the writings of Viollet-le-Duc, Pugin, and Quatremère de Quincy, Rykwert proceeded to an account of a controversial figure of the early nineteenth century, Jean-Nicolas-Louis Durand, whose thought, he argued, had been framed in conscious opposition to that of Marc-Antoine Laugier. At the beginning of chapter five, Rykwert arrived at a point where, in his words, "I cannot avoid a discussion of the text which all the writers I have quoted are forced to allude, and which must be regarded as the source of all the later speculations about the primitive hut: that of Vitruvius on the origins of architecture.[20]

Following an explanation of the influence of Vitruvian thought on fifteenth- and sixteenth-century Italian writers on architecture, especially Alberti, Palladio, and Filarete, Rykwert turned his attention to one of the two profoundly deeply rooted images of the "first building" as it has long been imaged in Western thought. Minimally documented historically but of great importance for cultural thought and religious practice, the "first building" in question was the ancient Temple of Solomon in Jerusalem. Having demonstrated the extraordinary significance of this building for generations of Western clerics, historians and architects, Rykwert described the intensive efforts made by a group of them between the sixteenth and the eighteenth centuries to devise a convincing reconstruction of the temple, one that would be compelling both as a project of contemporary archaeology as well as of durable religious conviction. Especially notable among those whose efforts are described are the sixteenth-century Jesuit scholar Juan Bautista Villalpando and the eighteenth-century Austrian architect Johann Bernhard Fischer von Erlach.

At the end of his "upstream" historical account, Rykwert turned to more anthropological matters. Chapters entitled "The Rites" and "A House for the Soul" make explicit what had been up to that point in his argument only a subtext: the sheer psychological, not to say ontological, urgency of the origin of architecture in Western European thought. It is no wonder then that Ernst Gombrich saw Rykwert in *On Adam's House in Paradise* as having adopted "the methods of the psychoanalyst".[21]

For all this, Rykwert never saw his project as a Platonic or a transcendental conception. Rather, he observed:

An object which has always been lost cannot—in any ordinary sense of the word—be remembered. The memory of which we speak, however, is not quite of an object but of a state—of something that was; and of something that was done, was made: an action. It is a collective memory kept alive within groups by legends and rituals.[22]

If Rykwert's method in *On Adam's House in Paradise* can be seen as a psychoanalytic and diachronic section through history, then that of his next major text was an equally ambitious, complementary one. *The First Moderns*, 1980 seeks to isolate a specific, synchronic layer of the history of ideas, this one being the intellectual and psychological prehistory of what we now think of in the broadest sense as Modernism in architecture.

The period during which this layer is formed is the eighteenth century. Thus, Rykwert's account focuses on arguments put forward by a diverse group of writers stretching from Claude Perrault at the end of the seventeenth century to Jean-Nicolas-Louis Durand at the beginning of the nineteenth. And as his account makes clear, the psychological anxiety about architecture that first manifests itself during those years still marks the substratum of what we think today.

Rykwert returned to a theme Giedion had explored in his *Spätbarocker und Romantischer Klassisismus* and began with an etymological account of the differences between the terms "classic" and "neoclassic" in accepted architectural history, quickly making it clear once again how labile the term "neoclassic" really is as a means of description and analysis. Indeed, reading *The First Moderns* as a coded account of the dilemmas concerning thoughtful architects today, in attempting to retheorise their praxis, one cannot help but see it as a Giedionesque effort to bring the unacknowledged subconscious of contemporary theory in architecture directly to the forefront of conscious understanding.

Rykwert used the project of reconstruction of the Temple of Solomon, one of the key themes of *On Adam's House in Paradise*, again in *The First Moderns* to launch a commentary on the complex series of disorienting revisionisms that typify the theory of architecture in the century and a half to follow. He cited the work of Fréart de Chambray, but only to set the stage for the revolutionary ideas of Claude Perrault, who, in his influential translations of Vitruvius of 1674 and 1684 and his *Ordornnance de cinq espèces do colonnes* of 1683, laid down challenges to European architects that haunt them still. Arguing that ancient precedent was no longer a sufficient guide for contemporary practice, Perrault put forward two new categories of "beauty", characterised as "positive" on the one hand and "arbitrary" on the other. Rykwert then used the disorientation caused by Perrault's intervention to characterise the anxious quest for a new ground of architectural certainty by some, and the frivolous but equally anxious play engaged in by others, in a series of episodes of style, theory, and polemic in architecture that typify the century and a half to follow.

The particular, relativist, and playful "orientalist" episode of chinoiserie is tabled, only to be set against an anxious new quest for a so-called universal architecture. But this effort at an ontological reconstruction is challenged in its turn by experiments described under the rubric of the "pleasures of freedom", including work of the painter François Boucher and, especially, the architects Juste-Aurèle Meissonier in France and Vanbrugh and Hawksmoor in England. Finally, the last stage of these parallel eighteenth-century trajectories is what Rykwert calls a "return to earnestness", typified in France by Servandoni's project for St Sulpice and in Britain by the later eighteenth-century work of the new "Palladians", Colen Campbell and William Kent.

And if this oscillation is not disorienting enough, it is followed by a pragmatic new philistinism at the beginning of the nineteenth century in the vastly influential work of Durand. Although Rykwert shows this to be a decisive conclusion to the vast synchronic portrayal of anxiety of the eighteenth century, Durand's new instrumentality is nonetheless not permitted to have the last word. In his conclusion, Rykwert takes considerable pains to refute it:

> Seen from the vantage point of the 1970s and 1980s, Durand's positive dismissal of the problems which engaged and worried seventeenth- and eighteenth-century architects does not seem quite final. The nature of our responses to the world of artefacts, the way in which groups and communities appropriate space, occupies sociologists and anthropologists, and we acknowledge these human scientists as important and wholly serious people. Yet their studies are, in the last reduction, almost inevitably about problems of form. Perhaps, if there is a place for the architect's work within a future social fabric, he will have to learn how to deal with such problems again.[23]

I will not here propose any analysis of *The Dancing Column*, but will instead essay a few provisional conclusions with respect to the intellectual influences that I see as contributing seminally to his intellectual formation, as well as to the structure of his typical methods, as I have been able to identify them.

Rykwert began with an intense interest in the new potentials of historical analysis in architecture as they were pioneered by Rudolf Wittkower in the late 1940s, and then went on to complement this interest with equally intense ones in the potentials of anthropology, archaeology, psychoanalysis, and phenomenological philosophy. It seems to me that it is in a complex hybrid of archaeology and psychoanalysis that we can delineate most aptly an image of the method that he was eventually able to formulate for himself, on the model of the one of Sigfried Giedion that he admired. These two disciplines have in common a method that always looks below the ostensible surface of things in an attempt to derive significance from that which lies beneath. What is more, both archaeology and psychoanalysis

share with anthropology a manifest interest only in an indirect relationship of cultural production to individual authorship.

It may by now go without saying that Rykwert shares in a generally understood *episteme* of our era that we call Foucauldian. That is, like most of his contemporaries, he has lost confidence in the efficacy or legitimacy of grand intellectual systems or systematic social or historical projects. By the same token, he is of a generation that abandoned teleological notions of progress in history and has particularly eschewed any interest in the once apparently potent forms of instrumentality in human affairs.

All this having been said, Rykwert's oeuvre, given the formulation of his characteristic method described above, has nevertheless been deeply marked by his conviction as to the power of the subconscious in history—in some respects, even of a subconscious that in some sense is collective. What is more, there is no doubt that he is also convinced of the powerful cause-and-effect relationship produced by that subconscious in the broad playing out of human events across time.

Thus, although his view of the sheer stuff of history is neither teleological nor deterministic, I think he sees it as possessing an apparently intractable density and thickness that commands the sustained attention and curiosity of the engaged intellectual. Indeed, I would be inclined to argue that it has been his lifelong intellectual project to employ the distinctive analytic methods he has devised, to bring to the conscious awareness of his contemporaries, the implications and potential consequences of the assumptions lying within the beliefs, social forms, and artefacts that form their horizon of existence, however individualised or however collective those forms may at first seem to be.

What is more, it seems to me clear that he sees those beliefs and forms as themselves being the product of a complex formation, as he put it, "altering in flavour and emphasis as the context of… ideas changed" and "polished by [centuries of use] as [are] the pebbles in a stream". Given this, and given the relatively modest roles particular individuals in history will have been able to play in their evolution, we may understand that the techniques of interpretation required to elucidate their significance will require a Rykwertian ellipsis. But this having been said, it will also be true that while not straightforward, such techniques will surely also be neither self-reflexive nor ironic.

Notwithstanding the difficulties of the tasks his methods have been formulated to address, it surely remains a matter for admiration that Rykwert continues to hold such high hopes for the project of architectural design in human affairs. Indeed, it can be said that he sees the relationship of interpreting to designing to be not only possible but even ontologically urgent. If, for Rykwert, it remains as true as it ever was that the project of architecture is to create a "house for the soul", then his intriguingly McLuanesque sympathy for the avant-garde conviction that "everything is art" (for him, it is admittedly only potentially so) comes to be understandable. For, in these terms, it is surely impossible ever to be able to determine in advance what the limits of any tectonic accommodation of the "soul" might be. Hence his keen curiosity in regard to the range of manifestations of creative activity extant in the world, furniture and fashion among them.

If this effort at a provisional delineation of Rykwert's historiography has succeeded in some measure, then it seems to me also that it can explain the absence of an obviously Rykwertian school in contemporary architecture or history. After all, the central analytic focus of his research is (speaking almost archaeologically) several levels below the operative layer within which most cultural and, even more particularly, design praxes have been promulgated by such contemporaries as Hejduk and Rowe. Indeed, Rykwert's distinct, intense, long-standing engagement with the long acculturation of architectural forms, coupled with his decidedly lesser curiosity with respect to the signature of the individual designer, make it clear that such readily visible praxes would not have been an appropriate result of his methodology in any event.[24] It seems to me instead that the Rykwertian school will surely lie for some indeterminate period of time largely operationally invisible, obscured in that very phenomenological thickness of history that I have called the central focus of his personal historiographical project. Only at some future historical moment will its effects be able to be clearly discerned.

In the end, it is for me the intensity of Rykwert's engagement with the sheer phenomenological thickness and historical embeddedness of reality that is so exhilarating. How astute it is of his Italian colleague Gregotti, at the end of *Body and Building*, to label him "an anthropologist of architectural history". There is no doubt that Rykwert's own oeuvre, like so many of the complex historical phenomena that have been the subject of his interpretative projects over the years, indeed constitutes "a promise as well as a memory".

1   The phrase "a promise as well as a memory" appears in the last sentence of Rykwert's *On Adam's House in Paradise* and has also been employed as an implicit reference to Rykwert's own writings in Gregotti, Vittorio, "Joseph Rykwert: An Anthropologist of Architectural History", *Body and Building*, Cambridge, MA: MIT Press, 2002.

2   Canetti is the author of *Auto-da-Fé, Crowds and Power*, and a three-volume autobiography. He won the Nobel Prize for literature in 1981. Illich is the author of numerous texts that challenge the tenets of Enlightenment rationality, including *Celebration of Awareness, Deschooling Society, Tools for Conviviality, Shadow Work, and In the Mirror of the Past*.

3   Rykwert's students include Bryan Avery, Timothy Bell, Richard Bulleyne, Mario Carpo, Patrick Devanthéry, George Dodds, Robin Evans, Homa Fardjacli, John Farmer, Donald Genasci, Vaughan Hart, Desmond Cheuk-kuen Hui, Peter Kohane, Inez Lamuniére, David Leatherbarrow, Daniel Libeskind, John McArthur, Mohsen Mostafavi, Lawrence Nield, Simon Pepper, Alberto Pérez-Gomez, and Robert Tavernor. Although I was not one of his students, I spent much time in discussions with him during my postgraduate studies in London in the mid-1960s.

4   Rykwert, Joseph, *The Necessity of Artifice*, London: Academy Editions, 1982, p 104.

5   Rykwert, *The Necessity of Artifice*, 1982, p 91.

6   Rykwert, *The Necessity of Artifice*, 1982, p 74.

7   Rykwert, *The Necessity of Artifice*, 1982, pp 75–76.

8   Rykwert, *The Necessity of Artifice*, 1982, p 7.

9   Rykwert 1986, "Sigfried Giedion and The Notion of Style", *Rassegna* 25, 1986, p 82.

10 Rykwert, "Sigfried Giedion and The Notion of Style", 1986, p 84.

11 Rykwert, 1967, p 465.

12 Evans, R, "Figures, Doors, Passages", *Translations from Drawing to Building and Other Essays*, Cambridge: MIT Press, 1997, p 55.

13 MacIntyre is the author of many texts, including *Marxism and Christianity, Against the Self-Images of the Age*, and *After Virtue*.

14 Rykwert 1982, p 23. "The Sitting Position: A Question of Method" was first published in Italian in *Edilizia Moderna* in 1964 and then in English in Jencks and Baird, 1969.

15 Rykwert, Joseph, "The Idea of a Town", *Forum*, 1963, p 100.

16 Rykwert, "The Idea of a Town", 1963, p 112.

17 Editor's Introduction to Rykwert, "The Idea of a Town", 1963, p 98.

18 Editors Introduction to Rykwert, "The Idea of a Town", 1963, p 99.

19 Rykwert, Joseph, *On Adam's House in Paradise*, New York: Museum of Modern Art, 1972, p 11.

20 Rykwert, *On Adam's House in Paradise*, 1972, p 105.

21 Gombrich, Ernst, "Dream Houses", *The New York Review of Books*, 29 November, 1973, p 35.

22 Rykwert, *On Adam's House in Paradise*, 1972, p 14.

23 Rykwert, Joseph, *The First Moderns: The Architects of the Eighteenth Century*, Cambridge: MIT Press, 1980, p 470.

24 At the end of my framing of this particular conclusion in respect to Rykwert's methods, especially his putatively lesser curiosity regarding the signature of the individual designer, it occurred to me to test my hypothesis by rereading "Two Houses by Eileen Gray" in *The Necessity of Artifice*. Rykwert was one of the first contemporary critics to rediscover Gray, and his essay certainly acknowledges the distinctiveness of her design approach. But on my rereading, I found it intriguing how he emphasises the way in which she has devised a "container for a carefully articulated way of life" rather than her "style". Indeed, he even laments what he calls her later "decline" to "what is now called Art Nouveau". In a provocative terminological choice, he also refers to her Roquebrune house as "one of the most remarkable 'ensembles' of the time". By choosing the word ensemble rather than the alternative *Gesamtkunstwerk*, Rykwert makes it clear that he sees Gray as operating in a quite different realm than, for example, Mies van der Rohe, to whose work he is famously averse. As he concluded, "Those of us familiar with latter-day proceedings, when an architect may think it in order to dictate the whole furnishing and even the details of the decoration to his client for fear that he might 'spoil' his building by use, may find some comfort in these proceedings. Eileen Gray built for herself; the houses were original, carefully considered, and matched to an open, relaxed way of life". Thus does Rykwert appropriate even such a stylist as Gray into his decisively anthropological conceptual framework for design.

Public Space

During the final preparation of the manuscript of my 1995 publication *The Space of Appearance*, it occurred to me that my thoughts about public space could be expanded further. An invitation in 1994 to contribute to a publication on the work of my Harvard colleagues, Rodolfo Machado and Jorge Silvetti, only deepened my interest in doing so. Two other subsequent texts amplify this growing interest of mine, which culminated in the publication of my 2011 book *Public Space: Cultural/Political Theory; Street Photography*.

On Publicness and Monumentality in the Work of Machado and Silvetti, 1994

Rodolfo Machado and Jorge Silvetti have long demonstrated a remarkable engagement with the possibility of a public monumentality for our time. This theme was launched in their 1978 project, the Steps of Providence, which first brought them to the attention of a broad architectural audience (as the result of its winning a *Progressive Architecture* Design Award). It has continued quite consistently since, notably in Silvetti's Four Public Squares for Leonforte of 1983, Machado's Sesquicentennial Park of 1986, and in their Piazza Dante for Genoa of 1989. The tenacity of the two designers in respect to public monumentality is all the more unusual in that it broadly distinguishes them from the generation of architects that preceded them, as well as from the generation that has followed. Forming their intellectual position in architecture in the wake of the startling events of 1968, Machado and Silvetti nevertheless sedulously avoided the literal politicisations of practice that became widespread among thoughtful young architects in the 1970s. Holding fast to a belief in the continuing efficacy of "form", they declared themselves very early to be primarily concerned with the importance of making concrete proposals for buildings to be built. At the same time, they also resisted the more popular modalities of so-called "Postmodernism" in architecture, especially its consumerist North American version. Their refusal to illustrate their politics in their work is thus political nevertheless.

Eschewing consumption, while still insisting on a practice oriented toward building, Machado and Silvetti found themselves dissenting from the emerging thrust of a younger generation, who similarly averse to consumption, chose to look to the art gallery rather than to the street as a viable venue for an integral architectural practice. In their resolute commitment to remain "in the street", Machado and Silvetti have found themselves necessarily confronting the question of the public dimension of architecture. Unlike their predecessors, who espoused orthodox Modernism, they have never been so naive as to suppose that architecture could establish a public territory in itself. But they have been too convinced of the essentially "social" basis of architecture ever to suppose that it could remain significant if it evaded a commitment to propound a visual discourse for some form of community-at-large. It is their almost unique combination of circumspection and insistent conviction that characterises the four projects that I will discuss in some detail.

View of Market Square and Memorial Steps at the Rhode Island School of Design, Providence, Rhode Island, 1978.

We may begin by considering the relative diversity of the sites of these interventions: Providence, Rhode Island; Leonforte, Sicily; Houston, Texas; and Genoa, Italy. In their evident geographic heterogeneity, the projects can be seen as methodologically exemplary. Two of the sites, for example, are European, and two North American. One of each pair is an energetic metropolis, while the other is a hinterland centre. All but Houston could be thought to be 'historical' cities, while Houston is self-consciously contemporary. Yet Machado and Silvetti's design techniques will disclose just how routinely modern Genoa can be—and how unexpectedly historical Houston can be. All these cities, of course, are equally contemporary in their evidence of urban displacement and fragmentation—generally as a result of the advent of the automobile and of the expediences of traffic engineering and parking lots. All manifest a similar loss of confidence in a once credible, but now historically unrecoverable, mode of civic space-making.

The Steps of Providence is an unsolicited proposal for an urban transformation of a portion of the campus of the Rhode Island School of Design. The Four Public Squares for Leonforte, interventions in the present-day city centre of this early seventeenth-century *città di fondazione*, were proposed on invitation from this provincial Sicilian city. The Sesquicentennial Park of Houston was a submission to a competition to celebrate Texas' anniversary. Finally, the Piazza Dante is an entry to a competition convened by Genoa to commemorate the 500th anniversary of the fateful voyage of Christopher Columbus to America.

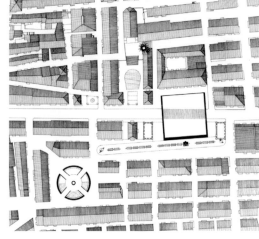

Aerial view of the proposal for the Piazza Dante, in Genoa, Italy, 1989.

Site plan showing the four public squares in Leonforte, Sicily.

Context

It seems to me that all four projects can be seen as "contextual", according to the usages of the term that followed from the work of Colin Rowe and his students in the 1970s. To be sure, one cannot call Machado and Silvetti's work definitively "contextual", since it never really took its urban theoretical lead from Rowe himself, having already been quite decisively formed by more European influences prior to their meeting him.[1] Still, "an overriding aim of [the Steps of Providence] design", state the authors, "has been to create tangible, positive, urban space where presently there exist only voids and leftover areas". The project inserts itself with skilful formal ingenuity into an existing urban-institutional fabric in ways that are as programmatically pragmatic as they are spatially lucid.

In the fabric of Leonforte, a subtly different challenge faced Silvetti. Here, the extant built fabric of the quarter was more cohesive than that of Providence, even if the social and functional role of its older part had deteriorated as a result of modern expansion. In Leonforte, Silvetti notes that the design proposes a modest "intervention in the modern expansion to address the issue of the regeneration of the historical centre". The contextual intervention in this case comprises subtle embellishments to a somewhat inchoate set of existing open spaces in the vicinity of a prominent church.

In the case of Sesquicentennial Park for Houston, the quest for context might seem an inappropriate, if not paradoxical, one. Yet here, too, the author's description of the project begins, "extended throughout

the site is a contextual grid". Even for such an ostensibly anti-urban setting as Houston, Machado insisted on finding—and on repositioning—a deep structural spatial referent, which, in turn, became a primary armature of his design. Looking closely at the compact form of the historical grid of downtown Houston, Machado satisfied himself that, even at this late date in the city's evolution, its grid was, in principle, extendible from one edge of the downtown core. And so he established an extensive extrapolation of it out into a strange no-man's land, which had once been part of a bayou, but which had been so invaded by the city's inner-city expressway system as to have become utterly inhospitable to pedestrian activity.

One might suppose that in Genoa the extant circumstances of urban context would provide more plausible generators of design than they would in Houston. Yet, despite the fact that the Italian city is far more urbane than Houston, the particular site of the proposed Piazza Dante was not. The site was near Genoa's centre, just outside the historic city walls, in a precinct substantially eroded by a series of partially implemented twentieth-century road 'improvements'. It was an idiosyncratic site, marked by various expedient circumstances of urban growth and evolution during the twentieth century. These circumstances fragmented the form of this historically vibrant European centre. The site was mostly open to traffic along two sides; the third side was blown open by earlier demolitions in a fashion that precluded any simple, Sittesque strategies of re-enclosure. As a result, such relatively straightforward

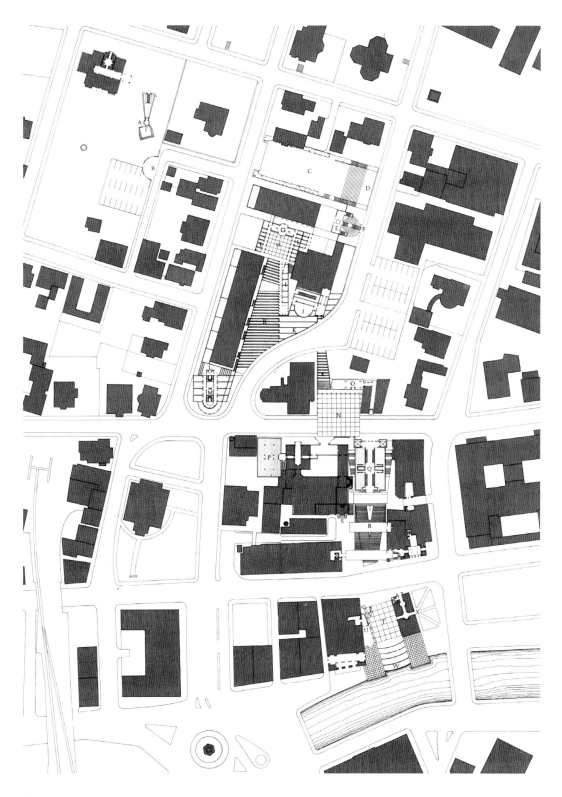

Context plan, showing the area of the campus of the Rhode Island School of Design where the Market Square and Memorial Steps were proposed to be located.

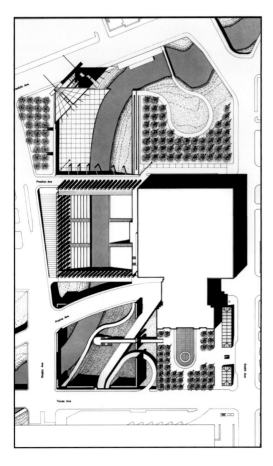

Site plan of the proposal for Sesquicentennial Park in Houston, Texas.

on perspective, Machado and Silvetti's urbanism is always as phenomenological as it is conceptual. Then, too, what distinguishes them from many of their contemporaries is their resolute insistence on fleshing out their urban prepositions with deeply committed material expressions.

Material Tectonics

Not for nothing have the two partners argued so insistently that architecture and urban design "are inseparable". Indeed, their urban design propositions have never been permitted to remain at the conceptual level of a diagram or a gesture. They have always conferred upon their urban designs the same material tectonic that has been characteristic of their architectural projects.

Thus the presentation for Steps of Providence characteristically encompasses sets of "before and after" drawings—very detailed, interrelated sets of plans, sections, and axonometrics, as well as carefully considered representations of stair tread-to-riser connections, paving patterns, and the like. These details have the cumulative effect of lending a starting tangibility to the scheme.

Similarly, at Leonforte the spatial phenomenology of the four piazzas finds its material expression in the now well-known tower, which has been rendered with such a degree of tectonic specificity as to enable us to read its masonry coursing, stair balustrade details, and cornice profiles.

Given the consistency of this emergent theme in the projects, it is hardly surprising that the Sesquicentennial Park exhibits a similar degree of material tectonic specificity, as seen in the rendering of the systems of support and cladding of the boardwalk balustrade, and of the greenery at the base of the colonnade.

In the case of the Piazza Dante, this material tectonic achieves its most powerful expression in the astonishing stair-amphitheatre-ship-fountain assemblage, which is the project's centrepiece. This brilliant apparatus—frame, filigree, and icon, all at once—makes it clear how the authors commitment to link architecture and urban design inseparably is not just a matter of their prodigious energy and commitment. Beyond that, it stands as a demonstration of the intense social and material realism their proposals manifest.

Typicality/Realism

With this reference to realism, my specific argument intersects with that of Michael Hays, who has understood

spatial gestures as sufficed for Leonforte would have been insufficient here. So Machado and Silvetti were driven to a set of elliptical and inferred volumetric refinements, making as much use of manipulations of the ground plane as they did of bounding surfaces, so as to posit a perceptible—and experientially convincing—spatial focus for their proposed Piazza Dante.

Now it is true, of course, that these varied and faithful strategies of contextual response, imaginative though they are, might be thought to be very similar to those that any number of capable protégés of Colin Rowe could have been expected to propose. But it seems to me that Machado and Silvetti's method is one that differs from the others' in several key ways. First of all, while it relies on the principles of figure/ground to establish its "tangible, positive urban spaces", it does not rely so predominantly on elaborations in plan as does the method of many of Rowe's followers. In its emphasis on elevation, section, and especially

Machado and Silvetti's term "unprecedented realism"
as providing a possible conceptual key to a general
understanding of their characteristic design practice.
What I want to point to in particular is the meticulous
political realism that these four projects represent
to me, precisely at the level of their response to and
acknowledgement of the detail of "object-types" as
they exist in the contemporary realm.

I frequently find myself engaged, as does any
architect extensively involved in the day-to-day
practice of contemporary urban design, in contentious
debates about the specifics of curb cuts, curvature of
road pavements at intersections, legalities of street
illumination levels, configurations and locations of
pedestrian crosswalks, and so on. How fascinating, then,
to see how Machado and Silvetti's commitment to
"types"—and to a realistic expectation of the possible
realisation of buildings—has led them to incorporate
within their proposals for public monuments the
conscientious utilisation of certain utterly familiar,
particular, and intransigent details of contemporary
'public works' design. In the early Steps of Providence
project, *sachlich* representations of street sidewalks,
curbs, and curb cuts form an implicit part of the virtual
realm of public activity portrayed.

In the Sesquicentennial Park project, this *sachlich*
commitment has intensified. The view of Preston
Avenue, for example, incorporates a series of standard
traffic control pavement markings as part of its relatively
spare approach to imagery. Then, too, the view of Bayou
Square looks across the top of a recognisable, 'standard-
issue' public works bridge balustrade. And interestingly
enough, the representations of these typical elements
lend them and their settings a certain 'delirious' quality.
Refining this design strategy further still, Machado has
proposed details analogous to those of the public works
bridge for the balustrade of the observation deck of the
tower. Ineluctable, typical apparatuses of public works
are thus not only allowed for within the conceptual field
proposed, but are also, by intent at least, redeemed
in their calculated redeployment within the project's
realms of metaphor.

Historically, literate architects have been well
aware of the powerful tradition of the object-type as
it stretched from the practice of Adolf Loos to that
of Le Corbusier. Less well known is the more recent
trajectory of an analogous kind in twentieth-century
American architecture, which would link Charles
Eames' inventions of new object-types (such as his

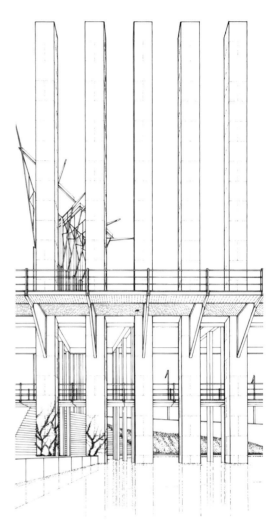

View through the Preston Avenue Colonnade towards the Tower
of Houston.

An elevation of the public stair proposed for the Piazza Dante
in Genoa.

View of the proposed Frazier Terrace on the campus of the Rhode Island School of Design.

plywood chairs of the 1950s and 1960s) to the new usages of 'banal' extant types (such as chain-link fencing) in the work of Robert Venturi and Frank Gehry. In the efforts to make the redeployment, bracketing, and elevation of the quotidian typologies of public-works objects in our time an integral component of their practice of monumentality, Machado and Silvetti have joined these distinguished lineages of architecture in our century. And this indeed constitutes "unprecedented realism" of a very high order.

Aspirations to Civitas

But at the same time that these 'typical' incorporations routinely bespeak the everyday, they are also strategic to the still larger ambitions of the projects' authors. Insofar as they do not just accommodate the *sachlich* everyday, insofar as they deploy the objects in question so pervasively, so realistically, so expediently—leading one to hypothesise their ready implementation, even in the philistine world of public-works practicality—Machado and Silvetti thereby produce the delirious effect I have noted.

The bracketing and the elevation of everyday elements provoke the passer-by to rethink the routine assumptions of inhabitation of this imagined world. And this rethinking, it seems to me, is the beginning of an enhanced public life-in-the-world that the projects, taken as a whole, surely evoke. To be sure, the two

designers sidestep a host of the clichés of wishful publicness that nowadays clutter our jaded streets. Never, for example, have Machado and Silvetti had recourse to any provision, or even allowance for, "public art". But at the same time that they have avoided "art", their calculated deployment of banal types assists them in their ambitions, in that their hortatory settings for possible public events readily present themselves to a lay audience as legible, as robust, and as exhilarating.

How eager the designers are to amplify the expansive public potentialities of the subconscious, sensory mobility of bodies in space! Surely it is not coincidental that all of these projects encompass complex systems of circumstantial and unprogrammed public movement. Elevated pathways, grand and rhetorical staircases, observation decks, amphitheatric ascents, and bleachers, all of which invite the distracted passer-by to engage in some seemingly incidental alteration of the consciousness of physical being-in-space, that necessarily exists in the presence of others.

It is important to note also that these manifold, elegant apparatuses of possible public exploration are not proffered gratuitously. In every case, they have the fascinating consequence of revealing to the distracted figure who happens to employ them some hitherto unforeseen aspect of the evidently routine urban reality of which one would otherwise be merely an

View from Sesquicentennial Park of the skyline of downtown Houston.

distinctive generational contribution they have made.

For they, through their adroit circumspection and ellipses, have succeeded in avoiding bathetic determinism or orthodox Modern architecture. At the same time, their insistent determination stands as a challenge to younger-generation skeptics who doubt the possibility of architecture to embody any sort of shared world successfully. We are well enough aware nowadays of the proliferation of a radically differentiated "otherness" being so forcefully propounded—claims that, if taken at face value, would render it impossible to suppose that a characteristic architectural practice could ever be relevant to Providence, Leonforte, Houston, and Genoa. Yet we also know that even such a loyal Heideggerian as Jean-Luc Nancy has made the poignant claim that being itself must be seen to be in "community".[2] And if Nancy is correct in this phenomenological supposition of the recent past, is it not also true that architecture will have to acknowledge its inevitable collective reality?

To be sure, the characteristic ethical risk of architectural practice—presumption and domination—remain as great a threat as ever. Yet, to their credit, Machado and Silvetti have consistently refused to concede that the successful avoidance of this dilemma would deny them the right ever to propound architectural proposals for a public life-at-large. In their work, Providence, Leonforte, Houston, and Genoa continue to have a great deal in common; adroit conceptualisations can be formulated to enhance their respective contemporary realities. It seems to me that Machado and Silvetti have succeeded, in all these complex urban settings, in invoking a public life that is neither naive nor sensational.

A final, personal observation: Machado's view across the proposed Sesquicentennial Park to the all-too-familiar high-rise towers of downtown Houston demonstrates so compellingly the generosity of its author's vision, the astuteness of the realism with which it was formulated, and the sobriety of the credible public life it so eloquently evokes.

unaware user. In Providence, for example, the observer will gain a new understanding of that city's complex relationship between history and topography; in Leonforte, slowly ascending the tower, one will slowly build up a phenomenological map of the evolution of the institutions of the whole city; in Houston and Genoa, one will comprehend a whole series of complex movements in three dimensions that invoke crowds, ceremonies, demonstrations, and festivals, not to mention a host of disclosures of the individual self-in-the-world.

I find the determination with which Machado and Silvetti have continued to insist on these elliptical possibilities of a public life, across such a surprisingly wide range of possible, existing urban settings both poignant and admirable. It is in this regard that I also find the

1   It is interesting to note that in a text published in 1983 Machado had already put a distance between himself and those mentors of his generation who, as he put it, had "learned to deal architecturally with the traditional city". In this text, Machado went on to confess—somewhat to his own surprise—that certain new urban realities radically question the extent to which the methods of "traditionalism" would suffice. In his enumeration of such realities, he cited automobiles as well as new building types such as the atrium, the underground, and "plus 15" walkways. Thus, already in 1983, Machado and Silvetti's practice was politically realistic in terms that transcended contextualism. See Machado, Rodolfo, "Domains of Architecture: Issues on the New City", Unprecedented Realism, Michael Hays ed, Princeton Architectural Press, 1994, pp 38–41.

2   Nancy, Jean-Luc, The Imperative Community, Minneapolis: University of Minnesota Press, 1991.

Review of "Free University Berlin: AA Publication/Exhibition in the Members' Room 21 May–18 June, 1999", 1999

In 1999 the Architectural Association released the third in an occasional series of publications it has entitled *Exemplary Projects*. The series began in 1996 with a slender volume of documentation on a contemporary project by Peter Zumthor: the much-admired thermal Baths at Vals in Switzerland. In 1997 it continued with a fatter publication, this one focusing on a series of projects by the Spanish architect Alejandro de la Sota, ranging from 1950s to the recent past. It now continues with the largest and most sumptuous volume in the series to date. Like the first volume, this one also examines a single building. But in this case the examination is far more ambitious in scope and detailed in its coverage, including a wide range of texts on different aspects of the building as well as a remarkable set of newly commissioned photographs. The building which is the focus of this meticulous attention is the increasingly legendary Free University of Berlin, designed by Candilis-Josic-Woods together with their colleague Manfred Schiedhelm, from 1964 on, with the first executed portion completed in 1973, and the second one shortly thereafter.

The launching of the *Exemplary Projects* series at Mohsen Mostafavi's initiative raises some intriguing ideological and polemical questions. For such an initiative, while in my view a commendable one, will surely be seen in many circles nowadays as out of date. According to the *Oxford English Dictionary*

Part of Diocletian's Palace in Split, as illustrated in *The Man in the Street* by Shadrach Woods.

the principal definition of "exemplar" is "a model for imitation". In the current theoretical climate this is not a characteristic of architectural projects which evokes much admiration. As far as I can tell, such a possibility has been precluded by a complex combination of recent circumstances, among which are the following: first, the now well-established backlash against Postmodernism; second, the ascendancy in much recent influential architectural theory of a stream of phenomenology which privileges radical authorial originality; finally, the hegemony of an architectural neo-avant-garde within the current international "culture industry". Together these circumstances have had the effect of making the use of "models for imitation" a disreputable design praxis.

This was not always so. Indeed, a key mission of second-generation Modernism, during the period of the global dissemination of its principles from the 1940s right through to the 1960s, was precisely to proffer such models. More recently, other movements advocating them have included European Rationalism, on the one hand, and Anglo-American Postmodernism on the other. Where for practitioners from those periods it was thought commendable to produce projects which

could be seen as "exemplary", nowadays it is usually thought far preferable to produce ones which are "authorially distinctive". Thus, for today's most prominent designers, it would be almost as poor form to design a project with the aim of "setting an example" as it would be to follow "a model for imitation".

Now one supposes that it has not escaped Mostafavi's notice that this climate of opinion is a propitious one in which to sustain media attention on the careers of star designers, as well as to highlight the "signature" qualities of their projects. One suspects also that such a climate is far less supportive of the institution of architectural education than it is of the currently ascendant neo-avant-garde. This would be especially so if he, like me, were to see the primary purposes of education as the teaching of transmissible procedures for design, as well as contributing to a culture of architecture that transcends the individual signatures of its leading practitioners.

This is the ideological and polemical setting in which I see Mostafavi's initiation of the *Exemplary Projects* series as anachronistic and commendable at the same time. Moreover, the Berlin Free University project is an

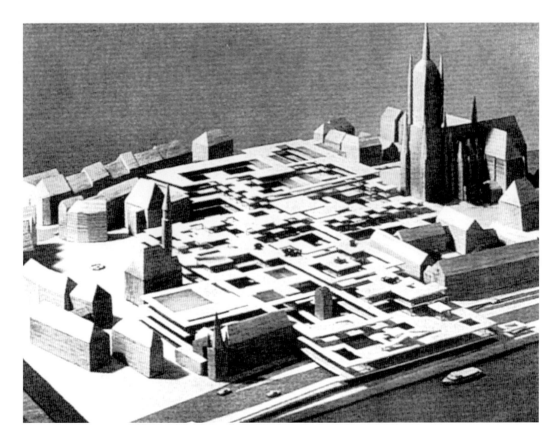

Frankfurt city centre competition entry by Candilis-Josic-Woods, 1963.

especially provocative topic with which to advance the
trajectory of such a series.

The Idea of the Building

First and foremost, the BFU is a project which offers up a
seminal architectural and urban idea from its period: the
"building as a city". Alexander Tzonis and Liane Lefaivre
make the lengthiest and most sustained contribution
to the volume, including key documentation in respect
of the emergence of this idea in the theorising of
Shadrach Woods, and in the built production of the
Candilis-Josic-Woods office.

1. The Lijnbaan

The first significant design precedent for the idea
that Tzonis and Lefaivre cite is the Lijnbaan project
in Rotterdam of van den Broek and Bakema, from
1951–1952. This famous proposal for a new urban
complex in war-damaged downtown Rotterdam is
one that Woods was familiar with on account of his
having participated with Bakema in the deliberations

of the Team 10 group. Indeed, the project stood as
an early icon of Team 10, introducing, as they saw
it, two key innovations. First, it left behind definitely
the "functionalist zoning" which had been typical of
earlier CIAM urban planning. Second, it proposed a
"linear pedestrian movement system" as a device to
organise the diverse urban functions it contained. As
Tzonis and Lefaivre put it in their essay:

> In this scheme, individual property lines and traffic
> routes were redistributed to fit within a mobility
> system; access points and services were organised
> in a linear pattern separating vehicular and
> pedestrian conduits.... An attempt was made to
> modernise commercial activities by 'Americanising'
> them. The old shopping street patterns were recast
> into a 'shopping mall'—an idea then just emerging
> in the United States—but in contrast to American
> planning which segregated users, the project mixed
> together retail and commercial activities, offices and
> residential areas.

Aerial View of Berlin Free University in 1974, soon after the completion of the first phase of construction.

2. "Stem"

To Shadrach Woods, the Lijnbaan also stood as an early realisation of an urban idea he had been working on for some time, as his own key contribution to the thinking Team 10 was evolving. Woods' idea was the "Stem": "a way of linking locations that accommodates human activity and interaction". Tzonis and Lefaivre describe it as "a support system, very similar to the network of paths in a traditional town". In a number of major urban projects of the Candilis-Josic-Woods office from the early 1960s, including Caen-Herouville and Toulouse-le-Mirail, Woods pursued several versions of the Stem idea.

3. Diocletian's Palace and Split

Bakema made a further key contribution to the evolution of Woods' thinking, in an influential account of the historical evolution—over a long time span—of the ancient Palace of Diocletian, on the east coast

of the Adriatic. Eventually the complex became the city we now know as Split. In his account, Bakema demonstrated how the ruins of the Roman palace were gradually infilled, becoming a complex urban entity incorporating an extensive pattern of multilateral streets. Where Woods' own Stem idea had tended to emphasise hierarchy within any given network of paths, the rough gridding of Split shifted the emphasis from a hierarchical movement-system to one that offered a multiplicity of routes.

4. Frankfurt Centre Competition, 1961

In 1961 a competition was held for a design to infill a war-damaged area in the centre of Frankfurt—a site, in fact, not dissimilar to that of the Lijnbaan in Rotterdam. In a seminal entry, Woods and his partners brilliantly brought to a culmination the line of urban thinking that has just been recounted. The mixed functions of the Lijnbaan, the network of Stem, and the multiplicity of choices represented by Bakema's reading of Split combined to produce an ingenious matrix of buildings. In a polemical volume of his writings published posthumously, Woods described the proposal:

> The underlying principle… was an extremely simple grid of pedestrian ways to which corresponded a servicing system, very like the street system which exists in most cities. Here, however the grid of circulation is scaled to the pedestrian while automobiles, lorries and buses are accommodated beneath the complex in an underground servicing system.

The five-acre site would be entirely built over. To an average height of three-storeys, and the circulation system is a multi-level grid of pedestrian ways, mostly enclosed, interconnected vertically by escalators. These ways give access to various uses such as museums, galleries, shops, offices and dwelling at the different levels. In principle, these pedestrian ways serve exactly the same functions as a street in the city, except that they are not required to carry any traffic other than pedestrian. As in a city street, the uses and the building which accommodate them can change over time. Modern building techniques make possible the demounting and reutilisation of practically all parts of the structure, which makes this scheme an ecologically and economically sound proposition. Natural light and ventilation, where needed, are provided by interior courts.

This scheme considers the centre of the city as an entirely built environment, pedestrian-oriented and multi-storyed, a layered web of open, covered or enclosed ways serving a mixed-use building. The city is considered as a building, and the scheme demonstrates one way in which it might be organised.[1]

It is one of the lost opportunities of mid-twentieth-century architecture and urbanism that this proposal for the centre of Frankfurt was not implemented.

5. Free University, Berlin

Woods and his colleagues went on to employ a number of the basic ideas from the Frankfurt design in their competition-winning design of 1964 for the proposed new Free University in Berlin. On this occasion the three-dimensional matrix was only two-storeys high, and it did not stack pedestrian circulation on top of vehicular. Then, too, it accommodates the programme of an academic university rather than the full range of urban functions that Frankfurt did. Still, the Free University

stands to this day as the only built manifestation of this mature idea of Woods, albeit somewhat modified from the Frankfurt prototype, and only partly executed.

The Building Itself

There is the "idea" of the building—in this case, one that is extraordinarily important in the recent history of European architecture and urbanism—and then there is the building itself, a physical artefact that exists in the real world. *Exemplary Projects* 3 also documents this aspect of the Free University. It includes extensive drawings of various stages of the project, from the competition submission through to technical details for construction. Mostafavi himself contributes an essay describing and analysing the building envelope, designed in collaboration with the distinguished French designer Jean Prouvé. In particular he explores the relationship of Prouvé's work to Candilis-Josic-Woods' own evolving ideas for the building during the two phases that were executed. As he states, the building envelope "was designed to be as flexible and responsive as possible to the various requirements of the programme".

But the most powerful evidence the volume includes of the reality of the building itself is a group of specially commissioned new photographs by Charles Tashima. The majority of these are black and white, but a small number are colour, and these depict sumptuously and in close detail the present condition of the "rusting hulk", as George Wagner describes it in his elegiac contribution to the volume. Tashima's photographs fall into three distinct categories. First there are the voluptuous colour images, which seem to present the building (when it is not a rusting hulk) in a state of luminous, serene abandonment. Then there are the typical black-and-white ones which are systematically documentary in character. These, in their restraint and their straightforwardness, manifest a resolute and utterly compelling sobriety, even inclining one to suppose that Tashima—who is also an architect must have been influenced by the sensibility of the school of contemporary German photographers who are followers of Bernd and Hilla Becher.

Finally, there is a very small group of images—also black and white—which depict the building inhabited by its contemporary student occupants. And they present to us yet another reading of the physical artefact. These shadowy occupants—how apt the word is to describe them—seem only provisionally present in the spaces portrayed. Indeed, they evoke all over again Woods' painful recognition, shortly after

View of one of the interior "gallerias" of the Berlin Free University.

the executed phase of the project was complete, and not long before his sadly premature death, of the rejection of the building by the first students who inhabited it.

The Free University's Current Significance

I have described the Free University as increasingly legendary. Virtually all the contributors to the volume would also do so. Yet, interestingly enough, the fact that the project holds such a status does not mean that it has not sustained serious criticism. Probably the best-known criticism was made by Kenneth Frampton, in his *Modern Architecture: A Critical History* of 1980:

> That the Frankfurt scheme as built out in the Free University of Berlin in 1973 lost much of its conviction stems largely from the absence of an urban context. In Berlin-Dahlem it was deprived of that urban culture for which it had been conceived and to which it would have responded had it been built in Frankfurt. However much a university may function like a city in microcosm, it cannot generate the animated diversity of the city proper.

This criticism of Frampton's intersects with an intriguing one by Tzonis and Lefaivre:

> Woods knew from the outset that the siting of such a high-density machinistic structure next to Dahlem, one of the wealthiest suburbs in pre-war Europe, would be contentious. In contrast to his Frankfurt scheme, which is integrated into the existing built environment, the university confronts a suburb with a piece of urban structure. The unhurried grand avenues of Dahlem are juxtaposed with the university's busy street-corridors: the sparsely populated garden settlement yields to high-density living and close contact settings, full of frequent chance encounters and human vitality.

> Woods said that the university's "gallerias", as he called its passageways, were intended to draw in the residents of Dahlem, to make them rethink their views, shed their suburban identity, and ultimately be converted to a more humanistic way of life. This never happened. Woods had succumbed to what we might call "environmental determinism", the architectural

profession's optimistic tendency to assume that environmental conditions can effectively change human behaviour and even belief systems. Woods, like other members of Team 10, was convinced that the circulation system of buildings could bring about social change....

The Free University encountered other problems which Woods found disturbing. The first phase of the building was completed at a time of student unrest and was not well received. When Woods confronted the students and suggested that if they did not like the building they might as well dismantle it, they responded that they were not interested in doing that. What they objected to was not the plan or the look of the university, but rather the fact that they had not been consulted during the development of the design.

It has been interesting for me, in attempting to contextualise, and to weigh the gravity of these criticisms, to reread parts of Woods' *The Man in the Street*. To be sure, his characterisation of what Tzonis and Lefaivre call BFU's "passageways" as "gallerias" receives corroboration there. For *The Man in the Street* makes utterly clear the powerful hold that their precedents in Milan and the "passages" of Paris had over him.

Perhaps even more telling than this was his grouping, in the book, of four demonstration urban projects by Candilis-Josic-Woods, a grouping which includes the Frankfurt competition entry but not the Free University. Interestingly enough, the other three are projects for the Bonne-Nouvelle district of Paris, for SoHo in New York, and for Karlsruhe.[2] From the vantage-point of today, these sit rather oddly with the scheme for Frankfurt. Whereas the latter still seems dense, finely scaled and intimately urbane, the other three seem much more megastructural, and much more monolithic in their basic form. In other words, while Frankfurt, and by implication the Free University, seems to point to the future, the others appear to stand as remnants of the utopian ambitions of orthodox Modernism. That Woods saw fit to group them together seems to me to reflect the limitations of his own view of the originality of the Frankfurt idea. Moreover, the fact that he has done so even inclines me to read certain utopian limitations back on to the projects for Frankfurt and the Free University.

He seems, for example, to have failed to appreciate the precise degree of applicability of the historical idea of the "galleria" to the contemporary projects he was working on, both in Frankfurt and in Berlin.

Frampton's commentary makes clear already that the close proximity of an existing urban context would have been necessary for the gallerias of the Free University to perform the urban—and urbane—role that was sought for them. The sheer abruptness with which they meet the perimeter of the building is utterly different from the seamlessness of the transition between the Parisian arcades and the street spaces of the city. But one could as easily point to the misunderstanding of their scalar role—and their sectional characteristics— in an urban fabric. For the dimensional scale of the historical galleria characteristically, and strategically, lies somewhere between that of the institutional corridor and that of the urban street. To my eye, the relatively small, and insufficiently differentiated, scale of the Free University passageways contributes to their tendency to collapse back into being 'mere' institutional corridors. And the fact that, unlike their Parisian precedents, they do not occur right at ground level, along with the surrounding pedestrian circulation system, contributes further to their unurban character.

Then there is the matter of the automobile. In the case of Frankfurt, the "public realm" of the project is restricted to pedestrians, and the automobile is relegated to an "underground servicing system". In the intervening years the negative impact of this excessive degree of segregation has become clear. In the case of the Free University the architects' statement accompanying their competition entry argued that "car parking has not been included within the university building, as we feel that the exigencies of the car are incompatible with the economics of the building". The statement did concede that "covered car parks may be provided, semi-underground, with playing fields on their roofs", and it also argued for a "travelator connection to the Dahlem U-Bahn station". But this half-hearted attitude to automobile use, on such a suburban site, has obviously contributed further to the condition of isolation in Dahlem that Frampton, Tzonis and Lefaivre have all lamented.

Then, too, there is the matter of the ownership of the land. All three urban projects grouped with Frankfurt in *The Man in the Street* presuppose widespread expropriation of privately owned land. And, despite its much finer urban grain, even the Frankfurt project was seen by Woods as working best "if it were all in public ownership". The events of 1968, in which the activities of paternalistic governments came to seem at least as suspicious as those of corporations, radically undermined the conviction of architects that expropriation was an unalloyed political good. Notwithstanding Woods' commitment to an emergent, urbane pluralism, he seems to have failed to anticipate this particular critique by the revolutionaries of 1968. Such anachronistic features make it clear, I think, the extent to which these projects all occupy a pivotal moment in between late high Modernism, on the one hand, and the various radical revisionisms that have typified architecture and urbanism since their era, on the other. No wonder, then, that Woods had no answer to the dissenting students at the Free University when they objected to not having been consulted. His residual convictions as to the utopian aspirations of Modernism being what they were (ironically, despite the consequences of many of his own deeply revisionist design inclinations) he was rendered politically impotent by the radicalisation of the opinions that had been precipitated in those turbulent years.

Still, from the perspective of the year 2000, these fallibilities of his position, and of the scheme for the Free University, pale in comparison with their strengths. For Woods and the BFU continue to offer us the model of a project that seeks to innovate simultaneously in the spheres of the social, the programmatic, the formal, the urban and the technological. It even opened an early door on to the possibility of what we might now think of as a potent kind of heterogeneous, pluralistic design practice.

Notwithstanding the powerful contemporary vogue for an international architectural avant-garde, it is clear enough that there is a renewed interest among members of a younger generation of architects in Candilis-Josic-Woods' powerful idea of a "building as a city". (Surely it is no coincidence that the facades of MVRDV's Villa VPRO are also reminiscent of the BFU.) It is true that this interest is often muddied by self-conscious gestures of avant-gardism. At the same time, the challenge that Woods and his partners faced in attempting to graft their concept on to an existing, living urban fabric remains as great as ever. Given such pregnant circumstances, one hopes that the book under review will contribute to a significant clearing of the polemical air in these regards, and will enable designers today to emulate the broad-based, socially committed and (relatively) clear-headed ambition that so distinguished the Team 10 generation. For, viewed from the perspective of this contemporary condition of our discipline, the work of Candilis-Josic-Woods surely does appear, in a word, exemplary.

1 Woods, Shadrach, *The Man in the Street*, London: Penguin, 1975, pp 123–124.

2 Woods, *The Man in the Street*, pp 129–145.

The New Urbanism and Public Space, 2007

It is a complex matter for me to comment on the phenomenon of public space in relation to the New Urbanism. I am neither a card-carrying member of the movement's Congress, nor a militant opponent of it. I am, however, keenly interested in the important question of the status of public space in our times.

To start with, I can say that I find many CNU (Congress for the New Urbanism) orthodoxies in respect to public space retrogressive. Reiterations of the historic forms of public space—especially in the suburban and exurban regions in which new New Urbanist neighbourhoods are so frequently created—are clearly problematic. For example, to reinvoke today the residential square that is so familiar in history, from Bloomsbury to Gramercy Park, necessarily makes one of two worrisome presumptions: either that obsolete forms of social life can be revived; or that the forms of public space can be manipulated on a purely formal basis without any ongoing consideration of the social forms that gave rise to them. A design methodology that does so has to be seen as either historicist or formalist.

But if the nostalgia of some New Urbanists for anachronistic urban forms is problematic, this is not to say that many of the characteristic stances of opposition to the New Urbanism are not also seriously misconstrued. The dystopic fascination of the opposed urban tendency that Douglas Kelbaugh has named Post-Urbanism with the scaleless systems of infrastructure that typify so much recently created regional urban form, is surely no less problematic than the misplaced nostalgia of the New Urbanists. If they are engaged in a hopeless effort to perpetuate historically superseded forms of public space, their opponents have succumbed to an equally problematic loss of confidence in the very idea of publicness in the city in our time—that is, of course, when they have not also lost confidence in the idea of the city itself. As a result of their dystopic fascination, in the worlds of architecture and urbanism we now find ourselves over and over again presented with image after apocalyptic image of highly complex urban highway interchanges (*S,M,L,XL*) of hugely scaled, multiple-lane highways traversing vast new urban territories (Pudong); or the characteristic forms of urban conurbation that typically result from the combination of the two (Tysons Corner).

Then, too, the tenor of the arguments the Post-Urbanists use to demonstrate the putative pertinence of such images to urban design in our time itself oscillates erratically between a masochistic professional self-abnegation on the one hand, and an apocalyptic eschatology on the other. According to the first version of this way of thinking, the architect, urban designer, and planner are powerless functionaries lacking any and all of the capacities of citizenship, such as those that might have a material effect on the future of the world in which they, like the rest of us, will live. Or, alternatively, these professionals are enjoined to cast off the old-fashioned garments of traditional professionalism, and to participate instead in the pleasurable, allegedly inevitable procedures of global capital at work in the urban realm. The current, highly evident professional oscillation between these stances has become so acute as to suggest that the ambiguous, febrile cultural interpretation typical of the writings of Jean Baudrillard has now been extended, in the eyes of Post-Urbanism, to encompass the entire arena of invention in contemporary urban form.

For those like myself, who seek to eschew such extremes of contemporary design discourse in regard to public space—those who still believe deeply in the importance of public space as a key component of contemporary urban form—there remains, of course (for our ongoing theoretical consideration and admiration), one particular, extraordinarily robust and resilient urban form of amazing historical durability. This is, of course, the "street". The residential square may now have become a historical anachronism, Post-Urbanism may be complicit in the creation of vast expanses of urban void, but the street everywhere endures, and continues to be—and deserves to be— the primary locus of publicness in architecture and urbanism today. In his seminal text *The Fall of Public Man*, Richard Sennett observed that the quintessential definition of a city is a place "where strangers are likely to meet".[1] To this day the street remains the central locus of such urban publicness, and while the rhetoric of neither New Urbanism nor Post-Urbanism has chosen to focus on it—it does, after all, lack both historic charm and apocalyptic charisma—neither has chosen to eschew it altogether, either.

For me, what distinguishes the street from the square—especially the square in its historic, residential format—is a set of key social and physical conditions: anonymity, a-focality, and interconnectedness. Anonymity because of the sheer possibility in the space of the street for "strangers to meet"; a-focality because the street, unlike the square, is not configured to focus the attention of its occupants in any particular way—indeed, it presupposes a certain Benjaminian distraction; and interconnectedness because every efficacious urban street always leads to numerous others. By contrast, the historic residential square was not really anonymous— indeed, many of the historic examples were even gated, so that only residents of the surrounding residences facing the square held keys to the gardens in their centres. By the same token, such a space is necessarily more focal, and less interconnected than the street, precisely because of this higher degree of familiarity of occupants with one another, as well as with the space of the garden in the square itself.

At the same time, the street is quintessentially distinct from the characteristic void that is the locus of Post-Urbanist theoretical fascination as well. The primary reason for this lies in its primary phenomenological condition of "boundedness". Typically, the street is not spatially limitless; typically it has edges. Especially

Garrison Woods, a New Urbanist project in Calgary, Alberta, Canada.

efficacious streets have edges that both contain and animate the citizenry moving about within them. It is for this reason that streets are such potent catalysts to urban assembly, and that they form such a powerful basis of the theory of retail marketing. (Even interior retail malls pretend to be streets for this reason.) Interestingly enough, the street is also a seedbed of politics. It is the characteristic spatial containment offered by the historic form of the street that provides the social condensation that makes for effective political protest. For this reason protest groups seeking to organise demonstrations always prefer to locate them within the system of streets close to the centres of cities. By the same token, in recent years it has become clear that police, and other administrative entities attempting to defuse such protest, have learned to seek to permit such protests only in those extensive, imprecisely "bounded" voids Ignasi de Solà-Morales taught us to call "terrain vague".

An academic colleague currently working together with me on an urban research project at the University of Toronto, Professor Robert Levit, shares a number of my predispositions with respect to efficacious contemporary urban form. Studying the typical form of existing suburbs of Toronto, Levit has found himself impelled to formulate a condition of space in the urban field that he thinks is a very desirable one. He calls it "interiority". Interiority, for him, is the characteristic condition of historical urban fabrics, wherein one finds evident significant, and perceptible modulation of spatial order. According to his line of argument, large-scale streets establish one tangible scale of inhabited spatial order for urbanites. Interconnecting with such streets are other, secondary ones that present them with a

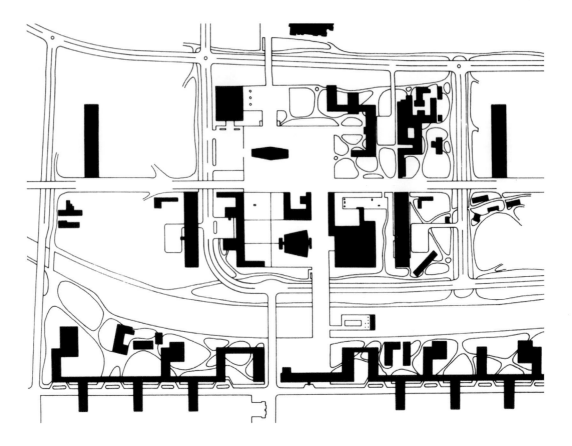

Figure-ground plan of Le Corbusier's project for Saint-Dié.

different, smaller-scaled, more intimate spatial order. Within the overall hierarchy of qualities of space within the urban fabric in question, then, this relative condition-at-a-smaller-scale, for Levit, constitutes interiority. One could illustrate his point by comparing two urban figure-ground drawings provocatively juxtaposed by Colin Rowe and Fred Koetter in their well-known urban design polemic, *Collage City*. The two are central Parma and the proposed city centre designed by Le Corbusier for the French town of Saint-Dié. Looking at the two together, one would quickly see that central Parma embodies an urban spatial condition of interiority, while Le Corbusier's proposed plan for Saint-Dié does not. Indeed, one can state that few contemporary projects—especially those of a Post-Urbanist orientation—possess little interiority at all. While working on our study, Levit found himself concluding that interiority was not discoverable in the recently built western suburbs of Toronto. Indeed—again, shades of Pudong—he even observed that Mississauga City Centre made him feel as though he were in China!

This last conclusion seems especially regrettable. After all, the historical Chinese city, with its complex patterns of streets, laneways, and courtyards, is a world cultural triumph of subtle urban space modulation. Observing this strange contemporary evolution of urban form in our time, I find myself driven to conclude that Camillo Sitte was correct after all when he mounted his famous critique of the urban development of the Ringstrasse in Vienna, seeing it as lacking adequate urban spatial definition. It is as though he has been vindicated by history, despite his dismissal by the heroes of Modernist urbanism, a century after his framing of his subtle "artistic principles" of urban space making.

Given these surprising recent realisations, it seems all the more odd that during the same period of time that such principles as Sitte's have been returning to the minds of some of us in the area of urban design theory, certain key figures within New Urbanism have been moving in an opposite direction. I have in mind here the revisionist position that has been elaborated by Andres Duany since the publication of his text on the concept

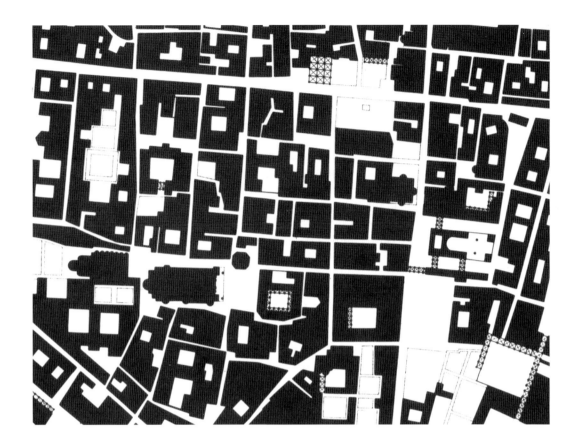

Parma figure-ground plan.

of the "transect". Followers of Duany's publications will recall his conclusion that a substantial group of the characteristic building types of the contemporary urban field, including shopping malls and big-box retail stores, simply cannot be integrated within the sort of desirably fine-grained urban fabric sought by New Urbanism. As a consequence, Duany has argued that any effort to modify the characteristic site plans of such facilities is a waste of designers' time, and that rather than attempt to domesticate them, wise and efficacious urbanists should simply do their best to relegate them to exurban locations, *fuori le mura* (outside the city walls), as it were.

Urbanists and urban designers in my own region of Toronto, Canada, have been puzzled by this turn of events in the New Urbanist camp. Our own recent historical experience suggests that this is an especially problematic and retrograde decision. A little local urban history is needed to explain our position. For many years now, we have found ourselves puzzled by the arguments of New Urbanism for increased gross and net residential densities. The reason for this

has been that in our own region such densities (for peripheral greenfield developments) were already high and continuing to rise. Indeed, the net residential densities for ground-related family housing in the region of Toronto have now become so high that it is difficult for many of us here to see how innovative design practice can make them much higher still. Instead, many of us working in the Toronto region are now in the process of realising that there are only two obvious further *loci* of realistic further potential density increases within the typical field of urban development overall—at least in our own region. One of these *loci* is a group of extant small urban centres in that region that are indeed capable of further densification, especially if they are served by adequate public transit. (It is understood, of course, that this densification will entail infilling with residential building forms of higher densities than those typically associated with ground-related family housing).

The other locus of potential further urban density increase—the more relevant one for the purposes of my current argument—is that vast areas of the urban field that does not comprise residential neighbourhoods at all. Indeed, it comprises everything else. (In the region of greater Toronto, it is estimated that this territory comprises well over half of the total field of urbanised land.) It is made up of larger-scale retail facilities (all the ones Duany is now proposing to exempt from the exigencies of New Urbanist site planning principles), employment lands, and the entire total of all forms of urban infrastructure: highways, utility corridors, transit corridors, public institutional, educational, and service uses, and so on. It seems to many of us here in the Toronto region that it is exactly this vast territory that needs to become the locus of the next threshold of urban design innovation. It is our view that this needed innovation should aim both at the more efficient utilisation of urban land as well as at the reconstitution of forms of public space in the city at a scale that can actually facilitate active public life by the citizenry. But what the appropriate form will be, both of the adapted urban form of such facilities and of accompanying new forms of public space among them, remains, in substantial measure, still to be determined.

In conclusion, let me draw a comparison between two recent urban projects that together fall more-or-less within the definition of New Urbanism, but which also exhibit significant differences. I am speaking, on the one hand, of the Duany Plater-Zyberk & Company project of a few years back: Kentlands, outside of Washington, D C and a recent one within the inner city of Calgary, Alberta, Canada. The Calgary project is called Garrison Woods, on account of the fact that it occupies the site of a former Canadian military base. Garrison Woods has clearly been deeply influenced by both the site planning principles and residential iconography of Kentlands. Similar street patterns, similar forms of local recreational space, and similar forms of secondary units on lots that formed part of the design for the earlier Kentlands can be found at Garrison Woods.

But Garrison Woods occupies an inner-city infill site (albeit a very large one), while Kentlands is located on a site that is almost exurban, as opposed to suburban. And this difference in regional location seems to have had a profound effect on the Garrison Woods overall site plan, generating a number of significant differences from Kentlands, despite the numerous obvious similarities. For example, along the streets which bound the site of Garrison Woods, new houses have been located facing the existing houses across the street. Thus, even though the site planning on the 'new' side of the street

is denser than that on the site that already existed, the completion of the street as a normally two-sided one significantly contributes to the integration of the precinct as a whole, into the one that surrounds it. Then too, the retail component of Garrison Woods is also more successfully integrated into both the new neighbourhood itself, as well as the larger precinct in which it sits. Surprisingly, the implemented version of the retail component at Garrison Woods resembles some of the early versions of those planned for its model Kentlands, but which failed to make it through to implementation there. Thus one finds that at Garrison Woods, there really does exist a traditional block of street related retail stores, such as was sought for at Kentlands. More remarkable still, one also finds a local shopping centre, the site plan for which succeeds in using ancillary pad retail facilities to bracket and contain the parking lot in the fashion also originally proposed for Kentlands, but not so tightly implemented there. Finally, the entire retail precinct is located on one edge of the Garrison Woods neighbourhood, oriented both inwards to the new neighbourhood, and outwards to the existing surrounding one, thereby contributing further to its integration into the larger urban fabric of the city of Calgary.

This heightened form of integration also plays a significant role in defining the character of the system of public space, both within Garrison Woods and within the larger urban fabric of its surroundings. Garrison Woods is not a gated community, and despite the fact that it offers a wider range of forms of street, residential form and open space than are found in the larger urban fabric surrounding it, its street systems are devised to facilitate continuous movement from the surrounding streets into Garrison Woods itself. Thus the system of public space is conceived as a binder of the new neighbourhood to the older inner city, rather than as one divided into an inner and an outer system.

Indeed, it may be appropriate to conclude by observing how tragically the idea of the gated community undermines the idea even of the urban safety that the continuous historic urban street system has traditionally provided. After all, the whole point of the 'gates' of the gated community is to keep the danger of the larger urban world outside at bay. But, of course, the very same gates that putatively keep the extant urban danger out paradoxically have the effect of slowing down any possible escape from any possible danger arising inside the compound. Ironically enough, the core idea of urban safety promulgated by Jane Jacobs all those years ago in *The Death and Life of Great American Cities*—eyes on the street—is undermined by the very idea of the gated community, on account of its reduced level of street activity, its reduced urban heterogeneity, and its self-induced conditions of domestic isolation.

In retrospect, it would seem that Sennett's observation remains as true today as it was when he made it in 1977. Quintessentially, a city remains "a place where strangers are likely to meet", and this condition is a primary and essential condition of publicness in urban life.

1   Sennett, Richard, *The Fall of Public Man*, New York: Random House, 1978, p 16.

On the "Critical" in Contemporary Architectural Theory

Criticality and Its Discontents, 2004

As I have already intimated, during the years I taught at Harvard, I became a reliable enough occasional contributor to the *Harvard Design Magazine* that its editor, Bill Saunders was eventually willing to give me considerable latitude to publish writings of mine on varying topics. So he did not demur when I suggested that I had been surprised by the text of Robert Somol and Sarah Whiting that had appeared in a then-recent issue of *Perspecta*, the Yale Architectural Journal, "Notes Around the Doppler Effect and Other Moods of Modernism", and that I would be interested in writing a critical commentary on it. I confess that I did not think of my text as a major piece of theoretical writing, but only as a topical commentary on a surprising turn of theoretical events in our field.

It was my friend Arie Graafland from the Technical University of Delft who recently pointed out to me that if one Googles "George Baird", one comes upon dozens of references to this 2004 text of mine. Despite all my other efforts, it is evidently the piece of writing I am most famous for. That may be justification enough for including it in this collection of texts. I may not have been attempting a major piece of theory, but I evidently touched a nerve.

Shortly before his untimely death, the Spanish theorist and critic Ignasi de Solà-Morales commented to me that "if European architects or architectural scholars wished to study contemporary architectural theory, they would have to come to the East Coast of the United States".

Is it still true that theory on the American East Coast holds such preeminence? I realise that it is one of the intentions of the Berlage Institute's new doctoral programme and of the creation of the new Delft School of Design to challenge this American hegemony— and recent events suggest that these challenges are meeting with some success. If America does retain some prominence in these matters, then it may be of interest to readers to know (or know more) about a significant divergence now appearing in the territory of contemporary theory there, a divergence that is triggering increasingly intense discussions such as have not been seen since the beginning of the polemical attacks of the protagonists of Deconstructivism on Postmodernism a decade and a half ago. The matter now coming into question is the concept of a "critical architecture" that has been promulgated in advanced circles in architectural theory for at least two decades. The conception can probably be said to have received a definitive early formulation in a text by my Harvard colleague Michael Hays, a text that Robert Somol and Sarah Whiting (two of the prominent recent participants in the discussion) have labelled "canonical": "Critical Architecture: Between Culture and Form", published in *Perspecta* 21 in 1984.[1]

Today "criticality" is under attack, seen by its critics as obsolete, as irrelevant, and/or as inhibiting design creativity. What is more, the criticisms that are increasingly frequently being made come from an interesting diversity of sources. To start to make sense of this emergent situation, we might try to locate the beginnings of the evident shift of opinion against this once-so-dominant theoretical discourse in architecture. One interesting precursor of current comment was an outburst by Rem Koolhaas at one of the series of conferences organised by *ANY* magazine, this one at the Canadian Centre for Architecture in 1994: "The problem with the prevailing discourse of architectural criticism", complained Koolhaas, "is [the] inability to recognise there is in the deepest motivations of architecture something that cannot be critical."[2] But if Koolhaas' complaint was a harbinger of things to come, probably the first frontal challenge to criticality was a text published by Michael Speaks, the Director of Graduate Studies at the Southern California Institute of Architecture, in the American magazine *Architectural Record* in 2002.[3] In a startlingly revisionist text, Speaks explicitly abandons the "resistance" that he had learned from his own teacher, Fredric Jameson, in favour of a model of a new, alternative, and efficaciously integrated architecture that would take its cues from contemporary business management practices.[4]

Before the dust from Speaks' polemic had settled, two other American theorists, Robert Somol of UCLA and Sarah Whiting of Harvard, mounted a subtler challenge. Their text, "Notes around the Doppler Effect and Other Moods of Modernism", appeared in *Perspecta* 33 in 2002.[5] In it, Somol and Whiting argue against the conception of a "critical architecture" that had been long promulgated by Michael Hays. In the place of the hitherto critical architecture, Somol and Whiting propose one that would be "projective".

Since Somol and Whiting's publication, the pace of publications on this theme and the number of participants in the discussion have increased. At the end of 2002, for example, Michael Speaks followed up his polemic with a longer text published in *A+U*.[6] Since then, additional partisans, such as Stan Allen, the Dean of the School of Architecture at Princeton, and Sylvia Lavin, the Chair of the Department of Architecture of the University of California Los Angeles, have joined the fray.

I have set myself the task of attempting to briefly clarify how the divergence I have described has unfolded to date and to summarise what is at stake in it, since it is my view that a great deal indeed is at stake.

Let me begin with a short account of the lineage of criticality. One of its most cogent and internally coherent renditions has been that of the practitioner —and no mean theorist himself—Peter Eisenman, accompanied by Hays. Together, over the past two

decades, these two have developed a position that has consistently focused intellectually on concepts of "resistance" and "negation". For Eisenman, the position derives primarily from the work of the Italian historian and critic Manfredo Tafuri, but it has been fleshed out in Eisenman's own mind by other prominent figures in contemporary thought, including Jacques Derrida, Gianni Vattimo, and others. For Hays, Tafuri is as important a figure as he has been for Eisenman, but he is accompanied by additional figures such as Georg Lukács, Theodor Adorno, and Fredric Jameson.

For Hays, following Tafuri, the paramount exemplar of negation in late Modernism was Mies van der Rohe. Like his mentor, Hays has seen the late Mies as embodying a "refusal" of the terms of contemporary consumer society in the very surfaces of his built forms. (In this regard, the Seagram Building is as important a case study for Hays as it is for Tafuri.) For his part, Eisenman has, over his career as a designer and thinker, welded precepts from Tafuri to others derived from the theories of Minimalist art practices, as they have been articulated by figures such as Rosalind Krauss. In his hands, this has produced not so much a series of built forms embodying refusal or resistance, but rather a design method that for Eisenman is more important as a process than it is for the architectural products resulting from it. Notwithstanding these differences in nuance, for the past two decades Eisenman and Hays have formed a formidable pair of advocates of resistance in contemporary architecture and architectural theory.

But an enumeration of participants in a recent *Harvard Design Magazine* "Stocktaking" symposium makes clear that Eisenman and Hays do not exhaust the modalities of criticality that have had influence in recent years.[7] For example, Kenneth Frampton's commitment to resistance to consumer society has been as resolute as that of Eisenman and Hays during the period in question, even if his intellectual lineage leads back more to Adorno and Heidegger than to Tafuri. Then there is Michael Sorkin, much more of a New York City 'street fighter', politically speaking, than any of the figures I have discussed so far. Sorkin is renowned in American design circles for his long standing courage in having mounted compelling attacks on prominent figures on the American design scene, from Philip Johnson to Daniel Libeskind. But despite widespread admiration for his critical writings, the substantive theoretical form of Sorkin's "resistance" is not seen to be centrally embedded in his own design production, as Mies' has been seen to be by Tafuri, or Eisenman's has been seen to be by Hays, And this has meant that Sorkin's criticism, powerful as it has been, has nonetheless been limited in its impact on the evolving forms of American design practice.

Perhaps the most distinctive critical American design practice has been that of two figures who did not take part in the *HDM* "Stocktaking": Elizabeth Diller and Ricardo Scofidio. For almost as long as Eisenman's and Hays' collaboration, Diller + Scofidio have produced a remarkable range of projects that have succeeded in embodying resistance in a fashion that bears comparison with the one Tafuri admired in the late work of Mies. Still, most of the work in question has comprised museum and gallery installations rather than buildings. And the museum has continued to be a more receptive venue for critical work than the street during the period in question, as witness the parallel art practices of the Belgian Marcel Broodthaers, the German transplant to New York Hans Haacke and so on. How interesting then, that the first major exhibition convened by the recently appointed architecture curator of New York's Whitney Museum, Michael Hays, should be of the work of Diller + Scofidio: surely a recent and can we perhaps say 'late' triumph of American criticality. What is more, it is interesting to note that in their Whitney show, Diller + Scofidio chose to exhibit many of the museum gallery projects that have made them famous and almost none of the building projects on which their recent design practice has focused, projects that will have to meet the more difficult test of being critical "in the street". It will be interesting to see how successful this firm will be in sustaining its compelling "resistance" in buildings rather than in installations and in the now-changing climate of American architectural theory.

What then can we say about this changing climate? What reasons can we adduce for the increasingly threatened state of criticality? And what are the key features of the approaches to architectural theory that are being offered up in its place? It seems to me that there are a number of strands to the story, most of them interesting, if not all of equal historical consequence.

One of them, as far as I can tell, is a purely biographical—not to say generational—predicament. It is a commonplace to note that Peter Eisenman has been a major influence in American architectural education since his founding of the New York-based Institute for Architecture and Urban Studies and of its in-house *Oppositions*, some three decades ago.

By now I think it can be said that Eisenman's influence on his protégés can be compared with that of his own mentor Colin Rowe on his. But Rowe, it would seem, was a more easygoing mentor than Eisenman has been able to be. As a consequence, getting out from under the influence of the master has been a much greater challenge for the protégés of Eisenman than it was for those of Rowe. I do not think it is a coincidence that so many of the protagonists of the currently proffered alternatives to criticality are former protégés of Eisenman, or at least figures at the edge of his circle. Stan Allen, Robert Somol, and Sarah Whiting all fall in to one or the other of these categories. To the extent, then, that Eisenman himself has maintained such obdurate loyalty to criticality over a long span of time, he has produced a corresponding tension among his followers in respect to their understandable career efforts to cut loose from him. I suspect that we could go even further and speculate that to the extent that he has also maintained a stance of continuing contempt for what he, following Rowe, has called "*decor de la vie*", he has opened the door to a revived interest in surface and texture—even decoration—on the part of some of his revisionist followers. Whatever the final answers to these intriguing biographical questions turn out to be, it is clear that an effort to transcend a certain Eisenmanian hegemony in the upper echelons of American architectural culture is one of the more personal current tendencies evident to observers such as myself.

What is more, it is probably no less coincidental that an alternate referent frequently turned to in the various discourses of "post-criticality" is Rem Koolhaas, For example Koolhaas performs a crucial bridging role in Somol and Whitings "Doppler Effect" text, enabling them to shift from a critical stance to a projective one. Then too, it is almost inconceivable that the post-utopian pragmatism so pervasive in leading Dutch architectural circles nowadays (and which one suspects, to some extent, has been imported to the United States by Speaks) cannot be tracked back to the influence of the stormy young Koolhaas himself on the early generations of his own protégés, in the late 1970s and 1980s.[8]

But this reference to Koolhaas brings me back to the short quotation from him I cited early in this text, which will serve to move us from biographical and generational considerations to more substantive ones. In the commentary in question, Koolhaas went on to speculate:

Maybe some of our most interesting engagements are uncritical, emphatic engagements, which deal with the sometimes insane difficulty of an architectural project to deal with the incredible accumulation of economic, cultural, political but also logistical issues.[9]

Here we see Koolhaas the ambitious real-politiker once again exhibiting his intense belief in the necessity of a professional, architectural efficacy. And for him, if it turns out that criticality constrains efficacy, then to that extent criticality must give way.

What is more, as the 1990s wore on, as it became apparent that Eisenman's own design interests would increasingly focus on process rather than products, and as it became apparent that the putative tropes of the then-ascendant "Deconstructivism" were much less critical than many had expected them to be, all this contributed to a dissipation of the robust energy that had earlier been embodied-theoretically at least—by the project of "critical architecture".

Then too, it is probably the case that the trajectory of the life of Manfredo Tafuri, from his retreat from contemporary criticism in the mid-1980s, to his death in 1994, contributed further to this shift of mood. After all, Tafuri had been the most assertive contemporary advocate of an architecture that would not accept the terms of reality as they were presented. Indeed, in an extended series of essays over the span of the 1970s, he formulated an utterly distinctive conception of the architectural "project", one which would at one and the same time propose a new architectural form, would do so on the plane of the entire urban entity in which it was to be located, and would, by inference, transform that entire urban entity itself into something new. Needless to say, there were not too many successful historical examples of this bold and ambitious method that he could point to (Le Corbusier's *Plan Obus* for Algiers being one of the few). Given that before he had retired to Venetian Renaissance history, he had already dismissed American avant-garde architecture as "architecture in the boudoir", it cannot be denied that by the time of his death his overall theoretical stance was a somewhat disheartening one especially for American audiences, who had had the dystopic side of Tafuri's sensibility so predominantly emphasised to them in earlier years.

In any event, with Speaks' polemic of early 2002, there commenced a stream of "counter-critical" texts that has continued up to the present day. Speaks' *A+U*

text of late 2002 is probably the most developed argument that he has contributed to the ongoing discussion to date. Entitled "Design Intelligence", it starts off with a calculatedly particular usage of the term intelligence—that of the American Central Intelligence Agency—and then moves on to argue that in the contemporary design world, "visionary ideas have given way to the 'chatter' of intelligence".[10] Speaks then goes on specifically to dissociate himself from a whole series of design tendencies he saw as obsolete, disparaging the influences of both Derrida and Tafuri along the way:

> Postmodernism, Deconstructivism, Critical Regionalism and a host of other critical architectures in the late 1980s and 1990s posed… as false pretenders to Modernism. Whether effetely Derridian or ponderously Tafurian, theoretically inspired vanguards operated in a state of perpetual critique. Stuck between a world of certainty whose demise they had been instrumental in bringing about, and an emergent world of uncertainty into which they were being thrown head long, theoretical vanguards were incapacitated by their own resolute negativity.[11]

Instead, Speaks argued for what he called a "post-vanguard" professional practice defined by "design intelligence, and not by any formal, theoretical or professional identity". He went on:

> Accustomed in ways that their vanguard predecessors can never be to open source intelligence (OSINT as it is called by the CIA) gathered from the little truths published on the web, found in popular culture, and gleaned from other professions and design disciplines, these practices are adaptable to almost any circumstance almost anywhere.[12]

Compared to the strongly pragmatic—even anti-theoretical—stance advocated by Speaks, Somol and Whiting's "Doppler Effect" remains a model of enduringly "theoretical"—not to say "philosophical"—nuance. They summarise their concern about what they label "the now dominant paradigm" by observing that in recent years "disciplinarity has been absorbed and exhausted by the project of criticality".[13] They employ the design production of Peter Eisenman together with the theory of Michael Hays to attempt to demonstrate this. In this respect, perhaps their most important claim is that:

For both [Eisenman and Hays], disciplinarity is understood as autonomy (enabling critique, representation and signification), but not as instrumentality (projection, performativity and pragmatics). One could say that their definition of disciplinarity is directed against reification, rather than towards the possibility of emergence.[14]

And they conclude this part of their argument by observing:

As an alternative to the critical project—here linked to the indexical, the dialectical and hot representation this text develops an alternative genealogy of the projective—linked to the diagrammatic, the atmospheric and cool performance.[15]

Perhaps not surprisingly, this schema leads them in turn to propose, as an alternative to the precedent offered by Eisenman, one they ascribe to Rem Koolhaas. In doing so, they contrast:

Two orientations towards disciplinarity: that is, disciplinarity as autonomy and process, as in the case of Eisenman's reading of the Domino, and disciplinarity as force and effect, as in Koolhaas' staging of the Downtown Athletic Club.

And they conclude:

Rather than looking back or criticising the status quo, the Doppler projects forward alternative (not necessarily oppositional) arrangements or scenarios.[16]

So even though they eschew the extreme polemical stance taken up by Speaks, they do not, in the end, differ all that fundamentally from the position he espoused. For his part, in his contribution to the *HDM* "Stocktaking", Stan Allen offered up a commentary broadly parallel to the two just cited. Like Speaks, Allen identified a need to "go beyond avant-garde models" and to make use of "popular culture and the creativity of the marketplace". Indeed, he explicitly endorsed both Speaks' and Somol and Whiting's arguments, citing both texts in his own.

Most recently, in parallel presentations at Princeton, Harvard, and Toronto, Sylvia Lavin has entered into the debate, and has made a distinctive contribution to it, calling for a new appreciation of and consideration for "the provisional" and the "ephemeral" in the world

of contemporary architecture and design. Characterising Modernism as excessively preoccupied with the "fixed" and the "durable" in the world, she argues that reconsideration of such qualities in the environment could be both liberating and productive of new design possibilities.[17]

What should we make of this unfolding divergence of opinion between two important generations of thinkers on the scene of American architectural theory? Let me conclude by offering a few observations of my own. First, let us step back a little from the front lines of this battle and take a closer look at figures that lie in the background. From my comments thus far, I think it is clear that Manfredo Tafuri looms large behind American formulations of a "critical architecture" and that, having long exhibited discomfort in regard to its implications, Rem Koolhaas has served as a model for some of the orientations to practice that have been proposed as alternatives to it. But there is an additional *eminence grise* looming in back of a number of the members of the camp who have criticised the influence of criticality. This is the American art critic and commentator Dave Hickey.

Not yet as well known in architectural circles as Tafuri once was, Hickey is a recently selected MacArthur Fellow who has written on a wide range of social and cultural issues in the United States and elsewhere. A keen observer of a wide range of popular culture and an art critic with a decidedly sceptical view of the continuing pertinence of the artistic tradition of Minimalism—this alone places him far from Eisenman—Hickey is cited by Somol and Whiting as the author of an interpretation that opposes the performing styles of two American film actors, Robert Mitchum and Robert De Niro. Interpreting Hickey on the two American actors, Somol and Whiting contrast the styles as, respectively, "cool" and "hot". While cooling suggests a process of mixing (and thus "the Doppler Effect" would be one form of cool), the hot resists through distinction and connotes the overly difficult, belaboured, worked, complicated. Cool is "relaxed, easy". Thus it is clear that Somol and Whiting are eager to employ Hickey as part of their effort to dispel the American legacy of Tafuri in our field.

For me—and let me say that I share the two authors' fascination with Hickey—this possibility is not so clear. I shall return to this in a moment, but first I want to review a few interesting paradoxes that arise within the overall spectrum of opinion I have outlined above.

To start with, let us take the matter of the design avant-garde (as Allen calls it) or vanguard (as Speaks does). Both commentators dismiss it as obsolete and irrelevant. This is clearly a rebuff to Eisenman, who has always seen a certain American cultural avant-garde as being the embodiment of resistance. Yet, interestingly enough, Tafuri himself declared the avant-garde in architecture obsolete and irrelevant long before the new critics of criticality did. So strong is the tendency of American theorists to see Tafuri through an Eisenmanian lens that they fail to take note of the fact that the American architects and planners he most admired were not avant-gardists at all, but rather such figures as Eliel Saarinen, Clarence Stein, and Henry Wright—not to mention the New Deal creators of the Tennessee Valley Authority. So preoccupied are Tafuri's American readers with "architecture in the boudoir", that they fail to pay comparable attention to "Socialpolitik and the city in Weimar, Germany", where Tafuri's impatience with avant-gardism and his strong commitment to professional "engagement" indisputably lie. So, in the first of our paradoxes we may observe that were he still alive, Tafuri would align himself with the disenchantment of the younger Americans with their own avant-garde and would support their desire for "a form of practice committed to public legibility, to the active engagement of new technologies, and to creative means of implementation".[18]

Then there is the matter of "instrumentality". At one point in their text, Somol and Whiting present "instrumentality" as the definitive opposite to "autonomy". And in doing so, as we saw above, they summarise under this term three of the key features of the new approach they are recommending: projection, performativity, and pragmatics. But of course, Tafuri was also deeply committed to the idea of projection; indeed, as I noted earlier in this text, his highly activist conception of the architectural "project" lay at the heart of his theoretical position. Similarly, to the extent that we can read "pragmatics" as having at least partly to do with architectural programmes, Tafuri was clearly as interested in programme as a medium of design innovation as Koolhaas has ever been. But like Socialpolitik, Tafuri's powerful commitments to projective efficacy and to programmatic innovation are hard to see through an Eisenmanian lens. (I concede that I do not find a comparable commitment to "performativity" in Tafuri's writings, but I do note that the political stance with which he was associated in the days of his journal

Contropiano, strategically distinguished itself from that of the Italian Communist party on account of its commitment to active participation by workers in the ongoing formulation of party positions, as opposed to the top-down party-line control advocated by the party leaders—and for this reason was labelled an operaista political tendency).

Let me return now to Hickey and to the possibility of his being enlisted for the polemical purposes of the younger generation disillusioned with criticality. To be sure, there is in his heteroclite sensibility a startling and engaging openness to distinctiveness that has attracted Somol, Whiting, and Lavin, and to which they in turn all seem to be committed. Hickey is even willing to engage the "decorative" in ways that would seem to lend support to some of the speculative comments Lavin has made in recent academic discussions. His characterisation of Mitchum's acting style and his interests in jazz reinforce further still his association with cultural stances that can be called "relaxed" or "easy".

But of course, it also remains the case that when all is said and done, Hickey himself continues to be engaged by an obdurate—if implicit—quest for "authenticity". At the first lecture I ever heard him give, he delivered an extended descriptive comparison of two southwestern American cities he knows well, Santa Fe (where his 2002 exhibition Beau Monde was held) and Las Vegas (where he lives). Summing up his critical assessment of the two cities, he made the dazzling observation that he prefers Las Vegas to Santa Fe because he prefers "the real fake to the fake real".[19]

Indeed, to the extent that the protagonists of any version of a post-critical project want to enlist him to challenge the legacy of Eisenman, a comment from his introduction to the Beau Monde show will give them pause. Discussing his selection of artists and works to be included in the show, he observed, "Rather than asking the post-Minimalist question: "How rough can it get and still remain meaningful?" I found myself asking the cosmopolitan question: "How smooth can it get and still resist rationalisation?"[20] So, we can now see, even the "cool" and speculative Hickey continues to be engaged by a form of "resistance". It seems to me that the provocative question he suggested he had asked himself about his Santa Fe show is one that one could easily imagine being asked in regard to a work of Diller + Scofidio, such as their Soft Sell 42nd Street installation of 1993.[21]

And speaking of 42nd Street, is it not interesting also to recall that the very figure with whom I began my account of the erosion of the dominant discourse of criticality was Rem Koolhaas? For Koolhaas himself, notwithstanding his interests in "creative means of implementation" and in other key parts of the post-critical agenda, has none-the-less participated in more than a few recent episodes of vigorous critical engagement. I could start by recounting the fascinating episode during which, having been brought to Harvard to attack Andres Duany and the New Urbanism, he declined to do so, waiting only for an appropriate moment to chastise Duany severely for his failure "as a prominent American architect" to speak out against the destruction of the distinctive street culture of Manhattan's 42nd Street as a result of its sweeping Disneyfication. And I would probably end with his recent attack on the Chinese authorities for their lamentable and all-too-pragmatic approval of the destruction of extensive historic residential districts of the city of Beijing.

Thus it seems to me that the political alignments and the theoretical complexities that this interesting divergence of opinions has brought to the surface to date do not so much constitute the conclusion of a story, but rather only the beginning. A number of important questions remain to be asked, it seems to me, before a truly robust and durable new professional stance will be able to be achieved. For example, while it is probably true that "relaxed" and "easy" cannot be reconciled with "difficult", it is not so clear to me that they cannot be reconciled with "resistant". And it is equally clear to me that a much more developed pursuit

of social and political parallels between architecture and cinema would be one potent way of articulating such subtle distinctions further.

Then too, I am very curious to see to what extent the putatively "projective" forms of practice being advocated by the new critics of criticality will develop parallel models of critical assessment with which to be able to measure the ambition and the capacity for significant social transformation of such forms. Without such models, architecture could all too easily again find itself conceptually and ethically adrift.

For example, while it is clear from a multitude of cultural perspectives that the "decorative" as a formal category can be integrated within new forms of practice, it is also clear that those forms run some risk of reducing to the "merely" decorative. Enough architectural episodes of the "merely" decorative have occurred to serve as a warning.

Most fundamentally, in my view, it is clear that a new projective architecture will not be able to be developed in the absence of a supporting body of projective theory. Without it, I predict that this new architecture will devolve to the "merely" pragmatic, and to the "merely" decorative, with astonishing speed.

May I conclude then by calling for much more careful reflection from us all, before the respective roles of critique, innovation, authenticity, and expanded cultural possibility can be integrated in an "operative" new theory of praxis for our times?

1 Somol, Robert and Sarah Whiting, "Notes Around the Doppler Effect and Other Moods of Modernism", *Perspecta 33*, 2002, p 73.

2 Rem Koolhaas quoted by Kapusta, Beth, *The Canadian Architect* 39, August 1994, p 10.

3 Speaks, Michael, "Design Intelligence and the New Economy", *Architectural Record*, January 2002, pp 72–79.

4 Upon hearing me present this text at a June 2004 conference at the Technical University of Delft, Stan Allen suggested that the Joan Ockman/Terry Riley pragmatism symposium held at MoMA in November of 2000 might be an earlier challenge to criticality than Speaks' polemic of early 2002. This may be so, but since I did not attend the conference and since it was devoted to pragmatism *per se* rather than to criticality, there is some question in my mind as to whether this challenge can appropriately be described as "frontal".

5 "Mining Autonomy", *Perspecta 33*, pp 72–77.

6 Speaks, Michael, "Design Intelligence: Part One, Introduction", *A+U*, December 2002, pp 10–18.

7 "Stocktaking 2004: Nine Questions About the Present and Future of Design", *Harvard Design Magazine* 20, spring–summer 2004, pp 5–52.

8 A number of forms of a post-utopian and post-critical European (and mainly Dutch) practice are described in an essay by Roemer van Toorn published in this issue of the *Harvard Design Magazine*.

9 Kapusta, Beth, *The Canadian Architect* 39, August 1994, p 10.

10 Speaks, Michael, "Design Intelligence and the New Economy Part One Introduction", *Architectural Record*, January 2002, pp 12.

11 Speaks, Michael, "Design Intelligence and the New Economy Part One Introduction", p 16.

12 Speaks, Michael, "Design Intelligence and the New Economy Part One Introduction", p 16.

13 Somol and Whiting, "Notes Around the Doppler Effect and Other Moods of Modernism", p 73.

14 Somol and Whiting, "Notes Around the Doppler Effect and Other Moods of Modernism", p 74.

15 Somol and Whiting, "Notes Around the Doppler Effect and Other Moods of Modernism", p 74.

16 Somol and Whiting, "Notes Around the Doppler Effect and Other Moods of Modernism", p 75.

17 Lavin, Sylvia, in lectures delivered during the spring 2004 at Harvard, Princeton, and the University of Toronto.

18 It is interesting to note at this juncture in my argument that in his contribution to the *HDM* "Stocktaking" Stan Allen himself observed that such forms of practice, as he is endorsing here can be found in a number of locations in Europe but have "so far resisted translation to the US". So perhaps the collectivist European legacy of Tafuri may remain stronger than has been acknowledged?

19 Hickey, Dave, "Dialectical Utopias", *Harvard Design Magazine*, winter–spring 1998, pp 8–13.

20 Hickey, Dave, *Beau Monde: Towards a Redeemed Cosmopolitanism*, Santa Fe, New Mexico: SITE Santa Fe, 2001, p 76.

21 *Soft Sell* is documented in Diller, Elizabeth and Ricardo Scofidio, *Flesh: Architectural Probes: The Mutant Body of Architecture*, New York: Princeton Architectural Press, 1994, pp 250–253.

Why Can't Architecture Just Be Happy? 2009

This text was invited by the editors of the Canadian academic journal *Architecture and Ideas,* Graham Livesey and Kelly Crossman. Contributors were asked to respond to the question: "Why Can't Architecture Just Be Happy?" The text below was my response. A relatively short text, it nonetheless brings together a number of the themes and the authors that have appeared in earlier texts in this collection.

On the face of it, the question you have posed reminds me of the hoary theological analogy from the Garden of Eden. If only Adam had not accepted the apple Eve offered to him! If only it were possible that the innocence that preceded the eating of the apple could be recovered? Well, we now know that the consequences of the eating of the apple are irreversible. "Paradise" truly has been lost.

Alternatively, we could adopt a historical perspective. My familiarity with ancient texts being limited, I can't really say whether the writings of Vitruvius constitute "architectural theory" as we would think of it nowadays. My modern—and probably insufficiently historical—eye finds them too pragmatic to constitute theory. My colleague Joseph Rykwert would probably not regard them as "theory" either, but in his case, this would be on account of his higher regard for Vitruvius than for "theory". Most of us would nonetheless agree that by the time of Alberti, the genre of writing by architects that we now know as architectural theory had undoubtedly come into being. By now, we can even go so far as to say that we architects are "condemned to theorise", whether we like it or not. Indeed, one does not have to be a Freudian to agree that the very Edenic "loss of innocence" cited above, also constituted the beginning of what we now know as "civilisation".

Theologically or historically then, the short answer to your question is no. Architecture can no longer just be happy—if, indeed, it ever could have been.

In considering this question further, I would be inclined to take a philosophical perspective. I hold in high regard the observation of Theodor Adorno from his famous text of 1960: "Functionalism Today": "Architecture worthy of human beings thinks better of men than they actually are."[1]

For me, this wise observation captures the phenomenological core of architectural praxis. Unless it is reduced to sheer instrumentality, or—worse still, sheer expediency—the act of conceiving the form of buildings is an inescapably 'edifying' one. (To be etymological for a moment, consider the root relationship of "edify" and "edifice". That tells us something about the ancient power of our discipline!) In the process of designing, we unavoidably imagine a better world than the one that already exists around us, and in constructing buildings, we inescapably participate in the process of bringing such a world into being. It is on this account that Hannah Arendt held in such high regard the figure of *homo faber*: the person who 'makes' things, since it is that 'making' which brings the 'world' we all inhabit together into existence.[2] Following Adorno, we can say that any architecture that is reduced to sheer instrumentality or sheer expediency, is indeed unworthy of human beings.

The question of architecture's putative relationship to actuality in our own time has recently been brought into sharp relief by the effort of a group of theorists— mainly in the United States—to formulate a method for contemporary practice to escape the strictures of so-called "critical theory".[3] In the first instance, the idea of a "critical architecture" has—for the past half-century or so—been associated with such figures as Peter Eisenman and Michael Hays. But behind Eisenman and Hays lie the philosophical luminaries of the so-called "Frankfurt School" of cultural theory, and among these luminaries is of course, the figure of Adorno himself.

This younger generation has come to find the long-standing effort of such figures as Eisenman and Hays to sustain a "critical architecture" an exhausted one. In its place, this generation has sought to conceive an architecture that it has named "projective" that would supersede the older, putatively "critical" one. Extending their disillusion to architectural Modernism itself, some advocates of the "projective" have gone so far as to argue for an architecture whose conception —and whose reception—would be "easy" as opposed to "difficult". Some of them have even taken this to relegitimise the "decorative" as a viable contemporary mode of design.

In an already published text, I have lent some support to the case for the "projective", pointing out that even Manfredo Tafuri believed in the importance of "the project".[4] But I also counselled caution. To the risks of the "purely instrumental" and the "utterly expedient" noted above, I added the troubling prospect of the "merely decorative". What I want to do in the conclusion of this short text is to attempt to disentangle the "projective" argument against the "critical" from the parallel one against the "difficult", and in doing so thereby to recontextualise the phenomenon of the "decorative".

It is true that much of the cultural production construed as "critical" can also be described as "difficult". From Eisenman's own designs, all the way back to Adorno's writings on music, a formal preference for the "difficult" over the "easy" has been clear. (In the earlier text in question, I even argued that in the arguments of the protagonists of the projective, a generational effort to escape the influence of Eisenman was obvious, even though unspoken). But here I would insist that the association of the critical with the difficult is far from being essential to critical theory. To cite only one obvious example, Kenneth Frampton's long-standing advocacy of "critical regionalism" in no way requires that the sought-after regional form be "difficult". To my own mind then, it might even be possible to conceive an architecture that was simultaneously "critical" in relation to the extant status-quo, at the same time that it was "projective" vis-à-vis future possibilities.

Indeed, as far as I can tell, this was more-or-less the position held by Tafuri.

To return to the question of the "decorative", let me cite the well-known critique of the Gesamtkunstwerk made by Adolf Loos in his text, "The Story of a Poor Rich Man", a text I discussed at some length in Space of Appearance of 1995.[5] Loos' argument, it seemed to me at the time—and indeed still does today—is irrefutable. Once an architectural setting has become a total work of art, it can no longer serve as a convincing support for human life. Yet after completing the text of The Space of Appearance, I found myself wondering about the absoluteness of Loos' polemical position. Clearly, domestic interiors and workspaces cannot viably be conceived as total works of art. But what about restaurants, or churches, or hotels designed by Philippe Starck? I am sure we have all had the experience from time to time of immersing ourselves in such Gesamtkunstwerke with great pleasure. The key to their success seems to be that these are settings in which we spend only very finite periods of time.

This way of thinking has led me to conclude that human experience of architectural space operates across a describable spectrum of consciousness. Some of the time—indeed, I would claim most of the time—we experience the architecture that surrounds us distractedly. But on occasion, we do indeed focus on it. In short, it would seem that we are prepared—indeed perhaps eager—to surrender to the power of design for finite periods of time, so long as the vagaries of our quotidian existence, are not unreasonably or indefinitely regimented.

And interestingly enough, this conclusion of mine leads me back to the "decorative". Consider the following provocative passage from the Spanish critic and theorist, Ignasi de Solà-Morales:

As it is most commonly employed, in the sense it has in the decoration magazines, in its everyday use, the decorative is the inessential. It is that which presents itself not as substance but as accident, something complementary that will even lend itself, in Walter Benjamin's terms to a reading that is not attentive but distracted, and which thus offers itself to us as something that enhances and embellishes reality, making it more tolerable, without presuming to impose itself, to be central, to claim for itself that deference demanded by totality.[6]

If Solà-Morales was correct in this intriguing speculation, it may be that the "spectrum of consciousness" I have hypothesised above, has room to encompass the "decorative", as one of architecture's wide range of modalities of human reception.

Accordingly, it might be the case that even if architecture itself "can't just be happy", it does have the capacity to find numerous, engaging ways to insert itself into the consciousness of its users, so as to evoke equally engaging responses, among which one might well be "happiness".

1   Adorno, Theodor W, "Functionalism Today", *Oppositions* 17, 1980, p 38.

2   See "Part III: Labour" and "Part IV: Work" in Arendt, Hannah, *The Human Condition*, New York: Anchor Books, 1959, pp 72–154.

3   Somol, Robert and Sarah Whiting, "Notes Around the Doppler Effect and Other Moods of Modernism", *Perspecta* 33, 2002, p 73.

4   Baird, George, "Criticality and Its Discontents", *Harvard Design Magazine*, no 21, Fall 2004-Winter 2005, p 16.

5   Baird, George, *The Space of Appearance*, Cambridge MA: MIT Press, 1995, pp 27–56.

6   de Solà-Morales, Ignasi, "Weak Architecture", *Differences*, Cambridge MA: MIT Press, 1997, p 70.

Index

A

Aalto, Alvar 4, 8–10, 61, 78, 79, 81–83, 85, 86–89, 91, 92, 96, 98, 99, 105, 169, 191, 217
    Enso-Gutzeit Headquarters 87–91
    Helsinki House of Culture 87
    Helsinki National Pensions Institute 78, 79, 84, 88, 91
    Otaniemi Institute of Technology 79, 80, 81, 82, 88
    Paimio Sanitorium 85–87, 89, 91
    Rautatalo office building 78, 79, 91, 92
    Säynätsalo town hall 79–81, 87, 88, 92, 289
    Seinäjoki town hall 81, 85, 88
    Sunila Cellulose Factory 84, 85, 87, 88, 91
    University of Jyväskylä 79–81, 88
    Vuoksenniska Church or Church of the Three Crosses 87, 88
    Wolfsburg Cultural Centre 82–84, 87
Adams, Henry 198
Adelphi Edizoni 230
Adorno, Theodor 148, 187, 263, 270–272
    "Functionalism Today" 270, 272
Alberta 255, 258, 274
Alberti, Leon Battista 230, 270
Albini, Franco 230
Alexander, Christopher 33, 34, 36, 44, 72, 75, 210
    Notes on the Synthesis of Form 72
Allen, Stan 16, 35, 263, 264, 266, 267, 269
Althusser, Louis 147, 156
American architecture 132, 191, 199, 204, 215, 218, 243
    American architects 55, 73, 267
American Central Intelligence Agency (CIA) 265
AMO 12
Ando, Tadao 191, 193
Anthropology 15, 19, 21, 22, 34, 39, 228–230, 232
Archaeology 231, 232
Archer, Bruce 44
Archigram 15
Architectural Association (AA), London 6, 19, 72, 161, 228, 246
    Exemplary Projects 246, 247, 250
Architectural Design (AD) 161, 166, 170, 172–175, 179
    "The Heroic Period of Modern Architecture", *AD*, 1965 179
Architectural Record 263
Architecture and Ideas 270
    "Why Can't Architecture Just Be Happy?" 270
Architecture and Urbanism (A+U) 263, 265, 269

Architecture New York (ANY) 175, 182, 263
    1994 *ANY* Conference Montreal 175
Arena 19, 20
Arendt, Hannah 7, 14, 34, 36, 38, 47, 51–52, 77, 148, 149, 151, 156, 204, 205, 207, 270, 272, 274
    The Human Condition 149, 204
    The Origins of Totalitarianism 149
Argentina 155
    President Nestor Kirchner 155
Arnold, Matthew 35
Art Deco 203
Asia 185, 187
Asplund, Gunnar 209, 211, 212
    Royal Chancellery, Stockholm 209
Assemblage 7, 11, 182, 208, 219
Atelier Bow-Wow 15, 146
    Made in Tokyo 152, 156
    Pet Architecture 152, 156
Aureli, Pier Vittorio 17, 74, 162
Australia 171
Avant-garde 16, 145, 154, 167, 175, 208, 214, 223, 233, 253, 265, 266, 267
    Neo-avant-garde 14, 16, 74, 154, 215, 217, 247
Aymonino, Carlo 8, 212

B

Bacon, Edmund N 54, 124, 131
    Design of Cities 124
Baird, George 6–17, 72, 166, 262
    "An Open Letter to Rem Koolhaas" 12
    "Built-Form Analysis" 110, 111
    "Carefully Reading Koolhaas" 184, 185
    "Criticality and Its Discontents" 15–17, 185, 272
    George Baird: A Question of Influence, 2012 6
    "Meaning in Architecture" 19, 20, 72
    Meaning in Architecture 6, 7, 9, 10, 38, 55, 60, 72, 73, 75, 148
    "*La Dimension Amoureuse*" 6, 9, 13, 20, 161
    "*Les Extrêmes qui se Touchent*" 12
    "OMA, Neo-Modern, and Modernity" 12
    "Onbuildingdowntown" 110, 111, 123, 274
    "Oppositions in the Thought of Colin Rowe" 11, 208, 219
    Public Space: Cultural/Political Theory; Street Photography 7, 237
    "Semiotics and Architecture" 15, 16
    "Studies on Urban Morphology in North America" 13
    The First Moderns 13, 230, 231

"Vacant Lottery" 7
Queues, Rendezvous, Riots 7
The Space of Appearance 7, 95, 146, 167, 196, 237, 271
"The New Urbanism and Public Space" 14
Bakema, Jaap 183, 248–250
Baldeweg, Juan Navarro 191, 193
Bangladesh 150, 275
Banham, Reyner 6–8, 31
Baraness, Marc 106
Barcelona 7, 190
Barenboim, Daniel 101–103
Barnett, Jonathan 125
"Urban Design as Public Policy" 125
Baroque 14, 48, 94, 95, 124, 227
Barthes, Roland 19, 21, 22, 24, 39, 40, 52, 71, 77
Elements of Semiology 71
Mythologies 71
Bartlett School of Architecture 6, 19, 20
Basler Nachrichten 223
Bathurst Street 113
Baudrillard, Jean 186, 254
Bauhaus 70, 84, 85, 200
BBPR Architects 230
Becher, Bernd 250
Becher, Hilla 250
Beck, Haig 161
Bel Geddes, Norman 162
Benjamin, Walter 60, 163, 271
Bense, Max 70
Aesthetica 70
Bentham, Jeremy 21, 95
Panopticon 21
Bercah, Paolo Conrac 196, 208
Bergamo 230
Berlage, Hendrik Petrus 181
Plan Zuid for Amsterdam South 181
Berlage Institute 7, 262
Berlin 8, 10, 85, 94, 95, 98, 100–103, 148, 151, 246, 247, 252
Dahlem 251, 252
Hansa-viertel 84
Berlin, Isaiah 210, 211
Bernstein, Eduard 148, 149
Bhalotra, Ashok 183
Bijvoet, Bernard 87, 182
Bjarke Ingels Group 16
Blake, Peter 57, 132
God's Own Junkyard 57, 132

Blau, Judith 73
Blondel, Jacques-Francois 30
Boas, Franz 41
The Kwakiutl Indian 41, 46
Boffrand, Germain 20
Bologna 149
Bonsiepe, Gui 70
Borges, Jorge Luis 206, 218
Borromini, Francesco 169
Boston 10, 13, 58, 63, 66, 125
Boston City Hall 58, 60, 171
Copley Square 66, 67
Boucher, François 231
Boullée, Étienne-Louis 30, 203
Bourdieu, Pierre 183
Bouw, Matthijs 180, 181, 183
"Disneyland with Euthanasia: The Vicissitudes of the New Welfare State" 180, 181
"Raw Power/No Fun" 180
Brasilia 14, 95, 96
Breuer, Marcel 78
Brinkman, Michiel 181, 183
Spangen Quarter housing 181
Britain 71, 73, 206, 207, 226, 230, 232
British Empire 72
Westminster 206
Broadbent, Geoffrey 73
Signs, Symbols and Architecture 73, 75
Broekhuizen, Dolf 179
Broodthaers, Marcel 264
Brown, Frank E 224, 226, 230
Brutalism 170, 171
Bunt, Richard 73
Burckhardt, Lucius 227
Burlington Magazine 226
Burroughs, William 32
Butterfield, William 168, 199, 218

C
Cadillac Fairview Corporation 109
Cage, John 31
Calasso, Roberto 230
The Ruin of Kasch 230
Calgary 255, 258
Garrison Woods 258
Calvino, Italo 206, 218
Cambridge University 148, 217
Campbell, Colen 232
Canada 6, 7, 106, 156, 255, 257, 258

Canadian Centre for Architecture (CCA) 263
Candilis, Georges 10, 151, 246, 248–250, 252, 253
Candilis-Josic-Woods 10, 151, 246, 248–250, 252, 253
    Caen-Herouville 249
    The Free University Berlin 246, 247, 250–253
    Toulouse-le-Mirail 249
Canella, Guido 208
Canetti, Elias 223, 228, 234
    Auto-da-Fé 228
    Crowds and Power 228, 234
Canton, Ohio 64
    The Canton flag 64
Caruso & St John 16
Casabella 223, 230
CBS building, the 20, 21, 24, 25, 27, 28, 30–32
CCTV 185
Central Business District (CBD) 108, 109
de Certeau, Michel 183, 276
de Chambray, Fréart 231
Chaplin, Charlie 27
Chermayeff, Serge 44, 54
de Chirico, Giorgio 203
Chevrolet 46
Chicago 121, 125, 155, 174, 177, 198
Chicago School, the 155
China 256
    Pudong 254, 256
Choay, Françoise 6, 72, 221
Choisy, Maryse 30, 31
Chomsky, Noam 73, 74
Cocteau, Jean 63
Coderch, J Antoni 191
Cohen, Stuart 55–57, 63, 65, 219
    "Physical Context, Cultural Context: Including
    It All" 56
Collage City 11, 124, 125, 131, 208–219, 256, 276, 283, 290
Collova, Roberto 193
Colquhoun, Alan 6–8, 19, 20, 72
    Essays in Architectural Criticism 8
    Modern Architecture and Historical Change 8
    Modernity and the Classical Tradition 8
    "Typology and Design Method" 20, 72
Columbia University 146, 147
Columbus, Christopher 239
Communication theory 21, 34
Congrès internationaux d'architecture moderne (CIAM)
    130, 191, 248
Conrad, Joseph 147
Constructivism, constructivist 164, 176

Contropiano 267
Cook, John 58, 59
Cook, Peter 19
Cooper Union Schools of Architecture 222
Coop Himmelb(l)au 182
Cornell University 9, 54, 63, 156, 172, 195, 196,
    207–209, 217, 218, 222, 276
    Harkness Fellowship 172
    Preston Thomas Lectures 54, 55, 195
de Coulanges, Festel 228
    The Ancient City 228
Crimson Architectural Historians 178
    Mart Stam's Trousers 5, 12, 178–183
Critical theory 148, 270, 271
    Post-critical 15, 16, 267–269
Crossman, Kelly 270
Culot, Maurice 172

D
Dalí, Salvador 162
Daly, Cèsar 199, 206, 207
    Revue generale de l'architecture 206
Davidson, Cynthia 189
    Writing Architecture 189
Davis Jr, Sammy 134
Deconstructivism, deconstructivist 15, 16, 74, 168,
    169, 172, 176, 262, 265
Deconstructivist Architecture 13
"Decorum", the theory of 9, 15, 55, 63, 64, 68, 214
Deleuze, Gilles" 190
    Differénce et Répétition 190
Delft 178, 180, 182, 262, 269
Delft School of Design 262
De Niro, Robert 266
Derrida, Jacques 74, 186, 263, 265
de Saussure, Ferdinand 19, 22, 39, 71, 72, 77
Design method, design methodology 44, 210, 263
Design Quarterly 106, 131
De Stijl 179, 182
Devillers, Christian 126, 131
Diller, Elizabeth 170, 264
Diller + Scofidio 264, 267
    Soft Sell 267, 269
Disney Corporation 73
    Disneyland 134, 141, 145, 180, 181, 210
Disraeli, Benjamin 207
Domus 223, 230
Dorfles, Gillo 72
Drexler, Arthur 162

Duany, Andres 174, 256–258, 268
Duchamp, Marcel 31, 223, 226
Dudok, Willem Marinus 181
Duiker, Jan 87, 181, 182
    Zonnestraal Sanatorium 87, 182
Duke University 146
    William A Lane Professor 146
Durand, Jean-Nicolas-Louis 230, 231
Dutch architecture 12, 178–183
    Dutch architects 4, 179
Dutch Forum 38
Dutch Modernism 180, 181

E
Eames, Charles 168, 243
Eames, Ray 168
East Germany 149
    Ulbricht regime 149
Eco, Umberto 71, 73, 75
    A Theory of Semiotics 71, 75
    La struttura assente 71, 73, 75
Edilizia Moderna 72, 234
van Eesteren, Cornelius 182
Eisenman, Peter 7, 8, 16, 38, 52, 73–75, 146, 162, 187,
    197, 207, 214–217, 219, 263–267, 271
    Inside Out: Selected Writing 1963-1988 8
Eliot, T S 33, 36
Elkisch, Franz 228
England 19, 72, 98, 125, 156, 169, 198, 199, 206, 231
    English Midlands 20
    HRH the Prince of Wales 73
Enlightenment, the 35, 203, 226, 234
Environmental design 44
Episteme 13, 94, 167, 168, 176, 205, 232, 277
von Erlach, Fischer 31, 231
Europe, European 7, 9, 11–14, 29, 72, 73, 78, 94, 95,
    106, 111, 120, 124–127, 129, 130, 135, 149,
    151, 172, 179, 182, 191, 196, 198, 201, 205,
    212, 213, 223, 230, 231, 239, 240, 247, 250,
    251, 262, 269
    The European city 14, 94, 127
    Northern Europe 179, 182
    Western Europe 127, 231
Evans, Robin 228
    "Figures, Doors, Passages" 228, 234
van Eyck, Aldo 10, 35, 38, 179–183, 191, 229
    "Rats, Posts and Other Pests" 179

F
Fadell, Tony 16
Fichter, Robert 150
    Freedom to Build 150
Ficino, Marsilio 34
Figini, Luigi 230
Filarete, Antonio de Pietro Averlino 230
Filler, Martin 78
Finland 99
First World War, the 121
Flavin, Dan 190, 192, 193
Flieg, Hans Gunter 78
Forum 38, 229, 230
Foucault, Michel 95, 167, 205
Fourier, Charles 43
Frampton, Kenneth 6, 7, 9, 16, 19, 64, 70, 72, 78, 222,
    251, 252, 263, 271
    "America, 1960-1970: Notes on Urban Images
    and Theory" 64
    Modern Architecture: A Critical History 251
Frankfurt 151
Frankfurt School, the 148, 187, 271
Franklin, Benjamin 95
Fretton, Tony 15
Freud, Sigmund 270
Friedman, Milton 155
Friedman, Yona 15
Fry Drew and Partners 230
Frye, Northrop 147
Fukuoka 172, 173, 186
Fuller, Buckminster 44
Functionalism 6, 12, 15, 34, 60, 190, 225, 229, 270, 272, 274
    Neofunctionalism 225
Furness, Frank 200, 218
Futagawa, Yukio 78, 98
de Fusco, Renati 71
    Archittetura come mass medium 71
    Reception theory 71

G
Gandelsonas, Mario 13, 73, 125, 126, 130, 131
Gans, Herbert 44
Garces and Soria 193
Gardella, Ignazio 191, 230
Garden of Eden, the 270
Garnier, Charles 43, 80, 126, 144, 162, 199
    The Paris Opera 80, 144
Garnier, Tony 13, 206
    Cite Industrielle 126

Gehry, Frank 8–10, 16, 98–101, 168, 191, 193
    Bilbao Museum 99
    Walt Disney Hall 8, 10, 98–103, 105
General Motors 46
van Gennep, Arnold 228
    Rites of Passage 228
George Baird Architects 123
Gesamtkünstler 21, 23, 24, 26, 28, 29, 34
Gesamtkunstwerk 21, 25, 26, 29, 32, 234, 271
Giedion, Sigfried 78, 226–228, 230, 231, 232
    Mechanization Takes Command 226
    Space Time and Architecture 227
    Spätbarocker und Romantischer Klassisismus
    227, 231
    The Eternal Present 227
Girard, Alexander 27
Gombrich, Ernst 21, 35, 231
Gomringer, Eugen 223
Gonggrijp, Remco 181, 183
Gothic Architecture 31, 52, 59
Graafland, Arie 262
Gramsci, Antonio 149
Grassi, Giorgio 172
Graves, Michael 54, 60, 73, 168, 174, 177, 219
Gray, Eileen 234
"Grays, the" 12, 173, 175, 176
Graz 7
Gregotti, Vittorio 230, 233, 234
Gropius, Walter 21, 78, 85, 202, 206
    Bauhaus at Dessau 85
Guadet, Julien 30
Guardini, Romano 191, 193
Guarini, Guarino 169
Guattari, Felix 190
Gutheim, Frederick 78

H
Haacke, Hans 264
Hadders, Gerard 178, 179, 181–183
Haldenby, Eric 94
Hamlin, Talbot 202, 205
    Forms and Functions of Twentieth-Century
    Architecture 202
Hans Scharoun, Bernhard 99–101, 103
    Berlin Philharmonic 98, 99, 101–103, 105
Harrison, Wallace 162, 163, 169, 173–175
Harvard Design Magazine 7, 15, 178, 185, 262, 263
    "Stocktaking" symposium 263, 264, 266, 269
Harvard University Graduate School of Design 6

Hawksmoor, Nicholas 168, 200, 231
von Hayek, F A 211, 213
Hays, Michael 8, 15–17, 242, 262–266, 271
    "Critical Architecture: Between Culture and Form"
    15, 16, 262
Heidegger, Martin 10, 38, 77, 190, 192, 245, 263
    "Art and Space" 192
Hellmuth Obata & Kassabaum 63
Helsinki 78, 84, 87, 88, 91, 92
Hertzberger, Herman 38, 52, 182
    Diagoon Housing, Delft 182
Herzog & de Meuron 15
Herzog, Jacques 191, 192
Hickey, Dave 185, 266, 267, 269
    Beau Monde (exhibition) 267
Hilberseimer, Ludwig 162, 170
Hitchcock, Henry-Russell 198, 207
    Architecture: Nineteenth and Twentieth Centuries 198
Hoffman, Dan 168
HOK Architects 171
Holberg International Memorial Prize 146
Holland 179, 180, 183
Hong Kong 156
    Hong Kong Island 156
Honig, Bonnie 149
Horkheimer, Max 148
Huet, Bernard 106
Humanism, humanist 180, 181, 251
Hume, David 31
Hungary 149
    1956 revolt against Soviet occupation 149
Husserl, Edmund 190

I
India 148
    Bhopal 148
Information theory 23, 24, 30, 35
Institute for Architecture and Urban Studies (IAUS) 7
Instrumentalism, instrumentality 14, 17, 95, 96, 232, 266,
    267, 270
International Congress of Modern Architecture 230
International Monetary Fund 155
Ireland 174, 206
Istanbul 151, 153
Italy 8, 15, 71, 95, 181, 208, 230, 239, 240
    Genoa 238–240, 243, 245
    Italian Communist party 267
Izenour, Steven 55–58, 60, 61, 63, 65, 68, 69, 72, 75,
    132, 143

J

Jacobs, Jane 150, 154, 259
    Arrival City 150
    Cities and the Wealth of Nations 154
    Death and Life of Great American Cities 150, 154
    The Economy of Cities 154
Jakobson, Roman 25, 27
Jameson, Frederic 146, 147, 148, 149, 151, 154
    "Architecture and the Critique of Ideology"
    146, 149
    "The Political Unconscious" 147
Japan 152
    Prime Minister Koizumi 152
Japanese architects 146, 156
Jencks, Charles 6, 15, 20, 55, 72, 73, 148, 161
    The Language of Post-Modern Architecture 73
Jerusalem 231
    The Temple of Solomon 231
Johns, Jasper 64
Johnson, Philip 13, 16, 31, 168, 177, 179, 263
Jones, Edward 7
Josic, Alexis 10, 151, 246, 248–250, 252, 253
Judd, Donald 190, 192, 193

K

Kant, Immanuel 34
Karlsruhe 185, 252
Kauffman, Stanley 52
Kelbaugh, Douglas 254
Kelly, Michael 70
Kent, William 232
Kesting, Hanno 228
Khan, Louis 203
    Trenton Bath House 203
Kim, Susie 216, 217
Kirkland, Michael 7
Klein, Naomi 154
    *The Shock Doctrine: the Rise of Disaster
    Capitalism* 154
Klein, Yves 12, 223, 225, 226
von Klenze, Leo 210
Klotz, Heinrich 58, 59
Knoll, Florence 21
Koenig, Giovanni Klaus 71
    Analisi del linguaggio archittetonico 71
Koetter, Fred 124, 125, 208, 216, 217, 256
Koetter/Kim 216, 217
Kohn Pedersen Fox 176
    125 East 57th Street, New York 176

IBM Headquarters Building, Montreal 176
Kolakowski, Leszek 52
Kollhof, Hans 148
Koolhaas, Rem 12, 14, 16, 111, 123, 126, 146, 148, 154,
    160–164, 166–178, 180–185, 187, 196, 263–269
    "Atlanta" 184, 185
    "Bigness" 184, 185
    Exodus 174
    "How Modern Is Dutch Architecture?" 180
    "Junkspace" 186, 187
    "Lipservice" 187
    "The Generic City" 185–187
    Voluntary Prisoners of the Architecture 174
    "Whatever Happened to Urbanism?" 186
Krauss, Rosalind 191, 263
Krier, Leon 172, 174, 212
Krier, Robert 172, 202, 204, 207, 212
    Urban Space 202
Kuroda, Junzo 152
Kwinter, Sanford 197

L

Labrouste, Henri 199, 218
Lahiji, Nadir 146, 147, 156
Lake Como 142
Lambert, Phyllis 187
Landsberg, Paul Ludwig 191, 193
Lapidus, Morris 173, 174
Lastman, Mel 153
Las Vegas 7, 13, 14, 64, 65, 132–145, 267
    Caesar's Palace 134, 138, 140, 141, 143
    Clark County 133, 137, 138
    Flamingo Avenue 135, 136
    Fremont Street 133
    Las Vegas Boulevard 133–138, 141, 143–145
    Las Vegas Convention Center 136–138
    Le Reve 143
    McCarran Airport 133
    New York New York 141, 142, 144
    Sands Avenue 135, 136
    The Aladdin 134, 141
    The Bellagio 134–136, 139, 141–143, 145
    The Desert Inn 134, 141, 143
    The Dunes 134, 139, 141
    The Flamingo 133
    The Mirage 134, 141, 143, 145
    The Paris 135, 141, 144
    The Sahara 137
    The Stratosphere 137, 138

The Venetian 138
Treasure Island 134, 141, 145
Tropicana Avenue 135–137
Laugier, Marc-Antoine 30, 31, 203, 230
Laurentian Library, the 80
Lavin, Sylvia 263, 266, 267, 269
Le Baron Jenney, William 199
First Leiter building 199
Le Corbusier 14, 42, 43, 52, 58, 78, 87, 95, 96, 151, 163,
167, 169, 171, 175, 179, 197, 202, 209, 210, 213,
216–218, 230, 243, 256, 265
City for Three Million 151
La Tourette Monastery 171
Plan Obus 265
Plan Voisin 151
Palace of the Soviets, Moscow 209, 210
Salvation Army Hospital, Paris 87
Towards a New Architecture 42
Unité d'Habitation 209
Villa Savoye 209, 212
Lefaivre, Liane 248, 249, 251, 252
Lefebvre, Henri 149
Léonidov, Ivan Ilich 162, 163, 168, 203
Le Pautre, Antoine 209, 213
The Hotel de Beauvais 209, 212, 213
Lévi-Strauss, Claude 13, 19, 21, 22, 33, 34, 39, 41, 43, 47,
71, 77, 147, 210, 211
Structural Anthropology 71
Levit, Robert 255, 256
Lewis, Mark 7
Libera, Adalberto 14, 96
EUR Congress Hall 96
Libeskind, Daniel 74, 234, 263
Lindsay, John 124
Livesey, Graham 270
Llewellyn-Davies, Richard 71
Locke, John 151
London 6–8, 19, 20, 40, 72, 78, 94, 161, 187, 197, 210,
221, 223, 228, 230
London Underground 40, 46
The West End 156
London Review of Books 148
Loos, Adolf 52, 196, 203, 205, 230, 243, 271
"The Story of a Poor Rich Man" 271
Los Angeles 8, 10, 99, 100–102, 125, 130, 133, 210, 215, 263
Grand Avenue 100
Loudon, John Claudius 31, 35
Lukács, Georg 263
Lutyens, Edwin 169, 198, 199

The Viceroy's House 199
Lyotard, Jean-François 212
Lytton, Lady Emily 198

M
Maaskant, Hugh 181, 183
Machado and Silvetti Associates 9, 10, 238–240, 242–245
Piazza Dante, Genoa 238–240, 242, 243
The Steps of Providence 239
Machado, Rodolfo 237, 238, 240, 243, 245
Sesquicentennial Park 238–240, 242, 243, 245
MacIntyre, Alisdair 228
Malaysia 155
Prime Minister Mahathir Mohamad 155
Maldonado, Tomás 15, 70, 71, 72
Manzoni, Piero 12, 223, 225, 226
Marcel, Gabriel 228
Marcuse, Herbert 46
Marshall, Richard 132, 145
Martin, Louis 17, 156
Martin, Reinhold 146–148, 154
Utopia's Ghost: Architecture and Postmodernism,
Again 147
Marxism, marxist 147, 148, 154
Marxist theory 148
Marx, Karl 156
Massachusetts Institute of Technology (MIT) 82, 170
Baker House 82
Maxwell, Robert 6, 19
McCartney, Paul 23, 32
McKim, Mead and White 200
William Low House 200
McLeod, Mary 16
McLuhan, Marshall 21, 29, 71
Medieval architecture 27, 33, 61, 94, 95, 227
"Mediterraneanism" 96
Meier, Richard 215, 216, 219
Douglas House 215
Getty Center, Los Angeles 215
Meissonier, Juste-Aurèle 231
Melnikov, Konstantin Stepanovich 168
Mendini, Alessandro 182, 183
Groningen Museum 182
Merleau-Ponty, Maurice 25, 26, 35, 38, 52, 77, 190, 221, 228
Merlin, Pierre 124
Morphologie urbaine et parcellaire 124
Mertins, Detlef 189
de Meuron, Pierre 191, 192
Meuwissen, Joost 180, 181, 183

"Disneyland with Euthanasia: The Vicissitudes of the New Welfare State"" 180, 181
Meyer, Hannes 31, 82, 85, 169, 172
    The Petershule project 82
Miami 164
    Miami Beach 174
Michelangelo 14, 80, 96, 169
Middleton, Robin 78, 98
Mies van der Rohe, Ludwig 78, 127, 162, 179, 189–193, 234, 263
    Farnsworths House 27
    Toronto Dominion Centre 127, 128
    The Seagram Building 263
Milan 8, 208, 209, 223, 230
    Milan Triennale 177, 225
Milan Polytechnic 208
Milwaukee 168
Minimalism, minimalist 190, 192, 223, 263, 266, 267
Minneapolis 106
Mirandola, Pico della 34
Mississauga 153, 256
    Mississauga City Hall 7
Mitchum, Robert 266, 267
MIT Press 7
Modern architecture 21, 45, 56, 58, 60, 61, 63, 65, 72, 85, 89, 91, 94–96, 150, 151, 162, 168–170, 174, 178, 179, 181, 183, 191, 196, 197, 200–203, 213, 216, 245
    Modern architects 58, 78, 89, 225
Modernism 9, 10, 14, 15, 25, 44, 63, 70–72, 85, 96, 126, 129, 141, 148, 154, 166–168, 170–176, 179–181, 185, 198, 201–206, 209, 210, 214, 215, 231, 238, 247, 252, 253, 262, 263, 265, 266, 269, 271, 272
    Heroic Period 13, 42, 44, 82, 85–87, 150, 151, 153, 154, 163, 178–180
    Modernist theory 127, 128
    Modernity 8, 12, 166, 167, 169, 171, 173, 175, 177, 274
    Modern Movement 68, 85, 91, 183
    Neo-Modernism 166–168, 175, 176, 185
Molière 205
Moneo, Rafael 126
Montreal 12, 106, 175, 176, 184, 187
Moore, Charles 73, 175, 176
Moran, Brendan 166
Morelli, Gustav 52
Moretti, Luigi 14, 96, 169, 210
Mori Building Corporation 152
Mori, Toshiko 185

Morris, Charles 70, 71
Morton, David 73
Moscow 12, 168, 210
Moses, Robert 163, 169, 174, 175
Mostafavi, Mosheen 234, 246, 247, 250
Mouffe, Chantal 149
    The Return of the Political 149
Mounier, Emmanuel 193
de Moura, Souto 15, 193
Munich 210, 216, 217
Muratori, Saviero 72
Museum of Modern Art, New York (MoMA) 15, 16, 179
MVRDV 181, 183, 253
    Villa VPRO 183, 253
Myers, Barton 106, 109

N
Nancy, Jean-Luc 245
Naples 203
Nazi Germany 149
Neo-Classical 63, 168, 175
Neo-Georgian 168, 175
Neo-Palladian 168, 175
Neo-Plasticism 63, 281
Neo-Positivism 41, 42
Neo-vernacular 168
Neuenschwander, Eduard 78
New England 206
New York 7, 12, 13, 20, 25, 41, 46, 61, 124, 125, 130, 146, 154, 174, 176, 179, 197, 203, 206, 252, 263, 264
    42nd Street 174
    Manhattan 28, 49, 111, 130, 142, 147, 268
    New Museum 154
    The New York Times 149, 154
    Times Square 41
    Rockefeller Center 49–51
    SoHo 252
    State University of New York 61
New York Five, the 168, 169, 197, 204
Nicolson, Benedict 226, 227
Nieman, Marcus 171
Nietzche, Frederic 149
Nolli, Giambattista 9, 63, 64
Norberg-Schulz, Christian 15, 35, 36
Norman Shaw, Richard 199
North America 7, 13, 14, 108, 124–127, 129–131, 138, 148, 196

O
Ockman, Joan 75, 184, 269
Office for Metropolitan Architecture (OMA) 10, 12,
      160–164, 166, 167, 169–175, 177, 185–187
      Barrels of Love 164
      Cronocaos 154
      Electric Bathing 164
      Elements of Architecture 12
      Hotel Sphinx 163
      Harvard Project on the City 12
      Melun-Sénart Euraille 186
      Residence of the Prime Minister of Ireland
      174
      National Football Hall of Fame 67
      Nexus World Housing, Fukuoka, Japan 186
      Roosevelt Island Competition 126
      S,M,L,XL 174, 177, 184, 186, 254
      Story of the Pool 164
      Strelka 12
Oppositions 38, 55, 264
Oud, J J P 179, 181, 183
      Kiefhoek housing estate, Rotterdam 181, 183
      Wytze Patijn 183
Ovaska, Arthur 148
Owings, Nathaniel 54
Oxford University Press 70
      Encyclopedia of Aesthetics 77
      Oxford English Dictionary 246

P
Pagano, Giuseppe 230
Palace of Versailles 95, 96, 210, 214
Palladian 65, 232
Palladio, Alberti 230
Panofsky, Erwin 34
Paris 7, 87, 94, 95, 124, 151, 187, 199, 252
      Bonne-Nouvelle district 252
      La Defence 124
      Parc de la Villette 186
      Place de la Concorde 95
      The Tuileries, 95
Pascal, Blaise 29, 212
Pawley, Martin 150
      Architecture versus Housing 150
Pérez-Gómez, Alberto 74, 75
      Architecture and the Crisis of Modern
      Science 74
Perrault, Claude 13, 29–32, 35, 231
      Treatise of the Five Orders of Architecture 29

Perret, August 209, 210
Persico, Edoardo 230
Perspecta 7, 10, 12, 166–168, 170–173, 175, 184, 185,
      262, 263
Phenomenology 9, 38, 52, 77, 190, 242, 247
Philadelphia 9, 13, 58, 66, 125
      Franklin Court 66
      Franklin House 66
Picasso, Pablo 227
Pierce, Charles-Saunders 43, 71
Pignatti, Lorenzo 95
Platonic 29, 231
Platonism 24
Polak, Michel 181, 183
Pollini, Gino 230
Pomo 74
Ponti, Giò 230
Pop Art 173, 176
Popper, Karl 11, 210–213, 219
      Conjectures and Refutations 213
      The Logic of Scientific Discovery 213
      The Poverty of Historicism 213
Porphyrios, Demetri 166
      "Pandora's Box" 166
Portman, John 162, 163, 169, 174, 175, 185
Portoghesi, Paolo 13
      The Presence of the Past 13
Positivism, positivist 70, 226
Postmodernism 9, 10, 15, 16, 55, 73, 74, 77, 148, 168,
      171, 175, 176, 208, 238, 247, 262, 265
Post-structuralism 77, 94, 167, 190, 205
"Potemkin village" 143, 145
Prangnell, Peter 52
Price, Cedric 17, 20, 21, 24–26, 28, 29, 31
      Potteries Thinkbelt project 20
Princeton University 72, 263, 266
Prouvé, Jean 250
Psychoanalysis 228, 232
Public space 7, 9, 13, 91, 92, 116, 120–122, 137, 237,
      254, 255, 258
Pugin, Augustus 230

Q
Quakers 61
de Quincy, Quatremère 230

R
Rational Architecture 172
Rationalism 77, 106, 171, 172, 204, 247

European Rationalism 106, 247
Technological rationalism 70
Rauch, John 9, 54–61, 63–69
Reason, Age of 95
Renaissance, the 14, 58, 265
Revisionism, revionist 12, 72, 162, 164, 168, 169, 171, 173
Rhode Island 200, 239, 241, 244
Providence 238, 239, 240, 242, 243, 245
Rhode Island School of Design 239, 241, 244
Richardson, H H 66, 199, 218
Marshall Field Store 199
Trinity Church 66
Ricoeur, Paul 147
Riegl, Alois 230
Rieman, Peter 148
Rietveld, Gerrit 179, 180, 182
Rietveld-Schroder house 179, 180, 182
Rio de Janeiro 151
Risselada, Max 178
Roche-Dinkeloo 148
Rogers, Ernesto 72, 230
Roman architects 95, 96
Romantic movement 227
Rome 8, 13, 14, 63, 94–96, 209, 210, 228, 230
EUR 96
Quirinale Palace 209, 215
Sant'Agnese 209
The Tiber 95
Trevi fountain 95
Villa Aldobrandini 200
Rossi, Aldo 8, 11–13, 72, 75, 111, 172, 212, 224, 225, 226, 229
Modena Cemetery 226
Rotterdam 7, 178, 183, 248, 249
Lijnbaan 249
Rousseau, Jean-Jacques 203
Rowe, Colin 6, 7, 9–13, 54, 55, 60, 63, 124–129, 162, 167, 183, 194–219, 222, 233, 240, 242, 256, 264
As I Was Saying 7, 202
"Character and Composition: or some Vicissitudes of Architectural Vocabulary in the Nineteenth Century" 55
Five Architects 11, 162, 183, 197, 198, 200–204, 209, 211, 215
"Mannerism and Modern Architecture" 197
"La Tourette" 197
"Lockhart, Texas" 198
"Robert Venturi and the Yale Mathematics Building" 200

The Architecture of Good Intentions 202
"The Mathematics of the Idea Villa" 197
"The Provocative Facade: Frontality and Contrapposto" 197
"The Vanished City, or Rowe Reflects" 201
"Transparency: Literal and Phenomenal" 197
Rowe, Peter 152
Emerging Architectural Territories in East Asian Cities 152
Royal College of Art, London 6, 221
Royal Institute of British Architects (RIBA) 179
Rudofsky, Bernard 33
Rudolph, Paul 58
Crawford Manor 58
Runciman, David 148
Rykwert, Joseph 6, 12, 13, 15, 19, 20, 38, 52, 70–72, 75, 161, 162, 220–234, 270
Body and Building 233
"Meaning in Building" 70, 223
On Adam's House in Paradise 222, 230, 231
The Dancing Column 229, 232
"The Dining Position: A Question of Method" 20
The First Moderns 13, 230, 231
"The Idea of a Town" 229, 230
The Necessity of Artifice 71, 223, 226, 234

S
Saarinen, Eero 17, 20, 21, 25, 26, 31, 32
Saarinen, Eliel 267
Salonen, Esa-Pekka 100
Santa Fe 267
Santayana, George 212
Sartre, Jean-Paul 228
Saunders, Bill 178
Saunders, Doug 149–151, 154
Scalvini, Maria Louisa 73
Scarpa, Carlo 27, 170
Schiedhelm, Manfred 246
Schinkel, Karl Friedrich 31, 35
Schweizer Werkbund 223, 225
Scofidio, Ricardo 170, 264
Scolari, Massimo 224
Scott Brown, Denise 4, 9, 13, 14, 54–61, 63–69, 72, 75, 132, 143, 171, 175
Scott, Gilbert 31
Scully, Vincent 199
Second World War, the 14, 127, 209, 210, 228
Semiology 6, 9, 15, 22, 23, 25, 31, 33–35, 39, 51
Semiotics 9, 15, 17, 55, 70–74, 166, 171, 214

Langue 22–26, 28, 30, 31, 35, 39–42, 46, 47, 51, 52, 72, 74, 176

Parole 22–24, 28, 30, 31, 35, 39, 40, 42, 46, 47, 51, 72, 74

Semper, Gottfried 230

Sennett, Richard 255, 259

    The Fall of Public Man 255

Servandoni, Giovanni Niccolo 232

    St Sulpice 232

Sheppard, Richard 230

Sicily 239

    Leonforte 238–240, 242, 245

Siegel, Bugsy 133

Siena 58, 198

Silvetti, Jorge 238–240, 242

    Four Public Squares for Leonforte 238

Sinatra, Frank 134

Sitte, Camillo 256

Situationists, the 191

Siza Viera, Álvaro 191, 193

Skidmore Owings and Merrill 147

Smithson, Alison 179

Smithson, Peter 179, 182

Soane, Sir John 168, 203

"Social architecture" 89

Socialism, socialist 151, 181, 183

Soeters, Sjoerd 183

de Solà-Morales, Ignasi 7, 8, 10, 11, 189, 190, 255, 262, 271, 272

    "Architecture and Existentialism" 190, 191

    "Difference and Limit: Individualism in Contemporary Architecture" 192

    Differences: Topographies of Contemporary Architecture 8

    "High Tech: Functionalism or Rhetoric" 190

    "Mies van der Rohe and Minimalism" 190

    "Place: Permanence or Production" 190, 191

    "Weak Architecture" 190, 192

Somol, Robert 16, 177, 184, 262–267, 269, 272

    "Notes around the Doppler Effect and Other Moods of Modernism" 262, 263

Sorkin, Michael 263, 264

de la Sota, Alejandro 246

Southern California Institute of Architecture 263

Souto de Moura, Eduardo 15, 193

Soviet Union 149

Spain 72, 170

Speaks, Michael 16, 178, 179, 181–183, 263–267, 269

    "Design Intelligence" 265

Split 249, 250

    The Palace of Diocletian 249

Stam, Mart 12, 178–183

    Drive-in Flats, Amsterdam 182

    Weissenhofseidlung housing estate, Stuttgart 182

Starck, Philippe 170, 271

Stein, Clarence 267

Steiner, Fritz 228

Stern, Robert 13, 54, 56, 60, 73, 125, 130, 131, 167, 175, 176

    New Directions in American Architecture 56

    "The Anglo-American suburb" 125

Stirling, James 11, 12, 19, 168, 169, 214, 216, 218

    Leicester Engineering Building 168

    Stuttgart Landesmuseum 216

Structuralism, structuralist 15, 38, 39, 40, 42, 51, 71, 72, 74, 77, 94, 105

Student Christian Movement (SCM) 228

"Style" 27, 167, 222, 234

Suburban 63, 106, 108, 111, 112, 132, 133, 148, 171, 251, 252, 254, 258

Superstudio 210

Switzerland 246

Sydney 171

Symbolism 16, 19, 20, 55, 56, 57, 59–61, 63, 64, 67, 68, 225

T

Tafuri, Manfredo 8, 9, 11, 16, 17, 167, 185, 224–226, 229, 263–267, 269, 271

Tashima, Charles 250

Tate Gallery, London 223

Taverne, Ed 182

    "The Only Truly Canonical Building in Northern Europe" 182

Team 10 10, 35, 172, 179, 180, 183, 191, 210, 229, 248, 249, 252, 253

Technical University of Delft 178, 262, 269

Teige, Karel 167

Tendenza, the 13, 224–226

Terrangni, Giuseppe 217

Tessenow, Heinrich 172

Texas 171, 198–200, 205, 206, 239, 242

    Houston 63, 210, 239, 240, 242, 243, 245

Thames & Hudson 98

The Architectural Review 228

The Art Bulletin 202

The Netherlands 179–183

    National Home Builders Association 182

    The Hague 179

The New Deal 267

Tennessee Valley Authority 267
Thomas Cubitt Lectures 201, 202, 205
Thomas, Preston 54
Tokyo 146, 152–154, 156, 199, 274
    Tokyo Midtown 152
    Ginza 152, 153
    Kagurazaka 152
    Roppongi Hills 152
    Shiodome 152
Toronto 6, 7, 13–15, 17, 20, 38, 74, 106–113, 115–117,
    119, 121, 123–130, 132, 149–151, 153, 154, 156,
    161, 166, 189, 195, 197, 255–258, 266, 269
    Bloor Street 113
    Central Area Toronto Plan 110
    City of Toronto Planning Board 110
    The Eaton Centre 109, 110
    Isabella Street 116
    Jarvis Street 111, 116, 120
    Lot Street 112
    Metropolitan Council 106, 107
    Monteith Street 116
    North Jarvis 111, 112, 116, 122, 123
    North Yonge Street 153
    Parliament Street 112, 113
    Queen Street 113
    Sherbourne Lanes 109, 110
    St Jamestown 111, 112
    The Globe and Mail 149
    Thorncliffe Park 151
    Wellesley Street 112, 116
    Yonge Street 112
    York Harbour 112
Trés Grandé Bibliotheque 185
Tsukamoto, Yoshiharu 152, 156
Turner, John 150, 230
    Housing by People 150
Typology, building 104, 116
Tzonis, Alexander 248, 249, 251, 252

U
ULM 15
    Hochschule für Gestaltung 15
    Hochschule theory 70
Unesco 12
Ungers, O M 13, 111, 123, 126, 131, 148, 162, 164, 172
Union Carbide 147, 148
United States of America (USA) 6, 7, 73, 138, 181, 182,
    198, 199, 201, 206, 208, 212, 248, 262, 264,
    266, 270

University College, London 19, 71, 72
University of California, Los Angeles (UCLA) 263
University of Essex 161
University of Pennsylvania 221
University of Toronto 6, 7, 38, 106, 197, 255, 269
    Meanings in Architecture: the early works of
      George Baird 1957–1993 7
Urban design 13, 15, 74, 109, 110, 124–126, 132, 154,
    172, 209, 210, 242, 243, 254, 256, 258
Urbanism 186
    Congress for the New Urbanism (CNU) 254
    Contextualism 12, 57, 125, 126, 212, 245
    New Urbanism 13, 14, 174, 182, 254–259, 268, 275
    Post-Urbanism 254, 255
Urban morphology 11, 13, 14, 72–74, 94, 106, 111, 112,
    116, 120–122, 124, 126, 128–130, 171, 212
Urban theory 126, 127, 129, 149, 152, 212, 218
Utilitarianism, utilitarian 25
Utopia, utopian, utopianism 4, 14, 15, 43, 68, 146–149,
    151, 153, 155, 156, 209–211, 224
Utrecht 87

V
Vanbrugh, John 169, 231
van den Broek, J H 181, 183, 248
Vanity Fair 100
Vanstiphout, Wouter 178–181
Vasari, Giorgio 209
Vattimo, Gianni 192, 263
Venezia, Francesco 193
Venice 8, 12, 16, 141, 177, 214, 224
    Venice Biennale 12, 16, 177
de Ventos, Xavier Rubert 73
Venturi, Robert 9, 11, 12, 13, 14, 16, 20, 21, 35, 54,
    55–61, 63–69, 72, 73, 75, 78, 98, 125, 131–133,
    135, 141, 143, 145, 162, 163, 168, 169, 171–173,
    175, 176, 182, 200, 201, 203, 204, 207, 244, ,
    Complexity and Contradiction in Architecture 9, 20,
    55, 57, 64, 65, 72, 98, 125, 169, 173, 200
    Learning from Las Vegas 9, 55–63, 65, 69, 72, 75,
    132, 135, 171
Venturi, Scott Brown and Associates 9, 13, 14, 59, 60,
    69, 132
    Brant House 56, 57, 60, 61, 64, 68
    Brighton Beach 163, 169
    Chestnut Hill House 68
    D'Agostino House 59, 68
    Guild House 9, 57–61, 63–67, 163, 169
    Lieb House 63

Trubek House 68
The Vanna Venturi House 56, 60
Yale Mathematics Building 200, 203, 204
Verona 27
Vico, Giambattista 95
Vienna 94, 95, 256
Ringstrasse 256
Villalpando, Juan Bautista 231
Viollet-le-Duc, Eugene 199, 218, 230
Virilio, Paul 186
Virno, Paolo 74
Vitruvius 230, 231, 270
Vriesendorp, Madelon 161, 162
Oysters With Boxing Gloves, Naked 162, 163

W
Wagner, George 250
Wagner, Richard 21, 200
Walker Art Center 106
Waterloo School of Architecture 94
Weeber, Carel 180, 181
"Raw Power/No Fun" 180
"Whites, the" 175, 176
Whiting, Sarah 16, 184, 190, 262–267
"Notes around the Doppler Effect and Other
Moods of Modernism" 262, 263
Wiener, Norbert 32, 33
Wigley, Mark 13, 16
Wilkins, Cassandra 178
Wittkower, Rudolf 226, 228, 232
Architectural Principles in the Age of Humanism 228
Wölfflin, Heinrich 227
Woods 246
Woods, Shadrach 9, 10, 151, 246, 248–253
The Man in the Street 247, 252
Wright, Frank Lloyd 68, 87, 168, 198, 199, 217, 230
Blossom House, Chicago 198
Imperial Hotel, Tokyo 199
Johnson Wax Building 168
Milwaukee Public Library, 198
Oak Park 68
Wright, Henry 267
Wynn, Steve 134, 135, 140–143

Y
Yale University 166, 175, 200, 203, 204, 262

Z
Zeebrugge Ferry Terminal 185

Zeidler Partnership 109
Zenghelis, Elia 111, 126, 131
Zentrum fur Kunst und Medientechnologie (ZKM) 185
Zodiac 11, 71, 208, 223
Zumthor, Peter 246
Vals Thermal Baths 246

Image Credits

22
Eero Saarinen, CBS building, 51 West Street, New York, NY, 1965: street entry. Photographer: Scott Hyde.

23
Cedric Price, Potteries Thinkbelt, North Staffordshire, England: perspective sketch of transfer area, 1966 gelatin silver print of photomontage, 24.4 × 47.5 cm. Cedric Price Fonds © Collection Centre Canadien d'Architecture/ Canadian Centre for Architecture, Montréal.

26
Cedric Price, Potteries Thinkbelt, North Staffordshire, England: axonometric of the Madeley Transfer Area, 1964, diazotype 60.1 × 84.8 cm. Cedric Price Fonds © Collection Centre Canadien d'Architecture/ Canadian Centre for Architecture, Montréal.

28
Eero Saarinen, CBS building, 51 West Street, New York, NY, 1965: interior view of a secretarial area. Photographer: Scott Hyde.

29
Eero Saarinen, CBS building, 51 West Street, New York, NY, 1965: interior view of a corridor. Photographer: Robert Damora, courtesy of the Robert Damora archive.

30
Eero Saarinen, CBS building, 51 West Street, New York, NY, 1965: exterior. Photographer: Robert Damora, courtesy of the Robert Damora archive.

32–33
Cedric Price, Potteries Thinkbelt, North Staffordshire, England: diagrammatic plan and section of Madeley Transfer Area, 1966, black ink on vellum, 35 × 88.4 cm. Cedric Price Fonds, © Collection Centre Canadien d'Architecture/ Canadian Centre for Architecture, Montréal.

46
Warren Chalk, Ron Herron, Control or Choice, detail section © Archigram 1967.

48
Henri Cartier-Bresson, *Sunday on the banks of the River Seine*, 1938 © Henri Cartier-Bresson/Magnum Photos courtesy of Magnum Photos.

56
Venturi, Scott Brown and Associates, The Vanna Venturi House, 1962–64: front facade. Photograph: Rollin R LaFrance. Courtesy of The Architectural Archives, University of Pennsylvania, by the gift of Robert Venturi and Denise Scott Brown.

57
Venturi, Scott Brown and Associates, Brant House, Philadelphia, Pennsylvania 1972: east facade. Photograph: Cervin Robinson. Courtesy of The Architectural Archives, University of Pennsylvania, by the gift of Robert Venturi and Denise Scott Brown.

58
Venturi, Scott Brown and Associates, Crawford Manor, New Haven, CT, 1966. © Robert Perron, photographer.

59
Venturi, Scott Brown and Associates, Guild House, Philadelphia, Pennsylvania, 1961: front elevation. Photograph: William Watkins. Courtesy of The Architectural Archives, University of Pennsylvania, by the gift of Robert Venturi and Denise Scott Brown.

63
Venturi, Scott Brown and Associates, The Lieb House, Long Beach Island, NJ, 1969. Photograph courtesy of The Architectural Archives, University of Pennsylvania, by the gift of Robert Venturi and Denise Scott Brown.

64
Venturi, Scott Brown and Associates: project for a town hallm for Canton, Ohio. Digital image courtesy of The Architectural Archives. University of Pennsylvania, by the gift of Robert Venturi and Denise Scott Brown.

65
Jasper Johns, *Three Flags*, 1958: encaustic on canvas, 78.4 × 115.6 × 12.7 cm. © Jasper Johns/ Licensed by VAGA, New York, NY.

66
Venturi, Scott Brown and Associates, Copley Square, Boston, MA: axonometric diagram. Digital image courtesy of The Architectural Archives, University of Pennsylvania, by the gift of Robert Venturi and Denise Scott Brown.

67 (top)
Venturi, Scott Brown and Associates, Guild House, Philadelphia, Pennylvania, 1961: exterior. Photograph: William Watkins. Courtesy of The Architectural Archives, University of Pennsylvania, by the gift of Robert Venturi and Denise Scott Brown.

67 (bottom left)
Venturi, Scott Brown and Associates, Franklin Court, Philadelphia, Pennsylvania, 1976. Photograph: Mark Cohn. Courtesy of The Architectural Archives, University of Pennsylvania, by the gift of Robert Venturi and Denise Scott Brown.

67 (bottom right)
Venturi, Scott Brown and Associates, National Football Hall of Fame, New Brunswisk, NJ, 1967: model. Digital image courtesy of The Architectural Archives, University of Pennsylvania, by the gift of Robert Venturi and Denise Scott Brown.

68
Venturi, Scott Brown and Associates, D'Agostino House, Clinton, NY, 1968: cross-section drawing. Digital image courtesy of The Architectural Archives, University of Pennsylvania, by the gift of Robert Venturi and Denise Scott Brown.

79 (left)
Alvar Aalto, National Pensions Institute, Door handle, Helsinki, 1948, 1953–57. Photograph: Maija Holma, 1996, courtesy of the Alvar Aalto Museum.

79 (right)
Alvar Aalto, Rautatalo Office Building, Door handle, Helsinki, 1951–55. Photograph: Heikki Havas, courtesy of the Alvar Aalto Museum.

80 (top left)
Alvar Aalto, Säynätsalo town hall. 1949–52. Stairs to the Council Chamber. Photograph: Maija Holma, 2014, courtesy of the Alvar Aalto Museum.

80 (bottom left)
Alvar Aalto, Jyväskylä University, 1951–78, Main building. Photograph: Heikki Havas, courtesy of the Alvar Aalto Museum.

80 (top right)
Alvar Aalto, Hall, Helsinki University of Technology, Espoo, 1953–65. Photograph: Eva and Pertti Ingervi, circa 1965, courtesy of the Alvar Aalto Museum.

81 (top)
Alvar Aalto, Säynätsalo town hall, 1949–52. Photograph: G E Kiddersmith, courtesy of the Museum of Modern Art, NY. New York. Museum of Modern Art (MoMA). © 2014. Digital image, The Museum of Modern Art, New York/ Scala, Florence.

81 (bottom)
Alvar Aalto, Säynätsalo town hall, 1949–52. Photograph: Heikki Havas, courtesy of the Museum of Modern Art, NY. New York. Museum of Modern Art (MoMA). © 2014. Digital image courtesy of The Museum of Modern Art, New York/Scala, Florence.

82 (top)
Alvar Aalto, MIT Senior Dormitory, Baker House, 1947–49: elevation drawing, courtesy of the Alvar Aalto Museum.

82 (bottom)
Hannes Meyer, Petershule Project, 1927: axonometric drawing, courtesy of Artur Niggli.

83 (top)
Alvar Aalto, Wolffsburg Cultural Centre, 1958–62. Photograph: G E Kiddersmith, courtesy of the Museum of Modern Art, NY. New York. Museum of Modern Art (MoMA). © 2014. Digital image, The Museum of Modern Art, New York/Scala, Florence.

83 (bottom)
Alvar Aalto, National Pensions Institute, Helsinki, 1948, 1953–57: library. Photograph: Heikki Havas, circa 1957, courtesy of the Alvar Aalto Museum.

84 (top left)
Alvar Aalto, Sunila Residential Area, Kotka, 1938. EKA House (Etelä-Kymin Asunto-osakeyhtiö). Photograph: Heikki Havas, circa 1950s, courtesy of the Alvar Aalto Museum.

84 (top right)
Alvar Aalto, Sunila Residential Area, Kotka, 1938: engineers apartments, 1936–37. Photograph: G E Kidder-Smith, circa 1930s, courtesy of the Alvar Aalto Museum.

84 (bottom left)
Walter Gropius, Bauhausgebäude Dessau, 1925–26, Südostansict des Alterlierhauses, (gelatin silver print, 14.8 x 11.6 cm). Photograph: Erich Consemüller © Dr Stephan Consemüller, courtesy of Bauhaus-Archiv Berlin.

84 (bottom right)
Alvar Aalto, Apartment buildings at the Hansa-viertel, Berlin, 1957. Photograph: Heikki Havas, courtesy of the Museum of Modern Art, NY. New York. Museum of Modern Art (MoMA). © 2014. Digital image, The Museum of Modern Art, New York/Scala, Florence.

85
Alvar Aalto, Paimo Sanatorium, 1928–32. Photograph: Gustaf Weline, 1932, courtesy of the Alvar Aalto Museum.

86 (top)
Alvar Aalto, House of Culture in Helsinki, 1952–58. © Rauno Traskelin, photographer.

86 (bottom)
Alvar Aalto, Säynätsalo town hall, 1949–52: floor plan, courtesy of the Alvar Aalto Museum.

87 (left)
Alvar Aalto, Vuoksenniska Church, Imatra, 1955–58. Photograph: Pertti Ingervo, circa 1960s, courtesy of the Alvar Aalto Museum.

87 (right)
Alvar Aalto, Säynätsalo town hall, 1949–52. Photograph: Martti Kapenen, 1982, courtesy of the Alvar Aalto Museum.

88
Alvar Aalto, Sunila Factory and the Residential area, 1937: site plan, courtesy of the Alvar Aalto Museum.

89 (top left)
Alvar Aalto, Seinäjoki town hall, 1958, 1959–1965: main building hall. Photograph: Maija Holma, circa 1997, courtesy of the Alvar Aalto Museum.

89 (top right)
Alvar Aalto, Jyväskylä University, 1951–78: main building hall. Photograph: Heikki Havas, courtesy of the Alvar Aalto Museum.

89 (bottom left)
Alvar Aalto, Enso-Gutzeit Headquarters, Helsinki, 1959–62. Photograph: Eino Mäkinen, circa 1960s, courtesy of the Alvar Aalto Museum.

90 (top)
Alvar Aalto, National Pensions Institute, Helsinki, 1948, 1953–57. © Suomen Ilmakuva Oy, photographer.

90 (bottom)
Alvar Aalto, Enso-Gutzeit Headquarters, Helsinki, 1959–62: second floor plan, courtesy of the Alvar Aalto Museum.

91
Alvar Aalto, Rautatalo Office Building, Helsinki, 1951–55: street facade. Photographer: Heikki Havas, courtesy of the Alvar Aalto Museum.

92
Alvar Aalto, Rautatalo Office Building, Helsinki, 1951–55: interior atrium Photographer: Eino Mäkinen, courtesy of the Alvar Aalto Museum.

99
Frank Gehry, Walt Disney Music Hall, Los Angeles, 1999–2003: interior. Photograph courtesy of Gehry Partners LLP.

100
Frank Gehry, Walt Disney Music Hall, Los Angeles, 1999–2003: cross section. Photograph courtesy of Gehry Partners LLP.

101
Bernhard Hans Scharoun, Berlin Philharmonic,1960–63: cross-section. Hans Scharoun Archiv, courtesy of Akademie der Künste, Berlin, Hans Scharoun-Archiv.

102
Bernhard Hans Scharoun, Berlin Philharmonic, 1960–63: interior hall. Photograph: Reinhart Friedrich, courtesy of Akademie der Künste, Berlin, Reinhard-Friedrich-Archiv.

110 (left)
Eberhard Zeidler and Bregman+ Hamann Architects, Toronto Eaton Centre,1977. Photograph courtesy of Zeidler Partnership.

110 (right)
Diamond and Myers, Sherborne Lanes 241–285,
Sherborne Street, 1976. © Ian Samson, photographer,
courtesy of Diamond Schmitts Architects, Toronto.

112 (bottom right)
Drawing of York Harbour, Toronto, Canada, 1793.
Courtesy of the National Archives, London.

113 (top)
James Cane, Topographical map of the city and liberties
of Toronto, 1842, courtesy of the City of Toronto
Archives MT 255.

113 (bottom)
© Lev Danko.

114, 115, 117–119, 121
Courtesy of The North Jarvis Group: James Brown,
John Chow, Paul Culpepper, Lev Danko, Paul Didur,
David Fujiwara, Robert Hodgins, Carol Kleinfeldt,
Roman Mychalowicz, Kevin Smith and John Stephenson.

125
Mario Gandelsonas, Representation of downtown Boston:
example of conceptual graphics. © Mario Gandelsonas.

128
John B Parkin and Associates, Bregman+Hamann,
Toronto Dominion Centre, 1967-1969. © Ron Vickers,
photographer. Photograph courtesy of TD Bank Group.

130
Donald Chong and Dathe Wong, Toronto Dominion
Centre, courtesy of Williamson Chong Architects,
Toronto, Canada.

133, 135 (right), 136, 139–140, 142, 144 (left)
All analytical diagrams are credited to the members of
the 2003 Graduate School of Design Option Studio,
Re-visiting Las Vegas: Shang-Wen Chiu, Sandy Chung,
Alexander Gill, Ross Hummel, Hyeseon Ju, Daniel
Kraffczyk, Jeanette Kuo, Vicky Lam, Vivian Lee, Michelle
Lin, Eriin Olson-Douglas, Seth Riseman, Jenny Stickles,
Timothy Wong, Aaron Young and Xiaodi Zheng.

135 (left top and bottom), 137, 138, 143–144
Courtesy of my former Harvard colleague,
Richard Marshall.

150
© Roger Keil, photographer.

152
© Elizabeth Baird, photographer.

169 (left)
Stirling and Gowan, Leicester Engineering Building, England,
1963. Courtesy of Stirling and Wilford Architects.

169 (right)
Hannes Meyer, Torten Housing Estate at Dessau:
site plan, 1928–30. Courtesy of Artur Niggli.

172
Courtesy of the Archives d'Architecture Moderne.

173
OMA, Fukuoka Housing Complex, Japan, 1990.
Photograph courtesy of OMA.

209 (left)
Le Corbusier, Marseille, Unité d'Habitation, site plan,
1946 © FLC/ ADAGP, Paris and DACS, London 2015.

210 (left)
Le Corbusier, Palais de Soviets, competition projet,
Moscow, 1931, © FLC/ ADAGP, Paris and DACS,
London 2015.

213 (right)
Le Corbusier, Villa Savoye, plans © FLC/ ADAGP, Paris
and DACS, London 2015.

217 (bottom)
Cover Image, Rowe, Colin and Fred Koetter, Collage
City, Cambridge Massachusetts: MIT Press, 1983.
Courtesy of MIT Press.

239–245
Photographs courtesy of Machado and Silvetti
Associates.

248–249, 251
© Charles Tashima, photographer. Courtesy of AA Files.

256
Le Courbusier, Plan for Saint Dié, © FLC/ ADAGP, Paris
and DACS, London 2015.

Acknowledgements

Thanks to Marc Baraness for giving me the idea to undertake the project on "Vacant Lots in Toronto".

Thanks to Marjo Holma at the Alvar Aalto Museum for her indispensible help sourcing images for this publication.

Thanks to Matthew Boxall, Leanne Hayman, Roberta Marcaccio, Hannah Newell, Kate Trant and Duncan McCorquodale at Artifice books on architecture, for their invaluable assistance in making this book a reality.

Artifice books on architecture
10A Acton Street
London
WC1X 9NG

T. +44 (0)207 713 5097
F. +44 (0)207 713 8682
sales@artificebooksonline.com
www.artificebooksonline.com

Designed by Matthew Boxall at Artifice books
on architecture.

British Library Cataloguing-in-Publication Data.
A CIP record for this book is available from the
British Library.

ISBN 978 1 908967 54 1

Artifice books on architecture is an environmentally
responsible company. *Writings on Architecture and
the City* is printed on sustainably sourced paper.

Silanes and Other Coupling Agents

Edwin P. Plueddemann